A HANDBOOK ON CANONS 573–746

Religious Institutes, Secular Institutes,
Societies of the Apostolic Life

A HANDBOOK
ON CANONS
573–746

EDITORS

Jordan Hite, T.O.R.
Sharon Holland, I.H.M.
Daniel Ward, O.S.B.

*Published under the auspices
of the Canon Law Society of America*

The Liturgical Press
Collegeville, Minnesota 56321

Published in the United States of America by The Liturgical Press, Collegeville, Minnesota.

Cover design by Don Molloy.

Library of Congress Cataloging in Publication Data

Main entry under title:

A Handbook on canons 573–746.

   "Published under the auspices of the Canon Law
Society of America."
   Bibliography: p.
   1. Monasticism and religious orders (Canon law)
I. Hite, Jordan F., 1938–   . II. Holland, Sharon.
III. Ward, Daniel J., 1944–   . IV. Canon Law
Society of America. V. Catholic Church. Codex Juris
Canonici (1983). can 573–746
LAW   262.9'4   85-10214
ISBN 0-8146-1403-5

Contents

The Contributors

THOMAS C. KELLY, O.P., D.D., is the archbishop of Louisville.

FRANCIS G. MORRISEY, O.M.I., J.C.D., is a professor of canon law at Saint Paul University, Ottawa, Canada, and former dean of the faculty of canon law.

ELLEN O'HARA, C.S.J., J.C.L., is the director of the marriage tribunal of the Diocese of Boise.

MARGARET MARY MODDE, O.S.F., J.C.D., heads the department of canon law in the division of legal services of the Catholic Health Association, St. Louis.

JOAN DE LOURDES LEONARD, C.S.J., J.C.L., PH.D., is a collegial judge on the tribunal of the Diocese of Rockville Centre and serves as a consultant to religious communities on canonical questions.

JORDAN HITE, T.O.R., J.D., J.C.L., formerly a professor of canon law at Saint Francis Seminary, Loretto, Pennsylvania, and director of formation, is now the director of personnel for Saint Francis Seminary.

DAVID F. O'CONNOR, S.T., J.C.D., is associate professor and chairman of the department of Church law at the Washington Theological Union, Silver Spring, Maryland.

RICHARD A. HILL, S.J., J.C.D., is a professor of canon law at Alma College/Jesuit School of Theology, Berkeley, California.

ELIZABETH MCDONOUGH, O.P., J.C.D., is an assistant professor of canon law at The Catholic University of America, Washington.

THOMAS E. MOLLOY, J.C.D., is the judicial vicar of the Diocese of Rockville Centre and a professor of canon law at the Seminary of the Immaculate Conception, Huntington, New York, and also at Mount St. Alphonsus Seminary, Esopus, New York.

CECIL L. PARRES, C.M., J.C.D., formerly a professor of canon law at Assumption Seminary, San Antonio; Kenrick Seminary, St. Louis; and St. Thomas Seminary, Denver, is an associate pastor of St. Catherine Laboure Parish in St. Louis.

DANIEL J. WARD, O.S.B., J.D., J.C.L.,, is an assistant professor of theology and government at St. John's University, Collegeville, Minnesota, and staff attorney at St. Cloud Legal Aid, St. Cloud, Minnesota.

SHARON HOLLAND, I.H.M., J.C.D., is on the staff of the tribunal and in the office for religious, Archdiocese of Detroit, and teaches canon law at St. John's Provincial Seminary.

MARY DAVID OLHEISER, O.S.B., J.C.L., PH.D., serves as defender of the bond and judge on the tribunal for the Diocese of St. Cloud.

Abbreviations

AA	*Apostolicam Actuositatem*
AAS	*Acta Apostolicae Sedis*
AG	*Ad Gentes*
AIE	*Ad Instituenda Experimenta*
C	1983 Code of Canon Law or canons therein
CanLawStud	*Canon Law Studies*, The Catholic University of America
CD	*Christus Dominus*
CDR	*Contemplative Dimension of Religious Life*
CIC	1917 Code of Canon Law or canons therein
CLD	*Canon Law Digest*
CLSAP	*Canon Law Society of America Proceedings*
CMSM	Conference of Major Superiors of Men
Comm	*Communicationes*
ConLife	*Consecrated Life*
CpR	*Commentarium pro Religiosis*
DC	*Dum Canonicorum*
EN	*Evangelii Nuntiandi*
ES I or II	*Ecclesiae Sanctae*
ET	*Evangelica Testificatio*
Jur	*The Jurist*
LCWR	Leadership Conference of Women Religious
LG	*Lumen Gentium*
MR	*Mutuae Relationes*
NCCB	National Conference of Catholic Bishops
PC	*Perfectae Caritatis*
PM	*Pastorale Munis*
PO	*Presbyterorum Ordinis*
RC	*Renovationis Causam*
RfR	*Review for Religious*
RL	*Religionem Laicalium*

9

RR	*Roman Replies*, Canon Law Society of America
SC	*Sacrosanctum Concilium*
SCCE	Sacred Congregation for Catholic Education
SCDF	Sacred Congregation for the Doctrine of Faith
SCOC	Sacred Congregation for the Oriental Churches
SCRIS	Sacred Congregation for Religious and Secular Institutes
StudCan	*Studia Canonica*
UISG	International Union of Superiors General
USG	Union of Superiors General
VS	*Venite Seorsum*

Foreword

One of the more pleasant features of my canonical formation was a brief sojourn at the University of Vienna in 1961. The atmosphere was quite different from that of the Angelicum, where I was then a student. There were famous historians, and a mostly lay faculty among whom were women professors of Church law teaching the canons on marriage, religious life, etc. The whole faculty was excited by Pope John XXIII's call, issued the previous year, for an ecumenical council. In the flow of subsequent philosophical exchange, a leitmotif was found in some words of Pius XII, delivered during a 1956 allocution to the professors and students of the University's law school, "Church life and Church law belong together." (*AAS* 48–498) That aphorism seemed uncommonly refreshing in a legal era not noted for homey wisdom, and I took it to be a sound approach for the revision of religious law, an enterprise even then being contemplated in the pontifical universities of the world.

Before pen could get to paper, however, Church life began to assert itself. With the encouragement of *Perfectae Caritatis*, religious began a process of renewal that gave a timeless Church an uncomfortable day or two. In *Evangelica Testificatio*, Paul VI pondered the results of that process, encouraged sound developments, and emphasized the deepest realities of religious life. He spelled out the Church's loving need for consecrated life, and as the drafts of the canons began to appear it was a source of much satisfaction to discover the dictum of Pius XII had prevailed: Church law and Church life had come together in a new and supportive way. By then I was working in the general secretariat of the United States bishops' conference and had an opportunity to see the approving, constructive comments of bishops and major superiors, canonists, and theologians. They found that the new canons faithfully reflected consecrated life as it had been renewed in the Church, with both traditional values and contemporary vitality. Flexibility, subsidiarity, respect for a wide range of traditions and charisms: all of this came to be successfully incorporated in the new law on institutes of consecrated life and societies of apostolic life.

As one draft succeeded another, canonists began to admire the spirit and craft of this section of the Code, and its canons are now among the most respected of the final texts promulgated by Pope John Paul II. There is a radical shift of perspective: instead of occupying a place of privilege, those embracing consecrated life are now seen to hold a place of service and ministry. There is a new emphasis on personal dignity and the responsibility of each member for the charism and life of the institute. Mutual discernment is regarded as a key value in formation, and there is a sensitive balance to personal and communal obligations and rights. The canons encourage as normative in the post-conciliar Church collaboration with bishops, priests, other religious and laity. Above all, the importance of the proper law of the institute is guaranteed, assuring the continuation of the founder's unique vision, charism, and gifts.

Lawyers now set themselves happily to the task of illuminating these canons, exposing the philosophy that undergirds them, and polishing the nuts and bolts of the structures of consecrated life. The Religious Affairs Committee of the Canon Law Society of America has assembled an impressive roster of talent for the first United States commentary on these canons. They have chosen authors well known for their experience, for the clarity of their teaching, and for their love of Church law. They offer extensive practical help, for which many of us will be most grateful. In the long run their greatest contribution may be to show that the canons protect the foundations of religious life, viz. that the evangelical counsels find their basis in the teaching and example of Christ, and that consecrated life belongs to the heart and holiness of the Church. More than ever, Church law and Church life belong together.

Thomas C. Kelly, O.P.
Archbishop of Louisville

Introduction

FRANCIS G. MORRISEY, O.M.I.

The promulgation of the revised Code of Canon Law by Pope John Paul II on January 25, 1983, marked the end of a process that had been nearly a quarter century in the making.[1] Indeed, from the day the project was first announced by John XXIII on January 25, 1959, to the day the Code went into effect, November 27, 1983, a period of twenty-four years and ten months had elapsed. While the promulgation of the new law marked the end of a process, it really was the beginning of another: a period wherein the Church would strive to live out the insights given it by the Spirit who continually guides the People of God toward their destiny.

The revised law, while striving to implement the orientations of Vatican Council II, also has to fulfill the role of any law: to guide the members of the society to the ultimate good for which that society exists. The law, as a means to an end, can only be justified if it fulfills its mission: providing freedom and a context wherein free choices can be made without the threat of the arbitrary hanging over everyone.

Paul VI has said that the law was to be an "instrument of grace,"[2] a means whereby the faithful could come to the Father without let or hindrance. The task of the canonist consists in deepening the work of the Spirit,[3] in seeing where the Spirit is leading the Church, and in providing means of enhancing the effects of this divine intervention. The law for institutes of consecrated life is based on the premise that the Holy Spirit, in distributing charisms in the Church, has been directly involved in the founding and development of consecrated life in its various forms. The law is there to make certain that the charisms have the necessary context wherein to operate freely and lead those who have received the gift to a particular mission in the Church. In other words, the law only can be understood—and accepted—in a context of faith. The faithful profession of the evangelical counsels finds its significance only in response to a God-given call to take up the cross and follow Christ.

Yet, even within this vision of faith, it must be recognized that the indiscriminate use of the law, without proper interpretation, could be a very dangerous thing in the life of the Church. Just as it is not always expedient to place the text of Scriptures in anyone's hands without the necessary annotations or explanations,[4] so too the code of law, if it is not to be used simply as a club or as a means of enforcing conformity, must be interpreted according to the principles used in its preparation, in the light of divine revelation, and the doctrine of the Church. It would be tragic for the Church if, after so many years of hard work and preparation, the law were to be used simply as a means of "restoring" order and uniformity. Instead, it must be envisaged as a means of consolidating the experience of the past to enable the Church and its members to look forward in joy and hope toward the future. The Code could be considered as the consolidation of the various experiences lived in the Church throughout its existence, those experiences which have proved to be beneficial to the community, and those which have not demonstrated their value. Thus, some prescriptions will be positive in their thrust, others negative.

The new law for institutes of consecrated life fits squarely into this perspective. It is one of the parts of the legislation that has been completely renewed. However, no matter how perfect the architect's drawings and designs, it is only when the building is lived in that its faults, if any, are noted. The same will be true of the new law. Only the test of time will reveal whether the project is apt to provide for the continual renewal of consecrated life in the line of particular community charisms and missions.

To determine to what extent the new legislation will be a suitably adapted instrument of grace and continual renewal, it will be necessary to review first the principles that guided its revision; then, the trends noticed in the revision itself can be examined. This would be followed by a comparative overview of the three published drafts of the text.

I. THE PRINCIPLES GUIDING THE REVISION

The Pontifical Commission for the Revision of the Code of Canon Law had drawn up a series of ten principles to be applied in the revision of the Church's legislation. These principles were approved by an overwhelming majority at the Synod of Bishops in 1967.[5] However, they were not sufficiently precise to direct each subcommission in carrying out the particular task assigned to it. Consequently, a certain number of additional ones were recognized as operative in revising the law for institutes of consecrated life and societies of apostolic life. Four such major principles were accepted, along with a number of secondary guidelines. They constitute the background for the study of the new law and provide certain criteria for any eventual evaluation of the legislation.[6]

1. The spiritual dimension of the law: the nature of consecrated life

Since law by itself remains sterile, it is not enough to base the existence of consecrated life simply on some form of outward observance. Indeed, while such observances are at times necessary if activities of religious are to correspond to an inner dynamism, the laws must nevertheless flow from a deep awareness of the spiritual dimension of consecrated life. Thus, the new Code specifically states that the following of Christ is the supreme norm of life for religious.[7] In one sense, this canon would be sufficient since it contains all; yet, on the other hand, it warrants development since there are many ways of following Christ, according to the particular charism and mission of each institute.

The subcommission had asked that the Code contain some pastoral norms, rules that would be seen more as guidelines than as strictly juridical prescriptions. We see such, for instance, in the canons which refer to the office and duties of superiors.[8]

But, what is more striking is the fact that the Code also contains a number of doctrinal canons, outlining the nature of consecrated life and of its various forms. Thus, the first canon in the section[9] reminds us that life consecrated by the profession of the evangelical counsels is a stable form of life by which the faithful, under the guidance of the Holy Spirit, follow Christ more closely, dedicate themselves totally to God, while striving for the perfection of charity. These and many other elements found in the canon have no minimal form of fulfillment. They call for a perfection that is never fully attained on earth.

Other theological elements of consecration are spelled out in CC 573–575, 607, 662, 663, etc. These remind us of the fact that consecrated life has as one of its purposes the building up of the Church, that it pertains to the life and sanctity of the Church, that the faithful receive a special call to embrace it, that the evangelical counsels, a divine gift, find their basis in the teaching and example of Christ.

One of the major consequences of this approach is that internal convictions, flowing from a faith response to a divine call, necessarily are seen as fundamental to the observance of any norms whose purpose it is to protect the gift received from God.[10] Of course, one of the dangers in such an approach is to turn the Code into a handbook of religious spirituality. This is not the case and the members of the subcommission, while respecting the spiritual dimension, were also very careful to make certain that the new Code was a text of law, in line with the first general principle approved by the Synod of Bishops.[11]

2. Respect for the special characteristics of each institute: its charism and mission

Another notion underlying the canons on consecrated life is that at the origin of each institute, there was a particular gift or charism of the Spirit. This charism, which varies somewhat from institute to institute, finds its expression, not only in the life-style of the members, but also in their mission. The laws of the Church have to allow flexibility so that each institute may live its own form of life and spirituality in accord with its charism. For instance, the laws on cloister are not applicable in the same way everywhere.

To foster respect for the special characteristics of each institute, the 1977 draft of the canons had tried to present a typology of apostolic institutes that would help clarify the distinctions found between conventual and integrally apostolic communities. In the conventual institutes, the apostolate is assumed by the community; there is stability in assignments, a strong sense of sharing, prayer in common, and a form of government that calls for greater participation. In the integrally apostolic institutes, the apostolate is carried out more by the individual members on behalf of the institute, mobility is a characteristic of apostolic commitment, the notion of obedience is strong, prayer life is more particularized, etc.

However, because of the difficulties faced by those who were trying to define the particular status of their institute in the light of their charism, and since few communities were able to fit directly into one category or the other, it was found preferable to drop the divisions. Thus, the 1983 Code has no direct reference to a typology of apostolic institutes, although the chapter on the apostolate contains some of the elements found in the 1977 draft (especially CC 674, 675). Nevertheless, if a community is preparing adapted legislation, it must know for what type of institute the law is being drafted. Thus, for instance, the norms on formation, on government, on community life, on prayer, on living the evangelical counsels, are all to be prepared in view of the functions to be assumed later on in the life of the institute.

Although the new Code does not retain a detailed classification of institutes, it still provides elements upon which to base particular legislation. Thus, it refers to the "patrimony" of the institute[12] which comprises the intentions of the founder, the nature, purpose, spirit, and character of the community, and its sound traditions. These elements find their doctrinal basis in the conciliar decree *PC* No. 2b. Many institutes have even been experiencing difficulties in determining who precisely is their founder or foundress, let alone the expression to give to their charism. This occurs because so many institutes are divisions of existing ones, either for diocesan reasons, or because of differences of language, culture, geography, etc. Furthermore, the missions of the institutes have necessarily changed with time in their practical expressions; works that were once identified with a certain community are now assumed by government or diocesan services; communities are no longer free to make appointments to schools or hospitals without going through elaborate personnel procedures. Therefore, the description of the nature and mission should not be hardened in law, or the institute would soon be boxed into a corner.

However, as a minimum, the law, in order to protect the special characteristics of each institute, calls for a faithful respect of the community's patrimony so that decisions are taken in a perspective of continuity and of fidelity to the call of the Spirit.

The norms on formation in the new Code bring out clearly the fact that the candidates are to be given a better knowledge and understanding of the institute and of its way of living,[13] and after first profession are to live the life of the institute in a more complete way and carry out its mission more fully.[14] These norms, among others, refer again to the special characteristics of the institute.

3. Principle of subsidiarity: use of proper law

One of the general principles invoked for the revision of the whole Code was that decisions were to be taken at the most appropriate level.[15] The general principle was viewed more in the light of a distribution of decision-making authority among diocesan bishops and episcopal conferences. However, in the subcommission on consecrated life, it was decided to apply this principle by providing for flexibility in institutes, without having the general law enter into endless details. This was carried out by a particular reliance on proper law.

The term "proper law" calls for some explanations. There are many levels of proper law in an institute. The fundamental code, or Book I, of the community spells out the patrimony of the institute, the basic norms regarding government and formation, membership, and the object of the vows. This enables each institute to protect its vocation and identity by enshrining them in the fundamental code. Such a code, once accepted by the general chapter of the institute, is approved by the competent ecclesiastical authority[16] and may only be changed with its consent.

In addition to Book I, the proper law of each institute is also expressed in other books or codes. The names given to such documents are of little import; what matters most is their content. Thus, Book II is usually called the "Rules." It contains the applications of the principles outlined in the constitutions and is more subject to change. This second book is approved by the competent authority of the institute,[17] usually the general chapter, and may be changed as necessary.

A third category of books, sometimes called directories, sets out more detailed prescriptions for application which are often not of import to the entire community. For instance, such directories can be concerned with formation,[18] chapter procedures,[19] financial policies,[20] and policies for superiors.[21] They are usually prepared by the supreme moderator and council.

A further application of subsidiarity at a fourth level can be found in codes approved for particular provinces or regions of an institute where situations are varied. Such local directories would be confirmed by the competent authority of the institute, according to the constitutions.

The new Code has very carefully applied the principle of subsidiarity. Indeed, some may even feel that too much was left to the institute and there will not be sufficient uniformity among communities. The problem is probably more acute in smaller institutes where human resources are not always available to prepare legal texts for the community. However, such institutes can always be helped by others who are willing to share their resources in such matters.

The 1983 Code definitively assigns to superiors certain powers that were previously delegated to them by indult or special papal dispensation. Thus, superiors by office may allow a religious to change the acts of cession of administration of goods and the last will and testament;[22] the supreme moderator can authorize a member to renounce personal patrimony, either in whole or in part. The constitutions can determine how an institute is to be divided into parts.[23]

Some points of the new law go even further than the experimental norms did in the period after the Council. The most striking example of this is exclaustration which may now be granted by the supreme moderator with the consent of the council;[24] this was previously reserved to competent ecclesiastical authority.

Another expression of subsidiarity—which is not without its problems—is found in the vocabulary used throughout this section of the Code. Neutral terms, such as supreme moderator, sacred bonds, fundamental code, proper law, members, were used, especially in the general part, to apply to all institutes who could then choose a term more in accordance with their traditions.

One expression of subsidiarity in the broadest sense of the term is found in the canons that refer to the autonomy of institutes and their relations with the diocesan bishops. C 586 spells out the general principle of autonomy, especially in matters of internal government. However, institutes are subject to the diocesan bishop in questions of liturgy,[25] apostolate,[26] particularly of education,[27] and care of souls.[28]

4. Coresponsibility in the government of the institute

PC (No. 4) has spoken of the necessity of representation and cooperation of the members of the institute, to make sure that they were involved in important decisions affecting the life of the community. The way such shared responsibility is fostered will depend to a great extent on the size of the institute, language and cultural factors, geographical distribution, etc.

Superiors are asked to listen freely to the members and encourage them to propose what they consider appropriate for the institute.[29] General chapters are to be established in such a way that they represent the entire institute.[30] When superiors are appointed and not elected, their choice is to be preceded by suitable consultation.[31]

C 633 provides for organisms of participation and consultation. No specific format or structure is prescribed; however, it is mentioned that such organisms should conform to the nature and purpose of the institute and that they shall be used in a discerning way. Accordingly, such assemblies would take on a quite different form in contemplative institutes and in apostolic ones.

5. Equality between institutes of men and of women

The Code Commission took great pains to eliminate what could appear to be discriminatory canons distinguishing between institutes of men and those of women. While such a policy was not part of the four guiding principles, it was one of the secondary guidelines observed by the subcommission.

Yet, because of the nature of institutes, some are described as clerical, others as lay. The major superiors in pontifical clerical institutes are Ordinaries for their subjects;[32] for lay institutes it is the Ordinary of the place where the house is situated. This will necessarily create a difference among institutes because some will have to have recourse to a local Ordinary for certain permissions, while others will be able to obtain the necessary authorizations within the institute itself. However, the difference is not based on sex, but on the exercise of sacred orders. An example of such differences is found in C 1288, where it is stated that the introduction of law suits and a response to them require the written permission of the proper Ordinary (likewise, the acceptance of foundations and their administration). [33]

C 606 outlines clearly the principle that what applies to institutes and to their members applies equally to both sexes unless otherwise provided; in the 1917 Code, it was stated that whatever applied to men also applied to women, unless the contrary was stated. The new formulation is better.

Thus, we no longer find norms regarding the confessions of sisters and special examinations of candidates for sisterhood. The visitation rights of the Ordinary are the same for both: [34] he can only conduct a visitation in houses of diocesan institutes; visitation rights for pontifical institutes are limited to specific matters regarding liturgy and the apostolate. Time alone will tell whether this prescription is for the well-being of institutes of women. Since the diocesan bishop has no general right of visitation in pontifical institutes, disputes or difficulties have to be referred to the Holy See; it might have been preferable to have provided for some type of arrangement whereby the matter could be resolved at the local level. Of course, nothing in the law prevents having recourse to the bishop if both parties agree to his voluntary intervention.

There are still a few canons in the Code concerning monasteries of nuns, the erection of such monasteries, and cloister for contemplative institutes of women. [35] However, these depend on the nature of the institute and should not be considered discriminatory. Indeed, many of the norms regarding monasteries refer also to communities of men.

This overview of five particular principles used to prepare the new law shows how they were observed in drafting the final text. Of course, it would be relatively easy to single out certain canons which might on the surface appear to go against one or more of these guidelines, but such is not our purpose here. Rather, in spite of some deficiencies, the law in general is very faithful to the principles; time alone will tell whether they were the right ones to apply. Everything at present seems to indicate that such is the case.

II. TRENDS NOTED IN THE REVISION OF THE LAW

In addition to agreeing on fundamental principles, a number of serious questions of substance had to be faced by the subcommission in revising the law for institutes of consecrated life and societies of apostolic life. One of the major issues concerned the place of such institutes in the overall plan of the Code itself. Others were related to the contents of the various drafts.

1. The place of CC 573–746 in the revised Code: the charismatic aspect of consecrated life

As the work on the preparation of the new Code progressed, it became evident that the place assigned to CC 573–746 in the law would express an underlying theology regarding consecrated life in the Church.

LG (No. 44) provides some insight as to where the canons were to be situated: "The state of life which is constituted by the profession of the evangelical counsels, while not entering into the hierarchical structure of the Church, belongs undeniably to her life and holiness."

The 1977 draft of the Code had thus placed the canons we are considering in the third section of Part II of Book II, "The People of God," under the heading "Institutes of Consecrated Life." This section was preceded in the second part ("Persons in particular") by sections on sacred ministers or clerics, and the hierarchical constitution of the Church. The fourth section referred to the laity. Many objections were raised against this plan because it still perpetuated the triple division between clergy, religious, and laity. The objections were centered on the fact that societies of apostolic life were considered to be institutes of consecrated life and were thus subject to the various norms regarding the evangelical counsels. Many such societies do not make a formal profession of the three counsels.

A new plan was then proposed in the 1980 draft, but this too caused serious difficulty. The canons were found in Part III of Book II, under the general title of "Associations." This now meant that religious life could be seen simply as a human society, without direct reference to the action of the Spirit. Vatican II had indeed recognized the charismatic state of those who were in such institutes and this dimension seemed to have been overlooked.

Consequently, in view of the objections raised against the revised plan, a new one was prepared which is found in the promulgated Code. This new division respects fully the charismatic nature of the Church. Book II is divided into three parts: the faithful, the hierarchical constitution of the Church, institutes of consecrated life and societies of apostolic life. Thus, after giving general principles regarding the faithful (laity and clergy), personal prelatures and associations of the faithful, the Code then considers the hierarchical and charismatic dimensions of the Church. By placing the canons on consecrated life and apostolic societies in this third part of Book II, the law recognizes that these forms of life do not pertain to the hierarchical nature of the Church, but nevertheless are distinct from the general associations and prelatures. This reminds us of the debate during the Council concerning the place of Chapter II of *LG*. The new plan renders a great service to consecrated life by recognizing its particular nature.

2. *The state of those who profess consecrated life: a canonical state*

Vatican Council II spoke about the legal sanction given to religious life and the raising of this form to the dignity of a canonical state.[36]

Three juridic prerequisites exist before a person can be considered in law to have entered a state of consecrated life: (1) the form of life must have been approved by the Church and recognized as an appropriate means of living out the Gospel;[37] (2) the institute itself must have been approved and recognized by legitimate ecclesiastical authority;[38] (3) the profession must be accepted by a legitimate representative of the institute.[39] In addition, the Code sets out other conditions for the validity of profession in C 656.

These three fundamental conditions immediately raise to mind the question of those institutes that desire to be noncanonical.[40] By removing themselves from the government authority of the Church, the members are no longer formally recognized as professed religious and no longer have the protection of law against arbitrary decisions. Furthermore, in addition to the lack of official union with the authority of the Church, the activities of the members often do not constitute an apostolate in the true sense of the term, since they are not carried out in a spirit of ecclesial communion.[41] The norms of the new law are very clear in regard to apostolic activity.

By entering into a recognized state of life, the member acquires a number of fundamental rights and assumes certain essential obligations. These are outlined in CC 662–672 of the 1983 Code. Not surprisingly, many of the obligations refer to spiritual matters. Each religious has the right to receive from the institute that which, according to the constitutions, is necessary to attain the goals of religious profession.[42] The law does not have parallel sections for members of secular institutes or societies of apostolic life, and their rights and obligations would have to be determined by analogy with those for religious.

3. *The form of consecration: vows and promises*

The new law adopts the position that religious profession is to be made by vows, either temporary or perpetual. [43] For a certain number of years, the practice of making promises to the institute had been authorized for the period of temporary commitment. [44] Yet, Vatican II had spoken of the possibility of a consecration that could become deeper with time [45] and thus become more perfect. Nevertheless, others spoke of consecration in terms of something permanent and definitive. The Holy Father eventually decided that vows would be used in religious institutes and promises or other sacred bonds in secular institutes and societies of apostolic life. [46]

As Abbot Primate Viktor Dammertz wrote: "The limitation inherent in temporary vows is understood in a way that is completely in accord with tradition: they presuppose a basic decision on the part of the person making the vows, which includes an intention of committing oneself irrevocably later on in perpetual profession, provided that in the meantime nothing happens to disprove the existence of a vocation from God." [47]

Although other possibilities could have been envisaged, there is no doubt that the formulation now found in the Code is in conformity with the teaching of the Council, even though communities that had authorized promises will have to make some changes in their practice.

4. *New forms of consecrated life: consecrated virginity*

The general introductory canons refer to the possibility of recognizing new forms of apostolic life. [48] Such could take on many forms: for instance, ecumenical or inter-faith communities, mixed communities of men and women, communities based on some form of temporary service, and so forth. The Church does not recognize such as constituting consecrated life at this time. Indeed, only the Holy See can approve any such new forms.

But, it is interesting to note that the general canons do speak of the eremitical life and of consecrated virginity. [49] While these forms of consecration are not directly placed among forms of consecrated life, since the eremetical life is seen as going beyond it, and consecrated virginity is presented as being similar to it, both have much in common with consecrated life itself. However, it could be asked whether these canons are in their proper place, especially the one on consecrated virginity. They might have been better placed elsewhere in the law.

The canon on consecrated virginity raises a number of canonical problems. What is the nature of the sacred *"propositum"* (commitment)? Does it constitute an impediment to marriage? How is it dispensed? What obligations does it entail? What is the responsibility of a bishop who accepts to consecrate a lay woman for the service of the diocesan church? These questions will probably only be answered with time, but they have significant consequences in law. A further question can be raised about lay men who wish to consecrate themselves to the service of the diocese. Has any similar rite been proposed for them?

At times it has been recommended that religious women who wish to leave their institute without losing their vows be consecrated as virgins. Such a practice should be seriously questioned, since consecrated virginity is a particular state of life in the Church and would require a period of preparation beforehand. A simple transition from one state to another is not advisable. The rite does not provide either for some form of temporary commitment, and thus the consecration is definitive, unless a person wishes to make private vows in the hands of the bishop. However, since we are still living in a period where the restored rite is considered as novel, it would be extremely important to make sure that it is placed on a strong footing and not seen simply as some second-class form of commitment.

5. Relationships with the local Church and its mission: exemption

We have already referred to the role of the local bishop regarding the apostolate of religious. However, there is still one canon[50] which raises the tricky question of exemption. Since religious are directly subject to the Ordinary in matters regarding the care of souls, liturgy and the apostolate, and since major superiors in clerical institutes now have the same authority as exempt major superiors in the old law, it can be asked what is the practical value of such an exemption. Possibly, the imposition of certain penalties might be reserved in the case of exempt institutes, but even this is not clearly stated in the law. For instance, C 1320 provides that religious may be coerced by a penalty in all those matters in which they are subject to the local Ordinary. Possibly, at some future date, specific legislation will be enacted referring to exempt communities. The matter might also be allowed to lie in peace!

Leaving aside this unanswered question, the theological notion of mission takes on prime importance in the new law. The threefold mission of Christ, to teach, sanctify, and govern, is also entrusted to religious and members of other institutes as they share in Word and sacrament, and provide for the internal government of the institute.[51]

Each institute, in addition to its charism, thus has its mission to carry out in the Church,[52] a mission to be adapted to the needs and circumstances of time and place. Institutes, no matter how great the need, cannot be called upon to carry out works not in conformity with their nature.[53] Because of the inherent tensions between mission and diocesan needs, members of institutes are to hold fast to their own spirit and to the patrimony of the institute, as the law clearly states.

These issues and others were faced by the subcommission as the various drafts of the canons were prepared.

III. THE DRAFTS OF THE NEW LAW

When the remarks on the 1977 draft canons on consecrated life were examined by Paul VI, he is alleged to have exclaimed: "This draft is fascinating; it was not understood; perhaps it was ahead of its time."[54]

The 1977 draft indeed appeared to be quite radical, even though it simply applied the vision of the Council. It seems that many people were afraid that too much was left to each institute and that the principle of subsidiarity was applied too readily. Once the principle was applied so extensively in consecrated life, they thought, there would be little reason why subsidiarity could not also be applied in the particular churches, and even in the parishes.

Other objections raised against the first draft referred to a danger of leveling all institutes; many were also opposed to the typology; it was said that the text did not insist sufficiently on community life and that it did not treat of the apostolate of religious. Then, it was alleged that the draft restricted somewhat the conciliar teaching on the *sequela Christi*, the following of Christ. Finally, it was stated by some that the notion of consecration was wrong, since it proposed this gesture as a response of the person to the divine call[55] and was not presented as a divine intervention.

Many of these objections could be readily answered. However, the spirit of the 1977 draft had not been clearly grasped by many of those who raised objections against it. Yet, the number of objections thus raised meant that there were indeed certain fundamental problems with the text that had to be addressed.

A revised version of the draft law distributed in 1980 was, then, a work of compromise. The general or common law would once again assume priority over the particular law, without however sacrificing the reliance on the proper law of each institute. This provided for greater uniformity. New sections were added on general chapters and on the apostolate of religious. The typology of 1977 was dropped.

The 1980 revision, which was substantially retained in the promulgated version, insisted on the ecclesial and eschatological significance of the admirable marriage established by God.[56] Religious life was seen above all as a consecrated life, a worship of love towards God. In this way, it goes beyond the virtue of religion and presupposes theological charity in a total gift of self to God. No longer do the vows suffice to identify the religious, since others can also make vows, but rather, the entire person is consecrated to the Lord; this too calls for fidelity.[57]

In addition the 1980 version proposed some interesting changes regarding admission to an institute. Henceforth, an indult from the Holy See would no longer be required if a person leaves the institute after making perpetual vows, having been duly dispensed, and now wishes to return to the community.[58] Likewise, that person does not have to repeat the novitiate[59] if the supreme moderator with the consent of the council does not judge it necessary; instead, the person undergoes a period of probation. These changes were retained in the final text.

The final version (1983) of the canons introduced a few more significant changes in existing legislation.

One such change concerns C 668, §5, on the renunciation of patrimonial goods. The 1980 version spoke of a professed religious who totally renounced any personal patrimony; such a person would henceforth be unable to acquire additional patrimony; anything received would belong to the institute. The promulgated version states that such a restriction applies only in the case of institutes which by their nature require the renunciation of temporal goods.

C 689 also contains a new clause to the effect that if a religious, during the period of temporary vows, becomes insane, even though a new profession cannot be made, that person cannot be dismissed from the institute.

Superiors were also given more leeway in cases of mandatory dismissal for faults against the sixth commandment,[60] provided the delinquent religious had repented and repaired in an appropriate way any scandal that had been caused. In such instances, it was not necessary to proceed with the dismissal.

Also, C 700 revised the procedure to be followed in the case of dismissal of religious. For validity, the decree must indicate the right of the dismissed person to have recourse to the competent authority within ten days from receiving the notification.

A cursory examination of the three drafts would reveal that they are quite similar. However, a detailed study reveals some significant differences. The promulgated version is more refined and decisive; it provides needed clarity without destroying the vision of the 1977 version.

IV. EVALUATION AND CONCLUSION

The promulgated text is set out as follows:

Section I: Institutes of consecrated life

Title I: Common norms for all institutes of consecrated life. Thirty-four general canons applicable both to religious and secular institutes, and also to some extent to societies of apostolic life, are found in this part (CC 573–606).

Title II: Religious institutes (CC 607–709). The matter is divided into eight chapters: religious houses, their erection and suppression; the government of institutes; the admission of candidates and the formation of members; the obligations and rights of members of institutes; the apostolate of institutes; separation of members from the institute; religious promoted to the episcopacy; conferences of major superiors.

Title III: Secular institutes (CC 710–730). Twenty-one canons which at times refer to the canons on religious.

Section II: Societies of apostolic life (CC 731–746). Sixteen canons which also refer abundantly to the canons on religious.

These new canons incorporate most of the changes that were authorized on an experimental basis during the post-conciliar years. In this regard the law contains few surprises.

Along with the section of the rights of the faithful and the law on sanctions, it is one part of the 1983 Code that has been completely recast. It exudes a new spirit: one of adulthood in a committed Church.

The law leaves a number of questions unanswered or gives rather ambiguous statements, but these will provide for future growth. Some of the questions still to be clarified are found in C 591 (exemption), C 595 (who approves constitutions for pontifical institutes), C 596 (the nature of the authority or power held in lay communities), C 602 (the modalities of common life), C 604 (the nature of consecrated virginity and its effects in law), C 608 (the "residence" when religious are unable to reside in a "house"), C 617 (the power of superiors), C 638 (the nature of extraordinary administration), C 687 (the dependency of exclaustrated religious on the local Ordinary), C 731 (the way in which societies of apostolic life are likened to institutes of consecrated life), etc. In some instances practical experience provides the answer to these queries; in others, such as with C 731, the subcommission took the most commonly held position.

There is no doubt that the law respects the gift of consecrated life in the Church, recognizes the unique character of each institute, provides for flexibility and subsidiarity, and offers means of promoting the participation of all members in the life and mission of the institute. It also clearly defines the object of the evangelical counsels, leaving particular specifications to individual communities. But, most of all, it traces a sure path that enables each member of an institute or society to respond to God's call in fidelity and love.

The new Code, in C 1752, ends by speaking of the fact that the supreme law is the salvation of souls. For religious, this is complemented by the supreme rule of life which consists in following Christ,[61] and in giving the testimony of consecrated life which is fostered by prayer and penance.[62] If such were observed and produced the much desired effects, then the efforts spent in revising the law will have been quite worthwhile. The challenge is given to each member of an institute of consecrated life or a society of apostolic life to respond to the divine call to the perfection of charity. The new law traces a clear path leading eventually to such a goal.

NOTES

1. John Paul II, Apostolic Constitution *Sacrae Disciplinae Leges*, pars II, *AAS* 75.
2. Paul VI, Allocution of February 8, 1973. *The Pope Speaks* 18 (1973–1974) 78.
3. Paul VI, Allocution of September 17, 1973. *Origins* 3 (1973–1974) 272.
4. C 825 §1.
5. *Comm* 1(1969) 55–56.
6. Many of the points in the following study as taken from the study prepared by Abbot V. Dammertz, "Institutes of Consecrated Life in the New Canon Law," *USG*, Circ. N. 33/82, October 27, 1982, 26 p. (ms).
7. C 662.
8. CC 618, 619.
9. C 573.
10. *Comm* 2 (1970) 170–71.
11. *Comm* 1(1969) 78–79.
12. CC 578, 587.
13. C 646.
14. C 659.
15. *Comm* 1(1969) 80.
16. Cf. CC 593, 595.
17. C 587.
18. C 650.
19. C 631, §2.

20. C 635, §2.

21. C 617.

22. C 668 §2. See *Cum Admotae* (Sec. St., Rescript, November 6, 1964) Nos 16 and 17, *AAS* 59–374 (Faculties of Superiors General of Pontifical Clerical Religious Institutes and of Abbots President of Monastic Congregations, *CLD* 6:147) and repeated in *RL*, etc.

23. C 581.

24. C 686, §1.

25. C 838, §4.

26. CC 675, §3; 678.

27. CC 801, 804.

28. C 678.

29. C 618.

30. C 631.

31. C 625.

32. C 134.

33. C 1302.

34. C 628.

35. CC 609, 614, 667, §2.

36. *LG* 45, §3.

37. *LG* 43, §1; C 573, §2.

38. C 573, §2.

39. C 656, §5.

40. See Richard A. Hill, "The Community and the Option of Non-Canonical Status," *RfR* 41(1982) 542–50.

41. C 675, §3.

42. C 670.

43. C 654.

44. *RC 34.*

45. *LG* 44, §1.

46. Secretariate of State, Prot. No. 41,829, August 12, 1980, in PONTIFICIA COMMISSIO CODICI IURIS CANONICI RECOGNOSCENDO, *Relatio complectens synthesim animadversionum* . . . , Typis polyglottis vaticanis, 1981, 133.

47. V. Dammertz, 4.

48. C 605.

49. CC 603, 604.

50. C 591.

51. See CC 204, 617, 758, 776, 801, 835, §4.

52. See C 677.

53. CC 674, 776.

54. J. Beyer, "Le deuxième projet de droit pour la vie consacrée," *Stud Can* 15(1981) 127. The 1977 draft of the canons is found in PONTIFICIA COMMISSIO CODICI IURIS CANONICI RECOGNOSCENDO, *Schema canonum de institutis vitae consecratae per professionem consiliorum evangelicorum*, Typis polyglottis vaticanis, 1977, xiii–37 p.

55. Cf. J. Beyer, 121–24.

56. See *PC* 12. The 1980 draft is found in PONTIFICIA COMMISSIO CODICI IURIS CANONICI RECOGNOSCENDO, *Codex Iuris Canonici, Schema Patribus Commissionis Reservatum*, Libreria editrice vaticana, 1980, CC 503–672.

57. Cf. J. Beyer, 96.

58. C 690.

59. C 690.
60. C 695.
61. C 662.
62. C 673.

BIBLIOGRAPHY

Beyer, Jean. "Le deuxième projet de droit pour la vie consacrée," *StudCan* 15(1981) 87-134.

Beyer, Jean. "Religious in the New Code and their place in the Local Church," *Canon Law Society of Great Britain and Ireland, Newsletter* (September 1982) 119-32.

Beyer, Jean. *Vers un nouveau droit des Instituts de vie consacrée.* Paris-Fribourg: Editions S. Paul, 1978, 352 p.

Dammertz, Viktor. "Institutes of Consecrated Life in the New Canon Law," *Union of Superiors General, Mensilis* (October 27, 1982) 26 p. (ms).

Gutierrez, Anastasio. "Schema Canonum a. 1980 emendatorum," *CpR* 61(1980) 193-207.

Hill, Richard. "The Community and the Option of Non-Canonical Status," *RfR* 41(1982) 542-50.

Kelly, M. Thaddea. "Religious Life and Law: The Implications," *The New Canon Law: Perspectives on the Law, Religious Life, and the Laity.* St. Louis: Catholic Health Association, 1983, 15-25.

Leduc, Jacques. "Principles of Common Law and the 1977 Schema of Canons on Institutes of Life Consecrated by Profession of the Evangelical Counsels," *StudCan* 14(1980) 405-22.

Leonard, Joan de Lourdes. "Religious Life and the New Code," *The New Canon Law . . . ,* 26-35.

Molinari, Paul. "Formation à la vie religieuse selon une dimension ecclésiale," *Vie Consacrée* 4(1979) 220-36.

Morrisey, Francis. "The Laity in the New Code of Canon Law," *The New Canon Law . . . ,* 36-48.

Morrisey, Francis. "The Spirit of the Proposed New Law for Institutes of Consecrated Life," *StudCan* 9(1975) 77-94.

O'Rourke, Kevin. "The New Law for Religious: Principles, Content, Evaluation," *RfR* 34(1975) 23-49.

Orsy, Ladislas. "A Theology of the Local Church and Religious Life," *RfR* 36(1977) 666-82.

Orsy, Ladislas. "A Theological Evaluation of the New Law for Religious," *The New Canon Law . . . ,* 62-67.

PONTIFICIA COMMISSIO CODICI IURIS CANONICI RECOGNOSCENDO, "Coetus Studiorum de Institutis Vitae Consecratae per Professionem Consiliorum Evangelicorum," *Comm* 11(1979) 22-26, 296-346; 12(1980) 130-87; 13(1981) 151-211, 325-407.

Said, Mark. "Particular Law of Institutes in the Renewal of Consecrated Life," *RfR* 36(1977) 924-47.

Norms Common to All Institutes of Consecrated Life
Canons 573–606

ELLEN O'HARA, C.S.J.

GENERAL COMMENTS

In reading the minutes of the *coetus* assigned to revise the 1977 draft proposal, one realizes that several decisions were made which affect the structure and content of the new law. (These minutes are in *Communicationes*, published by the Pontifical Commission for the Revision of Canon Law.) The first decision was to keep a first section on preliminary norms and then treat religious institutes, societies of common life, and secular institutes more specifically in later sections. There was a concern expressed both by members of the *coetus* and by several Sacred Congregations that the earlier draft would lead to a flattening out *(appiattimento)* of the forms of religious life and to a secularization of religious. Concern was also expressed within the *coetus* that a proper balance be struck between necessary detail and respect for proper law.

The *coetus* decided to let the preliminary norms (CC 573–606) stand as a separate section stating the fundamental elements of any life consecrated by profession of the evangelical counsels. Other decisions were to use 1917 Code terminology as much as possible and to use exhortations sparingly. There was some discussion over whether or not the requirement of *ES* that proper law suitably blend both theological and juridic elements also applied to the new Code. No final decision is recorded, but C 587, §3 requires just such a blending.

Three other matters should be noted: the term *ius proprium* was to be used whenever the new law would leave to the discretion of the institute the decision of where in their various legal documents different norms would be situated; the former term "dominative power" (used instead of jurisdiction in non-clerical religious institutes) has been superseded since all now can participate in the power of governance or exercise jurisdiction in accordance with the norms of law;[1] there was a notable attempt on the part of the *coetus* to be sensitive to the wording of these preliminary norms and their effect on secular institutes.

C 573

§1. Life consecrated by the profession of the evangelical counsels is a stable form of living by which faithful, following Christ more closely under the action of the Holy Spirit, are totally dedicated to God who is loved most of all, so that, having dedicated themselves to His honor, the upbuilding of the Church and the salvation of the world by a new and special title, they strive for the perfection of charity in service to the Kingdom of God and, having become an outstanding sign in the Church, they may foretell the heavenly glory.

§2. Christian faithful who profess the evangelical counsels of chastity, poverty and obedience by vows or other sacred bonds according to the proper laws of institutes freely assume this form of living in institutes of consecrated life canonically erected by competent church authority and through the charity to which these counsels lead they are joined to the Church and its mystery in a special way.

This canon is the essential canon for institutes of consecrated life. The sources for the canon are *LG* 43–45 and *PC* 6. One notable change from the equivalent Code canon is the omission of the phrase "in common" to describe the stable form of living. Not all secular institutes, which were officially and juridically recognized by Pius XII in an apostolic constitution on February 2, 1947, have a common life.[2] Neither do these secular institutes make public profession of the counsels; therefore, the word "public" was not used here. "Public" does appear in C 654 in reference to the vows of religious. The reference in §2 to "vows or other sacred bonds" is meant to encompass societies of apostolic life and secular institutes, neither of which take public vows. This is a change from interim law, which allowed members of religious institutes to make temporary profession by vows or other sacred bonds. In the Code the assumption is that religious make or renew profession by means of vows only (cf. SCRIS decree, February 2, 1984). Lastly, the term "consecrated life" in the canons applies to religious, secular institutes, hermits, and those consecrated by the rite of virgins.

C 573 is a combination of both theological and juridical elements. Following the wording of the canon, the choice for consecrated life is an explicitation of the prior choice for Christ in baptism. Both theologically and juridically, the choice for consecrated life is to be a total

ecclesial context as part of the Church's patrimony. This statement is the basis for the Church's authority in the next canon.

It is the teaching of Vatican II in *LG* that the practice of the evangelical counsels is incumbent upon all Christians. The practice is seen as an extension into the life of the individual Christian of the life-style of Jesus Christ. In the past, specific scriptural quotes have been taken out of context and used as proof texts for one or the other of the evangelical counsels. Modern Scripture studies show the danger of misinterpretation in taking such quotes out of context. Consequently, typical bases for the practice of evangelical counsels usually arise out of a study of the Gospels as a whole. Two recent books which deal with the biblical bases for the practice of the evangelical counsels within religious life are Francis Moloney's *Disciples and Prophets*[3] and John Lozano's *Discipleship: Towards an Understanding of Religious Life.*[4]

C 576

It belongs to the competent authority of the Church to interpret the evangelical counsels, to regulate their practice by laws, to constitute therefrom stable forms of living by canonical approbation, and, for its part, to take care that the institutes grow and flourish according to the spirit of the founders and wholesome traditions.

The source of this canon is *LG* 43 and 45. The canon has undergone several revisions which are important. Earlier, in the 1977 draft, reference was made to ecclesiastical authority's interpreting the counsels under the guidance of the Holy Spirit. This phrase was dropped in the revision of the canon because the committee felt that it could give rise to false interpretations as to the appropriate actions or interventions of hierarchy in the internal actions of a religious institute. In the 1980 draft and the promulgated text, the phrase about the spirit of the founders was enlarged to "and wholesome traditions" to indicate the value of authentic historical development. Finally, the phrase about the Church authority "on its part" was added to preclude an overly hierarchical interpretation, according to the *coetus*. This canon needs to be seen in concert with CC 578, 586, and 587.

C 579 deals with who is the competent authority to erect new *institutes;* C 605 deals with approving new *forms* of consecrated life. The first level of Church authority in this matter is the institute itself, which interprets and specifies the living out of the counsels in its proper law. The second level is that of the competent ecclesiastical superior, depending on whether the institute is pontifical or diocesan. The highest ecclesiastical superior is the Roman pontiff. Beyond the issue of ecclesiastical superiors, there is the mutual responsibility of religious and local ordinaries, discussed at great length in the document *MR*, 1978.

C 577

In the Church there are very many institutes of consecrated life which have different gifts according to the grace which has been given them: they follow Christ more closely as He prays, announces the Kingdom of God, performs good works for people, shares His life with them in the world, and yet always does the will of the Father.

In contrast to the preceding canon, which is wholly juridic, this canon is theological. In its wording, it gives both acknowledgement and legitimacy to the diversity of institutes of consecrated life. The reference to the multiplicity of institutes and their different gifts is a corrective to any attempt at an univocal concept of institutes of consecrated life. The canon is a corrective statement to the kind of "flattening out" which was feared in terms of regarding the diversity of charism and service which religious institutes offer to the Church. Likewise, the *Sequela Christi*, or "following of Christ" is pointed out as that which unifies institutes of consecrated life, despite their diversity.

C 578

The intention of the founders and their determination concerning the nature, purpose, spirit and character of the institute which have been ratified by competent ecclesiastical authority as well as its wholesome traditions, all of which constitute the patrimony of the institute itself, are to be observed faithfully by all.

The source of this canon is *PC* 2b. The wording of the 1977 draft was strengthened from "plans sanctioned by Church authority" to "approval by competent Church authority" and the phrase about constituting the patrimony of the institute wasn't there. The *coetus* rejected a suggested reference to the needs of the times because they felt that was included in the reference to traditions and because they didn't wish to encourage "too much continuing *aggiornamento*." This canon is important for several reasons: it requires that the institutes know their legitimate history, both of founders and graced development since then, and that legitimate historical changes be distinguished from historical accretions.[5]

In an emphasis on returning to discover the original charism of the founder, some institutes have discovered that there was no particularly original charism, but rather a response to the particular needs of a local community at the time of founding. An example of this might be a group of religious who were founded in a particular area of the United States to meet the needs of the immigrants in that area. Consequently, research into the intentions of the founders and their plans must include putting these within the proper context of ecclesiastical, historical, and cultural needs. The intention may remain the same, while the carrying out may entail involvement in different ministries or a different form of the apostolate at the present time.

The reality of the problems in trying to determine the founder's intention may be one of the reasons why the Code, following the documents of Vatican II, does not use the word "charism" with reference to the founding of an institute. Further, the Latin text speaks of "wholesome or authentic traditions" in the plural. In the Catholic Church, the concept of tradition has a time-honored place and involves the handing on not only of the content of the faith, but also time-proven ways for living out that faith. Within a religious congregation, the same could be said in terms of a searching out its authentic or wholesome traditions. The best judge of these would be the congregation itself, for the effect of such traditions is best seen in how they bear fruit within the community. At times, tradition can have value for the continuity it expresses with the past, and its continued relevance in the present; at other times, the original value and purpose of the tradition has been lost and the continued legalistic observance of such, merely for the sake of tradition, is counterproductive to the life of the community. The distinction into "wholesome traditions" rather than simply using the generic term "traditions" should be both a caution and a reminder to institutes in their continued living out of the responsibility of consecrated life within a particular institute, but for the purposes mentioned in C 573, i.e., the honoring of God, the upbuilding of the Church, and the salvation of the world.

C 579

Diocesan bishops each in his own territory can erect institutes of consecrated life by a formal decree, provided that the Apostolic See has been consulted.

This canon is almost identical to CIC 492; the addition is that the erection of such institutes must be by a formal decree as has been a required practice since 1922, by decree of the Sacred Congregation for Religious. [6] The canon also requires consultation with the Apostolic See prior to the decree of erection. This consultation is required *for validity*, since the Latin *dummodo* is used and the *coetus* also indicated that was the intent of the canon. For missionary dioceses, the contact with the Apostolic See is through the Sacred Congregation for the Evangelization of Peoples; for other dioceses, the contact is with the Sacred Congregation for Religious and Secular Institutes. [7]

In the older law only the Holy See could establish religious orders; diocesan bishops could only establish congregations (simple vows) or secular institutes. It remains to be seen whether the use of the term "institutes" in this canon will change this practice.

The document, MR 51, speaks of some cautions to be exercised by bishops in attempting to form or to recognize new institutes of consecrated life. In the United States the particular question has arisen as to the possibility of persons who are currently religious maintaining their public vows while joining a "pious union" (an association of the faithful) which intends to become a religious institute. The usual practice is to require the religious to seek an indult of departure and then profess new vows should the new group be recognized as a religious institute; however, exceptions to this rule have occurred within the past few years. Prior to erecting such new institutes, the concerns of stability of the group, financial stability, and the ability to attract and keep new members, would be important. Likewise, there is need to evidence that the group has indeed a gift given by the Spirit for the benefit of the Church (charism) and is not a ready "labor supply" to meet a particular need in a diocese. The possibility of a group's joining an already established institute should also be investigated.

C 580

The aggregation of one institute of consecrated life to another is reserved to the competent authority of the aggregating institute, always safeguarding the canonical autonomy of the aggregated institute.

There is no particular source for this canon. The *coetus*, in its discussion, decided not to define the term. The term "aggregation" in their discussion relates to either connection between a religious congregation or order and a secular institute, for example, for apostolic purposes, or to third-order relationships to a first or second order. The *coetus* voted (6–5) to stress both the authority of the aggregating institute and the continued autonomy of the aggregated group. This is a distinct phenomenon from mergers, federations, etc., discussed below in C 582. The proper law of the aggregating institute would specify who the competent authority within the institute would be; if the proper law is silent, determinations would have to be made in the individual case about who the competent authority is.

C 581

Dividing an institute into parts, whatever the parts are called, erecting new ones, joining previously erected parts or defining them in another way pertains to the competent authority of the institute, in accord with the norm of the constitutions.

This canon is the equivalent of C 494, §1 in the Code, but the authority has changed. This canon is one of the places where the promulgated text changed the 1980 draft by restoring the requirement that the competent authority be stated in the constitutions. A recent phenomenon, which is only indirectly related to this canon, is the formation of subgroups within the institute according to views on renewal, religious lifestyle or a similar basis. Some institutes are allowing this informally (e.g., by designating certain convents or geographical areas); others are allowing the subgroup to draw up names, agreements, etc. For one such example, cf. *CLD*, vol. 8, pp. 304–09.

C 582

Mergers and unions of institutes of consecrated life are reserved to the Apostolic See alone; confederations and federations are also reserved to it.

This canon is a specific juridic one. The source material for this canon can be found in *PC* 21–22 and *ES* II, 39–41. Separate phenomena are discussed within the one canon: Mergers, unions, federations, and confederations. In a "merger," one of the groups maintains its canonical identity while absorbing the other. At times the group which is being absorbed is totally absorbed into the other group; at other times, the group which is being absorbed maintains some sort of identity in the form of becoming a province or at least some identifiable structure within the other group. In the case of a "union," all of the groups involved relinquish their previous legal or canonical identities and form a new public juridic person. All of the groups involved in the union enter the formation of the new institute as equals. Until recently mergers were more common and usually involved the absorption of a smaller group into the canonical structure of a larger group. Documents used as a source for this canon emphasize that the scarcity of members and lack of reasonable hope of further development are reasons to consider a merger. In both documents, the similarity of goals, spirit, law, and customs is to be considered in a proposed merger of institutes. The requirement of *ES* should be carefully noted, particularly with regard to adequate and careful preparation and the freedom of choice of each member.

Two recent examples of approved mergers involving the absorption of one group into another are mentioned in *CLD*[8]. The *Digest* also includes examples of approved unions.[9] It should be noted that in the case of a merger and in the case of a union, the members of the institutes retain their identity as religious. In the case of a union, there is a simultaneous extinction of the former canonical identities of the religious institutes and the erection of a new public juridic person of the new institute.

This canon also speaks of federations and confederations. In the United States the term "federation" is used in several ways. At times, it refers to separate religious institutes who come from the same historical roots and founding charism. The uniting factors among these autonomous institutes are history and charism. Often, the federation participates in joint meetings or projects, but federation officers have no authority over member institutes, who are free to withdraw from the federation at any time. A second type of federation exists when the term is used as it is for the groupings of Benedictine communities of men and women in the United States. In these cases the communities maintain a great degree of autonomy, but at the same time have a juridic relationship with the federation and some common proper law. The term "confederation" refers to the joint meeting of two or more federations. At the level of confederation, the relationships are usually non-legal. The wording of the canon indicates that any merger or union of religious institutes or the establishment of federations or confederations is reserved to the Holy See. Whether the reservation to the Holy See would apply to the merging or uniting of federations would depend upon how the term "federation" applied to the legal personality of the institutes involved.

C 583

Changes in institutes of consecrated life which affect matters which have been approved by the Apostolic See cannot be made without its permission.

This canon is also a strictly juridic canon. There is no particular document that forms the source material for this canon, but the canon is consistent with the general principle and tradition of law that the one who has the authority to effect something legally is also the source of the authority for making changes. In the earlier drafts of this canon, mention was made only of needing the *beneplacitum* of the Holy See; the promulgated text requires the permission of the Apostolic See. The term *beneplacitum* refers to the goodwill or pleasure of the one in authority, indicating that only the acquiescence of that authority (either stated or tacit) is necessary. The switch to the word "permission" indicates a stronger, more definite, and more juridic involvement is necessary for the changes. One example of current importance as institutes revise their proper law is that Book I, usually referred to as the fundamental code or constitutions, requires approval of the competent ecclesiastical authority. For pontifical-right institutes, this means approval by the Apostolic See; therefore, future changes in this book would also require such approval.

C 584

§1. **Suppressing an institute pertains to the Apostolic See alone, to whom also it is reserved to determine what is to be done with the temporal goods of the institute.**

This canon is listed as 1, but there is no 2 in the edition currently available. There is a similar canon, CIC 493, in the 1917 Code, but the old canon had an additional phrase about wills and intentions of donors being safeguarded. There are two important juridic matters to be noted here. The first is that this canon is an exception to the general principle that the authority which creates can also extinguish: a diocesan bishop can erect a diocesan institute, but he cannot suppress it. Second, the canon will need to be interpreted in the light of C 123, which states that when a public juridic person is extinguished, the destination of its goods is ruled by law and by its statutes, always observing the will of founders and donors and acquired rights. Only when these statutes are silent does the determination about the goods fall to the immediately superior juridic person. For a pontifical right institute, this would be the Holy See, but for a diocesan institute, the immediately superior juridic person is the diocesan bishop. Therefore, this canon is an exception in the law itself to the statement of C 123.

C 585

Suppressing parts of an institute pertains to the competent authority of the institute itself.

The source is CIC 494 of the 1917 Code. In the earlier Code, the Apostolic See was needed to suppress parts of an institute of pontifical right: this right for *all* institutes will now reside with the competent authority of the institute. Who the competent authority is to be will have to be decided in the proper law of that institute (although it need not appear in the constitutions, since this is not specified in the canon). The competent authority of the institute could be a chapter or, depending on the size of the part and the consequent effects on the members, the supreme moderator, with consent of the council. Such an action is clearly an act of extraordinary administration and should follow the laws for this. When the suppressed part had juridic personality (e.g., the suppressed part was a province, which was a separate moral or juridic person), laws for the extinction of juridic persons have to be followed. The laws for extinction of juridic persons are found in CC 120 and 123. In addition, if these parts enjoyed a civil legal identity (i.e., were incorporated), the appropriate civil actions need to be taken.

C 586

§1. For individual institutes there is acknowledged a rightful autonomy of life, especially of governance, by which they enjoy their own discipline in the Church and have the power to preserve their own patrimony intact as mentioned in can. 578.

§2. It belongs to local ordinaries to safeguard and protect this autonomy.

There is no specific source from which the text of this canon was taken. The just autonomy of the institute is the necessary corrective to unwarranted hierarchial influence. The level at which real collaboration, communication, and cooperation should take place cannot be mandated in law: these living relationships are far more complex and need greater attention than a legal minimum. It is interesting to note that the 1977 draft gave this responsibility to the Apostolic See and bishops and used the verbs "to sanction and safeguard." The 1980 draft gave the responsibility to bishops and chose the verbs "to protect and foster"; the new law uses the verbs "to safeguard and protect." The changes suggest some lack of clarity about the exact role, but greater clarity may need to evolve rather than be defined!

C 587

§1. In order to protect more faithfully the particular vocation and identity of each institute, its fundamental code or constitutions must contain, besides what must be observed according to can. 578, fundamental norms about the governance of the institute and the discipline of members, the incorporation and formation of members, and the proper object of sacred bonds.

§2. A code of this kind is approved by the competent authority of the Church and can be changed only with its consent.

§3. In this code spiritual and juridical elements are to be suitably joined together; however norms are not to be multiplied unless it is necessary.

§4. Other norms established by the competent authority of the institute are to be suitably collected in other codes, which can moreover be fittingly reviewed and adapted according to the needs of places and times.

The sources for this canon are *PC* 2 and *ES* II, 12–14. This is the canon about the revision of the proper law of an institute. The proper law includes this first book or constitutions, the second and any other books (e.g., policy or procedure books), acts and decrees of chapters within the limits of their authority, and legitimate precepts of superiors. Some confusion exists as to the status of these revised books before final approval of the competent authority: they have the interim authority of proper law once passed by legitimate authority of the institute. Section 1 speaks of the content of the first book.[10]

In the 1983 Code the section on religious life makes references to various items which must appear in the *ius proprium* of the institute. This would be the institute's own law, or proper law. At times, the Code is more specific and requires that a particular item appear in the constitutions. This is usually what is referred to as Book I, as mentioned above. In development of new documents, institutes should keep in mind these distinctions and be aware that those things which are required to be in the constitutions must appear in the Book I of their proper law. Items which are to appear or be specified in the institute's own law may appear in the constitution, Book II, or in other policy or procedural books which the institute has developed. Specifically, those matters which the Code requires to appear in the constitutions are the following: the competent authority to erect or divide parts of the institute (C 581), specific topics which must be covered in the constitutions (C 587), the bishop to approve and grant dispensation from the constitutions for diocesan communities (C 595), the definition of the powers of superiors in chapters (C 596), the specific mode of living out the evangelical counsel within the institute (C 598), the specific mode, in particular, of living out the vow of obedience (C 601), the authority competent to erect houses of the institute (C 609), the autonomous nature of houses of canons regular and monks (C 613), the governance of nuns whose institute is connected to an institute of men (C 614), the power of a superior in an autonomous monastery (C 615), the authority competent to suppress houses of an institute (C 616). In addition, the Code specifies that these items also be specified in the constitutions: the requirements for major superiors (C 623), the exception to the term of office for the supreme moderator and local superiors (C 624), the mode of election of the supreme moderator in the institute and the confirmation of other superiors (C 625), provision for councils to assist the superiors (C 627), the authority of the general chapter (C 631), the limitation of rights with regard to temporal goods if there are any (CC 634 and 668), the allowance for periods of apostolic activity during the novitiate (C 648), the specification of how the following of Christ is to be lived in the institute (C 662), definition of how cloister is to be observed for nuns whose life is not wholly ordered to the contemplative (C 667), and the definition of which necessities the institute must provide for its members (C 670).

Section 2 refers to the competent authority to approve codes. Only Book I technically needs approval by the higher ecclesiastical superior, but both or all the necessary books are usually submitted this first time to allow for examination for completeness. For diocesan congregations, the competent authority, according to C 595, is the bishop of the diocese in which the principal seat of the institute is located. If the institute has spread to several dioceses, the bishop is to consult with the other diocesan bishops before approval. This consultation does not require their consent.

For institutes of pontifical right, the process is more involved. After a process which has involved all of the members of the institute, the documents should be ratified by the general chapter of the institute. Several copies of the document are then sent to SCRIS. The institute then enters a period of dialogue with SCRIS, during which a group of consultors (known as a *congresso*) studies the documents and makes suggestions for clarifications or changes. In most institutes, this process involves a period of dialogue during which the documents may be returned to the institute one or several times for the recommended changes and clarifications. While the process is the same in general, variations in emphases occur among institutes. Areas in which clarifications or changes are usually requested include the definition of the content of the vows, specification about spiritual practices such as prayer and other devotion, as well as reception of the sacraments, and the exercise of authority, particularly the personal authority of the superiors at every level within the institute. (The Leadership Conference of Women Religious in the United States has begun to publish an information bulletin on the experience of the process of approbation by several of its member institutes.)

C 588

§1. The state of consecrated life by its very nature is neither clerical nor lay.

§2. An institute is said to be clerical if, by reason of the purpose or design intended by its founder or in virtue of legitimate tradition, it is under the supervision of clerics, it assumes the exercise of sacred orders, and it is recognized as such by church authority.

§3. An institute is called lay if recognized as such by church authority, by virtue of its nature, character and purpose it has a proper function defined by the founder or by legitimate tradition which does not include the exercise of sacred orders.

This canon is both theological and juridical. The source of §1, a theological statement about consecrated life, in *LG* 43. There are no direct sources for the other two paragraphs. An earlier draft of §1 spoke of institutes of consecrated life as being neither clerical nor lay, but the committee writing the law felt it was more accurate to speak of the *state* of consecrated life, rather than institutes, and so revised the paragraph. The statement is a logical consequence of the teaching of *LG* that religious life, while belonging to the holiness of the Church, is not part of its essential structure. The state of consecrated life in itself involves a further specification of the baptismal commitment and response to the call of the Lord. Hence, there can be lay religious and clerical religious, depending upon whether the individual religious has received the sacrament of orders or not. At the same time, a specific institute may be clerical or lay by virtue of its founding and tradition. The definition of clerical and lay institutes is the basis for the rest of this canon.

In §2, the phrase "under the regulation of clerics" was added to the 1980 draft and to the promulgated version. Two different issues emerge here. One is the request by several previously clerical institutes to allow non-clerics (e.g., brothers) to assume offices of authority in the institute, even as major superiors. This idea has surfaced among Jesuits, Franciscans, and Passionists, for example, but has not met with general agreement in Rome. In 1967, the general chapter of the Order of Friars Minor voted to regard all members "as friars" so that any distinction in eligibility for office among members would be eliminated. This was submitted to SCRIS for final approval, and on November 27, 1969, SCRIS issued *Clericalia instituta*. In this decree the decision is that in clerical institutes of consecrated life, the nonclerical members may hold administrative offices, the function of councilor at any level, but specifically *not* the office of "superior or of vicar, general, provincial, or local." [11] Several years later, the Order of Friars Minor Capuchin requested an exception to this decree, in order to allow a nonclerical member to serve as vicar of a local superior. This was granted by the Sacred Congregation on November 12, 1974. [12] Later, SCRIS also granted an indult allowing a nonclerical brother to be a local superior in a clerical community. Despite such exceptions, it appears the intent of the law is that the same basic position is held, namely, that nonclerical members may not in fact be superiors in clerical institutes, except by way of limited exception.

Within this canon, it is also interesting to note the difference in priority of Church recognition between clerical institutes and lay institutes. While Church recognition appears as the last criterion of a clerical institute, it is listed as the first criterion for a lay institute. This is at least partially attributable to the surge in the founding of new institutes, a practice which the Apostolic See has tried to discourage outside of mission areas.

C 589

An institute of consecrated life is said to be of pontifical right if it has been erected by the Apostolic See or approved by a formal decree of the Apostolic See; on the other hand an institute is said to be of diocesan right if, after having been erected by a diocesan bishop, it has not obtained a decree of approval from the Apostolic See.

The source of this canon is CIC 488, §3 of the older Code. The distinction between diocesan and pontifical institutes was introduced by Pope Leo XIII in the Constitution *Conditae a Christo*, issued in 1900. Although the law does not specifically stipulate this, there was an original intention that all diocesan institutes would eventually become pontifical if they continued to grow. This has not been the case and some congregations have chosen to remain diocesan. There have also been instances where a province in the United States has separated from the original institute and become a separate institute of consecrated life of pontifical right immediately.

C 590

§1. Institutes of consecrated life, inasmuch as they are dedicated in a special way to the service of God and of the entire Church, are subject to the supreme authority of this same Church in a special manner.

§2. Individual members are also bound to obey the Supreme Pontiff as their highest superior by reason of the sacred bond of obedience.

There is no particular text as source for §1; §2 is taken from CIC 499, §1 of the old Code. The supreme authority of the Church by definition includes the Roman Pontiff and the college of bishops (cf., CC 330, 331, and 336). The only distinctions in §2 from the equivalent Code canons are the switch from Roman to Supreme Pontiff and the substitution of "sacred bond" for "vow" to encompass those in institutes of consecrated life who do not profess vows. In times of societal and ecclesial stress, a canon such as this can easily lead to misunderstanding or abuse. §1 particularizes the way in which institutes are subject as a result of their recognized juridic state in the Church. §2 speaks of individuals, but the context is that of the bondvow of obedience. The *content* of the vows differs within different institutes, as does the interpretation of the will of the superior; for example, whether or not one can disagree with a superior's decision and whether or not interior conformity of the will is part of the vow.

What can be commanded by a superior under the vow of obedience has legal parameters both in canon law and in civil law. In canon law the legal parameters are those which are stated in the proper law of the institute, as well as those which appear in canon law, and beyond that, anything which would involve sinfulness. In the United States, as well as in some other countries, the question of conscientious objection sometimes arises. This discussion has both theological and cultural factors involved. The theological question is complex, involving the basic duty of the individual to follow his or her own conscience, while at the same time trying to ensure that that conscience is well-informed and that the decision has been made on a sound basis.

Within some traditions, the possibility of objecting to the command of a superior is possible. Francis allowed for it in his early rule, while Ignatius specifically required interior conformity of the will as well as external conformity. Thus, in addition to the complexity of moral issues involved in the possibility of objecting to the command of a superior, the question of the tradition of the institute and its spirituality is also a factor.

The issue in itself is too difficult and complex to address in the limited space here, but the issue does need to be faced. For those in the United States and other countries with an Anglo-Saxon heritage of law, the right to dissent and to have that dissent protected by law is often coupled with an assumed right to conscientious objection in terms of practice. Such is not the case in the tradition of law within the Church. In an address given in 1977, Pope Paul VI, in speaking of the goals of canon law, said, "wherefore, *conscientious objection*, which would do away with ecclesial obedience, is out of place."[13]

The other question, also needing discussion, is that of members of institutes of consecrated life who, as citizens of a particular nation, choose to be civilly disobedient in order to maintain obedience to a higher moral principle. In dealing with these issues, institutes of consecrated life need to be particularly sensitive to evolving a common agreement among their members, the effect of acts of civil disobedience on the corporate witness of the institute in a particular area, and the implications of such a decision for the communal understanding of the living out of the evangelical counsels. At times, it may be necessary to suggest to a particular person that his or her actions are not consonant with the communal position, while at other times and in other institutes, the same actions may be very much a part of the institute's corporate commitment. The question of the interpretation and application of this canon is part of larger unresolved issues, one of which is that of the bases and exercise of authority within a changed ecclesiology. It is important to remember that this is not solely an issue of *religious* law.

C 591

In order to provide better for the good of institutes and the needs of the apostolate, the Supreme Pontiff, by reason of his primacy over the universal Church and considering the common good, can exempt institutes of consecrated life from the governance of local ordinaries and subject them either to himself alone or to another ecclesiastical authority.

This canon states again the principle of exemption and its source is CIC 448, §2 of the old Code. Some changes should be noted. First, reasons are given for exemption, the same reasons mentioned in *CD* 35, although primary emphasis there is given to the reason of the internal organization of the institute. Second, the old Code and both previous drafts of this canon used the word "jurisdiction." The new law replaced the word with "governance." This is more legally correct since all religious, including the exempt remain under the diocesan bishop's jurisdiction in many important areas: liturgy, apostolate, establishment of a house, care of souls, fund-raising (as distinct from the privilege of begging), etc.

An understanding of the history of exemption is important to its context. Basically, the notion of exemption had to do with removing certain orders and congregations from the jurisdiction of the local bishop in order to enable them to carry out their mission more effectively. In the documents of Vatican II and subsequent documents, this emphasis on the pastoral value of exemption has been reconfirmed, although some of the specific aspects of mission have come under the jurisdiction of the local bishop again, as was mentioned above. Traditionally, exemption has meant that the institute involved was subject directly to the Roman Pontiff. Other possibilities exist but are not common.

C 592

§1. In order that the communion of institutes with the Apostolic See be better fostered each supreme moderator is to send a brief report on the status and life of the institute to the Apostolic See in a manner and at a time determined by the latter.

§2. The moderators of every institute are to promote knowledge of the documents of the Holy See which affect members entrusted to them and be concerned about their observance of them.

Both paragraphs of this canon restate juridic obligations which appeared in the previous Code. §1 of this canon is from the previous Code's CIC 510, §2, from the previous Code's CIC 509. Specifications will need to be made about the time and method of reporting by the Apostolic See. In reviewing the reports of the committee which wrote this section on religious law, two disagreements appear: whether or not this applies to diocesan institutes also and, in reference to §2, whether or not this applies to communications sent to superiors about particular situations within the community. In the latter case the committee agreed to suggest that the accompanying letter to the superior in question specify in a particular case as to whom the contents should be made known. §2 was expanded from the draft versions to include the phrase "and see to their observance" thereby extending to superiors' or moderators' responsibilities. In bringing attention to various documents from the Holy See, care will need to be taken that respect for the document not be confused with its juridic value. Documents of unequal juridic value will need to be perceived as such. [14]

C 593

With due regard for the prescription of can. 586, institutes of pontifical right are immediately and exclusively subject to the power of the Apostolic See in internal governance and discipline.

The basic source (with some changes) of this canon is CIC 499, §1 of the 1917 Code. The canon has been substantially revised in each draft (1977 and 1980) and in its promulgated version. Section 4 of the earlier drafts appears now as C 679. The minutes of the *coetus* indicate that they dropped some of the material with the intent of adding a new paragraph, which does not appear. The Canon Law Society of America had suggested changing power *(potestas)* to authority, but the word was kept. The content of "discipline" will probably give rise to a variety of interpretations and practices which will need to be resolved in individual cases. This canon does not change the fact that members and institutes of pontifical right remain subject to diocesan bishops in various areas. [15]

C 594

With due regard for can. 586, an institute of diocesan right remains under the special care of the diocesan bishop.

The source material for this canon is to be found in the previous Code's CIC 492, §2 and 493. The special care of the diocesan bishop to which the canon refers means that institutes of diocesan right, besides acknowledging the diocesan bishop as the competent ecclesiastical authority, also have other obligations to him, such as the annual financial report mentioned in C 1287. In addition, the diocesan bishop has a more special responsibility for the administration of temporal goods in general with respect to diocesan institutes (C 1276) and a closer concern for the spiritual and physical well-being of such members. Again, the working out of such a relationship can never completely be defined by law: elements of trust, respect for the autonomy of the institute, as well as for the diocesan bishop, and communication are essential. Likewise, the Code provides that this bishop preside at the election of the supreme moderator of institutes of diocesan right, [16] extend indults of exclaustration, [17] and impose exclaustration if necessary. [18]

C 595

§1. It belongs to the bishop of the principal seat of the institute to approve the constitutions and confirm any changes legitimately introduced into them, except in those matters in which the Apostolic See has intervened; it also belongs to him to deal with business of greater importance which affects the whole institute and which are beyond the power of its internal authority; he does so after consulting other diocesan bishops if the institute has spread to several dioceses.

§2. The diocesan bishop can grant dispensations from the constitutions in particular cases.

This canon is strictly juridic and applies only to institutes of diocesan right. The source for §1 is CIC 495, §2 of the previous Code, with one notable change: the bishop of the diocese of the principal seat needs only to *consult* the other bishops, if there are any; he does not need to obtain their agreement or approval. §2 is an example of the canonical principle that one who has the authority to approve law may dispense from it. The wording of §2 would allow for any of the diocesan bishops in whose diocese members of the institute are to grant dispensations in particular cases.

C 596

§1. Superiors and chapters of institutes enjoy that power over members which is defined in universal law and the constitutions.

§2. Moreover, in clerical religious institutes of pontifical right they also possess ecclesiastical power of governance for both the external and the internal forum.

§3. The prescriptions of cann. 131, 133 and 137-144 are applicable to the power referred to in §1.

The source of §1 and §2 is CIC 501, §1 of the 1917 Code. These paragraphs have remained the same throughout the revision drafts; §3 has been added since the 1980 draft. Here again, the Canon Law Society of America had recommended a change in the wording of "enjoy that power" (*gaudent ea potestate*). This power or authority effects what may be a matter of precept under the vow of obedience: it should more accurately state "universal or proper law," since the assumption of membership in an institute binds the member to acceptance of the law of the institute, not just the constitutions. §1 is applicable to all levels of superiors and chapters within the institute: general, provincial or equivalent, local.

§2, while having its source in the 1917 Code, changed that canon. The previous canon limited this power to exempt clerical institutes; the new law grants the power to clerical institutes of pontifical right. Further, the older canon spoke of ecclesiastical jurisdiction; this canon speaks of the ecclesiastical power of governance *(potestas regiminis)*. This is consistent with the thinking expressed earlier that one cannot properly speak of jurisdiction of superiors in secular institutes whose members remain incardinated in their dioceses.[19] Nevertheless, the new terminology may give rise to some problems of its own. A *forum* in canon law refers more to where an action takes place than to a physical place. The *external* forum refers to actions known or provable in public and having definite juridical effects. The *internal* forum refers to actions of conscience: it is private and has no specific juridic effects unless specifically provided for (e.g., by the Sacred Penitentiary). Internal forum actions may or may not involve the sacrament of Penance as their context. One of the principles of revision adopted by the 1967 Synod of Bishops was to reduce the conflicts between actions in the two fora. It is more technically correct and easier to speak of jurisdiction for the internal forum than to speak of governance in the internal forum. Does this mean that precepts may be given for matters of conscience or matters discussed within the sacrament of Penance? This was probably not the intent of the canon, but it may give rise to some difficulties before the authentic interpretation is ever made known. §3 refers the reader back to the section in Book I on the power of governance (CC 129–144). The canons mentioned have to do with the definition and scope of ordinary and delegated power of governance (subdivided in C 135 into legislative, executive, and judicial).

C 597

§1. Any Catholic, endowed with a right intention, who has the qualities required by universal and proper law and who is not prevented by any impediment can be admitted to an institute of consecrated life.

§2. No one can be admitted without suitable preparation.

The source of this canon is CIC 538 of the previous Code. In the revision of the 1977 draft, the *coetus* intentionally put reference to right intention and lack of impediments back into the text. "Right intention" is of particular significance today when there has been a noticeable increase in several types of applicants: young people with little or no formal training in Catholicism and rather rigid ideas of what religious life "should" be to meet their needs, recent converts or those who have had a recent conversion experience, divorced persons seeking to escape the trauma of failed relationships, and members of other institutes of consecrated life who desire transfer in reaction to something occurring in their own institutes. The impediments of universal law are listed in CC 641–645: these are impediments to admission to the novitiate because the new law does not treat the period prior to novitiate, which is the beginning of religious life. C 643, §2 states that the proper law of an institute may establish further impediments. Later canons in the sections on novitiate and training of religious deal more specifically with the meaning of "suitable preparation."

C 598

§1. Each institute, keeping in mind its own character and purposes is to define in its constitutions the manner in which the evangelical counsels of chastity, poverty and obedience are to be observed for its way of living.

§2. All members must not only observe the evangelical counsels faithfully and fully, but also organize their life according to the proper law of the institute and thereby strive for the perfection of their state.

There is no particular text as a source for §1; §2 is based on CIC 593 of the previous Code. Two things should be noted here: the *coetus* made a deliberate decision to name the counsels as chastity, poverty, and obedience. Secondly, the canon stipulates that each institute define in its first book, usually called constitutions, the manner of living out the counsels which is consonant with the institute's goal and character. This requires both research and study on the part of the institute and a greater awareness on the part of the institutional Church and some writers that the living out of the counsels among members of institutes of consecrated life is not intended to be uniform. In a private reply published in *CLD*, vol 7, p. 478ff., some suggestions are offered by SCRIS for expressing the content of the vows. It should be noted that expressing the content of the vows and the appropriate manner of living out the counsels has been one of the areas of continued discussion between institutes of pontifical right and SCRIS in the process of trying to obtain approval of proper law. In the reply mentioned previously, SCRIS leans heavily on the exhortation *ET* for its emphasis on the content of the vows. While stressing that a clear definition of each vow is necessary, these suggestions include the use of chastity or consecrated celibacy, not virginity; specifying the content of each vow as including positive action or positive emphasis; and the communal element in the living out of the vows. Specifically, with respect to the content of the vow of poverty, the simplicity of life-style, actual sharing and dependence upon the congregation, and accountability are to be included. With respect to obedience, the necessity for consultation and cooperation should be mentioned, as well as the obligation and right of the superior to exercise personal authority when necessary. §2 is an important corrective to some members of institutes who deny or denigrate the value of the proper law of their institute in favor of their own interpretation of how consecrated life should be lived.

C 599

The evangelical counsel of chastity assumed for the sake of the kingdom of heaven, as a sign of the future world and a source of more abundant fruitfulness in an undivided heart, entails the obligation of perfect continence in celibacy.

The source of this canon is *PC* 12. The style of this and the following two canons seems to be a theological statement about the counsel followed by some of the juridic content of the same counsel. The theological or first part is akin to what used to be known as the virtue, while the latter half is akin to the vow in the older commentaries and instructions which distinguished between the vow and virtue of each of the counsels. Of note juridically is the choice of the name chastity (although some have suggested or requested other options) and the "perfect continence in celibacy" as a requirement.

C 600

The evangelical counsel of poverty in imitation of Christ who, although He was rich became poor for us, entails, besides a life which is poor in fact and in spirit, a life of labor lived in moderation and foreign to earthly riches, a dependence and a limitation in the use and disposition of goods according to the norm of the proper law of each institute.

The source of this canon is *PC* 13. Earlier draft of this canon referred to the *sequela Christi*, but this has been changed to the "imitation of Christ." The juridic emphasis is on poverty of life-style and limitation with respect to temporal goods. The theology of poverty as "availability" is not apparent here, but that may be because of its limited evolution within only some of the more developed countries of the Western rite. Most of the specifications are left to proper law. Some of these may appear in the two books being developed as constitutions and Book II, but other matters could easily be left to policy manuals, e.g., use of budgets, personal allowances, travel, criteria for study, gifts, etc. CC 634–40 are more specifically directed to religious, C 718 to secular institutes, and C 741 for societies of apostolic life.

C 601

The evangelical counsel of obedience, undertaken in a spirit of faith and love in the following of Christ who was obedient even unto death requires a submission of the will to legitimate superiors, who stand in the place of God when they command according to the proper constitutions.

The source is *PC* 14. In this canon, as opposed to the previous canon, the earlier wording of "example of Christ" was changed to the *sequela Christi*. Earlier drafts spoke of dedication of the will, but the promulgated text chose "submission of the will." *PC* used the term "dedication"; "submission" is used in *ET* 27. The expression "taking the place of God" appeared in *PC*, but not in *ET*. There were several suggestions to remove this phrase, but its continued inclusion and the other wording changes in the canon are consistent with a very strong emphasis on authority present in the whole new Code. The draft wording was also changed to read according to particular *constitutions* because the *coetus* felt that profession is made according to the *constitutions*. There is obviously some unclarity about this term.

C 602

The life of brothers or sisters proper to each institute, by which all members are united together like a special family in Christ, is to be determined in such a way that it becomes a mutual support for all in fulfilling the vocation of each member. Moreover by their communion as brothers or sisters, rooted in and built on love, the members are to be an example of universal reconciliation in Christ.

The basis for this canon is found in *PC* 15. This canon calls attention to the positive witness value of the corporate aspects of consecrated life. The canon, which in its way is both an exhortation and an expression of a value, specifies that the communal life of an institute is to be lived with regard to the law and traditions of that institute, as well as its charism, and is to include a special bonding among the members that goes beyond legal minimum. This canon places the responsibility for the living out not only of personal vocation, but the vocations of the other members of the institute in such a way that mutual support is obvious. This canon is exhortatory in that it always calls for a movement beyond the present toward a greater openness and positive action to the up-building of community.

C 603

§1. Besides institutes of consecrated life, the Church recognizes the eremitic or anchoritic life by which the Christian faithful devote their life to the praise of God and salvation of the world through a stricter separation from the world, the silence of solitude and assiduous prayer and penance.

§2. A hermit is recognized in the law as one dedicated to God in a consecrated life if he or she publicly professes the three evangelical counsels, confirmed by a vow or other sacred bond, in the hands of the diocesan bishop and observes his or her own plan of life under his direction.

The basic source for this canon is *VS* I. The discussion of the *coetus* indicates that they used the verb "recognizes" *(agnoscit)* to intend official ecclesiastical juridical recognition. §2 offers a legal definition of a hermit. In practice, the terms "hermit" and "anchorite" are used almost synonymously. The *New Catholic Encyclopedia* nuances the difference slightly by distinguishing hermits as those who "retire to a place far from human habitation" to live the religious life and anchorites as those who live a solitary religious life in cells adjacent to a community. The revival of the eremitic form of life is occurring in various parts of the world, including areas of the United States. This canon offers a new possibility for those seeking such recognition. Care must be taken in moving ahead too quickly: the episcopal conference in consultation with other interested groups like LCWR or CMSM in the United States may want to issue suggested guidelines and a discussion of the ramifications. Certainly a period of approbation or temporary commitment is called for before the public profession mentioned in the canons. In particular, practical details such as financial responsibilities, regular contact, provision for sacraments, etc., should be worked out in advance. The term "religious" now applies to individuals with no obligation to common or community life and no relationship to an institute. Groups could use the category of associations of the faithful to have ecclesiastical identity if they wish.

C 604

§1. Similar to these forms of consecrated life is the order of virgins, who, committed to the holy plan of following Christ more closely, are consecrated to God by the diocesan bishop according to the approved liturgical rite, are betrothed mystically to Christ, the Son of God, and are dedicated to the service of the Church.

§2. In order to observe their commitment more faithfully and to perform by mutual support service to the Church which is in harmony with their state these virgins can form themselves into associations.

The basic source for this canon is the Rite for the Consecration of Virgins (May 31, 1970), 1 and 5. Historically, groups of widows and virgins are seen as antecedent forms of consecrated life. Some juridical matters to be noted: it is the *order* which is considered a form of consecrated life, not just individuals; connection to a diocesan bishop is stressed (as it was with hermits); dedication to the service of the Church is an element.

This order or consecration is available to both men and women;[20] in some institutes, individual members have made such a consecration. The canon does not require a public ceremony. §2 was the source of discussion within the *coetus*. This paragraph basically restates the more general right of Church members to associate, or form associations. More discussion and clarification will be needed in terms of the forms and status of such associations if any are formed. Two kinds of association are envisaged in the new law: public and private, both of which must have statutes and are under the supervision of ecclesiastical authority (cf. CC 298–329).

C 605

Approving new forms of consecrated life is reserved to the Apostolic See alone. Diocesan bishops, however, should strive to discern new gifts of consecrated life granted to the Church by the Holy Spirit and they should aid their promoters so that they can express their proposals as well as possible and protect them with suitable statutes, utilizing especially the general norms contained in this section.

The distinction in this canon is approval of new *forms* of consecrated life, not simply new institutes. This takes account of the phenomenon occurring in various parts of the world where groups of both men and women, sometimes both clerical and lay, join together in the pursuit of a new form of consecrated life. Some examples of new forms have already emerged, including Catherine Dougherty's group in Combermere, Ontario (which has the technical status of pious union, but which has never moved to more specific status of institute of consecrated life), or the *Seguimi*.[21] In the *CCD* (vol. 8, pp. 318–20) this *Seguimi* is referred to as "an institute of perfection" and also as a "new form" because it does not fit into the already established categories for institutes of consecrated life. The following of the evangelical counsels is more general than in forms of consecrated life and there is no formal agreement for incorporation. Finally, the *Seguimi* have no particular apostolate, and the main purpose for the organization is the spiritual perfection of the members. In a sense, the *Seguimi* are not very different from the concept emerging in the United States of associate membership or other groups which affiliate themselves to religious institutes in a similar way.

C 606

Whatever is determined about institutes of consecrated life and their members applies equally to either sex, unless the contrary is apparent from the context of the wording or nature of the matter.

The basic source of this canon is CIC 490 of the previous Code. The difference would be that the phrase "and their members" was added after the first draft of this canon, so that the equal applicability of the law applies both to the institutes as juridic persons and to the members as individual religious. One example of where the contrary might be apparent from the "nature of the matter" would be in laws dealing with religious in clerical institutes, and specifically dealing with the clerical aspects of their lives.

NOTES

1. See C 129, §2.

2. See the commentary on C 714.

3. Francis Moloney, *Disciples and Prophets*. New York: Crossroads, 1981.

4. John Lozano, *Discipleship: Towards An Understanding of Religious Life*. Chicago: Claretian Publishers, 1980.

5. On the notion of the patrimony of an institute, see the comments of SCRIS in establishing the USIG, December 6 and 8, 1965, on "Loyalty to Founders," 6 *CLD* 462–64.

6. See 1 *CLD* 269.

7. See 7 *CLD* 458–59, which has two private replies: one lists documents needed for erection of a diocesan institute, and the other discusses the need for the approbation of the SCDF in missionary areas.

8. 8 *CLD* 324 and *Supplement* for 1978 under C 493.

9. 6 *CLD* 445–46 and *Supplement* for 1978 under C 493.

10. See Miriam Cerletty, "Some Practical Helps for the Development of Constitutions," 14 *StudCan* 155 (1980).

11. See 7 *CLD* 468–71.

12. 8 *CLD* 342–43.

13. 6 *Origins* 602–05.

14. A good reference for learning how to deal with the legal value of such documents is the booklet written by Francis Morrisey, "The Canonical Significance of Papal and Curial Documents," published by the Canon Law Society of America.

15. See the commentary on C 591.

16. C 625, §2.

17. C 686.

18. C 686, §3.

19. C 588.

20. The present liturgical rite, however, is for women only.

21. 8 *CLD* 318–20.

Religious Houses and Governance
Canons 607-633

MARGARET MARY MODDE, O.S.F.

Introduction

Who has the authority for religious institutes? How is that authority exercised? CC 607–633 respond to these questions. They introduce the section on religious institutes: what they are (C 607), how they are established (CC 608–616), and how they are governed (CC 617–633). As a whole these canons are generally referred to by religious as the canons on government. They determine which communities in the Church have the authority to act as an institute of the Church and which members of these communities have the authority to act personally for an institute or for one of its major parts or houses.

According to their basic subject matter the canons on government divide into two unequal parts. How a community may obtain and use authority in the Church is the main topic of the nine canons titled *Religious Houses and Their Erection and Suppression*. How a member of the community may obtain and use personal authority in the institute is the main topic of the seventeen canons titled The Governance of Institutes. These twenty-six canons, plus the introductory canon which describes religious institutes, have their counterpart in forty-six canons similarly located and titled in the 1917 Code (CIC 488; 492–498; 499–537).

Basic to the use of this section of the Code is a socio-historical understanding of Church authority. Both Codes apply the overall Church construct of hierarchical authority in relation to institutes. This construct is commonly known as the pyramid model for organizations. More recently it is known, with negative connotations, as the authoritarian model. The model shows supportively ascending levels and areas for the exercise of collegial authority. Each part, and the pyramid as a whole, comes together under a single head. Often the pyramid is represented by naming only the "heads." The model fits historically with the enduring scriptural paradigm of the Church as the head and body of Christ. [1]

What is new in the Code is the infusion of the traditional pyramid model of organization with spiritual understandings of the collateral dynamics of a trinitarian God. [2] The integration of spiritual matter with basic organizational and juridical matter recontextualizes and, therefore, revitalizes the use of the model for asking and answering questions about the authority of religious institutes and its nature, essence, modes, and operational circumstances.

Since Vatican II, and its renewal of the pyramid model, critical questions on the fact and use of authority in the Church and in all its parts and areas have been aided by applying key words from Vatican II to test this model. The same words have become bywords for religious institutes and their design of structures of authority, namely, their structures of government and governance. What religious is unfamiliar with the concepts and applications of such key words as communion, community, mission, dialogue, collegiality, subsidiarity, participation, co-responsibility, service, mutuality, collaboration—and others? [3] Each concept a key word conveys has had some influence on the renewed structures of institutes. Each has influenced the Code on government as well. Through the exploration of these key words numerous changes are evolving in the fact and use of Church authority as a collaborative service. [4]

To assure renewal of the Church the Code does more than apply a spirituality of authority. It also proceeds from a different starting place than that of the 1917 Code to describe the use of authority. [5] Through Vatican II's attention both to the socio-historical signs of the times and to the timeless evangelical witness of the mission of Jesus, the Code unites an ecclesiology to a theology of authority. Authority for the Church as a people of God is viewed as a unique participation in the universal authority of Jesus (LG 1-4; LG 19-20; CD 4). Obtaining and using this authority entails receiving the gift of service to a people from God through the Spirit and offering this gift in an orderly union with others in Christ (LG 4; AG 2, 9, 15). Religious institutes share in this authority through receiving the gift of the evangelical counsels for a closer following of Christ in his mission (PC 1,13-15, 20).

Applying Vatican II's spiritual understandings of authority has variously affected the renewal and restructuring of the Church's government and law. [6] What is true for the universal Church is also true for the local church and for institutes, societies, and associations in the Church. Religious institutes in particular confront the renewed dimension of authority in the Church as they continue renewal of their life and its governance.[7]

Expressing the spirit of Church authority as gathered from various documents,[8] the Code directs the fact and use of a spiritual authority in Church institutes through appropriate attention to their government. It guides each institute's particular statement of its spirit and law, referred to as its proper law. Over half the canons on government mention details that an institute must decide in its constitutions or in other parts of its proper law, such as in its chapter directives, provincial statutes, special decrees, and administrative policies. Attention to these details further refines for the institute its use of authority from what it has learned in its own tradition through lived experience.

The relationship of an institute's structures of authority to the practices of obedience in institutes is not fully resolved in the Church.[9] Questions about the advisability and practicality of some post-Vatican II innovations or provisions by institutes are still being raised.[10] The Code does not provide ready answers for these issues. It does, however, guide the major decisions an institute must make about its own authority by comprehensively presenting the universal norms for the life of the Church as developed from Vatican II's reflection on the lived experience of the whole Church. It is in this spirit of offering some guidance to institutes in their decision-making about their way of life together that the canons on government are discussed here.

RELIGIOUS INSTITUTES

Title II of the Code, Religious Institutes, continues the development of Section I, Institutes of Consecrated Life. Following Title I, Norms Common to All Institutes, Title II presents 103 norms specific to religious institutes. Some of the norms of Title II are incorporated into Title III's twenty-one canons for secular institutes and Section II's sixteen canons for societies of apostolic life. Roughly one-fourth of the norms of Title II treat authority for religious institutes. The first of these defines religious institutes.

In the 1917 Code religious institutes are defined in the second of five introductory canons on religious (CIC 488, 1°). That canon contains seven other definitions for various types of religious and their institutes and superiors. Many of the terms used in those definitions are not carried over into the terminology of the new law. These 1917 definitions include terms for the distinctions between orders and congregations, solemn and simple vows, and regulars and sisters. The distinctions are now subsumed to a remarkably simplified concept of religious institutes viewed as one of two forms of consecrated life to which the Christian faithful may be called. C 607 gives the details.

C 607

§1. Religious life, as a consecration of the whole person, manifests in the Church a wonderful marriage brought about by God, a sign of the future age. Thus religious bring to perfection their full gift as a sacrifice offered to God by which their whole existence becomes a continuous worship of God in love.

§2. A religious institute is a society in which members, according to proper law, pronounce public vows either perpetual or temporary, which are to be renewed when they have lapsed, and live a life in common as brothers or sisters.

§3. The public witness to be rendered by religious to Christ and to the Church entails a separation from the world proper to the character and purpose of each institute.

C 607, the lead canon for Title II, serves as an introduction to eight chapters on religious institutes. The lead canon's three parts carefully, yet simply, define religious life and religious institutes according to their essential elements of spousal and sacrificial consecration, public vows, community life, and special witness. The paragraph on religious life which begins the canon should be read as the basic condition and goal for a religious institute. It is a progression from the earlier paragraphs on consecrated life and its various forms (CC 573, §1; 577).

Special note should be taken of the canon's focus on religious life as an involvement in sacrificial worship and of the canon's use of the traditional spousal imagery to describe religious life. What is new to the understanding of religious life is the canon's addition of the connection of religious life to the future age.

The spousal imagery of the canon is derived from *LG*, which recalls it from the tradition of the Church for the Council's introduction of the role of the Holy Spirit in the Church (*LG* 2). The concept of sacrificial worship is introduced by the Council in its description of the role of the Son on mission from the Father (*LG* 3). Mention of both the spousal and sacrificial aspects of religious consecration emphasizes the relation of the religious to a trinitarian and communitarian God of three persons, and not to Jesus alone.

§2 of the canon, which specifies the element of vows for religious institutes, reverses the post-Vatican II trend in religious institutes to substitute promises for temporary vows. The practice of promises was suggested by the 1969 instruction on the renewal of religious formation (*RC* 34, I and II). Promises met the practical problem of hesitation on the part of new members regarding commitment by vows. Now commitment other than by vow is no longer allowed members of a religious institute. The perpetual renewal of temporary vows, a practice of some institutes, is allowed only by Church approval of an institute's proper law. For approval the law of such institutes must contain a specific prescription for perpetual temporary vows and must also indicate their purpose.

The element of community life prescribed as a mark of religious institutes in §2 of the canon is carried over as an element of religious life from the 1917 Code's definition of the religious state (CIC 487), and not from its definition of the institute itself (CIC 488,1°). The wording of the new canon combines two understandings of community life. The first one emphasizes a familial dimension as amplified in C 602. The other, a provisional dimension, is implied in CC 665 and 670. The provisional dimension emphasizes the common life of a house.

Both the familial and provisional dimensions of community life have a long history in the Church. However, legislation for religious over the past several centuries has highlighted the provisional aspect. Through emphasis on its legal aspects community life for the religious often came to be understood as common life, namely, as having the same or similar things for each religious in terms of housing, clothing, food, and other necessities. The Code restores the complementary dimension of community, the dimension of persons relating to each other familially through having and sharing everything in common.

Treated in context with other parts of the law the familial element of community life is also given a spiritual dimension—that of essential witness to the nature of the Church. The community is viewed as a unified and unifying communion of persons whose life is "a new and eternal life acquired by the redemption of Christ" (*LG* 44 and 7, C 602). There is no counterpart in the 1917 Code to suggest a similar spiritual dimension for community life.

The third part of the canon refers to a special provision for the spiritual dimension of witness reflected by community life. Such witness entails a separation from the larger community of the world. This section of the canon at first appears regressive in its emphasis on the separation of the religious from the world. However, the purpose of this part of the canon is to call each institute to determine in its proper law its contemplative dimension.

This third section of the canon should be read with C 603 on hermits and anchorites, where emphasis is on separation from the world by solitude. It should also be read with C 667, which carries with it the vestiges of the Church's long tradition of cloister, but which actually functions to provide for the need of religious for a place to be alone individually and as a community.

In no way should §3 of the canon be read restrictively and as confining religious. The proper perspective in the use of this canon is particularly important for religious institutes who are engaged in an active apostolate as described in C 675. Religious institutes are to protect the solitude at the core of their ministry and their identity. Without this solitude the institute cannot hope to give public witness to the nature of the Church as a communion of persons.

As a whole C 607 is a remarkable synthesis of the sacramental or sign value of religious life in the Church. It does not focus on juridic exigencies through concrete provisional means, as did the 1917 Code. From the canon's spiritual contexts it is clear that religious institutes are to give public, namely visible, testimony or witness to Christ and the Church. They do so essentially by their members coming together in a community clearly separated from the world.

As other Church documents show, the separation of a religious community from the world is most evident by the community's spirit of prayer, solitude, and penance (EN 69; *CDR* 4). The degree of emphasis placed on this sacramental dimension of an institute derives from the particular character, purpose, and tradition of the institute, as C 607 indicates. This degree of sacramental emphasis, rather than a definitive typology of institutes, determines the distinctive kind of community an institute is in the Church (*CDR* 6).

RELIGIOUS HOUSES AND THEIR ERECTION AND SUPPRESSION

Nine canons constitute the first chapter of Title II on religious institutes. They determine how a religious community of an already established institute for religious life (C 579) obtains and uses its own authority to live and work in houses of the institute. Basic for applying these canons is the awareness that most institutes divide themselves into smaller communities of various numbers for the achievement of various purposes.

If an institute as a community divides itself into smaller communities, each community has a specific place, namely, its own house, where it lives and works and where it relates with a superior of the community who has authority for the smaller community according to the institute's proper law.

In their treatment of the opening and closing of the houses of an institute, these canons differ significantly from the companion set of canons in the 1917 Code (CIC 492–498). They proceed from the understanding of a house of an institute as a place where the community of the institute lives (C 608) rather than as a certain type of house (CIC 488,5°) which an institute may establish as a part of the institute.

C 608

A religious community must live in a house legitimately constituted under the authority of the superior designated according to the norm of law; each house is to have at least an oratory in which the Eucharist is celebrated and reserved so that it truly is the center of the community.

C 608, a juridic and not a spiritual canon, reflects the Church's essential spiritual concept of religious life as a sacramental community. The word "house" as used in the canon has a specific juridic meaning as the place where the community lives. The word must be read with the essential qualification which follows it in the canon. Namely, there must be a superior who, according to the ordinary practice of the institute, as stated in its proper law, has authority for the community, as stated in the universal law (CC 617–630).

The point of the canon is not that a community live in a house rather than in a trailer, or in an apartment, or in a cave. The point is that every religious community, wherever it lives, in whole and in part, has a law that says who its superior is and how it is accountable to this superior. Moreover the law of the community on who the superior is must be in accord with the universal law of the Church on who may be a religious superior.

The wording of this first part of the canon precludes the need for the Code to specify, as it previously did, various kinds of religious houses according to the number of persons and according to the degree of dependency on another house of the institute for its juridic acts, namely, its valid legal acts. That dimension of a religious house is now determined in the Code by CC 113-123 on who or what is a juridic entity in the Church.

Specifically, the Code requires that a juridic person in the Church involve at least three persons (C 115, §3) and be established either by the law or by the competent person who has lawful authority to do so (C 116, §2). The application of this juridic understanding of "house," which may include the capability of owning and administering goods (C 634), does not necessarily apply to every house of a religious institute. When it does it should be defined in the proper law of the institute.

Also the canon requires that there be at least an oratory in every religious house. In order to reserve the blessed sacrament in this oratory

CC 934–943 must be observed. If these observations are not possible it is not prudent to implement the requirements of the canon. The Church's main purpose in this canon is to call the religious community to an explicit awareness of the centrality of the Eucharist in its life. Given certain living conditions prevalent today, the complete implementation of this canon would be most imprudent. Where prohibitive conditions exist, the community should be challenged to name specific ways in its law to nourish its sacramental awareness. This awareness develops a religious community's closer ties with the divine life and holiness of the Church (*LG* 43 and 44).

C 609

§1. Houses of a religious institute are erected by the competent authority according to the constitutions with the previous written consent of the diocesan bishop.

§2. In order to erect a monastery of nuns the permission of the Apostolic See is also required.

C 609 applies the Church's principle of internal autonomy. Any religious house has the right to internal government (C 611, 1°) if it is established by the internal authority of the institute according to its proper law. The consent of the diocesan bishop where the community as a whole or as a part is to be established honors the bishop's right to internal autonomy through exercise of authority for all those who participate in sacramental worship and in the works of the apostolate in his diocese (*LG* 26, 34, 42, and 45; CC 386 and 394).

In addition to obtaining the written consent of the diocesan bishop to set up a house, a monastery of nuns who wish to open a new monastery must also have the consent of the Holy See before the new monastery may be established. This part of the canon is applied in light of the proper law of a monastic order when a monastic federation or congregation begins a monastery of nuns. If a group neither affiliated with a monastic order nor with an autonomous monastery wishes to set up a monastery of nuns, the bishop would first follow the canons and procedures for setting up a diocesan institute (C 579).

In particular instances the Holy See can establish an autonomous monastery of nuns which is not affiliated to a federation, or a congregation, or a diocese (C 615). These autonomous monasteries are governed by special norms of the Holy See, by their own proper law, and by CC 615; 625, §2; 628, §2, 1°; and 637.

C 610

§1. The erection of houses takes place with due regard for their usefulness for the Church and the institute and safeguarding those things which are required for the correct living out of the religious life of the members according to the specific purposes and spirit of the institute.

§2. No house is to be erected unless it can be prudently judged that the needs of the members will be suitably provided for.

An institute's primary witness of consecrated life and the sacramental function of this witness in the local church is the major concern of C 610. There can be an overabundance of religious houses in some areas of the Church and none or too few in others. Institutes share responsibility with bishops to adjust particular situations for a more equitable distribution of religious in such cases.

Particularly in cases of houses with limited sources of income, care should be exercised that the religious institute and the diocese are capable of providing what is necessary for the appropriate living of consecrated life as a witness.

Both the religious superior and the bishop in consultation with each other share a responsibility to the Church-at-large that the establishment of a religious house is for the good of the Church and of the institute. It is also to be ascertained that the members residing in the house can live out their lives in accord with the spirit and goals of the institute. Otherwise the sign value of religious witness is lost to the Church. Living as sign requires that the needs of members be met for prayer, solitude, penance, Eucharistic worship, and adaptation to current understandings about the role and value of religious life in the Church, as the Church's various documents on religious life suggest.

§2 of C 610 echoes CIC 496 and has as its intent the meeting of the material needs of the religious as a complement to meeting the spiritual needs suggested by §1 of the canon. In the past many parishes and dioceses provided houses for members of religious institutes whose members worked in the diocese. Now in some instances, especially where there are fewer religious, the parish or diocese provides instead a stipend adequate to meet this need.

A problem of need today not common at the time of the 1917 Code's writing is an institute's concern for the disproportionate numbers of aging religious caused by longer lifespans of religious and by decreased membership in religious institutes. With increasing frequency bishops and superiors are collaborating to seek creative ways to meet the needs for personnel and finances both in the dioceses and in the institutes. The dual focus of needs expressed in C 610 provides a framework for meeting this problem.

C 611

The consent of the diocesan bishop to erect a religious house of any institute brings with it the right:

1⁰ to lead a life according to its own character and the purposes of the institute;

2⁰ to exercise the works proper to the institute according to the norm of law, with due regard for any conditions attached to the consent;

3⁰ for clerical institutes to have a church, with due regard for the prescription of can. 1215, §3, and to perform sacred ministries, observing what is by law to be observed.

C 611 is strictly juridic. It sets up a relationship between an institute, the religious house, and the Church through the diocesan bishop. Working through the diocesan bishop is a practical measure in Church law and an application of the organizational principles of collegiality and subsidiarity promoted by Vatican II. The primary right of members of a religious house is to live in accord with their particular form of consecrated life. The diocesan bishop must abide by this right of internal autonomy.

In giving a religious institute the right to establish a house in his diocese, the bishop's consent includes the right for members of the institute to exercise the institute's apostolic works in accord with the proper law of the institute. However, the bishop may set some conditions on the exercise of these works in his diocese.

For clerical institutes the right to have a church and perform sacred ministries is included with a bishop's consent to establish a house. Similar rights are specified in CIC 472, §2, but not the right to live the form of life proper to the institute.

In this canon, and in the Code as a whole, the specification of the primary rights of members of the institute in relation to the primary rights of the bishop provides a foundation from which a harmonious mutual relationship may be built. Through a relationship built on respect for the autonomy proper to each, both bishops and superiors can more fully promote the mission of the Church (see MR 8, 10, and 15).

In examining the mutual rights established by the erection of a religious house, it does not seem misplaced to call attention to various sets of rights operative within a diocese. Religious, as well as bishops, in the application of the principles of collegiality and subsidiarity, need to be sensitive to the rights of other groups as well as to their own rights.

The moderation in the law on the role of subsidiarity made between the 1977 and 1980 draft canons suggests that a balance in rights is more necessary in the Church.[11] Many in the Church need the assurance of the Church's concern for their basic Christian rights and an appropriate balance of these rights as an important complement to the mission of the Church as well as an important complement to human dignity and equality of persons.

Again, it does not seem amiss to mention here that religious can also benefit from a greater consciousness of rights between groups of members within their own institutes. The concern all should have for the right of the institute to be what the founder intended is a complementary area for active concern (C 578). As all work to apply this canon, the Church can expect a new flowering of justice.

C 612

In order that a religious house be converted to apostolic works different from those for which it was established the consent of the diocesan bishop is required; but this is not so if it is a matter of a change which refers only to internal government and discipline, with due regard for the laws of the foundation.

The matter in C 612 is treated in CIC 497, §4, and no new setting is given the canon in the Code. If the competent authority of a religious institute as named in its law wishes to change the apostolic work for which a religious house was established, the consent of the diocesan bishop is required. This need to have the bishop's consent for a change in work makes sense because the consent of the bishop was given for a specific work at the erection of a house. He may also have required certain conditions according to the needs of the apostolate. It is reasonable to expect, therefore, that a change in a specific work may involve a change in the conditions set for the establishment of a house, as in C 611, §2.

With the rapid changes observable today in social and economic conditions, this canon on conversion of works gains in importance and use. An increasing number of institutes find themselves changing the apostolic works of the community. An example of a current change in work which substantially changes the purpose for which a house was originally established would be the conversion of a school owned by an institute and made into a retreat center or into a center for the mentally handicapped.

The consent of the bishop is not needed if the conversion of a house for other purposes involves one established for a need of the institute and then afterwards converted for another need of the institute. An example would be a house established as a novitiate and later converted into a provincialate or into a home for the institute's retired members. In both cases the apostolate is internal to the institute and to its governance and discipline.

As a rule-of-thumb it is prudent for any institute which is planning the conversion of a house to consult the bishop, even if the conversion affects only the internal matters of the institute. Through mutual collaboration and planning the misson of the Church gains as a whole.

C 613

§1. A religious house of canons regular and monks under the governance and care of its own moderator is autonomous unless the constitutions state otherwise.

§2. A moderator of an autonomous house is by law a major superior.

This canon recognizes the autonomous nature of monasteries of canons regular and of monks. C 613 further recognizes that in certain monastic groupings, according to their constitutions, the individual houses of such monasteries are not autonomous but are subject to superiors in a way similar to other religious houses.

§2 of C 613 seems unnecessary, since the fact of who is included in references to major superiors of religious occurs in the section on government which treats superiors at length (see C 620).

C 614

Monasteries of nuns which are associated with an institute of men maintain their own order of life and governance according to the constitutions. Mutual rights and obligations are to be so defined that the association is spiritually enriching.

Once more a separate canon attends to a particular form of religious life which has particular needs, especially in the area of autonomy. Some religious families include monasteries for women as well as for men. Of these families some have maintained especially close relationships. These relationships may include obedience to the same higher superiors gathered under the same rule.

Some monasteries of women are under the care of monasteries of men and their superiors for observance of the rule of the founder and for promotion of the spirit of the entire religious family of the founder. The canon especially addresses this latter situation.

Two features permeating the Code for the establishment of autonomy between groups perceived as formerly unequal are highlighted by C 614: a clear definition of mutual rights and obligations and a clear indication of the purpose and condition for these rights as spiritual enrichment. The canon and the Code avoid the pitfall of a declaration of rights for the sake of rights alone.

C 615

An autonomous monastery which has no other major superior beyond its own moderator and is not associated with any other institute of religious in such a way that the superior of the latter enjoys true power over such a monastery determined by the constitutions is committed to the special vigilance of the diocesan bishop according to the norm of law.

C 615 can be read as a legal protection for members of an autonomous monastery which is not subject to the general supervision of a federation or congregation (see C 609). The canon establishes that the diocesan bishop exercises special vigilance according to universal law toward this type of monastery.

Besides the general relationship of bishops to autonomous monasteries as established by law, the diocesan bishop specifically presides at the election of the superior (C 625, §2). The bishop also has the right and duty to conduct a visitation of the community even regarding the monastic discipline (C 628 §2, 1°). However, the canon does not give the bishop authority over the community either to legislate or to govern, even if he finds areas of concern.

The basic autonomy of the monastery is respected by the law. The bishop may strongly try to persuade a community or superior to act a certain way, but if either refuses his only recourse is to the Holy See. The decision on dismissal of a member of an autonomous monastery, however, does belong to the diocesan bishop. If the monastery is of pontifical right the dismissal must be transmitted to the Holy See for confirmation (CC 699, §2; 700).

The practical benefits for autonomous monasteries of C 615 are more obvious than its juridical and spiritual benefits. A bishop can be especially helpful in many practical areas of decision-making about meeting the goals and needs of the institute in educational and financial matters.

C 616

§1. A legitimately erected religious house can be suppressed by the supreme moderator according to the norm of the constitutions after having consulted the diocesan bishop. The proper law of the institute is to provide for the goods of the suppressed house, with due regard for the wills of the founders and donors or for legitimately acquired rights.

§2. The suppression of the only house of an institute pertains to the Holy See, to which is also reserved the right to determine what is to be done in that case with its goods.

§3. The suppression of an autonomous house, such as that described in can. 613, belongs to the general chapter, unless the constitutions state otherwise.

§4. The suppression of an autonomous monastery of nuns pertains to the Apostolic See, with due regard for the prescriptions of the constitutions with regard to its goods.

The preceding canons have prepared the way for C 616 on the closing of a religious house and the redistribution of its goods. This canon clearly holds to the principle that whoever is the competent authority to establish a house is also the competent authority to suppress it. In contrast to C 616, C 609 requires that for the establishment of a religious house the competent authority of the institute must have the consent of the bishop. However, in the closing of a religious house, only consultation with the bishop is required and not his consent, which is a change from CIC 498.

Once more the role of the proper law of the institute is invoked. Specifically the institute must decide in its law how the goods of a suppressed house are to be distributed. Those who make the decision to suppress a house are also obliged to consider the sources of these goods. If these were external to the institute, and if certain rights of the donors were established in the acceptance of the goods, these rights must be attended to. As in CC 634–640 and in other related canons throughout the Code, religious who receive goods from the faithful are obliged to fulfill any conditions for which these goods were given. Requirements of civil law should also be attended to before the goods of a suppressed house are distributed.

§2 of C 616 treats the suppression of a last remaining house of an institute. Its suppression is equivalent to the suppression of the institute. There is no change in the requirement of this norm from CIC 493. Only the Holy See has the right to suppress a last house and to distribute its goods.

On the whole §2 appears to repeat C 584 on the suppression of an institute. Nevertheless, it complements the understanding of religious houses. CC 579 and 584 refer to the bishop's right to establish an institute of consecrated life. It covers those institutes which have divided into smaller communities and then dwindled to or reverted to one community and a single house.

C 616, §§ 3 and 4 attend to the situations of suppressing an autonomous house of canons and monks, some of which may be similar in their structure to institutes in their number of houses, and of suppressing an autonomous monastery of nuns. For the former the general chapter can suppress the house unless the constitutions state otherwise. This norm changes CIC 493 regarding the suppression of an autonomous monastic house. That canon required a decree from the Holy See. For the suppression of an autonomous monastery of nuns, the Code reaffirms that the Holy See alone can act, but with due regard for the members, the constitutions, and the goods of the monastery.

With the change in the law regarding the suppression of autonomous houses, it would seem that federations and congregations to which these houses may belong should restudy their constitutions to ascertain whether changes may be needed. Areas of concern for possible change include the distribution of any assets of the community and provisions for transfer of vows in the event of suppression.

C 616 closes the canons on religious houses and their establishment and suppression. To summarize this chapter, it can be observed that although the autonomy of religious institutes, of bishops, and of the Holy See is emphasized in the law, mutual collaboration is called for. The changes in the Code are attempts to implement this kind of relationship in the total mission of the Church.

THE GOVERNANCE OF INSTITUTES

In twenty-four canons the second chapter on religious institutes replaces the thirty-two canons of CIC 499–530. The new canons, as those of the 1917 Code, direct religious to govern themselves through the proper use of superiors, councils, chapters, and temporal goods (CC 617, 622, 627, 631, and 636). In contrast to the 1917 Code, the 1983 Code through re-titling this section links superiors with councils and not with chapters. The change emphasizes the proper role of each of these groups in relation to that of superiors.

From its overall structure, it can be seen that Chapter II of the canons on government focuses exclusively on the internal exercise of authority in a religious institute. The most striking difference from the 1917 Code is the deletion of the chapter of twelve canons on confessors. The final canon on superiors (C 630) treats this topic in terms of the superiors' promotion of a member's freedom of conscience.

Like the first chapter of the canons on government, the second chapter has a spiritual dimension not present in the 1917 Code. The first three canons are the spiritual fountainhead of the section. The first canon relates the fact that the power bestowed on superiors is within the limits set by universal law and by proper law of the institute. Taken as a whole both laws form a law of the Spirit. The two canons which follow give detailed means for a superior's development of a spiritual relationship with members. These are complemented with a similar but much briefer canon for members (C 627, §3). Together these canons help religious to develop a relationship of listening and trust as basic to their government (*LG* 46; *PC* 14). This spiritual relationship is restated in sacramental terms in the last canon on superiors (C 630).

All the remaining canons of Chapter II are juridic with the exception of the canon on election of the superiors. That canon directs all members of the institute to action in accord with their inmost conscience (C 626).

Superiors and councils

Although the title of these canons suggests otherwise, only one of the fourteen canons on superiors treats councils (C 627). It is a very significant one given the overall structure of these canons. The first three canons (CC 617–619) treat the fact and manner of a superior's exercise of power. The next seven canons (CC 620–626) identify which superiors are major superiors and how superiors are elected or appointed. Introducing the final four canons (CC 627–630) on the specific obligations of superiors is the canon on councils.

C 617

Superiors are to fulfill their duty and exercise their power according to the norm of universal and proper law.

C 617, notable for its brevity, gives superiors the power to govern the institute's members in accord with universal and proper law. The term superior includes superiors of all forms of religious institutes in whole or in part.

The terms universal and proper law are to be properly understood by superiors. A universal law is one that binds anywhere in the world those for whom it is enacted. Proper law is enacted for a specific religious institute and binds only those who are members.

Some examples of universal law are the Code, conciliar and papal decrees, a *motu proprio*, and all other types of papal pronouncements[12] for the Church as a whole. Examples of proper law include the institute's constitutions, directories, chapter acts, and policies.

In the use of both universal and proper law, it is important that the user clarify the legal impact or force of a new pronouncement and that the faithful school themselves in distinguishing between what is Church legislation and what is an individual view.

C 618

Superiors are to exercise their power, received from God through the ministry of the Church, in a spirit of service. Therefore, docile to the will of God in carrying out their duty, they are to govern their subjects as children of God and, promoting their voluntary obedience with reverence for the human person, they are to listen to them willingly and foster their working together for the good of the institute and of the Church, but with the superiors' authority to decide and prescribe what must be done remaining intact.

C 618 repeats in part Vatican II's decree on the appropriate renewal of religious life (*PC* 14). It cautions individual superiors to use the power given them for service and ministry to the institute's members. Superiors are to respect the individual human person by listening to members while securing their collaboration for the good of the institute and of the Church. The canon, nevertheless, clearly emphasizes the personal authority of the superior for discerning and initiating what is to be done.

Although it is clear that the personal authority of the superior does not exclude, but invites, respect for members of the institute and consultation with them, it is important that members of the institute do not confuse the "style" of exercising authority and an individual manner of communicating with the superior's clear right and obligation to act. Reflection on this canon suggests that prudence, discretion, and goodwill are necessary ingredients for action by any superior.

That the role of the superior not be confused with the connotations associated with particular names given the role is the chief implication of C 618. It makes no difference whether the superior is called abbot, abbess, general, brother, father, mother, sister, custodian, guardian, moderator, animator, president, coordinator, servant unifier, minister, or contact person. [13] It is the manner of carrying out the role that is important in the Church norm and the superior's personal responsibility for governance or guidance of an institute, province, or local community. [14]

C 619

Superiors are to devote themselves to their office assiduously and, together with the members entrusted to them, they should be eager to build a community of brothers or sisters in Christ in which God is sought after and loved before all else. Therefore, they are to nourish the members frequently with the food of the word of God and lead them to the celebration of the sacred liturgy. They are to be an example to the members in cultivating virtues and in the observance of the laws and traditions of the particular institute; they are to meet the personal needs of the members in an appropriate fashion, look after solicitously and visit the sick, admonish the restless, console the faint of heart, and be patient toward all.

C 619 lists the important qualifications for a superior's exercise of power. The power is exercised with the cooperation of all the other members. The goal of this mutual exercise of power is the co-creation of a communion wherein God may be sought after and valued in preference to anything else (see C 573, §1). The superior encourages this close communion particularly through providing members with the Word of God which prepares them for the liturgy of the Word.

The role of the superior as indicated in C 619 is a pastoral one. It focuses on and seeks the good of everyone involved in the creating of the community, especially those in need of pastoral care: those ill, restless, lacking in courage, or needing ordinary patience. Key to the exercise of this pastoral role is the personal relationship established between superiors and members through their cultivation of attitudes of listening and trust, as indicated in the preceding canon and in CC 628, §3 and 630, § 5. But these practical virtues necessary for human relations and reverence for the human person are to be complemented with the unifying force of the Word of God which is provided by superiors and celebrated liturgically. Lacking this spiritual example and leadership, superiors fail in their basic call to build community, the essential witness of the institute (see C 607, §2 with CC 573 and 673).

C 620

Major superiors are those who govern a whole institute, a province of an institute, some part equivalent to a province, or an autonomous house, as well as their vicars. Comparable to these are the abbot primate and superior of a monastic congregation, who nonetheless do not have all the power which universal law grants major superiors.

The Code through C 620 designates which superiors may be called major superiors. The term includes those who govern the whole institute or a specific province of the institute and does not exclude those who govern a part of the institute similar to a province, such as a region, directorate, or vicariate, together with those who govern an autonomous house. The term also includes the vicars of these major superiors and, with some restriction of power, the abbot primates and superiors of monastic congregations. These latter have the powers granted them by proper law and any other power which may be specifically given them through the universal law. Further interpretation of this canon comes through attention to the canons that follow.

C 621

The grouping of several houses under the same superior which constitutes an immediate part of the institute and which has been canonically erected by the legitimate authority is called a province.

C 621 supplies some clarifications needed to interpret C 620. The union of several houses under the same superior is called a province. A province is treated as a particular part of the institute. Traditionally it has its own chapter and statutes. The establishment and suppression of provinces is within the competence of the authority designated in an institute's constitutions (CC 581 and 585).

There are various opinions expressed about the proper number of members or of houses needed to constitute a province. Canon law does not state either. It would seem that the competent authority of the institute would look at the need for provinces or parts rather than at specific numbers of members or houses. The competent authority should also look at the proportion of major superiors needed for other superiors and members and at the institute's overall need for religious personnel in internal and external ministry.

Two reasons which may justify a division of an institute into provinces are an institute's having a single form of government when there are large property holdings involved in diverse geographic areas and an institute's needing to overcome the distance of a substantial number of members from the principal house of the institute or from the generalate.[15]

A province as a distinct unit of the institute requires a certain autonomy in government and ministry. Yet a province maintains a close relationship to the generalate of the institute and to every other province of the institute. This relationship takes the form of adherence to the constitutions of the institute and to the decisions of the general chapter to further the institute's response to its founding mission and the needs of the Church. Some of the powers given over to the superior of the institute in universal law may be delegated to the superior of a province (see *RL* and areas of the law which specify major superiors).

Every province can be a juridic person in its own right if it is lawfully established, and it can be recognized as a legal entity both in Church and civil law. A juridic person is created by operation of the law or by competent authority; it receives its mandate and purpose, and its powers and rights, within the context of the law from which it receives its existence (CC 113–123). In view of this fact, the rights and duties of the provincial chapter, of the provincial superior, and of the provincial council are determined by the institute, that is, by its general constitutions and proper law, and by the provincial statutes. These latter must receive approval by the provincial chapter and by the superior and council for the whole institute.

An institute may have a distinct unit of the community which, due to some particular reason, requires some autonomy but cannot be independent in personnel or finances. In this instance the competent authority designated by the constitutions may create a unit, often referred to as a region. A region is governed by a regional superior whose authority is dependent upon the delegation of the superior for the whole institute and the council. The powers given to a regional superior are specified in the regional directory.

In establishing either provinces or regions the competent authority of the institute is cautioned to take into consideration the good of the members and of the institute as a whole and not to unduly multiply the structures of the institute and consequently the number of persons needed in positions of leadership in the institute.[16]

C 622

The supreme moderator holds power over all provinces, houses and members of the institute, which is to be exercised according to proper law; other superiors enjoy power within the limits of their office.

The key terms in C 622 are "supreme moderator" and "proper law." The supreme moderator as head of the institute holds power over all the provinces, even though these have major superiors at their head, and over every house and member of the institute. The proper law of the institute determines how this power is exercised in the institute. Other superiors enjoy power only within the confines of the roles to which they are appointed or in which they are confirmed, again in accord with the proper law of the institute.

This canon confirms the personal authority of a supreme moderator, or head, for the entire institute. "Supreme moderator," a titular referent carried over from the Latin of the 1917 Code, covers various titles held by heads of institutes, such as abbot, abbess, president, general coordinator, minister general, general superior, community coordinator, and others. This canon also affirms the concept that no part of the institute is autonomous; each is part of the whole. The supreme moderator governs the entire institute, safeguards the good of all members and parts, promotes the vitality of the institute as a whole, and fosters cooperation among all the parts of the institute.

C 623

In order that members be validly appointed or elected to the office of superior, a suitable time is required after perpetual or definitive profession, to be determined by proper law, or if it is a question of major superiors, by the constitutions.

The Code no longer determines a minimum chronological age for superiors. For the validity of a nomination, election, or appointment of a superior, the Code requires that the institute's proper law determine a specific time after perpetual profession for a member's eligibility as a superior. Moreover, the years after profession required for eligibility as a major superior must be stated in the constitutions. Some institutes prefer a shorter time and others a longer time after perpetual profession for major superiors than for other superiors.

This canon does away with CIC 504 and later laws on superiors (*AIE* 3), which list other requirements for validity of an election of a superior. CC 174–179 guide Church elections in general.

C 624

§1. Superiors are to be constituted for a certain and appropriate amount of time according to the nature and needs of the institute, unless the constitutions state otherwise for the supreme moderator and for superiors of autonomous houses.

§2. Proper law is to provide in suitable norms that superiors constituted for a definite time do not remain too long in offices of governance without an interruption.

§3. Nevertheless they can be removed from office during their term or transferred to another office for reasons determined in proper law.

Superiors serve for a definite and appropriate length of time as the constitutions determine in accord with the nature and need of the institute. Exceptions to this norm may be made for the supreme moderator or for superiors of autonomous houses. This exception, if made, must be stated in the constitutions of the institute.

The law cautions that persons not remain in the service of governance for a long time without intermission. The canon can be seen to warn against the practice of a constant rotation of the same persons as elected or appointed superiors. The same caution should be applied to the rotation of councilors, except in smaller communities where fewer persons are available for service to the community.

Superiors can be removed from their time of service or they can remove themselves by resigning. They may also be transferred for another service during their designated time for reasons stated in the proper law.

For further treatment of religious superiors in regard to their loss or change of office CC 184–196 should be consulted.

A supreme moderator who wishes to resign from office may do so before an assembled extraordinary general chapter.[17] A supreme moderator who wishes to resign other than during a chapter presents the reasons to the Holy See and awaits its decision.[18]

If it is necessary to remove the supreme moderator from office, the council of the supreme moderator submits the reasons to the Holy See and awaits its decision (see C 193, §3).

The companion norm of this canon in the 1917 Code (CIC 505) stipulated no more than two three-year terms in succession for a "lower local" superior in the same house. An earlier draft canon, in 1977, legislated no longer than nine years in succession as a superior (DC 28, §2), but that canon was dropped. It seems a more reasonable approach that institutes examine their particular needs for superiors in proportion to their membership and set well considered means in their constitutions to encourage the effectiveness of members in these roles.

C 625

§1. The supreme moderator of an institute is to be designated by canonical election according to the norm of the constitutions.

§2. The bishop of the principal seat presides at elections of the superior of an autonomous monastery, mentioned in can. 615, and of the supreme moderator of an institute of diocesan right.

§3. Other superiors are to be constituted according to the norm of the constitutions, but in such a way that if they are elected they need the confirmation of the competent major superior; if they are appointed by the superior, a suitable consultation is to precede.

C 625 combines the points of CIC 507, §1 and 506, §4 on the election of supreme moderators and adds a point concerning the constitutional determination of other superiors. The supreme moderator must be chosen according to the canonical election procedures described in the constitutions of the institute. When the constitutions do not cover the matter, the appropriate canons from CC 164–179 apply.

Some religious institutes implement a process of discernment in their election procedures. Such processes are not denied by the law, but the discernment must be confirmed by a canonical election as described in the constitutions of the institute.

In general, for canonical elections the Code requires sufficient advance notification to each elector on the time and place of elections, free and secret written votes according to the provisions in the institute's constitutions, or, failing provisions, according to C 119, and, when required by law, acceptance of the election by the competent authority. To elect someone who has a canonical impediment the laws of postulation apply (see CC 180–183). The canonical impediments include election of someone for an extended term not possible through the constitutions or of someone who has not completed the years after perpetual profession as required by the constitutions.

The diocesan bishop where the principal house of the institute is located presides at the election of the supreme moderator of a diocesan institute and of an autonomous monastery. The law no longer requires the presence of the diocesan bishop at the election of a supreme moderator of a pontifical institute (CIC 506, §4).

The constitutions of the institute determine the method for choosing other superiors, such as the provincial and local superiors. If provincial superiors are elected by a provincial chapter, the constitutions designate which next higher superior confirms the election, and they state whether the council of the next higher superior must also give its consent. If a regional or a local superior is elected by members of the region or of the local community, the election is confirmed by the superior who is indicated in the constitutions.

C 626

Superiors in the conferral of offices and members in elections are to observe the norms of universal and proper law, abstain from any abuse or partiality and name or elect those whom they know in the Lord to be truly worthy and suitable having nothing in mind but God and the good of the institute. Moreover, in elections they are to avoid any procurement of votes either directly or indirectly for themselves or for others.

C 626 directs the attitude and spirit of superiors in the conferral of office and of members in elections to office. Both are to choose those persons they judge before God to be best suited to govern the institute. The canon's caution that votes should not be procured for one's self or another should not be read in a way that eliminates preparation of oneself or of the institute for informed participation in elections in the institute.

The prohibition against voting for oneself (CIC 170) is no longer mentioned in the Code. Therefore, such a vote is not forbidden by canon law in cases where one judges onself as the most suitable person for election. Proper law frequently limits a fourth ballot in elections to two persons, both of whom may not vote. Through this precaution one's vote for oneself cannot be decisive.

C 627

§1. According to the norm of the constitutions, superiors are to have their own council, whose assistance they are to use in carrying out their office.

§2. Besides the cases prescribed in universal law, proper law is to determine cases in which consent or counsel is required in order to act validly, which must be obtained in accord with the norm of can. 127.

C 627 is the only one to treat councils, the co-topic of the chapter on superiors according to its title. Through its placement C 627 introduces the final four canons on superiors and heads the list of the four major duties of superiors. Unlike its predecessor, CIC 516, §1, this canon does not include the topic of bursars in the same canon. Through these changes in titling, placement, and focus, C 627 highlights the role of councilors in institutes and their close relationship to the superiors they assist.

According to the canon all superiors have councils to assist them in their service to the institute. The institute's constitutions should provide for such councils, the minimum number of councilors, their method of election or appointment, and their terms of service. In C 699, on the necessity of the vote of councilors in cases of dismissal of members, the law specifies at least four councilors for validity. If there are fewer than four councilors, the council adds the necessary members when acting in dismissal cases.

The proper law of the institute in accord with the universal law specifies the instances when the superior in order to act validly is required to seek the deliberative or consultative vote of the council (C 127). The deliberative vote refers to the consent of the council for the superior to act. The consultative vote refers to the advice of the council to assist an action for the good of the institute. Some actions cited in the universal law of the Church that require the deliberative vote of the council and that are reserved to the supreme moderator and may not be delegated to other superiors include:

C 647   the erection, transfer, and suppression of a novitiate;

C 684   allowing a member of the institute to transfer to another religious institute;

C 686   granting an indult of exclaustration to a perpetually professed member, but not beyond three years; requesting the Holy See to impose exclaustration of a member of the religious institute;

C 688   allowing a sister in temporary profession to leave the institute; and

C 690   admitting a person to the institute who has legitimately left it after completion of the novitiate or after completion of a time of profession.

Those actions in the universal law which require the superior to consult the council include:

C 689   excluding members from subsequent profession; and

C 697   initiating the process of dismissal for a member of the institute.

The determination of the need for a deliberate or consultative vote for the validity of acting is left to the proper law in some instances. These instances include:

C 638 §1   the transaction of extraordinary business in the name of the institute;

CC 656–658 admitting a novice to temporary profession and admitting a member to perpetual profession.

When the law calls for a deliberative vote of the council, it is understood that the superior cannot act validly without the consent of the council. There is, however, no obligation to act for a superior who has obtained the consent of the council. For example, the superior who obtains in accord with the law the consent of the council to alienate a piece of property is not obliged to alienate the property after having obtained the consent of the council. The prevailing principle is that the council may restrain the superior from acting, but it cannot force the superior to act.

Although the superior is not forced to act by either a deliberative or consultative vote of the council, it seems unwise for a superior, without serious reasons of conscience, to act differently from the expressed understanding of the council. In context with the whole of the section of canons on governance, the superior is directed by the Church to listen to the other members of the institute, to earn their trust, and to foster their responsive and responsible cooperation for the good of all (see CC 618; 619; 628, §3; 630, §5; 559 §1). The council is a select group of these members.

To achieve the intent of the law of governance, most superiors meet regularly with their councils. Some institutes in their particular law specify the minimum number of times for these meetings. On the local level the determination of councils and their meetings with the local superior ordinarily depends on the need of the local community.

When seeking the deliberative or consultative vote of the council, the superior is moreover required to act in conformity with CC 127 and 166. C 127 treats valid juridic acts by a superior. If the law prescribes consent or advice from the council, or any group, the superior must convene it according to C 166 unless proper law allows otherwise for acts requiring only advice. In matters requiring advice the superior must seek it from each one in the group; in matters requiring consent the superior must obtain it from an absolute majority of those present. If the law prescribes further consent from certain individuals, the superior is obliged to obtain it. If only advice is required, it suffices that the superior hear it. A superior should not act contrary to advice received, except for overriding reasons. Those who give consent or advice should do so sincerely and should maintain secrecy on matters which require it. The superior, moreover, may oblige them to secrecy.

C 166 requires that the superior convoke the council by notifying each member. If a member of the council is overlooked in the notification, the meeting is nevertheless valid. Upon the insistence of the member overlooked, however, together with proof of the oversight, any decision of the council made without that member, even if confirmed by the superior, must be overturned by the competent authority if it is juridically established that recourse to the competent authority was made within at least three days from the member's receipt of the notice of the action being taken. If more than one-third of the council was overlooked, any action taken by the remainder of the council is null and void by law unless all those overlooked were nevertheless present for the acts of the council.

CC 127 and 166 support the participation of members in key decisions of the institute. They also provide for dialogue by the superior and the greater competency of the superior in the exercise of authority.

To further the participation of members in assisting the supreme moderator, some religious institutes have introduced what is often called the enlarged or extended general council. The enlarged or extended council can promote on a broader basis a jointly responsible participation by the members of the institute in their life and in the on-going renewal of the institute. More so than other groups, an extended general council is an organ of collaboration with the supreme moderator and the general council. Its purpose is a better exercise of authority and of shared responsibility in dealing with the more important issues of life in the institute. Its *ex officio* members usually include the supreme moderator and the general council, the provincials, or other superiors, and also the general treasurer and the general secretary. Other individuals may be invited to participate as observers or presentors.

The enlarged or extended general council is an advisory and consultative body distinct from the general council. It is a structure to aid the supreme moderator and the council and not a structure to impede their work. Constitutions should define clearly and precisely the function and power of the extended council if such a body is desired or already exists. [19]

C 633 governs the enlarged or extended general council and cautions a wise discretion in its use and its way of proceeding.

Probably the most important point to keep in mind on councils is that the role of its members is that of councilor to the superior. The advice given to superiors comes from hearing the concerns of members.

C 628

§1. Superiors who are designated for this function by the proper law of the institute are to visit the houses and members entrusted to them at the times designated by the norms of this same proper law.

§2. It is the right and the duty of the diocesan bishop to visit even with respect to religious discipline:

1° autonomous monasteries mentioned in can. 615;

2° individual houses of an institute of diocesan right situated in his territory.

§3. Members are to deal in a trusting manner with a visitator, whose legitimate questions they are obliged to answer according to truth in love; moreover no one is permitted in any way to divert members from this obligation or otherwise to impede the scope of the visitation.

C 628 states the second major duty of religious superiors. They are to visit the houses, members, and works of the institute. Members are to cooperate with their religious superiors to achieve the purposes of these visitations. Proper law determines the times for these visitations.

Visitations by higher superiors have a long history in religious life. This practice is viewed both negatively and positively by superiors and members of institutes. It seems significant that the Code retains the practice for religious institutes. Visitations can be seen as opportunities for a mutual exchange of understandings and an honest evaluation of the life of the community. The visitator's role often includes reviewing the life and work of members of institutes, their spiritual and financial condition, and the fidelity of the community to its spirit, charism, traditions, and constitutions. Proper law determines these details.

The purposes of the visitation frequently include the offering of service to a member or community by providing an objective point of view. The visitator may be of assistance to individuals to realize their potential and to clarify their ideals. The visit can in itself be a freeing force for the member or the community.

Visitations can also be an effective structure for accountability of members to their profession. They can cause a member or community to examine their particular goals and value systems as well as to assess who they are as juridic persons and who they wish to become. Visitations can also cause a member or community to face certain difficult questions. In some cases a visitation does not achieve its purpose because of the lack of preparation. For this reason visitators and the community should prepare themselves in advance of a visitation.

A visitation may serve the whole Church by helping a community of the institute to see how it relates to the institute and the Church as a whole. Through well-planned visits the visitator can encourage a better use of talents by causing the individual and the community to examine whether they should enlarge or restrict their horizons.

A visitation is often placed in a faith context. Such a context requires spiritual preparation on the part of the visitator and on the part of the community being visited. A good visitator asks the community to prepare for the visit by clarifying its spiritual ideals and goals and by sending this data in advance of the time scheduled for the visit. During visitations, a visitator, as any superior, is not concerned with the internal manifestation of conscience by members. The focus is kept on external life and work.

A visitator should be a person who is well informed and experienced in the life of the institute and one who relates well with persons of different and varying types of personalities. Sometimes a team of visitators is good, since the members of the community then have a choice of one with whom to speak.

The obligation of the visitator includes the task of making judgments based on the oral and written data received from the visitation. Other tasks concern the promotion of growth in the community through advice given to members, convincing community members of their potential, helping the community with ways and means of self-correction, assuring implementation of decisions arrived at during a visit, submitting a formal report to the highest superior, and obtaining a response from those to whom the formal report is submitted. If the visitator's tasks are done well, visitations are generally perceived as helpful by members.

The religious superior is not the only person with the right of visitation. For an autonomous monastery of C 615 and for houses of diocesan right in his diocese, the diocesan bishop has the right and obligation for visitation. C 683 speaks of the bishop's visitations to churches, oratories, schools, and other works of the diocesan apostolate entrusted to religious of various institutes. In visitations of these works, the bishop focuses on the work as it relates to the diocese and not on the institute or its internal life and work.

Members of institutes are required by the last part of the canon to receive a visitator trustingly and to answer the visitator's questions with truth and love. C 628, §3 clearly forbids any member to impede other members in presenting the truth as they see it or to block the purposes of the canonical visitation in any way.

The last paragraph of C 628 also calls religious to assist their superiors in their role of accountability for the life and work of the institute and in their role for the service of authority in the Church. Through mutual participation in self-evaluation and in self-criticism, with honesty and love, religious can expect an increasingly effective role in the Church.

C 629

All superiors are to reside in their respective houses and not absent themselves from it, unless according to the norm of proper law.

This short canon on the third major duty of superiors should be read in light of the major duties of a superior and in light of Vatican II's call to the implementation of the principle of subsidiarity and the service of authority. Superiors are to be available to those they serve. To do this they need to live among those they serve as one of them. But in no way should this canon, which repeats its forerunner, CIC 508, be read in a restrictive manner as its forerunner sometimes was. Not every house necessarily needs a superior in residence. If the superior is readily available to a designated house and members, the requirement of the canon seems to be met.

The role and need for presence of a superior at a specific place depends very much upon the other members of the group at that place. Motherhouses, novitiates, houses of study, and retirement houses perhaps need a resident superior; obviously, smaller houses and more experienced and able groups do not. Particularly in small groups of two or three members, there may be a superior who is not resident with the group but to whom the group is accountable.[20] Local members can easily assume the administration for the house in many instances without a superior being present at all times. The role and presence of a local superior should be determined by the situation, need, values, and capabilities of the group. Proper law specifies this role.

Local superiors, whether they have residence in the local house or not, do have personal authority. After dialogue and consultation with other members, they may make decisions which are for the good of the group or of its individuals and for the good of the institute as a whole in regard to the group. By their vow of obedience, members are obliged to obey the directives of the superior for implementing the decisions made (C 601).

The principle of subsidiarity can best be implemented through members' fostering a proper attitude toward the role of local superiors in the institute. A local superior fosters unity. Having a person to exercise personal authority in the local area of the governmental structure is an attempt to promote greater dialogue and trust among members, yet it allows for recourse to a higher superior when necessary. It relieves major superiors of a significant amount of day-to-day "care-taking" and allows them more time to decide upon and to implement short- and long-range plans of the institute. It also develops individuals for service as superiors in all areas of governance.

C 630

§1. Superiors are to recognize the due freedom of their members concerning the sacrament of penance and the direction of conscience, with due regard however for the discipline of the institute.

§2. According to the norm of proper law superiors are to be solicitous that suitable confessors to whom they can confess frequently be available to members.

§3. In monasteries of nuns, in houses of formation and in more numerous lay communities there are to be ordinary confessors approved by the local ordinary after consultation with the community; members nevertheless have no obligation to approach them.

§4. Superiors are not to hear the confessions of their subjects unless the latter request it of their own initiative.

§5. Members are to approach superiors with trust, to whom they can express their minds freely and willingly. However, superiors are forbidden to induce their subjects in any way whatever to make a manifestation of conscience to them.

The thirteen canons on confessors which formed the second chapter on governance in the 1917 Code are now collapsed into this one canon. C 630 appears to affirm the freedom of conscience of the individual member.[21] This affirmation reflects Vatican II's development of the Church's fundamental doctrine of religious freedom. From this principle of freedom flows the function of the Church to enable the spiritual and human development of all people.[22]

To further the development of an individual's freedom of conscience, superiors are to be solicitous according to proper law that suitable confessors are made available to members. No particular faculties are now required by the Code for hearing the confession of members of institutes nor are members under obligation by law to present themselves to any specific confessor.

In monasteries of nuns and in houses of formation or other lay communities with numerous members, ordinary confessors are to be made readily available for those persons living there. The appointment of these confessors by the Ordinary is done only after conferring with the particular community.

In order to protect both members and superiors against any violations of the internal forum, C 630 requires that superiors of clerical orders not hear the confession of another member of their group unless requested to do so by the member. On the other hand the canon once more encourages the members of the institute to approach their superiors with trust. This initial goodwill may lead them to share with each other the Spirit within them. Although the canon highlights the pastoral role of the superior, it simultaneously protects members from receiving care they may not want by clearly stating that the superior may not in any way induce the member to reveal matters of conscience.

Chapters

The article on chapters, which includes the three canons numbered 631–633, is new. In the 1917 Code there are only broad references to chapters in the canons on government of institutes (CIC 501, 506, 507). Their definition and operation is assumed. The 1983 Code defines chapters by their function and by their distinction from other participative and consultative bodies within the institute. It does not, however, determine the many practical details such meetings of the institute involve. Proper law is responsible for determining such detail (C 631, §2). Details should be in accord with the universal law in its determination of the power of governance for the institute (see especially CC 131, 148, and 166).

C 631

§1. The general chapter, which holds supreme authority in the institute according to the norm of the constitutions, is to be so formed that, representing the entire institute, it should be a true sign of its unity in love. Its foremost duty is this: to protect the patrimony of the institute mentioned in can. 578, and promote suitable renewal in accord with this patrimony, to elect the supreme moderator, to treat major business matters and to publish norms which all are bound to obey.

§2. The composition and the extent of the power of the chapter is to be defined in the constitutions; proper law is to determine further the order to be observed in the celebration of the chapter, especially regarding elections and procedures for handling various matters.

§3. According to norms determined in proper law, not only provinces and local communities but also any member at all can freely send his or her wishes and suggestions to the general chapter.

A general chapter is constituted in such a way that the spiritual character of the institute is evident. It is a sign of an institute's unity and love. It represents all the members and holds the highest authority in the institute during the time it is in session. Through its basic constitution it is a collegial body whose members have identical rights and who therefore share authority for the laws and for the extraordinary government of the institute. Its authority, however, neither derogates nor conflicts with the ordinary authority of the superior, who by right is president of the chapter.

The function of the general chapter is fivefold. It first guards the institute's particular patrimony, designated in C 578 to mean the nature, end, spirit, character, and traditions of the institute. It promotes an updated renewal of the institute in accord with its needs and means. It also elects the supreme moderator and treats major business matters. Finally, it draws up the necessary norms with which all are held to comply.

The constitutions are required by the universal law to state the composition and the extent of power of the general chapter (C 587). Proper law details the order to be observed in the chapter, especially that for elections and other business. Further details usually are contained in directories of policies of the institute.

The supreme moderator may delegate someone to preside at the chapter. This arrangement can release the superior for fuller participation in the discussions and deliberations of the chapter. The chapter moderators appointed by the supreme moderator do not need to be chapter members. Some religious institutes employ moderators from other religious institutes in order that the sessions of the chapter can be conducted with the greatest possible objectivity on the part of the moderator.

A pre-chapter committee on planning for the chapter is usually appointed by the supreme moderator in consultation with the council. Other ways for selecting a pre-chapter committee may be used. The committee should not be too large and should be representative of the institute. The usual duties of the committee include preparing the agenda and the chapter process and obtaining appropriate presentors and staff for the chapter. All the work of the committee is done in conjunction with the supreme moderator and the council. When the chapter convenes for its first session, the members of the chapter usually approve or disapprove the proposed agenda, process, presentors, and staff.

Resource persons may be invited to attend the chapter sessions. These persons have neither vote nor voice in decisions by the chapter. A chapter may object to giving the supreme moderator and the council the authority to select resource persons. However, given the necessity to engage resource persons a year to two years in advance of a chapter, a practical approach must be taken by chapter members toward this situation. Chapter members, nevertheless, after they convene as a chapter always retain the right to approve or disapprove the selection of resource persons.

The second point of the canon requires that the constitutions of the institute further determine the *ex-officio* members of the chapter. The general chapter sets the number of elected delegates for the next chapter and the method of their election, unless the constitutions state otherwise. In some institutes the number of elected delegates and the method of their election is left to the discretion of the supreme moderator and the council. Canon law sets no guidelines for this decision but leaves it to the proper law of the institute.

The composition of general chapters has been a source of questions in many institutes. This issue mainly centers on the advantage or disadvantage of a delegate chapter vis-a-vis a full participatory chapter. An institute may not have a full participatory chapter unless it has been approved in the constitutions of the institute or unless the institute has obtained a special indult of the Holy See. The decision to allow such a chapter is usually based on the tradition of the institute or on the fact that the institute is fewer than one hundred members who are geographically situated in such a way that all may attend the chapter sessions.[23]

It is imperative to safeguard the active and passive vote of each perpetually professed member of the institute to elect chapter delegates and to be elected as a delegate to the chapter. Active and passive voice is a vested right of a member as designated by the constitutions and cannot in any way be arbitrarily denied a member.[24]

In order to have more participation and input into delegate chapter deliberations, some institutes have designed a process for the general chapter to involve the non-chapter members in dialogue previous to any decision-making by the chapter members. Such a process can more easily be done in nationally contained institutes rather than in large international institutes.

Chapters sometimes conduct a session on elections separate from meetings on business affairs and legislation. To provide for a smooth transition of persons elected to particular services, some institutes hold their chapter of elections previous to the chapter of affairs. This practice should be noted in the consitutions of the institute, and the elections should not be held sooner than six months before the day of vacancy of the office (C 153). Institutes who conduct the chapter of affairs in advance to the chapter of elections claim the advantage of electing those members most qualified to implement the decisions of the chapter. Nothing precludes an institute's deciding for itself how best to arrange its sessions of elections and affairs.

The merit of on-going chapters versus chapters held every three, four, or six years to coincide with the chapter of elections has been an issue in religious institutes. It is to be remembered that a general chapter or a provincial chapter is an event in the life of the institute or province. Neither a greater frequency of chapters nor the practice of on-going chapters allows for implementation and evaluation of the work of the chapter. Nor do frequent or on-going chapters allow for adequate in-depth preparation for the next chapter. Through these deficiencies the impact of the chapter on the institute is lessened and members, in general, pay less attention to the chapter. The general chapter thereby deteriorates as a sign of unity and love in the whole institute.

As a rule chapters ought not extend beyond the time necessary to accomplish their respective tasks. Once the time needed to accomplish its task is completed, the chapter should be closed, and the implementation of the decisions should be entrusted to the persons elected to administer the institute. At the close of the chapter, the delegates and *ex-officio* members of the chapter have no further capitular authority. The constitutions ought to provide for an extraordinary chapter in addition to the ordinary ones to decide on unforeseen business of an extraordinary nature.

Every member of the institute should be aware of contributing to the work of a chapter. Any province, local community, or individual may freely send wishes and suggestions to the general chapter. Chapter members in receiving these suggestions will need to sort out carefully those suggestions that fit into the scope and competency of the chapter.

In meeting the tasks of the chapter, institutes may need the reminder that Vatican II called institutes to renew their structures, but it did not tell them to overdo structural reorganization in ways that become ends in themselves and their purpose lost. The process of reorganization should further Christ's reign. It should not damage the gifts of persons or of goods organized to achieve this end. This caution applies equally for superiors, members, chapters, and other bodies of the institute.

C 632

Proper law is to determine clearly what pertains to other chapters of the institute and other similar gatherings, namely, regarding their nature, authority, composition, mode of procedure and time of celebration.

In addition to the general chapter, an institute may have provincial, regional, or local chapters. These are to be clearly defined in the proper law of the institute and distinguished from other gatherings of members which are representative of the membership. Each gathering has its own nature, authority, composition, mode of procedure, and time of celebration as determined by proper law.

Provincial and regional chapters are convoked and conducted in a manner very similar to general chapters in most institutes. Frequently the constitutions of an institute with provinces states that the province conducts its own chapter, elects its own provincial, and determines its own statutes subject to the approval of the supreme moderator and the council of the supreme moderator. The decisions of the province are not to contradict the laws of the institute in any way but are to support the purpose of the institute.

The constitutions of the institute also state the powers of a provincial superior in relation to those of the supreme moderator. A regional superior may have fewer delegated powers due to a greater dependency of regions on the institute for personal and material resources. Regions established by the institute in other countries may be granted powers similar to those of a province to allow a quicker and more apt adaptation to local customs in matters such as admissions of new members and conduct of business affairs.

Some institutes have a tradition of local chapters for conducting the business of a local house, and even for electing a local superior subject to the approval of the major superior. If local chapters are not the practice of an institute, many institutes through their proper law have set a structure of regular house meetings for determining goals, practices, and rules of the local house. Usual areas for decisions at such meetings include provisions for regular community prayers and participation in the sacramental life of the Church, designation of times and places reserved for the community, setting of an annual house budget, and ways for ameliorating personal conflicts.

As in general chapters, chapters of other kinds in the institute are best conducted in an explicit faith context. A scriptural theme for the year or for the meeting challenges the attention of the group. Times for prayer, hymns, meditation, reflection, and faith-sharing may well be a regular part of the meetings as links with the life of the institute as a whole. Because emphasis is on community life in such local meetings, rather than on government, the conduct of local meetings is often treated in the constitutions of the institute under the title of community life.

Aside from chapters conducted in various parts and houses of the institute, similar gatherings of a collegial nature are conducted in some institutes to renew and enrich the spirit and charism of the institute in some way. Some institutes host "community days" several times a year for the institute as a whole. Others set meetings for parts and houses of the institute. Still others conduct a "general assembly" of all members every two, three, or four years, or "forums" of parts and houses of the institute. Like the chapters of the institutes, each of these gatherings has its particular role carefully delineated by the institute in its proper law.

C 633

§1. Organs of participation or consultation are to carry out faithfully the duty entrusted to them according to the norm of universal and proper law and to express in their own way the concern and participation of all members for the good of the entire institute or community.

§2. Wise discretion is to be used in establishing and using these means of participation and consultation, and their procedures are to conform to the character and purpose of the institute.

The Church through C 633 encourages organs of the institute for participation and consultation in an institute. These are to be delineated and guided by the proper law of the institute. They should express the involvement and concern of all the members of the community for the good of the whole (*PC* 14,ff). The powers of these organs as consultative or legislative must be clearly defined in the proper law of the institute.

Chapters may establish on-going and ad-hoc commissions, boards, panels, and committees to study certain areas such as ministry, admissions, finances, and elections. If so, the chapter should designate their consultative function by directing their establishment and use in general and by indicating to whom each group is accountable.

To promote an awareness of individual and human rights in institutes, some chapters have established an organ for resolving inter-community grievances. These are often referred to as instruments for conflict resolution or for reconciliation. In the establishment of such organs in institutes, particular care should be taken that the rights of superiors in accord with universal and proper law are in no way contradicted or diminished. Those who exercise power in any way in the use of such organs must be familiar with the universal and particular law on the nature of religious life and they should be competent in demonstrating spiritual as well as practical solutions for interpersonal conflict. Otherwise, institutes risk supporting willfulness and self-righteousness in members more so than developing their awareness of individual and human rights.

A final word is in order for the governance of religious life. In planning organs for participation and consultation, an institute should guard against overstructuring. Simplicity is still a desirable norm for living religious life structurally as well as spiritually. Too much participation and consultation, as well as too little, can dull the enthusiasm of members for the vital life of the institute. An appropriate balance of organs of authority with organs for participation and consultation is necessary.

NOTES

1. For a critique of the pyramid model of the Church see Kress, R., "Membership and Leadership in the Church," *Jur* 42 (1982) 29–69, esp. 34–42. For a critique of the paradigm of the head and body of Christ, see Dulles, A., *Models of the Church* (New York: Doubleday, 1974) esp. 20–21 and 46–57, and NCCB, *As One Who Serves* (Washington: USCC, 1977) II, A, 3. Although both models, as all models, have weaknesses, they also have strengths. The faithful in general are familiar with them, and for this reason alone they can be more useful than others to describe the Church's use of authority and to indicate its proper use. The paradigm of the head and body of Christ is applied to describe Church government in the brief study, Modde, M., "Governance in Institutes of Consecrated Life," *CLSAP* 43 (1981) 184–93.

2. Both Dulles and NCCB, *supra*, recognize Vatican II's use of the image of the People of God as a helpful corollary to the Church's traditional image of itself as Body of Christ. A similar corollary occurs in *LG* where the image of the Trinity is presented in *LG* 2–4 as a broadened image of Christ the Light of Nations, the foundational image in *LG* 1. These interacting images prepare for the introduction of the Church as both the mystery of Christ, *LG* 4–8, and as the People of God, *LG* 9–17. Kress, 50–51, affirms the importance of the concept of the Trinity in the history of democratic governments. Through the doctrine of the Trinity, Christian monarchies can be seen to develop beyond the monotheistic imperialism and totalitarianism of oriental and non-Christian monarchies. Attention to this fact and to Vatican II's use of trinitarian imagery in *LG* 1–8 can aid further development of Christian forms of government.

3. The presentation of many key words of Vatican II is undertaken by J. M. R. Tillard's "Restructuring Government," an appendix to R. Voillaume's *Religious Life in Today's*

World. Vita Evangelica, no. 4 (Ottawa: CRC, 1970) 285-301. The key word "co-responsibility" is the subject of twelve essays in J. Coriden, ed., *Who Decides for the Church?* (Hartford: CLSA, 1971).

4. See Dulles, A., "The Church," *The Documents of Vatican II,* ed. W. Abbott (New York: Guild Press, 1966) 12. Noting the overall structure of *LG* to present the dignity and responsibilities of lay Christians, Dulles explains the overall role of authority in the Church to be one of service for the Church's total mission. This concept is frequently assumed in discussions of Church authority.

5. Dulles, "The Church," 12, and J. C. Murray, "Functions of Authority in the Church," in *Code, Community, Ministry,* ed. J. Provost (Washington: CLSA, 1982-1983) 1-11, esp. 7. Dulles points to Vatican II's starting with people, not structures and government, in the development of its concept of Church; Murray notes a different arrangement by Vatican II of the traditional four themes on Church, and its beginning with the concept of Church as community rather than the concept of Church as society. From these new starting places a different approach to the meaning of the Church and its authority is made possible.

6. *Ibid.,* and Huizing, P., "A Methodological Reflection on the Section 'Institutes of Consecrated Life' in the *Schema Codicis Iuris Canonici,"Jur* 42 (1982) 180-91. With a discussion group of seven Huizing examines the changing methods of Church law, the blending of theological and spiritual elements with the juridical, and the weaknesses in the new methods of law-making from the standpoints of clarity and legal force, of creative processes and local initiatives, and of religious identity and spiritual power. Huizing sees introduction of spiritual elements into law as self-defeating unless there is a future legal system founded on theological constitutional principles.

7. Linscott, M., "The Service of Religious Authority," *RfR* 42 (1983) 197-217, esp. 217. Linscott presents an exegesis of the authority of Jesus for application by religious. A yet broader understanding of the spiritual dimensions of authority needed by religious is given by R. Voillaume, 164-65. For the achievement of humanity's essential task to govern existence Voillaume sees the need to join the laws of Christ with that of divine transcendence of human limits to direct life as a whole.

8. For the kinds of documents of the Church which may contain law, see Morrisey, F., *The Canonical Significance of Papal and Curial Pronouncements* (Hartford: CLSA, 1974). Morrisey lists and explains thirty-one types of papal pronouncements and fourteen types of curial documents. The binding force of the documents increases in proportion to the legislative nature of a document as contrasted with its doctrinal nature. For specific post-Vatican II documents presenting religious law, see *CLD* on CIC 487-681 (New York: Bruce, 1963-; Chicago: Chicago Province S. J., 1968-; Mundelein, Chicago Province S. J., 1973-) and documentary services such as *ConLife* (Boston: Daughters of St. Paul, 1977-).

9. See Murray, 11; also see Fleming, D., "Hope-filled Deeds and Critical Thought," in *Religious Life Tomorrow, Donum Dei,* no. 24 (Ottawa: CRC, 1978) 49-50 and 53-54; Schneiders, S., "Toward a Theology of Religious Obedience," in *Starting Points,* ed., L. A. Quiñonez (Washington: LCWR, 1980) 59-85, esp. 62-63; and Schillebeeckx, E., *Ministry* (New York: Crossroad, 1981), esp. IV: 4, and 99. Each of these sources treats post-Vatican II concerning authority and obedience in Church life. S. Holland details specific tensions in authority for religious in "Governmental Stumbling Blocks," *New Catholic World* (May-June 1983) 122-24.

10. See Linscott, esp. 314-17; Minutes, *Consilium "16",* 79: 12/22; 80: 1/25; and 80; 2/29; and Couesnongle, V., "Structures of Participation and the Future of Religious Institutes," in *Mass Media and the Future of Religious Life, UISG* 25, no. 3 (1972) 25-39. Each of these sources discusses basic inadequacies in structures for religious government.

11. See Griffin, B., "Subsidiarity and the Church Lawyer" and "National Church Structures," in J. Provost, ed., 47 and 48–52, esp. 51–52, with Morrisey, F., "The Significance of Particular Law in the Proposed New Code of Canon Law," *CLSAP* 43 (1981) 1–17. The first author summarizes the second. Both encourage consistent use of the principle of subsidiarity in applying the Code's concessions to proper law, the latter being the Code's way to relieve tensions created by the universal law. Both authors, however, foresee new tensions developing through applying the principle of subsidiarity because of multiple national, regional, and local church structures; divergent local values; slow consensus; and a general tendency, esp. for Americans, to over-legislate. The new Code, as shown by McDermott, R., "Schema: Revision or Update?" *CLSAP* 42 (1980) 129–30, uses the principle of subsidiarity more moderately than in the draft canons. Further studies such as Kinney, J., "Rights and Duties of the Faithful in the Schema," *CLSAP* 42 (1980) 107–14, and Provost, J., "Rights for Christians," *New Catholic World*, (May–June 1983) 110–12, show that the Code incorporates into the text rights of the faithful which were formerly proposed as a separate document, i.e., *Lex Fundamentalis*. This shift lessens the focus on making decisions and laws in the development of Church relationships and increases the focus on honoring various persons and groups and their basic dignity and responsibility as Church. C 611 clarifies the fact of appropriate rights and areas for subsidiarity for institutes and dioceses.

12. See Morrisey, F., *Pronouncements*, and Alesandro, J. "Particular Legislation," in J. Provost, ed., 24–27, esp. A, B, C, and F. 5. The universal law guides statements of proper law. Particular law has many forms and sources. The law of one specific local unit is more precisely known as its proper law.

13. See O'Connor, D., "Government," Seminar on Religious Law, *CLSAP* 40 (1978), 91–99. A number of O'Connor's points on the fact and role of a superior's exercise of authority are summarized here. See also Modde, M., *Manual for Writing New Constitutions* (Zumbrota, Minn.: Sommers Printing, 1979) 55–56.

14. *Ibid.*, and S. Holland, 123. Both O'Connor and Holland treat the importance of a superior's style of exercising authority.

15. Cf. Creusen, J., *Religious Men and Women in Church Law* (Milwaukee: Bruce, 1958) 34. Other practical reasons may determine an institute's decision to divide into smaller units.

16. See Minutes, *Consilium "16"*, 80: 2/29.

17. *CLD* 8, 356.

18. *Ibid.*

19. See O'Connor, 96 and *ConLife* 2 (1978), 149–51.

20. *CLD* 8, 347.

21. M. Modde, 186.

22. See Murray, J., "Religious Freedom," in Abbott, 672–74, and fnn. 3–5, 676–79. The principle of religious freedom is fundamental to the development of doctrine itself and to objective truth. This freedom is not identical to freedom of conscience; such identification can lead to subjectivism. It does not, however, contradict freedom of conscience. Rather, this traditional understanding of religious freedom is placed within proper perspectives of con-joined Church and civil orders.

23. *CLD* 8, 357. A useful study of the conduct of chapters to include input from all members appears in *ConLife* 2 (1978) 175–84. See also O'Connor, and Modde, *Manual*, 57–61.

24. Neither CC 208–23 nor CC 662–72 bestows the right of active and passive voice to religious. However, C 687 on exclaustrated members mentions the curtailment of this right and thus assumes its universality.

BIBLIOGRAPHY

Abbott, W., ed. *The Documents of Vatican II*. New York: Guild Press, 1966.

Alesandro, J. "Particular Legislation." In *Code, Community, Ministry*, 24–27. J. Provost, ed. Washington: CLSA, 1983.

Consilium "16". Minutes: 79:1222, 80:125, 80:229.

Coriden, J., ed. *Who Decides for the Church?* Hartford: CLSA, 1971.

Couesnongle, V. "Structures of Participation and the Future of Religious Institutes." In *Mass Media and The Future of Religious Life*. UISG 25, no. 3 (1972) 25–39.

Cruesen, J. *Religious Men and Women in Church Law*. Milwaukee: Bruce, 1958.

Dulles, A. *Models of the Church*. New York: Doubleday, 1974.

Dulles, A. "The Church." In *The Documents of Vatican II*, 9–13. W. Abbott, ed. New York: Guild Press, 1966.

Fleming, D. "Hope-filled Deeds and Critical Thought." In *Religious Life Tomorrow*. Donum Dei, no. 24, 41–56. Ottawa: CRC, 1978.

Griffin, B. "Subsidiarity and the Church Lawyer." In *Code, Community, Ministry*, 47. J. Provost, ed. Washington: CLSA, 1983.

Griffin, B. "National Church Structures." In *Code, Community, Ministry*, 40–52. J. Provost, ed. Washington: CLSA, 1983.

Holland, S. "Governmental Stumbling Blocks," *New Catholic World* (May–June 1983) 122–24.

Huizing, P. "A Methodological Reflection on the Section 'Institutes of Consecrated Life' in the *Schema Codicis Iuris Canonici.*" *Jur* 42 (1982) 180–91.

Kinney, J. "Rights and Duties of the Faithful in the Schema," CLSAP 42 (1980) 107–14.

Kress, R. "Membership and Leadership in the Church," *Jur* 42 (1982) 29–69.

Linscott, M. "The Service of Religious Authority," *RfR* 42, no. 2 (1983) 197–217.

McDermott, R. "Schema: Revision or Update?" *CLSAP* 42 (1980) 124–31.

Modde, M. "Governance in Institutes of Consecrated Life," *CLSAP* 43 (1981) 184–93.

Modde, M. *Manual for Writing Constitutions*. Zumbrota, Minn.: Sommers Printing, 1979.

Morrisey, F. *The Canonical Significance of Papal and Curial Pronouncements*. Hartford: CLSA, 1974.

Murray, J. C. "Freedom, Authority, Community." In *Code, Community, Ministry*, 1–11. J. Provost, ed. Washington: CLSA, 1983.

Murray, J. C. *"Religious Freedom."* In *The Documents of Vatican II*, 672–74. W. Abbott, ed. New York: Guild Press, 1966.

National Council of Catholic Bishops. "In the Church," *As One Who Serves*, II., A., 3. Washington: USCC, 1977.

O'Connor, D. "Government." Seminar on Religious Law. *CLSAP* 40 (1978) 91–99.

Provost, J., ed. *Code, Community, Ministry*. Washington: CLSA, 1983.

Provost, J., ed. "Rights for Christians," *New Catholic World* (May–June 1983) 110–12.

Schillebeeckx, E. "Tensions between Actual Church Order and Alternative Practices in Ministry." Chapter IV in *Ministry*, 75–99. New York: Crossroad, 1981.

Schneiders, S. "Toward a Theology of Religious Obedience." In *Starting Points*, 59–85. L. A. Quiñonez, ed. Washington: LCWR, 1980.

Tillard, J. M. R. "Restructuring Government," appendix to *Religious Life in Today's World*, R. Voillaume. *Vita Evangelica*, no. 4, 285–301. Ottawa: CRC, 1970.

Voillaume, R. "The Freedom of the Children of God." Chapter X in *Religious Life in Today's World. Vita Evangelica*, no. 4, 157–77. Ottawa: CRC, 1970.

Temporal Goods
Canons 634–640

JOAN DE LOURDES LEONARD, C.S.J.

As an aspect of the governance of the institute, article 3, CC 634–640 (corresponding to CIC 531–537), deals solely with goods corporately owned and administered by the religious institute; it does *not* apply to goods that may be personally owned or acquired by the individual religious. These latter goods do not belong to the religious institute, although, in some instances, the institute may agree to assume the management of these patrimonial goods as a trust and a service in behalf of the religious. Personally owned goods are governed by the requirements of the vow of poverty, especially C 668, which is treated elsewhere in this volume.

NOTION OF TEMPORAL GOODS

Temporal goods may be defined as material things of a corporeal nature, whether movable or immovable, as well as incorporeal things of a monetary value, whether real or personal, such as legal rights and obligations, titles, offices, annuities, etc. Spiritual things are not included in the category of temporal goods, although they constitute the essential patrimony of the Church, e.g., divine worship, the sacraments, etc. Yet, material resources are necessary in order to give support to the spiritual purposes of the institute and provide a degree of stability for the pursuit of temporal and eternal goals.

PATRIMONIAL GOODS

The term "patrimonial goods" has sometimes been applied to the temporal goods of the Church. In the revision of the Code, however, this expression was specifically rejected when the members of the Commission were reminded that "patrimony" is much wider than temporal goods.

ECCLESIASTICAL GOODS

The term "ecclesiastical goods" is used instead of "temporal goods" whenever the canons are dealing with the goods of a public juridic person in the Church (C 1257, §1). It is not, however, usually applied to the goods of a private juridic person (C 1257, §2).

JURIDIC PERSONS

CC 113–123 distinguish between physical and juridic persons. However, juridic persons, like physical persons, are the subjects of rights and responsibilities which accord with their nature as set forth in the law (C 113). A juridic person is constituted either by prescription of the law itself or by a decree which is expressly given by the competent authority. Whether made up of persons or things, the juridic person in canon law bears some analogy to the corporation in civil law. It is a corporate entity made up of persons or things, which, within the scope of its competence, has the right, as a public juridic person, to act in the name of the Church; lacking this right, it is known as a private juridic person which acts in its own name. As a legally constituted entity, apart from the individual persons who comprise it, the juridic person carries on its corporate business, in accord with the norms of law, through duly appointed agents who enjoy competence to act in the name of the body, within the limits of the respective roles assigned them by constitutive or statutory law. They have responsibility and accountability for carrying out the formalities required either by particular or universal law for the validity of juridic acts.

C 634

§1. Institutes, provinces and houses, insofar as they are juridic persons by the law itself, are capable of acquiring, possessing, administering and alienating temporal goods, unless this capacity has been excluded or restricted in the constitutions.

§2. Nevertheless, they are to avoid all appearance of luxury, immoderate wealth and amassing of goods.

RELIGIOUS INSTITUTE AS PUBLIC JURIDIC PERSON

The basic premise underlying the religious institute's right to acquire, possess, administer, and alienate temporal goods is that it has been constituted a public juridic person i.e., it has been given a corporate existence apart from the individual persons who comprise it. Therefore, in canon law, it is the subject of rights and obligations which accord with its nature and purpose (C 113, §2). This canonical status is conferred on the institute as a whole by an ecclesiastical process of erection and approval according to the prescriptions set forth in this same Code (CC 576, 578, 579, 586, 587, 609, etc.). In addition, the provinces and houses of the institute erected by the competent internal authority become capable of acquiring and administering temporal goods as specified in the institute's proper law.

It may be noted that in the Church no ecclesiastical property can belong to an individual physical person; rather, all property belongs to one public juridic person or another. Individual administrators may hold legal title to assets of a juridic person, but they do not own them in an absolute sense. Rather, they hold these goods for the benefit of the juridic person and, therefore, exercise a role of stewardship. They act as human agents of the juridic person in a relationship of trust, and they are held accountable.

§1

The law of a particular institute may exclude or limit this right; e.g., the Capuchins may not by rule possess any temporal goods, so that whatever they have is owned by the Holy See. It is also possible for the general or provincial government to make some of the local houses fiscally dependent on it, e.g., house of novitiate, or house of retirement, or even some very small local communities. However, larger houses should be able to carry on their own local management of financial affairs subject to whatever obligations toward the provincial or general government that are set forth in the proper law of the institute.

INCORPORATED APOSTOLATES AS JURIDIC PERSONS

The apostolic works of the religious institute, even when separately incorporated by civil law, are, from the canonical point of view, usually part of the one public juridic person which is the religious institute which sponsors it. Hence, while these apostolates are subject to civil law, they are also subjects of canonical rights and obligations inherent in the juridic person of which they are a part. Therefore, administrators are required by C 1284, §2 to see that ownership of ecclesiastical goods is safeguarded in civilly valid ways, such as civil incorporation. It is important, also, for the administrators of such entities to realize that they must have concern for the canonical as well as the civil obligations of the incorporated apostolic work. This is true even where the administration of the work is not directly under the control of the religious institute that sponsors it. For example, the canonical requirements for alienation of ecclesiastical property must still be carried out by the religious institute. It is, therefore, prudent for the religious institute to create a civil corporation in such a way that the institute is enabled to carry out its canonical responsibilities with respect to the corporation.

§2

This norm, together with C 635, §2 and C 640, gives emphasis to the concern of Vatican II, which sees religious life as giving public witness to Christ's love for the poor. "Religious should be poor in fact and in spirit, having their treasures in heaven" (*PC* 13). In addition, *ES* II, 23 asks the general chapters of religious institutes to promote concretely the spirit and practice of poverty, devising new forms "which may make more effective the practice and witness of poverty today." The wording of this canon is actually an incorporation into the Code of the last sentence of *PC* 13. The poverty of religious institutes varies, according to charism, from institute to institute, and is described in the proper law of an institute. However, *PC* 13 has added the notion that "it is by no means enough to be subject to superiors in the use of property," and *ET* 22 speaks of the evangelical exigency of a lifestyle that witnesses to the Gospel and is not just preoccupied with "appearing to be poor."

C 635

§1. The temporal goods of religious institutes, since they are ecclesiastical goods, are regulated by the prescriptions of Book V, *The Temporal Goods of the Church*, unless it is expressly stated otherwise.

§2. Nevertheless, each institute is to determine appropriate norms for the use and administration of goods so that the poverty appropriate to the institute is fostered, protected and expressed.

APPLICABILITY OF BOOK V NORMS

The whole of Book V is on "Temporal Goods of the Church." C 635, therefore, specifically obligates the administrators of religious institutes to implement, where applicable, the norms set forth in this book, since the goods owned by religious institutes are properly designated as "ecclesiastical goods."

Book V makes clear that the temporal goods of the Church are designed to serve its spiritual purposes. The very first canon of this book, which proclaims the inherent right of the Church to own temporal goods independently of the state (C 1254, §1), also sets forth the purposes for which the temporal goods are requisite, namely, divine worship, the maintenance of clerics and other ministers, the works of the apostolate, and the exercise of charity, especially with respect to the needy (C 1254, §2). Towards these all-important ends, the Church has the right to acquire, possess, administer, and alienate the goods which it legitimately owns (C 1254, §1). This right is understood as extending to the universal Church, to the Apostolic See, to the particular churches, and to all juridic persons, public and private, recognized by Church law (C 1255). Such goods belong to the juridic person which has legitimately acquired them. Ultimately, however, the ownership of all such goods is under the supreme authority of the Roman Pontiff (C 1256).

The principles of stewardship, accountability, and subsidiarity are all integrated into Book V and, hence, are normative for religious institutes as well as other juridic persons in the Church.

§1

Book V (fifty-seven canons), after setting forth four introductory canons (1254–1257) on the subject of the ownership of goods, deals with three titles: the Acquisition, the Administration, and the Alienation of Temporal Goods, plus a final title on Pious Wills and Foundations. Much of this material applies to the governance of temporal goods in religious institutes as well as the Church at large, e.g., C 1288 which forbids administrators to carry on a case in the civil courts without written permission given by the Ordinary; or, C 1286 which requires the implementation of the Church's principles on justice to employees and merchants by administrators of the Church's goods. This latter principle has been strongly asserted in Church documents; now it is mandated by law.

The Code describes two categories of juridic persons: public and private. Only the goods of the former are denoted as ecclesiastical goods, subject to the prescriptions of Book V. The goods of the private juridic person belong to that person and are governed by its own statutory law. They are not considered to be ecclesiastical goods unless it is expressly provided otherwise (C 1257, §1, §2).

Since religious institutes are by law public juridic persons, they are subject to the norms of Book V, and each of the titles of Book V must be seen as applicable to the governance of the temporal goods of religious institutes unless the subject matter indicates otherwise.

§2

Like C 534, §2, this prescription is significant for two reasons: first, it places the responsibility for expressing the particular poverty of the institute on the proper law of the institute itself. This is both a respect for differences of charism and also a commitment to the principle of subsidiarity. The Code makes it the immediate responsibility of the religious institute to incarnate in its proper law its motivating ideal in a way that accords with the founding vision and the legitimate tradition of the institute as it is to be lived in the contemporary world (C 587). In so doing one institute will be seen as differing from another in the mode of living its poverty: one will put major emphasis on divestment of goods; another, on work as the common vocation; another, on sharing of goods and facilities with others; another, on availability in service, etc. The proper law of the institute must take great care to integrate the universal norms governing temporal goods with its own particular spirit so that neither element will be lost in the effort at implementation.

This canon is another effort to implement Vatican II, emphasizing that material goods are viewed as means to higher ends, not as things to be sought for themselves. An ostentatious life is a contradiction to the simplicity of the Gospel and to the following of Christ which is the supreme law (C 662); on the other hand, the law indicates that every institute is required to provide for the needs of its members (C 670) and to safeguard the stable patrimony of the institute.

C 636

§1. In each institute and likewise in each province which is governed by a major superior there is to be a finance officer, distinct from the major superior and constituted according to the norm of proper law, who carries out the administration of goods under the direction of the respective superior. Even in local communities there is to be a finance officer distinct from the local superior to the extent that it is possible.

§2. At the time and in the manner determined by proper law finance officers and other administrators are to render an account of their administrative actions to the competent authority.

SEPARATION OF ROLES AND ADMINISTRATIVE ACCOUNTABILITY

The emphasis of this canon is on the need for the Church to have competent and trained administrators for its temporal goods, persons who will know and follow the prescriptions of both civil and canon law, recognizing themselves to be accountable for the goods of the poor.

§*1*

In the universal law, the diocesan bishop, having heard his consultors and the council on economic affairs, is required to name a finance officer who will provide experienced and expert advice and service in the economic matters of the diocese (C 494, §1). Expertise and consultative decision-making are as necessary for the governance of religious institutes in fiscal matters as they are for diocesan administration. That is the import of this canon governing religious institutes.

While the major superior has responsibility for the fiscal management of the temporal goods of the religious institute, the superior cannot and should not be immediately and directly responsible for carrying on the daily transactions of business. Rather, a treasurer or financial officer should be constituted for this purpose not only at the general level of government but also at the provincial, and where possible, every local house should have its own bursar, apart from the local superior. This distinction of roles with a shared responsibility is also fostered by the law's requiring, in specific cases, that the superior must obtain the consent of the council or, at least, must consult with the council, thus providing a wider base for decision-making in important matters (C 627).

§2

This canon not only reinforces the importance of accountability in the Code, but it further highlights the significant role given by the Code to the proper law of the institute. Every administrator of Church property is responsible and accountable for actions under the law and is answerable to those being served as well as to those in higher authority. It is necessary that the religious institute recognize this serious responsibility as being important for the good of the government and welfare of the institute, making it concrete and practical in terms of the life of the particular institute.

This canon is directed toward internal accountability just as the following canon (C 637) deals with external ecclesiastical accountability. The proper law of the institute should spell out the times and manner of reporting. There should also be a job description for the financial officers at all levels of government giving them a statement of those actions which flow from the role and therefore may be undertaken without special permission of the superior, as well as those actions which require explicit permission.

C 637

Autonomous monasteries mentioned in can. 615 must render an account of their administration once a year to the local ordinary; moreover, the local ordinary has the right to know about the financial reports of religious houses of diocesan right.

Substantially, this is the same requirement as CIC 535, but there are several differences. It is significant that whereas the latter was specifically directed to "every monastery of nuns," this canon is more generally directed to self-governing monasteries as defined in C 615 (i.e., those monasteries which, in addition to their proper superior have no other major superior, and are not connected with another religious institute in such a way that the superior of that institute enjoys true constitutional power over it) and to religious houses of diocesan right, both of which are committed to the special care of the diocesan bishop (CC 615, 594). Thus, ecclesiastical dependency and concern, rather than sex, are the basis for this monastic reporting to, and fiscal review by, the diocesan bishop, as set forth in C 637.

CIC 535, §1, 2° specified that the Ordinary could take action directly against fiscal remissness, or indirectly through a regular superior, even to the extent of removal from office. C 637 gives no such indication. However, C 1279 speaks of the administration of goods as belonging to the one immediately governing the juridic person, "saving the right of the Ordinary to intervene in cases of negligence by administrators."

CIC 535 spoke of the local Ordinary's right, on the occasion of his visitation to other institutes of women, to examine "the administration of the property constituted by the dowries." In the Code there is no mention of dowries.

C 638

§1. It is for proper law, within the scope of universal law, to determine acts which exceed the limit and manner of ordinary administration and to determine those things which are necessary to place an act of extraordinary administration validly.

§2. Besides superiors, officials who are designated for this purpose in the proper law can validly incur expenses and perform juridic acts of ordinary administration within the limits of their office.

§3. For the validity of alienation and any other business transaction in which the patrimonial condition of a juridic person can be affected adversely, there is required the written permission of the competent superior with the consent of the council. If, moreover, it concerns a business transaction which exceeds the highest amount defined for a given region by the Holy See, or items given to the Church in virtue of a vow, or items of precious art or of historical value, the permission of the Holy See is also required.

§4. For the autonomous monasteries mentioned in can. 615 and for institutes of diocesan right it is additionally necessary to have the written consent of the local ordinary.

ORDINARY AND EXTRAORDINARY ADMINISTRATION

In the administration of ecclesiastical goods, the distinction between ordinary and extraordinary administration is very important for the validity of acts. Ordinary administration refers to acts which may be carried out in the usual course of business by the administrator in virtue of holding a particular office or by virtue of delegation of power. In the matter of fiscal affairs, ordinary administration includes such things as: making and receiving payments for goods, depositing money in the bank, investing free capital, accepting or making donations or gifts, reserving money for particular purposes, etc.

On the other hand, extraordinary administration refers to acts which exceed the limits and extent of what is ordinary. It, therefore, requires particular permission from the competent superiors or from ecclesiastical authority, or both, in order to act validly. Acts of conveyance or alienation almost always are acts of extraordinary administration.

§1

Significantly, this canon puts the responsibility on proper law, within the limits of universal law, for establishing the dividing line between ordinary and extraordinary administration in terms both of dollars and of types of actions undertaken. Furthermore, it requires the proper law to set forth carefully those things which are required for the validity of an act of extraordinary administration. This should not be just an abstract statement, but rather, should rest on distinctions and requirements which flow from the nature of the institute and its needs and operations. Obviously, ordinary upkeep of the physical assets of an institution, including some on-going provision for ultimate replacement of goods, differs both in dollars and intent from a physical development program which is an extraordinary effort by the institution. If the latter requires the incurring of indebtedness, it may need both ecclesiastical and internal permission depending on the amount of indebtedness.

§2

Ordinary administration, which has been described above, includes those transactions which inhere in the daily carrying out of the office for which one is designated. Ordinary administration also includes all those juridic acts normally required for the preservation and improvement of goods and property as well as the use of the fruits arising therefrom. In addition to superiors, proper law should designate others who may perform specific acts of ordinary administration, such as treasurers, investment officers or committees, fund-raisers, administrators of apostolic institutions: schools, hospitals, etc.

§3

The canon applies to both acts of alienation and other acts which adversely affect the condition of the juridic person. Both are usually considered to be an act of extraordinary administration and require special authorization by competent superiors.

There are nine canons in Title III of Book V which govern the process of alienation (CC 1290–1298). Many of these apply to religious institutes and should be considered in any act of alienation.

These canons reflect the Church's cautious attitude toward alienation and acts which adversely affect ecclesiastical property. C 1293 sets up additional requirements for alienation, namely, a just cause such as "urgent necessity, evident usefulness, piety, charity, or some other serious pastoral reason" (C 1293, §1, 1°) and an expert evaluation in writing of the thing to be alienated (C 1293, §1, 2°). Moreover, the thing to be alienated should not ordinarily be sold for less than the evaluated sum (C 1294, §1). Proper canonical formalities are also prescribed not only for alienation but also for any transaction which could cause a loss of ecclesiastical goods (C 1293, §2).

Requests for alienation or conveyancing permission should contain answers to the following questions if they are relevant to the transaction:

a) Who is requesting the permission? Since all ecclesiastical property pertains to a public juridic person, the purpose of this question is to ascertain the identity of the public juridic person involved.

b) What is being alienated? This question requires a description of the property that is being sold. Permission is required only for alienation of immovable goods or fixed capital. Real estate should be described by metes and bounds and should include a description of any buildings thereon. Stocks should be specified as to number of shares and company, bonds by amount and issuer. (Stocks and bonds are fixed capital when they have been previously dedicated to a specific purpose.)

c) What public juridic person has ownership rights in the property? Normally, the answer to this question would be the same as to the first question above. It could happen, however, that more than one public juridic person has ownership rights in property being alienated (e.g., both a provincial house and a local house or both a diocese and a parish). In such a situation, the more inclusive public juridic person would apply for conveyancing permission, but the less inclusive public juridic person should also be named as having ownership rights in the property.

d) How was the property originally obtained? The answer to this question would specify the means by which the property being alienated became the property of the public juridic person now requesting alienation permission. Property is usually obtained by purchase, by gift, or by testamentary bequest.

e) What is the original cost of the property being alienated? If the property was purchased, this question requires disclosure of the purchase price. There is no cost of acquisition if the property was obtained by gift or by bequest.

f) What is the appraised value of the property being alienated? Canon law requires two separate appraisals of the property to be conveyed. Such appraisals could be the same as those for insurance or tax assessment purposes. Where these are unavailable, independent appraisals by conscientious and recognized experts must be obtained.

g) What are the reasons for selling the property? Anytime an enduring part of the patrimony of a public juridic person is to be conveyed, it is critical that good and sufficient reasons exist for the conveyance. Examples are: (i) when the property has become a liability to the public juridic person (real estate in irremediable disrepair); (ii) when the public juridic person is no longer involved in the apostolate for which the property is used (a religious congregation that is no longer able to sponsor a hospital and wishes to deed it away); (iii) when the public juridic person has other uses for the assets that are more critical than those to which the assets are currently dedicated (a religious congregation wishes to sell some real estate in order to obtain funds for the operation of one of its public charities).

h) Who is the buyer and what is its reason to buy the property? It is the intent of this question to avoid scandal (e.g., when a religious structure would be sold to another group that is not in a position to honor the religious history of the property).

i) Who is the broker and what is the broker's commission? As in the previous question, the purpose of this question is protective: to assure that there is no self-dealing or conflict of interest and no unwarranted commission.

j) What are the down payment and general terms of sale? This question is addressed by attaching a copy of the pertinent sales agreement. This inquiry also seeks to ascertain that the terms of sale do not deprive the public juridic person of the benefit of the bargain or that they do not tie the public juridic person into an on-going commercial relationship with the buyer (e.g., where the public juridic person finances the sale by taking either a note or mortgage as part of the purchase price).

k) What are the protocol numbers for previous alienations granted by the Holy See to the public juridic person seeking this alienation permission? This item is self-explanatory. In practice, only those protocol numbers for the previous ten years need to be submitted.

l) Has the consent of the provincial and/or general council been obtained? Both permissions are required when the province is the alienating party; otherwise, only the generalate need consent. All applicable consents should be in writing and attached to the alienation request.

m) Has the Ordinary (bishop) of the location of the property consented to the transaction? This item is normally answered by a letter from the bishop that is attached to the alienation request.

The requirement applies to an institute of diocesan right or an autonomous monastery (C 615). For institutes of pontifical right it has been the practice of SCRIS to request an opinion from the diocesan bishop in whose jurisdiction the property is located to ascertain if there would be any effect within the diocese if the property is alienated. There is, however, no canonical requirement for the consent of the bishop.

n) What is the current financial condition of the public juridic person seeking the alienation permission? The public juridic person should provide a summary financial statement that normally includes a balance sheet listing both the assets and liabilities of the public juridic person.

Two things seem noteworthy about the Code's treatment of alienation of ecclesiastical goods. First, subsidiarity is applied in designating the competent superiors for the granting of permission to alienate below the amount approved by the Holy See (in 1981 the amount set for religious institutes in the United States was $1,000,000). Second, the civil law of the country, where not contrary to divine or canon law, is to be followed in the making of contracts (C 1290). The contradictions, however, between the civil and canon law may engender problems for the administrator of ecclesiastical goods, but canon law cannot be ignored on that account. This problem becomes more clear by studying the situation of incorporated apostolates.

The civil corporation and the ecclesiastical public juridic person may not be identical entities. For example, a hospital is usually civilly incorporated as an entity distinct from the religious institute. However, in canon law the hospital is usually not a separate public juridic person but part of the religious institute which is a canonically established public juridic person. Thus, while the hospital property may be owned civilly by the hospital corporation, it is owned canonically by the religious institute.

Since an incorporated apostolate is subject to both civil law and canon law, the religious institute and the incorporated apostolate must be careful to observe both canon and civil law. In order to avoid potential conflict, civil documents should take into account canonical norms.

For the validity of alienation of property or goods belonging to the stable patrimony of the religious institute, as well as for the validity of any action that can weaken the patrimonial condition of a juridic person, permission given in writing by the competent superior with the consent of the council must have been previously secured (C 638, §3).

As has been said, in the United States, if the value of the property to be alienated is more than $1,000,000, permission for alienation must be sought from the Holy See as well (C 638, §3).

The chief intent of all this legislation is that property belonging to the Church and its entities should not be lost to another, thus depriving the Church of resources needed for its mission, and especially for the service of the poor in the spirit of Christ.

§4

This is the same requirement as that of the 1917 Code (CIC 534). C 1276, §1 of the 1983 Code requires the Ordinary to "sedulously watch over the administration of all goods which belong to public juridic persons subject to him." That means the two groups mentioned in the canon, namely, self-governing (not subject to higher internal authority) monasteries located within the diocese, and institutes of diocesan right which, by the law, are particularly under the care of the local Ordinary, must get his written consent. Pontifical right institutes are not subject to the local Ordinary for their financial accountability.

C 639

§1. A juridic person which has contracted debts and obligations even with the permission of the superior is bound to answer for them.

§2. If a member with permission of the superior has made a contract concerning personal goods, the member must answer for it, but if the business of the institute was conducted by order of the superior, the institute must answer.

§3. A religious who has made a contract without any permission of superiors must answer for it, but not the juridic person.

§4. It shall be a fixed rule, nevertheless, that an action can always be brought against one who has profited from the contract entered into.

§5. Religious superiors are to be careful that they do not permit debts to be contracted unless it is certain that the interest on the debt can be paid from ordinary income and that the capital sum can be paid off through legitimate amortization within a time that is not excessively long.

LIABILITY

This canon, in part, touches on the question of "agency." In this regard, the law is saying that only authorized persons may make contracts in the name of the juridic person which is the religious institute. Each of the articles of the canon tries to establish the locus of responsibility and liability in carrying on business by a member of the institute or in behalf of the institute.

In general, what is very important here to the juridic person, from the civil law viewpoint, is that once persons have been given actual authority as agents, they always bind the principal (i.e., the religious institute in this case) when they act within the scope of their agency. Moreover, unless specifically directed otherwise, agents have implied authority to act in accordance with general custom or usage of the affairs with respect to which they are expressly authorized to act.

Religious institutes should, therefore, be especially careful in creating new "titles" and new "job descriptions" for their members. The currently popular practice of borrowing terminology from the business world deserves special scrutiny. The incautious misuse of terms commonly used in the business world may constitute a "holding out" of a member of an institute as a person apparently authorized to bind the institute in transactions in ways that the institute does not intend to authorize the member to act.

§1

What is emphasized is that the superior who gave permission is not personally liable for the indebtedness because such a person acted in a corporate role and not in a personal capacity. It is the juridic person who is liable. This was also included in CIC 536, §1.

§2

The only change from the Code of 1917 is that the distinction between a member with solemn vows and a member with simple vows has been eliminated. Since the universal law does not, in the Code of 1983, make this distinction, the first sentence of CIC 536, §2 has been dropped. Such a distinction, however, may remain as part of the proper law of an institute. The basic point of this canon, however, is the distinction between whether members acted on their own behalf with permission, or acted on the institute's business by the superior's command. In the first case, the liability is personal; in the second, the liability belongs to the institute.

§3

When the member contracts without permission of superiors, the member is solely responsible. There is no question of acting as agent of the institute. Yet, there are circumstances that could make the institute liable. Should the institute fail to communicate to a third party that a particular member, in a given situation, has not been authorized to bind the institute, the institute may conceivably find itself bound by the member's acts, especially if a third party had come to believe that the agent possessed authority from the institute to place the act and this had not been denied in any way by the institute.

§4

In every case, the rule obtains that an action can always be brought against the one for whom the contract has been a source of gain, whether individual religious or corporate body. Once again, it is important to remember that civil law suits cannot be entered into without ecclesiastical permission.

§5

All of the above sections are based on the principles of justice. All, furthermore, distinguish between corporate and individual responsibility. All make clear, too, that no individual person has a legal capacity for contracting in the name of the corporation unless the latter has made that person an agent or given a power of attorney.

C 640

Taking into account local conditions institutes are to strive to give, as it were, collective witness of charity and poverty and are to contribute what they can of their own goods for the needs of the Church and the sustenance of the poor.

This is a direct quote from *PC* 13. It clearly shows the impact of Vatican II. The previous Code was much more cautious in its approach, saying in CIC 537 that "donations from the goods of the house, province, or institute are not permitted unless by reason of almsgiving, or other just cause, by will of the superior and according to the norms of the constitution." By contrast, the 1983 Code takes a positive stance in favor of a quasi-collective witness to poverty and charity, and calls upon religious institutes to contribute something of their own goods for the other needs of the Church and the sustenance of the poor. Stewardship and accountability for sharing of the goods that support life have become ascendant in the law.

The Code also requires administrators of ecclesiastical goods who employ workers to observe the civil laws concerning labor and social policy, according to the principles handed down by the Church (C 1286, §1). They are also required to pay an equitable and decent wage or salary so that they may provide for the workers' needs and those of their families (C 1286, §2). This is a new canon which has appeared in many documents, but, until this time, has not appeared in the law of the

Church. Religious administrators, whether in their religious institutes or their incorporated apostolates, are bound by these norms.

The Code makes it clear that the Church intends to show itself to the world as the Church of the poor. Within the universal law, each institute, therefore, must consider for itself how its corporate poverty can best be lived and protected from on-going erosion. Although the Church recognizes that institute will differ from institute in this regard, it nevertheless obligates all religious institutes to some kind of corporate witness to poverty, arising from, and appropriate to, their own tradition and vision.

When, however, religious institutes come to reflect on how they will dispose of and invest their temporal goods, they should reflect on their own charism and tradition, along with the needs of the world in which they live, in order to develop policies and practices which will be in harmony with their tradition. In this way, their stewardship in behalf of the poor will best be realized.

BIBLIOGRAPHY

Hite, Jordan. "Religious Vows and the NLRB," *RfR* 37, no. 6 (November 1978) 20–34.

Hite, Jordan. "The Status of the Vows of Poverty and Obedience in the Civil Law," *StudCan* 10, no. 1 (1976) 131–93.

Maida, Adam, and Cafardi, Nicholas P. *Church Property, Church Finances and Church-Related Corporations.* The Catholic Health Association of America, 1984.

Maida, Adam. *Ownership, Control and Sponsorship of Catholic Institutes.* Pennsylvania Catholic Conference, 1975.

McCoy, Alan. "Fiscal Management and Christian Stewardship," *RfR* 41, no. 5 (September–October 1982) 734–37.

Morrisey, Francis. "The Conveyance of Ecclesiastical Goods," *CLSAP* 38th Annual Convention. Philadelphia (October 1976) 123–37.

Morrisey, Francis. "New Canon Law on Temporal Goods Reflects Vatican II's Influence," in *The New Canon Law: Perspectives on the Law, Religious Life, and the Laity,* CHA, 1983, 49–61. Originally published in *Hospital Progress* (March 1982) and subsequently revised in the light of the promulgation of the Code (January 1983).

O'Rourke, Kevin D. "Lay Sponsorship: a Right, a Trust," *Hospital Progress* (September 1981) 40–44, 66.

Admission of Candidates and Formation of Members
Canons 641–661

JORDAN HITE, T.O.R.

INTRODUCTION

The law governing the formation of members of religious institutes has undergone major revision three times in the twentieth century. First, in the 1917 Code, second, in *RC* in 1969, and third, in the 1983 Code.

The 1917 Code, which was the initial codification of Church law, established common norms for religious in all areas of life including formation. The renewal initiated by Vatican II for religious in *PC* brought with it the need to review and update religious formation. SCRIS was presented with requests from institutes and organizations representing institutes to revise the canonical regulations governing religious formation. It was recognized that contemporary attitudes, conditions of modern life, and new apostolic needs along with the special charism and purpose of each institute called for changes in formation.

SCRIS responded in 1969 with *RC* in an instruction that was a combination of pastoral and juridic norms. The instruction was understood to be for the interim, since work on the new Code had already begun. Based on the new guidelines institutes began what has amounted to a period of experimentation in formation. The tenor of the instruction was to reduce or relax legal norms, provide pastoral considerations for renewal, and transfer authority regarding formation to the institute.

The result was to produce a wealth of new approaches and information about formation which would form the basis of the new law governing formation. Before *RC*, canon law regulated formation in institutes by means of a series of detailed laws which covered a variety of ways of life. *RC* drew out and identified the fundamental principles of formation while allowing institutes to develop their own formation program

115

by applying the principles so that they fit the charism and purpose of the institute. The sense of the instruction was to offer choices rather than imposing one choice on institutes. In offering choices to institutes several of the canons of the 1917 Code were repealed or modified. The repeal or modification was always in the direction of more freedom for institutes to resolve issues in formation.

RC noted it was increasingly difficult to promulgate laws which would apply to every institute considering the differing conditions in which institutes live throughout the world and the diversity of institutes and their works. It especially mentioned the fact that the formation and education will not be the same in institutes of men as in institutes of women or in institutes of contemplative life as in those devoted to the apostolate.

RC established that:

1. Formation should be extended over a longer period of time.
2. Candidates should be prepared to enter novitiate.
3. For institutes devoted to the apostolate, greater attention should be paid to preparation for the institute's life and work.
4. Temporary vows may be replaced by another bond of commitment.
5. Former members who have completed novitiate may return without repeating the novitiate in accord with conditions established by the institute.

All of these directions were carried over into the new law except that of replacing temporary vows by another bond of commitment.

The 1983 Code underwent two major drafts before promulgation. Although there were substantial changes from the 1977 draft to the 1980 draft, the changes in the area of formation were minor. The major change was that the 1977 draft followed RC in permitting other bonds, while the 1980 draft and the 1983 Code returned to the term, temporary vows.

The practical result of the idea that institutes should develop and apply the general principles of formation was that the number of canons on formation was reduced from fifty-one to twenty. [1] The prescriptions of the former law that are omitted are now left to individual institutes to decide if any of the former laws apply to them in part, or not at all, and then to take whatever is useful and place it in their proper law. It can be noted that the omission of the detailed prescriptions does not mean they are not useful. In fact, as the following commentary notes, institutes would do well to review them to see if any of them in their present or some adapted form would serve the needs of the institute.

The commentary for the most part reviews the previous law, its repeal or modification in RC and is followed by an explanation of the new law.

The major omission regarding the process of formation itself is that of postulancy. Both the 1917 Code and *RC* covered postulancy. Pre-novitiate programs are now entirely in the hands of the institute. The wide variety of pre-novitiate programs are guided only by the criteria for admission contained in C 642. Whatever program an institute has should prepare a candidate to enter the novitiate.

Two major additions to the law focus on the responsibilities of the professed members of an institute, first to the process of formation and second to their own formation. In C 652, §4 the responsibility of prayer and good example is broadened beyond formation directors and those living in houses of formation to all the members of the institute. This is in recognition of the powerful positive or negative witness members provide in the process of formation. Responsibility for on-going personal formation is highlighted in C 661, which envisions formation as a lifelong process. Both the individual member and the superior have a serious obligation for a member's lifelong growth and development.

This new law on formation will probably be easier to adjust to than other areas because much of what is contained in the new law has already been part of the practice and proper law or policy of most institutes. Although questions will continue to arise, most of them will be within the authority of the institute to resolve, since the weight of responsibility has now been shifted to individual institutes. This should satisfy the desire of institutes to develop programs that form people in accord with its nature and charism.

ADMISSION TO THE NOVITIATE

CC 641–645 establish (1) the right of major superiors to admit candidates to the novitiate; (2) the qualities that a candidate should have in order to be admitted; (3) the causes which make admission to the novitiate invalid or illicit; and (4) the testimonies required to be admitted. There are fewer impediments and fewer required testimonials, although each institute is free to establish its own impediments and to require testimonies or information it would find helpful.

C 641

The right of admitting candidates to the novitiate pertains to major superiors according to the norm of proper law.

This section of the law begins by establishing admission to the novitiate as the juridic act of admission to the religious life. The act of admission belongs to the major superior to be exercised in accord with proper law.

The institute in its proper law may require either a deliberative or consultative vote on the part of the council for admission.

By making the novitiate the beginning of religious life, the law leaves it to the discretion of institutes to provide a pre-novitiate program. *RC* contained guidelines and recommendations for pre-novitiate which are helpful; however, the institute is free to develop norms and policies that suit the life of the institute in order to prepare candidates for the novitiate.

In institutes which have a novitiate longer than one year, the act of admission pertains to the canonical requirement of twelve months and should take place prior to the beginning of the canonical period.

C 642

Superiors are to be vigilant about admitting only those who, besides the required age, have health, suitable character and sufficient qualities of maturity to embrace the particular life of the institute; this health, character, and maturity are to be attested to, if necessary by using experts, with due regard for the prescription of can. 220.

The opening clause of the canon reminds superiors of the important responsibility they have in fulfilling the task of admitting candidates to the novitiate. It then outlines three areas that need to be considered in order to admit an applicant; health, suitable character, and sufficient maturity for the particular life of the institute. These qualities are a further specification of the general requirements of C 597, which permits admission of any Catholic who has the right intention, the qualities required by universal and proper law, and is not held back by any impediment.

The health of the candidate can be verified by a physical examination by a medical doctor chosen by the candidate or the institute. In cases in which it is necessary to clear up doubt or gain further insight into a candidate's medical condition, the institute may request an additional examination. An institute may avoid difficulty later on by refusing admission if a candidate has a chronic or debilitating illness that will prevent living the life of the institute. However, the health requirement should not be interpreted to bar the admission of the handicapped who can live the life of the institute.

C 645 outlines the mandated and optional means an institute may employ to ensure that a candidate is of suitable character.

Sufficient qualities of maturity and more particularly mental health have over the past years been investigated by means of psychological testing and interviews. It seems clear that in most cases serious psychological illness or organic disease can be detected, but such testing is not predictive of future perseverance in religious life. Institutes should obtain the proper releases to review the data from both medical examinations and psychological testing, which should ensure a candidate that the information will be kept confidential. The release or an accompanying explanation should clearly state the purpose of the examination, who is to see the report, and what happens to the report after its initial use. In some cases the report may be given to the superior and/or council, while at the same time the candidate is given a copy of the report or a "read out" of its contents. It is helpful for the psychologist to instruct those who will read the report on the nature, uses, and limitations of the information in the report.

Discretion should be used in giving reports to candidates so they are not given false impressions about themselves because of a lack of understanding of the material. On the other hand, the report can often be helpful to the growth and development of the candidate whether admitted or not. In some cases these reports are shared with formation directors so they can better understand the candidate and more skillfully promote growth and development. If this is the case, it should be explained to the candidate and permission secured. Since these reports lose validity with the passage of time and the growth of the individual, they should be destroyed when they are no longer valid.

Institutes should also develop their own internal admissions standards in order to provide a consistent, well-considered approach to admissions that reflects the specific requirements of the institute. Candidates who have experienced previous difficulties such as alcohol or drug addiction, child abuse, sexual experiences that will impair the ability to live the vowed life, marriage (followed by a decree of nullity) but who now believe they have a vocation should find institutes well prepared to deal honestly with persons from their particular background if they decide to admit the person.

Interviews by a vocation director or an admissions board, visits to the candidate's home, extended visits by a candidate to a house or houses of the institute are all procedures that can help in preparing a competent report on a candidate.

The canon notes that the institute or experts employed by the institute are to conduct their examination without prejudice to the right of a person to protect his or her privacy. This is an important consideration for institutes to use in guiding experts so that they do not use methods that would violate privacy or in any way harm the reputation of the institute. At the same time institutes would do well to employ experts who have an understanding of the religious life so they can make their report more relevant to the needs of the institute and the candidate. If an expert does not already have this understanding, the institute may need to provide some education regarding its life and needs and the specific characteristics it believes to be desirable and undesirable. An institute may wish to provide written guidelines for the expert. If there is information that an institute cannot have access to except by violating or seeming to violate an individual's right of privacy, it should forego seeking the information, but it should not place itself at a disadvantage by granting admission on inconclusive evidence of suitability.

The admitting superior, with or without the council, needs all relevant evidence of suitability in order to make a proper decision regarding admission. If the institute has a pre-novitiate program, a variety of material may be presented to the admitting superior. It can include the reports and recommendations of the vocation director or admissions committee and a psychological report. If a council is involved in the decision by either a consultative or deliberative vote, they should have access to the relevant information in order to make a good decision.

The counsel to superiors from RC 14 appears in this canon in advising superiors to be on their guard and not accept candidates who do not show the right temperament and maturity to enable them to live the life of the institute. Institutes should not expect the desired qualities to be in an advanced stage of development; however, they should be sufficiently developed so that the institute has a reasonable hope that during the full period of formation the candidate will grow into a mature, responsible, and contributing member of the institute.

In the negative sense superiors in exercising their responsibility must consider the potential harm that can be done to the candidate and the formation program or institute by admitting to the novitiate someone who is unqualified or unprepared to undertake the life of the institute. It is better to delay admission until these qualities are sufficiently developed, possibly even developing a plan for the applicant so that an interested individual may grow to the point where admission is appropriate. Delay and/or working with an applicant is better than premature admission.

C 643

§1. One is invalidly admitted to the novitiate:

1° who has not yet completed the seventeenth year of age;

2° who is a spouse, during a marriage;

3° who is presently held by a sacred bond with any institute of consecrated life or who is incorporated in any society of apostolic life, with due regard for the prescription of can. 684;

4⁰ who enters the institute as a result of force, grave fear or fraud, or whom the superior receives induced in the same way;

5⁰ who has concealed his or her incorporation in any institute of consecrated life or society of apostolic life.

§2. Proper law can establish other impediments to admission, even for validity, or can add other conditions.

§1

There are five conditions or impediments which would cause the admission of a candidate to the novitiate to be invalid. In the previous law there were eight. Four of the previous impediments or their close parallel are included in the present law, while four are omitted.[2]

The new impediment is that of concealing incorporation into another institute of consecrated life or a society of apostolic life. This condition is a softening of the previous impediment which invalidated the admission of anyone who had been bound by the bonds of profession.

§1,1°

A candidate must have completed seventeen years of age. According to C 203 a person is seventeen at the end of the day of the person's seventeenth birthday. A candidate's age can be verified by a birth certificate or a baptismal certificate. In the United States a birth certificate can usually be obtained from a state bureau of vital statistics or its equivalent. Although this is an age younger than most institutes in the United States have for admission, it is set at such an age to allow institutes throughout the universal Church to have flexibility in the admission of candidates. Each institute by proper law may set a suitable age for admission which can take into account the culture, relative age of maturation, and the demands of the life of the institute.

§1,2°

A person may not be admitted while the marriage bond continues to exist. This section does not apply to those who have obtained a decree of nullity. However, in the case of a decree of nullity the institute should have some internal criteria that allows it to determine if the cause of the break-up of the marriage is one that would impede the person from entering religious life at that time. In the case of a decree of nullity, a candidate may be asked for permission to review the annulment sentence. This would reveal the cause of the termination of the marriage and would also reveal whether the tribunal issued a prohibition or conditions that should occur before entering another marriage. These same comments would be helpful in determining the readiness of a person to enter a religious institute.[3]

This section applies to a person who is party to a still existing marriage which has not been annulled. As with CIC 542 an institute can apply to the Apostolic See for a dispensation from the impediment. Previous petitions have required the following information: (1) has a civil divorce been obtained and if so include a copy of the decree, (2) the number of children, if any, their age, and the provision that has been made for their care (the most recent custody and support decree as well as a statement by the petitioning party and in some cases the former spouse or the party who has custody regarding the adequacy of care is appropriate here), (3) has the candidate contributed to the break-up of the marriage? (4) is there evidence that the former spouse had forfeited his or her marital rights? In a recent case SCRIS responded to a petition by an institute for a dispensation for a divorced woman to enter.[4] SCRIS stated that "the fact that the petitioner received a civil divorce or that her husband presents no objection to her becoming a religious is not sufficient in the eyes of the Church to establish that he has forfeited his rights to the marital life. There must be evidence of the partner's infidelity by reason of remarriage, cohabitation, or adultery in the sense of CIC 1129." SCRIS continued that "unless the above points were stated and somewhat proven, there is no hope of obtaining the dispensation that the petitioner is seeking." The institute forwarded the further proof SCRIS wanted and the dispensation was granted.[5]

§1,3°

A person who is bound by a sacred bond to another institute of consecrated life or who has been incorporated into a society of apostolic life may not be admitted. The fact of being bound to one precludes being bound to another. A person who wishes to enter another institute or society must be free to do so. The only exception is the process of transfer described by CC 684 and 685. A religious who is transferring from one institute to another retains the vows pronounced in the former institute until profession in the new institute.

In the 1917 Code this impediment included all those who had been bound by a previous temporary or perpetual profession even though they had been granted a dispensation from their vows. Previous profession is no longer an impediment.

According to RC 38 a member who lawfully left an institute at the expiration of temporary profession or by dispensation could seek re-admission to the institute with the permission of the superior general and the agreement of the council without the obligation of repeating the novitiate. The superior general was to impose a period of probation of not less than one year or not less than the period of temporary probation which was still needed to complete the time necessary to make perpetual profession at the time the member left the institute. A longer period of probation could be prescribed at the discretion of the superior general.

C 690 grants additional discretion. If a member has completed novitiate or made profession and departed legally, the member can be readmitted by the supreme moderator with the consent of the council. The novitiate need not be repeated. The difference between *RC* 38 and C 690 is that instead of defining the period of probation it is left to the supreme moderator to determine a suitable period according to the norm of CC 655 and 657. This would mean at a minimum a former member should make up the additional time necessary to profess perpetual vows. For example, if a member left two years prior to eligibility for perpetual profession, the period of probation could not be less than two years.

§1,4°

This section applies to two situations in which admission is invalid: force, grave fear or fraud on the part of the candidate or on the part of the admitting superior.

Each of the prohibited influences has its particular effect on the freedom of consent of either the candidate or the admitting superior, which like any other juridic act in the Church must be freely made (C 125). Force, grave fear or fraud depending on its effect on the will may destroy or diminish consent. In either case it invalidates it.

Force[6] is the coercion or violence exerted by an outside agent which moves a person to act because of a threat of evil so that the person consents to the act in order to avoid the evil. Force is uncommon but cases of kidnapping or physically handing over a candidate to an institute would be examples of prohibited conduct.

Grave fear is the intimidation which results from the threat of evil. In order to be invalidating, it must be grave and causative. Fear is absolutely grave when it would induce a reasonable, prudent, well-balanced person to enter an institute against his or her will. Absolute fear would be caused by threat of death or physical harm to the person or someone else, imprisonment, loss of great wealth, or disinheritance. Fear is relatively grave if the threat is brought to bear on an anxious or immature person so that a smaller objective threat of evil results in great fear.

Since the section does not distinguish between extrinsic and intrinsic fear, it seems that whether the fear is produced by an outside agent or merely the result of an interior fearful state of mind, the result would be invalidating. Extrinsic fear would be a case of a young person entering because of fear of a parent. For example, parents may help a child in choosing a vocation but may not threaten expulsion from home if a child fails to enter an institute. An example of intrinsic fear would be fear of punishment by God for failure to enter. Fear is causal if the person chooses to enter the institute in order to avoid the threatened evil.

Fraud is the knowing concealment or false assertion of an important factor regarding suitability for religious life. The factor would have to be so important that the person would not have been admitted if it were known or the false statement or materials served to support an admission that would not have been made except for the untrue statement. Concealment of physical disability, previous psychiatric care, or admission to an institute of mental health, dishonorable discharge from the armed services, homosexual relationships, drug or alcohol dependency, and previous arrests are some of the important areas that would be covered by the term fraud. These are all areas that should be covered in an interview with the candidate with a record kept of the answers so that if the issue of deceit arises at a later time a record of the candidate's responses are available. In fact the candidate may have dealt with and resolved any of the above areas in his or her life. Matters of great importance that would seriously affect the ability of the candidate to live the religious life need to be disclosed so the institute can assess them and arrive at an appropriate decision. Many of the above are sensitive areas, and unfortunately an undeserved and long lasting stigma may be attached to them. Investigation into these areas must be prudent and considerate of the confidentiality of the candidate while at the same time protecting the life of the institute.

An example of a false statement or materials that might be substantially supportive of admission would be providing a false diploma or transcript without which the person would not have been admitted.

§1,5°

This section covers the specific concealment of incorporation into another institute of consecrated life or a society of apostolic life. This is different from CIC 541, §1, which invalidated admission of someone who had been bound by a previous bond of religious profession. The focus of this section is the act of incorporation. Canonically this would refer to the act of incorporation described in C 654. However, because many institutes have extensive pre-novitiate programs and make decisions based on considerable evidence, an institute would do well to have such information from a previous institute in order to review it. The failure of a candidate to provide information predating the juridic act of incorporation would not be invalidating under this section. The concealment of such information could be made an impediment under C 643, §2 if an institute considered it of sufficient importance.

The record of the candidate in the previous institute and the reason for departure or dismissal form an important part of the information an institute may rely on in determining the suitability of the candidate for the life of the institute.

Since this section covers concealment of incorporation, a candidate who does not wilfully conceal but forgets, misunderstands, or inadvertently fails to provide such information does not fall under the impediment of this section.

In regard to the application of C 643, §1 to novices, the institute upon discovery of an invalidating impediment may petition SCRIS for a dispensation, allow the person to depart, or follow the process for dismissal (C 653). If professed, the member may apply for a dispensation from vows or be subject to dismissal (CC 694–704).

§2

An institute is free to establish its own impediments for admission which may also invalidate admission or establish conditions for admission. This section refers to three types of regulations: first, impediments that would make admission invalid; second, impediments that would make admission illicit; and third, conditions that would be a basis for refusing admission. For example, an institute may desire a higher age than seventeen for admission. It can make the age limit for validity, liceity, or merely a basis for refusing admission.

The 1917 Code provided for six conditions which made admission illicit but not invalid. Two of these are provided for in C 644. The others are conditions that an institute may wish to provide for in its proper law if they would be important considerations for an institute. The omitted conditions are: (1) those who are liable to furnish accounts or are implicated in situations from which the institute may have reason to fear lawsuit or annoyance; (2) persons who are needed to provide assistance or support for parents, children, or relatives; (3) for clerical institutes, those who would be barred from ordination by a canonical irregularity or impediment; and (4) orientals, who may not be received into institutes of the Latin rite without the permission of the Sacred Congregation for the Oriental Churches.

Those who are liable to furnish an account would be public officials, guardians, trustees or executors, and those with a power of attorney. A practical approach should be taken to persons with such obligations. If the duties of the office and the responsibility to render an account will not interfere with the ability of the person to live the life of the institute, it should not bar them from entering. On the other hand, if the responsibility is time consuming or could be substantially diverting in other ways, an institute may wish to defer entrance until a person is free.

In regard to actual or potential lawsuits, an institute should take the same practical approach. If the suit would call for extensive consultations or court appearances or be a cause of anxiety that would distract the person from living the religious life, entrance should be delayed. If a suit would not result in the above or justifiably harm the reputation of the person, the institute may wish to admit someone involved in a lawsuit.

A person involved in a lawsuit because of holding one of the above-mentioned offices in which an account is to be rendered may be considered sufficiently detached from financial responsibility if he or she is insured for the actions undertaken while holding the office.

The support of parents, children, or relatives is an important issue. If a candidate is a parent, the institute should be assured that the children no longer need the financial or emotional support of the parent. If children are of school age, even if the financial needs can be met, there is still the question of parental guidance and emotional support. The primary duty of a parent is to support and educate their children, and a vocation may have to be deferred until that responsibility is fully met.

The support of parents usually arises when a candidate is the sole or primary support of the parents. More discretion here can be given to the assessment of the candidate regarding alternate means of support. However, if the institute is satisfied that the parent(s) can be properly supported, it should not be a bar to entrance. The same would apply to relatives on a less stringent basis and usually only when a candidate has actually been the sole support of a relative.

Clerical institutes would have an interest in whether candidates for ordination would be encumbered by an irregularity or impediment to orders. There are additional conditions attached to ordination that do not bar a person from religious life such as commission or cooperation in voluntary homicide or procuring an abortion, serious mutilation of self or another, or performing an act of orders (C 1041). While the person may receive a dispensation for an irregularity, an institute may desire that the dispensation be requested prior to investing its time and resources in the candidate.

The law no longer requires an Oriental rite Catholic to obtain the written permission of the Sacred Congregation for the Oriental Churches in order to join a Latin rite institute. To help the candidate make a good decision an institute may wish to discuss the option of joining an Oriental rite institute with the candidate so he or she is apprised of all the options. If the candidate is intending to receive orders, the present practice is to permit the candidate to be ordained to the Latin rite and grant bi-ritual facilities.[7] It is not the practice of the SCOC to grant permission for a transfer of rite for a seminarian. It is preferred to have the candidate retain his baptismal rite and function within the Latin rite.

The purpose of C 643 is to retain the most important conditions as causes for invalid admission and to permit each institute to determine both additional conditions and their legal severity in proper law. This means an institute may make such conditions invalidating, a cause of illiceity or merely a policy which will prohibit a candidate from being accepted. For the most part there seems to be wisdom in the approach of the universal law in not multiplying invalidating conditions. There is a flexibility in placing such matters at the policy level that allows them to be thoroughly investigated and permits the institute to make the decision that is most appropriate for itself and the candidate seeking admission.

C 644

Superiors are not to admit to the novitiate secular clerics if their local ordinary has not been consulted or those who, burdened by debts, cannot repay them.

This canon establishes two conditions that bar admission to the novitiate. First, a superior should not admit a secular cleric to the novitiate if the cleric's local ordinary has not been consulted. Clerics in this case would include both priests and deacons. When a priest or deacon is ordained, he becomes incardinated into a particular diocesan church. A cleric may not leave the jurisdiction of the bishop or his church without the bishop's permission. Normally, the initiative for the consultation should rest with the secular cleric who has informed the bishop that he desires to enter the novitiate of an institute. However, the consultation called for by this canon is between the local Ordinary and the appropriate admitting superior of the institute. The fact that the secular cleric has informed the bishop of his intention is not sufficient to meet the requirements of this canon. The permission of the bishop is not required by this canon. However, since a cleric may not freely depart from the jurisdiction of the local Ordinary, if the bishop does not grant permission, the cleric may appeal the decision to the Sacred Congregation for the Clergy.

A superior is also not permitted to grant admission to persons burdened by debts they cannot repay. There are a variety of conditions of debt that an institute should give consideration to prior to admittance, but only those in which it can make the judgment that the individual cannot repay the debt fall under this canon. For example, in the United States persons burdened by debts they are unable to repay may petition for voluntary bankruptcy. If an institute has an applicant who has chosen to undergo this process, the institute should be aware that even if the candidate has obtained a bankruptcy discharge there are certain matters the discharge does not cover.[8] An institute would be prudent to consult with its own attorney in reviewing the application of someone who has received a bankruptcy discharge. In addition, since there is a deeper question of equity and fairness in regard to former debts, an institute should assure itself that former creditors have been treated fairly so it does not give the appearance of culpably or through ignorance of cooperating in a process that denies someone a just claim.

A more common instance of debt is that of a college student or recent graduate who desires to enter an institute but has loans outstanding that were used to obtain an education. These may be loans on which the student is personally liable or loans on which the parent may be liable. Institutes have adopted a variety of practices to meet this situation. Some have permitted individuals to obtain employment and use the wages to pay on loans. Other institutes have met interest and/or principal payments themselves during the period of novitiate and temporary profession, agreeing to pay the loan should the person profess perpetual vows in the institute. However, should the person leave, the unpaid debt reverts to the individual. In some cases the individual is obligated to repay the institute for any debt payment made during the course of formation. When institutes and individuals make such agreements, it is prudent to have the agreement in writing so that the mutual obligations of the parties are clearly set out.

C 645

§1. Before they are admitted to the novitiate, candidates must show proof of baptism, confirmation and free status.

§2. If it is a question of admitting clerics or those who have been admitted to another institute of consecrated life, a society of apostolic life or a seminary, there is further required the testimony of the local ordinary or major superior of the institute or society or of the rector of the seminary respectively.

§3. Proper law can demand other testimonies about the requisite suitability of candidates and their freedom from impediments.

§4. If it appears necessary superiors can ask for other information, even with the obligation of secrecy.

There is certain basic information which can be attested to by documentation and by requesting parties who have had an official relationship with a candidate to provide testimony regarding the candidate. The purpose of this information is to provide evidence of freedom and suitability to enter a religious institute.

§1

Each candidate in order to be admitted must show evidence of baptism, confirmation, and free status. Certificates of baptism and confirmation may be issued by the church where the sacrament was celebrated and be signed in the name of the pastor or administrator and sealed with the parish seal. These certificates should be issued at a reasonable date before admittance (three to six months) so that the institute is receiving up-to-date information. If certificates are not available because records have been destroyed or lost, the testimony of a reliable witness such as a parent, brother, sister, guardian, celebrating bishop, priest, or deacon would be satisfactory. If the candidate had received the sacraments at an age when he or she could offer reliable testimony, the testimony of the candidate could be received but should usually be corroborated by another source unless it is not possible.

The baptismal certificate should contain the record of other sacraments, orders, or membership in an institute of consecrated life or society of apostolic life and would be evidence of a candidate's free status. If there is information regarding previous orders, marriage, or membership in an institute of consecrated life or society of apostolic life whether from the baptismal certificate, the candidate, or outside sources, further documentation attesting to free status should be obtained. For those previously married a divorce decree (if granted) should be obtained. [9] For those previously in orders the rescript of laicization is necessary, and for those who made profession in an institute of consecrated life or society of apostolic life a rescript of dispensation should be obtained. Should an institute decide to accept someone previously dismissed from an institute of consecrated life or society of apostolic life, a copy of the decree of dismissal would be a helpful record.

§2

This section covers three former affiliations, candidates who formerly were clerics, those who had been in another institute of consecrated life or society of apostolic life, and former seminarians.

For those who were formerly clerics, meaning those who had received the order of deacon or priest, the institute must obtain the testimony of the local Ordinary or several local Ordinaries if the cleric has been incardinated in more than one diocese. It may also be helpful, although not canonically required, to obtain letters from local Ordinaries where a cleric was assigned for lengthy periods of training looking forward to ordination or was on loan for a substantial period of time. This provision is a change from the former law (CIC 433, §2), which required all male candidates to present testimonial letters from the local Ordinary of the place of birth and the Ordinary of any place they lived for a morally continuous year after completing their fourteenth year. The previous requirement became too burdensome to fulfill in a society as mobile as that in the United States and other areas. Along with the testimonial, the institute should also request a copy of the certificate of ordination of the cleric.

The language of the phrase applying to institutes of consecrated life refers to those "who had been admitted to an institute or society"; thus it is different from C 643, §1, 5°, which speaks of concealing incorporation. Being admitted to an institute or society would not apply to any formal pre-novitiate program such as a postulancy. Although it would be helpful to know if a candidate was a postulant, affiliate, or participated in an active contact program in which spiritual direction and periodic sessions took place, such programs do not fall under the coverage of this canon. The failure to obtain this information is not invalidating as is concealing admission to another institute or society but it does mean candidates should not be admitted unless the required testimonial is submitted. The testimony is to come from the major superior although in fact it will probably be a composite report from the directors of formation and the major superior which will be much more valuable as testimony of suitability.

In regard to those who have been in a seminary, the canon requires the testimonial of the rector of the seminary. In cases in which the candidate was a student for a particular diocese, the institute may also wish to obtain the testimonial of the bishop. A seminary in this canon refers to theological studies and college studies if part of a seminary program. It would not refer to preparatory or high school programs. For former members of institutes of consecrated life or societies of apostolic life who attended a seminary separate from the institute or society, the admitting institute may ask for a testimonial from the rector of the seminary.

§3

Besides the testimonies required by the common law, the institute may in its proper law require additional testimonies regarding the suitability of candidates and their freedom from impediments. Other testimonies which might be helpful would be those from the pastor or associate of the candidate's parish, recommendations from former employers or business associates, school administrators or teachers, as well as transcripts, degrees, certificates of study, and military discharge or termination papers.

In certain cases a testimonial from a spiritual director may be helpful. Since this is a confidential relationship the institute should ask the candidate to request the testimonial or secure the written permission of the candidate to make the request. In requesting information from a spiritual director, the candidate and the institute should agree on the information that the director will be permitted to relate. This will protect the candidate, the spiritual director, and the institute.

Proper law can either specify additional testimonials or institute policy can develop a detailed checklist of helpful testimonials that a vocation director or admitting superior can review with each candidate and choose to request those which are most relevant to the candidate's situation. For some institutes a combination of the above may be the most helpful.

Testimonials from a variety of sources give the institute an insight into the character, personality, attitudes, values, and work habits of the candidate from several points of view which along with other materials can paint an accurate profile of the candidate.

§4

In cases of necessity superiors can ask for additional information, even secretly. It is a serious responsibility to admit a candidate to an institute. A superior should be able to resolve any serious doubts or concerns regarding any important areas of a candidate's life.

Additional information simply refers to any information that a superior believes that it is wise and prudent to procure in order to make a good decision, that is not otherwise required by the canon law, proper law, or even other institute regulations, statutes, or policies.

The additional information the superior is seeking may be sought in a secret manner, which is different from attempting to obtain secret information which this canon does not permit. To seek information secretly means that the candidate is unaware that the superior is seeking the information. In such cases the superior should be motivated by a sufficient cause. Sufficient cause would be reliable testimony regarding a matter that would bar admission or even testimony not considered reliable about a serious matter that it would be imprudent to overlook. Normally, these matters should first be brought to the attention of the candidate in order to try to resolve them, unless there is cause to believe that reliable testimony would be obstructed by being brought to the candidate first.

There are matters of public record or quasi public record that may be obtained without knowledge of the individual. Records of birth, marriage, divorce, death, arrests, convictions, credit rating, membership in an organization may be a matter of public access or obtainable on request. Even though these may be easily available, an institute should not request them without serious cause. For example, a candidate may be suspected of trying to hide a criminal record by stating that he or she was never convicted, but someone who knew the candidate previously had casually commented on the previous conviction of the candidate. An institute may be justified in secretly seeking the record instead of embarrassing the candidate or itself in case the person who made the casual comment is mistaken.

NOVITIATE AND THE TRAINING OF MEMBERS

CC 646–653 establish the purpose of the novitiate, the manner of its erection, transfer and suppression, requirements of time and place for validity, the qualifications of the novice director, the responsibilities of the novice director and the members of the institute for formation, and provision for departure, dismissal, or extension of the time of novitiate.

Several of the provisions in this section are adopted from RC totally or with modifications. These will be noted in the commentary on the individual canons.

C 646

The novitiate, by which life in the institute begins, is ordered to this, that the novices better recognize their divine vocation and one which is, moreover, proper to the institute, that they experience the institute's manner of living, that they be formed in mind and heart by its spirit, and that their intention and suitability be tested.

The novitiate is the formal and legal beginning of religious life.[10] The purpose of the novitiate is to provide for its beginning, and as the canon notes life in the novitiate is to be ordered to this purpose. The canon states both the objectives of the novitiate and the means to accomplish the objectives.

In the novitiate the novice is to consider the two basic elements of his or her vocation, namely, that it is a divine call from God issued personally to that individual and that the call is particular to the institute. The call that is particular to an institute is the specification of the divine call. The responsibility of the director and the novitiate program is twofold. First, to discern and test the actuality of the divine call which may or may not be to that institute, but if a divine call exists, it is still to be nurtured and discerned with the novice. Second, to discern and test whether there is a call to the institute. This is to take place by means of experiencing the life of the institute and being formed in the life and spirit of the institute.

Thus, the development of an appropriate novitiate program is to begin with these premises and specify them to express the life and needs of the institute. The specific elements of the program should be outlined in written form. The purpose and general requirements of the novitiate can be placed in the constitutions and directory, but the program and its policies should be placed in a form of proper law that is easy to change, since they may require constant monitoring and adjustment.

C 647

§1. The erection, transfer and suppression of a novitiate house are to take place through a written decree of the supreme moderator of the institute with the consent of his or her council.

§2. In order to be valid a novitiate must be made in a house properly designated for this purpose. In particular cases and as an exception, by concession of the supreme moderator with the consent of the council, a candidate can make the novitiate in another house of the institute under the guidance of an approved religious who assumes the role of director of novices.

§3. A major superior can permit a group of novices to live for a stated period of time in another house of the institute, designated by the same superior.

§1

This section provides for the erection, transfer, and suppression of the novitiate, which is to be accomplished by the written decree of the supreme moderator with the consent of the council. This is a change from CIC 554, §1, which required pontifical institutes to seek the permission of the Holy See to erect a novitiate. The source of C 647,§1 is RC 16, i, which gave this power to the superior general with the approval of the council. RC 16, i further gave the superior general the authority to determine the character and pattern of life in the novitiate as well as deciding the particular house to be used as the novitiate. The present law only gives the supreme moderator the authority to decide the place of the novitiate. Thus, it rests with the proper law to indicate who has the remaining authority. In institutes divided into provinces, it may be more practical for a provincial and/or council to determine the character and pattern of life of the novitiate. Provinces may take the initiative in petitioning the supreme moderator to erect a novitiate, or the initiative may come from the supreme moderator after assessing the need of the province.

In omitting the latter provision of RC 16, i, the present law allows each institute to apportion responsibility on the details of the novitiate to the appropriate level of authority.

Transfer and suppression of the novitiate also belong to the supreme moderator and council. Transfer may occur simply because a more apt place has been found for the location of the novitiate. Suppressing a novitiate would occur because of events that would lead the supreme moderator and council to believe that the novitiate was not being operated in accord with the law of the Church or the institute and the best solution would be to close it because the situation is not easily correctable. The lack of novices is not cause for the suppression of the novitiate.

This canon does not cover the situation described by RC 17, which permitted the superior general with the approval of the council and after consultation with the appropriate provincial to establish several novitiates in the same province should the need arise. According to CIC 554, §2 a special apostolic indult was needed in order to have several novitiate houses in the same province.

The rationale behind CIC 554, §2 was apparently that two or more novitiates in the same province could cause division or compromise unity. However, there are situations in which two or more novitiates would be appropriate. In situations where an institute or province has a mission that is geographically distant and/or culturally distant, another novitiate is proper. In cases where an institute or province has a large number of candidates in each of several countries where there may be diverse culture, language and customs, other novitiates may be needed in order to fulfill the responsibility of an appropriate formation.

This canon places no restrictions on the practice of having one novitiate for several provinces, especially in cases in which there are not enough novices or sufficient competent formation personnel to justify separate novitiates. This is accomplished by the decree of the supreme moderator. If different pontifical institutes desire a common novitiate, they should petition SCRIS, since at least some of them would not be using a house of the institute for the novitiate.[11]

RC 18 emphasized the importance of community life in the formation of novices. Wherever the group of novices was too small to form a community in itself, the superior general was charged with setting up the novitiate in another community capable of supporting the novice community. Since novice classes are often small or consisting of only one novice, it may be necessary to have the novices live in a house of professed members. When erecting such a house as a novitiate, the superior should realize that not all houses are suitable for a novitiate. A particular apostolate or the life-style of some of the members may render a house unsuitable where the members of a local community are too busy or lead schedules that do not permit communal relationships with novices or there is a lack of fidelity in leading the life of the institute that would provide a negative witness to those beginning religious life.

§2

A novitiate must be made in the house expressly designated as a novitiate in order to be valid. The term religious house is not always coterminous with novitiate. A particular house may be a novitiate, but a novitiate may also be part of a house. It is the entity that is the novitiate that is described in the canon.

By concession a supreme moderator with the consent of the council can allow the novitiate to be made by a candidate in another house of the institute under the guidance of an approved religious who assumes the role of novice director. This provision presumes there is already a designated novitiate and this special action is providing for a novitiate to be made outside of the designated house. This may occur because of the special background of the novice such as age, experience, orders, or the promotion of a special charism of the institute that would make a particular house more suitable for an individual's novitiate.

This section is taken from *RC* 19, which altered CIC 555, §1, 3° requiring that for a novitiate to be valid it had to be made in the novitiate house. This change was made in *RC* 19 because SCRIS had received requests to allow the novitiate to be made in another house of the institute.

A supreme moderator and council considering such a request will need to consider whether the purpose of the novitiate can be accomplished in another house. Important considerations would include the presence of a supportive community life, the faithful example of the religious, the availability of on-going training in spirituality and the history and traditions of the institute, and an atmosphere of prayer and recollection that may not be present in other houses of the institute. Depending on travel considerations, the formal training or classes in the spiritual life and the history and tradition of the institute may be conducted at a designated novitiate or by a religious who is capable and available for such instruction. It is the "spiritual atmosphere" that may be a more difficult consideration in permitting a novitiate to be made in another house of the institute. This will be both the responsibility of the religious assigned to the alternate house and the director of the novice who must be qualified and have time available to direct the novice.

§3

In contrast to the first two sections of C 647, the major superior rather than the supreme moderator can permit a group of novices to live in another house of the institute for a stated period of time. The house is to be designated by the major superior, but the major superior need not have the consent or consultation of the council although proper law may so provide.

This section does not state either the reasons (for a particular experience of prayer or spirituality) or the weight of the reasons (for a serious cause). Therefore, the major superior may permit the novices to live in a designated house for any appropriate reason. Again, the formation policy of the institute may list some of the reasons for living in another house of the institute.

Examples of appropriate causes for living in another house of the institute would be to live in a house of prayer or retreat, to attend special conferences in spirituality or religious life, to live with a community that engages in a special apostolate, or even to provide a period of rest or vacation. The only qualification is that a stated period of time be lived in another house of the institute. For most institutes the reasons for granting permission to live in another house should follow the spirit of C 646 in providing a better experience for the life or varieties of life in the institute or to provide an important formational experience for the novices.

When this section is read in conjunction with C 648, §2, it can be seen that it is not intended to provide for a series of diverse apostolic experiences. Nor is it intended to cover an experience for an individual novice, since the canon speaks of "a group of novices," unless, of course, there is only one novice. It does not seem that it is necessary for the entire novitiate group to live in another house, since the canon applies to a "group of novices." Thus, for example, in a group of twelve, three groups may be sent to four different houses. There is a presumption of the move being made by a community or part of the community of novices rather than individual novices. This is realistic, since a particular house may not have room for an entire community of novices.

In light of C 648, §1, providing for twelve months in the novitiate community itself, the permissions granted in virtue of this section should not be so numerous as to interrupt the stability cf the twelve-month novitiate.

This section is a change from *RC* 16, ii, which auhorized the superior general to allow the novice community to reside for certain periods of time in another house of the institute if this would be appropriate for the formation of the novices. The changes from *RC* 16, ii, to C 648, §3 are twofold. First, the authority is now in the hands of the major superior rather than the superior general. Second, *RC* authorized the move to allow for the more appropriate formation of the novices, while the present section provides no rationale but leaves supplying of a rationale to the institute or major superior.

C 648

§1. In order that the novitiate be valid it must include twelve months spent in the community of the novitiate itself, with due regard for the prescription of can. 647, §3.

§2. To complete the formation of the novices, in addition to the time mentioned in §1, the constitutions can determine one or several periods of apostolic exercises to be spent outside the novitiate community.

§3. The novitiate is not to extend beyond two years.

This canon describes the minimum and maximum length of the novitiate and provides for special training or apostolic experiences outside the novitiate community. It is important, since it modifies the prescriptions of *RC* regarding the same matters.

§1

A novitiate must include twelve months in the novitiate community in order for it to be valid. The time period is substantially the same as CIC 555, §1, 2°. However, the period of twelve months is different than the previous requirement of over a full year, which was understood as at least a year and a day. The condition of CIC 555, §1, 2° that the year be continuous is omitted. If this section is read with C 647, §3 and C 649, §1, it seems clear that a valid novitiate requires twelve months in residence in the designated novitiate, except for the period of time that may be spent in another house of the institute with the permission of the major superior.

The requirement of twelve months has been maintained to emphasize the importance of the novitiate. The omission of the requirement that the twelve months be continuous seems to mean that the periods of apostolic activity described in C 648, §2 may occur as interruptive of the twelve months though they are to be added on to the twelve months. Even the permitted periods of time to be spent outside the house should not be so extended or so frequent as to disrupt the novitiate. Realistically, twelve months is a relatively short time for an institute to lay a foundation for the spiritual life and to discern the vocation of the novice. Experience shows that it often takes several months for a novice or community of novices to adjust to the new life and that it is only after this initial period that the more serious matters may be fruitfully undertaken. The whole atmosphere of prayer, study, reflection, and some minimal ministry takes time to bear fruit for the novice. If it is frequently interrupted, even for the purpose of ensuring the novice has a more complete experience of the life of the institute in all its varieties, which is helpful in its own right, the novitiate can become a series of short experiences in and out of the novitiate community that may be an obstacle to the deep prayer and reflection necessary during this period. An institute should not be overly ambitious in trying to ensure an experience of everything during the twelve months, but it should view its entire formation program as a unit which emphasizes certain areas during each period of formation so that the novitiate is an important beginning but not a time during which everything must be accomplished.

§2

If an institute believes that more than twelve months is needed to properly train the novices, it can provide in its constitutions for one or more periods of apostolic exercise to be done outside the novitiate community.

This section is an outgrowth of RC 23, i, but covers in less detail the principles, means, and limitations that were offered in RC 23, 24, and 25 in regard to periods of time outside the novitiate, some of which are wise considerations should an institute develop a program in accord with this section.

The first difference between C 648, §2 and RC 23, i concerns authorization of the periods of time beyond twelve months. RC 23, i authorized a two-thirds majority of the general chapter to permit such activities, while C 648, §2 requires that it be in the constitutions. From the wording of this section, it does not appear that this power can be delegated to a province or a special committee within the institute. However, in order to have flexibility the constitutions may provide for periods of apostolic exercises outside the community and leave the details to the province and other forms of proper law. This would provide the necessary flexibility in using the opportunities granted by this section.

It would also be consistent with the sound advice of RC 23, which left to the novice director with the approval of the major superior whether such periods would be advantageous for formation.

The second difference between RC 23, i and C 648, §2 is that C 648, §2 speaks of periods of apostolic exercises, while RC 23, i spoke more generally of appropriate formative activities. In itself C 648, §2 is more limited than RC 23, i; however, since C 648, §3 provides that a novitiate may extend up to two years without describing what activity may take place during this extra period of time, it seems that other appropriate formative activities that are not specifically apostolic or that can be provided for under C 647, §3 may be provided for beyond the twelve-month period.

RC 23, ii further provided that such periods of time may involve one, several, or a whole community of novices, but as far as possible an individual novice should not spend this period in isolation. This is consistent with the spirit of C 647, §3, which emphasizes the notion of community by speaking of a group of novices. Again, this is an important consideration for a community in planning apostolic exercises. Community support is important; however, if there is an important experience that can only be gained individually or the institute is involved in numerous individual assignments, then it may be appropriate for a novice to have an individual period of apostolic exercise.

RC 23, iii expressly provided that during these periods the novice was still subject to the novice director. This requirement would be retained according to the general authority granted to the novice director by CC 650, 651, and 652.

RC 25, i considered the purpose of the periods of time. First, it should be in accord with the aim of the institute and the character of its work. Second, the purpose must be formative and in some cases enable the institute to make a better judgment regarding the suitability of the novice. It mentions several purposes such as progressive preparation for apostolic work, bringing the attention of the novice to poverty and hard work, offering them a deeper knowledge of people, strengthening their wills, making them aware of the work of the institute, and giving them the opportunity to strive to live faithfully in the midst of an active life. These are all important factors an institute should consider in planning for periods of apostolic exercises.

The combination of RC 24, i and ii, allowed these activities to take place within the context of a twelve-month novitiate; however, the periods of time could not be counted toward the twelve-month period of novitiate. In addition, they had to be structured so that the novice began with three months in the novitiate, had six continuous months in the novitiate, and then returned at least a month prior to profession. The structuring of the time periods is now left to the institute.

RC 24, iii provided for an institute to prescribe a period of formative activity prior to the beginning of the novitiate. This could include living in a house of the institute or an extended retreat or period of recollection to prepare for entrance into the novitiate. An institute may continue such a practice as a matter of proper law.

§3

The total length of a novitiate should not extend beyond two years. This is a shorter version of CIC 555, §2, which was more explicit in allowing institutes to prescribe in their constitutions for a novitiate of longer than one year; however, the extra time was not required for validity unless the constitutions stated otherwise. The previous law did not have a two-year limit, which was introduced by *RC* 24, i.

According to this section an institute may provide for a novitiate of any period of time between twelve and twenty-four months; however, twelve of the months must be spent in the novitiate community for validity according to the universal law. Since the universal law does not prevent it, the proper law of the institute may provide that the additional period of time required by the proper law be for validity as well. As indicated above, although an institute is authorized specifically to include additional periods of apostolic exercises in accord with C 648, §2, it may also provide for any other additional period of formation activity so long as it does not extend the novitiate beyond two years.

C 649

§1. With due regard for the prescriptions of cann. 647, §3, and 648, §2, absence from the novitiate house which lasts more than three months, either continuous or interrupted, renders the novitiate invalid. An absence of more than fifteen days must be made up.

§2. With the permission of the competent major superior first profession can be anticipated, but not by more than fifteen days.

The two sections of this canon define the two instances that a novice need not be present at the novitiate without the time being made up. These are limited absences and anticipation of profession. Other absences must be made up, but if beyond the limit, they cannot be made up and render the novitiate invalid.

§1

Any absence from the novitiate except those covered by C 647, §3 and C 648, §2, which lasts more than three months, whether continuous or interrupted renders the novitiate invalid. Any absence longer than fifteen days must be made up.

This is a change from CIC 556, §1, which provided that an absence of more than thirty days interrupted the novitiate; thus, the entire novitiate had to be repeated. *RC* 22, i modified CIC 556, § 1 and is the source of the present law. In accord with *RC* 22, i, the period of absence is extended to three months. Until this time the law governing absences was interpreted as being a combination of *RC* 22, i and CIC 556, §1 because *RC* 22, i did not repeal the section of CIC 556, §1 which described the instances in which the novitiate was interrupted by dismissal by the superior or departure without the superior's permission and not intending to return. Thus *RC* 22, i was interpreted as being limited to situations in which the absence of the novice was with the permission of the superior.

Since this section does not specify the causes of absence it seems that any absence with or without permission is included in the wording of this section. Thus, even if the absence is due to dismissal or departure without permission if the time limits are not exceeded the novice may be received back into the novitiate. An institute may prefer to regulate such situations in proper law. Given the seriousness of dismissal and departure without permission, such reasons would be cause for serious consideration before giving a novice permission to return.

Since the absences may be continuous or interrupted, there will be a need to calculate the time of absence which may be slightly different depending on whether the absence is continuous or interrupted. If the absence is continuous,[12] it would be counted by the days of the calendar. For example, if an absence began on May 15 and was continuous, it should end August 15 for the novitiate to be valid. If a novice has several absences, the time of absence should be counted in accord with C 202, §1, which provides that a month is a period of thirty days. Thus, if the total number of days that a novice is absent exceeds ninety days, the novitiate is invalid. If the absence is continuous, the number of days may exceed ninety if there are one or more thirty-one day months, but the novitiate will still be valid as long as the absence terminates on the proper date of the month.

RC 22, ii provided further that if the absence were less than three months, the major superior, after consulting with the novice director and taking into account the reason for the absence, could decide in each individual case whether or not to have the novice make up the time of absence by extending the time of novitiate. This was a change from CIC 556, §2, which required absences of more than fifteen days but less than thirty-one days to be made up to the exact day, while for an absence of less than fifteen days the superior had discretion in deciding whether the absence should be made up, but it was not necessary for validity.

The final sentence of C 649, §1 is a return to the former law in declaring that an absence of over fifteen days must be made up. The fifteen days refers to both continuous or interrupted absences. For example, if a novice is in the hospital for twenty days or for two periods of ten days each, five days must be added to the length of the novitiate for it to be valid.

There is no restriction on the causes for absences. It could be extended absences for the illness of 'the novice, a funeral or illness in the family, vacation, or special counseling or spiritual direction that is not a regular part of the novitiate program. Any cause that is not provided for in the previous canons would be limited by the restriction of fifteen days and must be made up. The sense of the canon seems to be that it must be made up to the exact number of days. Therefore, if a novice is absent thirty days over the limit of fifteen days, the time to be made up would be thirty days.

§2

First profession may be anticipated by up to fifteen days with the permission of the competent major superior. This is a change from CIC 555, §1, 2°, which made no exception to the rule that for a novitiate to be valid it had 'to extend continuously over one full year. This section is based on *RC* 26. There is no restriction on the reason for allowing profession to be anticipated. Thus, a major superior may grant permission for any reasonable motive or even mere convenience. For example, the profession can be anticipated so it falls on the day of a particular liturgical feast of the Church or a feast that is important to the institute, the novice class, or the novice. The permission will also be useful if the novices did not enter on exactly the same day so that a common day of profession can be chosen for a novice class. Permission can also be granted for the convenience of allowing families, guests, or the novices a better time for travel or to permit the novice to meet a particular date for assignment or further training.

CIC 574, §2 required that vows be professed in the novitiate house. *RC* 20 permitted the major superior for good cause to allow first profession to be made outside the novitiate house. The present law has no such restriction; therefore, an institute is free to have the profession made at any suitable place. For example, the institute may wish to hold profession at the motherhouse, a place central to the institute, or at a place which could hold a large number of people. The place of profession could also be chosen because it was special to the novice or close to the family of the novice, especially if it were difficult for a family member to travel because of illness or handicap. The value of having profession at the novitiate, the motherhouse, or elsewhere should all be weighed so as to arrive at an appropriate decision.

C 650

§1. **The scope of the novitiate demands that the novices be formed under the guidance of a director according to the program of training to be defined by the proper law.**

§2. **The governance of novices is reserved to one director under the authority of the major superiors.**

Beginning with C 650 there are a series of provisions in CC 650–652 dealing with the novitiate program, the qualities of the novice director and assistants, the responsibility of the novices, and the responsibility of members of the institute to the novices.

§*1*

The first section covers two points. First, the novices are to be formed under the supervision of a director. Second, the novices are to be formed according to a program of training defined by the proper law.

The idea that novices are to be placed in the care of a director is completed by C 650, §2, which reserves the responsibility to one director. This section is rooted in CIC 561, §1 and *RC* 30. The emphasis here is on the scope of the program, which is implemented by the director as opposed to the notion of governance covered by C 650, §2. The sense of this section is to provide a unity in the novitiate program that would not be obtainable if the authority to implement the program were divided. Besides preserving unity in placing the program under the supervision of the novice director, unity is also fostered by giving the novice director the responsibility of forming the novices according to the program of the institute.

This section places major importance on the novitiate program as defined by the proper law. It does not call for the program to be outlined in the constitutions, and in order to retain flexibility it should probably be placed in a lesser form of proper law so it can be revised according to the needs of the institute.

§2

The governance of novices is reserved to one director under the authority of major superiors. In addition to the novice director's responsibility for the program of training mentioned in C 650, §1, this section complements that authority by placing the governance of the novices under one director. Thus, personal authority in regard to the novices rests with the director. The purpose of this section is to try to provide an atmosphere of harmony and unity in goals and means, which is an important ingredient at the beginning of religious life. This section means that members of a formation team may not be allocated equal amounts of authority or that one person on a team may have complete authority over a particular area of the program. Even though supervision of an aspect of the training of the novices may be delegated to someone else, ultimate authority resides with the novice director.

This would especially apply in situations in which novices are part of a larger community where the local superior has overall responsibility for the house. CIC 561, §1 directly addressed the matter by providing that the government of the novitiate belonged to the novice director, and no one could intervene in these matters except superiors who had authority over the novice master. The novice director and the novices were subject to the local superior in matters concerning the house at large. Since these matters are omitted from the present law, it would be up to the institute to state in proper law or policy the balance or areas of authority in a clear manner so that the novice director can properly meet the responsibilities of the office.

The last clause of this section places the governance of novices by the director under the authority of major superiors. It is the responsibility of the major superior to ascertain whether the novice director is following the institute's program of formation. It can be a delicate task to oversee a program while not interfering with it. This would probably mean occasional visits to the novitiate and discussions with the novice director in order to be informed about the operation of the program. This is necessary because if the program is not being followed or the novice director is unable or unwilling to meet the important responsibilities of the office, then it is up to the major superior to correct the director or in some cases to replace the director.

The wording of this section speaks of major superiors in the plural. In cases where there is a common novitiate of several provinces, authority would rest with the several major superiors. The principles and methods of exercising authority where more than one major superior is involved should be clearly outlined in order to avoid fragmentation and duplication of lines of authority for the novice director.

A novice is under the authority of both the novice director and the superiors of the institute. Thus, the novice is obliged to obey the director and superiors. This obligation is not based on the vows, since profession has not yet been made but on the acceptance of the novice of undertaking the responsibilities of religious life upon being received into the institute. In the past this has been likened to a quasi contract, which is apt in the sense that the novice and the institute have agreed to commit themselves to a series of mutual responsibilities, but the term may be a bit mundane to apply to a response to a divine call.

C 651

§1. The director of novices is to be a member of the institute who has professed perpetual vows and is legitimately designated.

§2. If there is a need, assistants can be given to the director to whom they are subject regarding the governance of the novitiate and the program of training.

§3. Members who have been carefully prepared and who, not impeded by other duties, can carry out this duty fruitfully and in a stable manner are to be in charge of the training of novices.

The subject of this canon is the qualifications of the novice director, assistants to the novice director, the preparation of the directors and assistants, and the limitation in regard to other duties.

§1

The minimum requirements for a novice director are that the director should be a member of the institute, professed perpetual vows, and be legitimately designated.

The requirement of membership in the institute was presumed rather than stated in the former law. The requirement of membership means that institutes that send novices to another institute for their novitiate must get a dispensation from SCRIS for pontifical institutes and the bishop for diocesan institutes in order to do so.

The requirement of perpetual vows is a change from the former qualifications of being at least thirty-five years of age, professed ten years from the date of first profession, distinguished for prudence, piety, charity, fidelity to regular observance, and if the institute was clerical, the director had to be a priest. The only requirement now is that the member has professed perpetual vows. All other qualifications that an institute desires belong in the proper law.

§2

In case of need, assistants can be appointed to aid the novice director. Assistants are subject to the director in regard to both the governance of the novitiate and the program of training. In the former law there were also qualifications of age and time of profession that just as for the novice director are now matters for proper law.

This provision incorporates the opportunity to utilize a team concept of formation that so many institutes have found beneficial, with the understanding that the assistant or team is subject to the novice director. The fact that assistants are subject to the director should not prevent a true spirit of cooperation and designation of special areas of responsibility for assistants.

The use of assistants is not only helpful when dealing with a large number of novices, but appointing assistants will broaden the scope of talent, competence, and service available to novices. It is difficult for one person to bear the total responsibility of formation, even if the director is exceptionally talented. Team members with education and experience in spirituality, the history and charism of the institute, the Scriptures, liturgy, spiritual direction, counseling, or other helpful areas would be useful members of a formation team.

There is also an advantage of having assistants in providing a more complete living witness to the life of the institute. A variety of positive role models will impart a lesson that can have a powerful impact on novices.

Since the novice director is required to render reports and evaluations, the presence of assistants will add a dimension and perspective to the reports and evaluations that would not be possible with only one person. The ability to discuss one's impression of a novice and to hear another's impression is beneficial in compiling a composite evaluation that provides a more complete picture. A novice director and assistants may confirm one another's evaluation or disagree with it. Even if an assistant adds a section to a report that is not in agreement with that of the director, it still provides those who have the responsibility of admitting a novice to vows a perspective that should aid them in making their decision.

Another benefit in appointing assistants to the director is that of providing mutual support for those who have been given the duty of forming novices. If a director is alone in fulfilling the responsibilities and has no one within easy reach to communicate with either in regard to the task of formation or even at a brotherly or sisterly level, the responsibilities of formation can be a heavier burden than if there is someone with whom to share them.

§3

In order for the director to carry out the training of novices in a fruitful and stable manner, this section declares that only those who have been adequately prepared and who are not burdened with other duties should be appointed to the office.

The careful preparation of members for roles in the formation of novices can be carried out in a variety of ways. There are formal programs of study and training in the ministry of formation or programs that would be beneficial to an important aspect of the formation of novices such as studies in spirituality, spiritual direction, special studies in the history and charism of the institute or its tradition, and counseling. Practical experience such as teaching, spiritual direction, counseling, working with young people, along with experience in the apostolates of the institute, can be important preparation. Although the canon seems to speak of preparation in terms of prior preparation, it is also important to plan a program of continuous updating and meeting with other people in the ministry of formation to stay abreast of developments in the field of formation.

The novice director and assistants are not to be burdened with other duties so that the primary responsibility of training the novices is not deterred in any manner. This directive was also found in CIC 559, §3. The intent of this qualification is to emphasize the importance of the responsibility of the novice director and assistants and to caution them not to voluntarily undertake tasks or assignments that undermine their primary obligation. The same caution applies to superiors, major and local, not to assign the director and assistants tasks that interfere with formation. One commentator said of the norm of CIC 559, §3 that it would be contrary to it to place the same religious over three classes of candidates such as aspirants, postulants, and novices.[13] With the small numbers in formation groups, such an assignment may not be burdensome because of the number of people to be formed, but it may be burdensome because it fragments the duties of the director or because it places candidates in formation under the care of one person for too long a period of time.

It may seem to some that a novice director has a large amount of free time and should be available for ministry. This may be misleading in regard to availability for other work, since the duties of the director require much time for prayer and thought in order to offer insightful advice and direction to novices as well as perceptive reports and evaluations to superiors.

C 652

§1. It is for the director and assistants to discern and test the vocation of the novices and to form them gradually to lead correctly the life of perfection proper to the institute.

§2. The novices are to be led to cultivate human and Christian virtues; they are to be introduced to a fuller way of perfection by prayer and self-denial; they are to be instructed to contemplate the mystery of salvation and to read and meditate on the Sacred Scriptures; they are to be prepared to cultivate the worship of God in the sacred liturgy; they are to be trained in a way of life consecrated by the evangelical counsels to God and humankind in Christ; they are to be educated about the character and spirit, purpose and discipline, history and life of their institute; and they are to be imbued with a love for the Church and its sacred pastors.

§3. Conscious of their own responsibility, the novices are to collaborate actively with their director so that they may faithfully respond to the grace of a divine vocation.

§4. Members of the institute are to take care that on their part they cooperate in the work of training novices by the example of their life and by prayer.

§5. The time of novitiate mentioned in can. 648, §1, is to be employed properly in the work of formation and therefore the novices are not to be occupied with studies and duties which do not directly serve this formation.

The five sections of this canon describe the mutual responsibilities of the director and assistants and the novices during the course of the novitiate, the importance of the good example of members, and the appropriate use of the time in the novitiate.

§1

It is the responsibility of the director and the assistants to discern and test the vocation of the novices and to gradually form them to faithfully lead the life proper to the institute.

The first charge to the director and assistants is to discern and test the vocation of the novices. This is a further specification of the direction indicated in C 646. The source of such discernment and testing is in the institute's understanding of its own vocation and presenting it clearly to the novices. A vocation in the institute should be described as clearly as possible so that a novice is able to identify him or herself within the institute. Admittedly, the mystery surrounding a vocation, the variety of expressions of a vocation within a particular institute, and the on-going growth, development, and self-understanding of the institute prevent every little detail from being presented. On the other hand failure to describe a call to the institute will leave the director and the novices without clear goals or guidelines and can be a source of confusion and contention if each director and/or novice feels he or she must supply their own notion of vocation.

The idea of testing a vocation refers to the cumulative experiences of the novice in being introduced to the life of the institute. Past notions of testing a vocation that had little to do with faithfully living the life of the institute are now understood as being more of an obstacle to coming to a decision regarding a vocation than a help.

The final clause of this section connects two ideas. The first is that the novices are to be formed gradually. This is a counsel based on a realistic pattern of human growth. To expect a novice from the very beginning, or too quickly, to meet demands for which the novice is unprepared will impede growth rather than aid it. Moreover, each person grows at his or her own pace so that notion of gradual growth must be refined to accommodate the growth of a particular novice. This gradual formation is to take place in the context of forming the novice to lead the life of the institute. It is especially important that in addition to forming the novice as an individual that the whole program of formation be adapted to the life the novice will lead after having professed vows in the institute.

Each institute will need to develop a program to guide the director and assistants in fulfilling the directives of this section. A program of interviews, evaluations, conferences, retreats, work, apostolic, and spiritual experiences are all methods at the disposal of the director and the assistants.

§2

This lengthy section offers a seven-point program for the instruction of novices to ensure each institute touches the foundation of religious life in its training.

The roots of this section are in CIC 565, §1 and *RC* 15, iii, iv, and 31. This section is more positive in tone than the former law and much closer to the sense of *RC* 15. The areas of instruction are divided into those which form the foundation of the Christian life (human and Christian virtues, prayer and self-denial, reading and meditating on the Scriptures, devotion to the liturgy, and a love of the Church and its pastors) and those pertaining especially to the religious life (the life of the evangelical counsels and the character, spirit, goal, discipline, history, and life of the institute).

Having offered the direction of the training to be undertaken in the novitiate, it is up to the institute to accomplish the training by the means best suited to it.

Commentators on the previous law recommended that a complete copy of the rule and constitutions, not merely a summary, should be given to novices at the beginning of the novitiate. The reception of novices in some institutes includes the handing over of the rule and constitutions of the institute to the novice with the counsel to study it. This section speaks generally of the life of the counsels and the discipline of the institute; however, the principles of the life of the institute are collected in the rule and constitutions. Without adopting a legalistic spirit by handing over the rule and constitutions with the injunction to obey what is written, it should be understood that the constitutions represent the common understanding of the life of the institute and oblige every member including superiors and formation personnel. Therefore, they do need to be introduced and studied at an appropriate time during the course of the novitiate, since the profession of vows is a promise to live the life as set out in the rule and constitutions.

§3

Novices have a responsibility to actively collaborate with the director so they can faithfully respond to the grace of their vocation. This section is an outgrowth of *RC* 32, which offered a sequence of principles that led to the conclusion that novices should both cooperate with positive and responsible obedience and be able to act on their own initiative. *RC* 32 began with the premise that there should be a harmony of outlook and approach between superiors, the novice director, and novice. These relationships were to be marked by gospel simplicity, loving kindness, respect for the dignity of the person, and mutual trust. The conclusion was that the director encourage the novices so they would be able to be both obedient and act on their own initiative.

This section has a slightly different emphasis, since it places the responsibility squarely on the novice rather than expecting the director to encourage the novices in these attitudes. That does not mean that the director should avoid encouraging the novices, but rather that the novices have a personal responsibility that is not entirely dependent on the director. Active collaboration at its minimum means that passivity, reverential fear, and distance should not characterize the relationship. Instead mutual trust, eagerness to apply oneself, and honesty should mark the relationship between director and novice. As this section points out, the purpose of this active collaboration is so the novice can respond faithfully to the grace of a divine vocation. Although, the human relationship is real and should have a good foundation, the divine call is the reason the novice came to the institute and should be sufficient motivation in and of itself for the novice to exercise personal responsibility in active collaboration. It may also be noted that since novices for the most part are older than they were in previous years, they may be more capable of exercising the personal responsibility called for by this section.

§4

Members of an institute are to cooperate in the training of novices by their exemplary life and prayer. The importance of this new provision in the law on formation cannot be underestimated and should be applied beyond the level of the novitiate. This section is not limited to only those who live in the same community with the novices but every member.

The life of the members of the institute is probably the most powerful witness and impetus that novices can receive either to live fully the life of the institute or not to live the life of the institute. Young religious observe and absorb the lessons they are taught to them by the lives of their brothers and sisters. They compare these observations with the ideals they are being taught and which are usually so well stated in the rule and constitutions. Taking into account human failure and sin, young religious are deeply impressed by those who have preceded them. The work of formation is no longer solely for the formation staff. Members have a most important obligation expressed in the law.

For a long time institutes have enacted proper law requiring that only those religious of "exemplary life" be assigned to live in houses of formation. Although this is important, this section acknowledges that the greatest impact on those in formation is the corporate life of the institute.

§5

The twelve months of the novitiate are to be directed to the formation of the novices; therefore, the novices should not be occupied with studies and duties which are not for the purpose of formation.

A similar provision is contained in CIC 565, §3, and more specific guidelines were given in *RC* 29. In *RC* 29 the general chapter was empowered to permit or even prescribe studies if they furthered the formation of novices. If the studies were doctrinal, they were to be directed to a loving knowledge of God and to strengthen the life of faith. However, during the canonical year all studies including theology and philosophy were forbidden if the purpose was to obtain a degree or prepare a novice for a special work. These are helpful considerations for an institute in deciding how to apply this section.

It is clear the novitiate is a school in the sense that novices can attend classes that further their spiritual and religious formation. It is equally clear that academic, professional, or career oriented studies are not to be undertaken. Since many novitiates are now combined with retreat houses, infirmaries, institute headquarters, or other missions, although the novices may help in the work of such houses, they should not be appointed to duties that take them away from their primary state of being in formation. Interpreters of CIC 565, §3 permitted a limited time to be devoted to other studies, such as Latin, Greek, a foreign language, music, or theoretical nursing. This limited training was justified on two grounds: (1) the novice should be able to review knowledge already obtained so it is not lost, and (2) during this period it is helpful for the director to test the talents and abilities of novices. [14]

Unlike RC 29 the power to permit, prescribe, or prohibit certain studies is not reserved to the general chapter; therefore, it may be regulated at a lower level in accord with this section.

Again, it should be noted that this section refers only to the twelve months of the novitiate described in C 648, §1. Beyond this time the training of the novices may include whatever program the institute believes would be beneficial to the novice.

C 653

§1. A novice can freely leave an institute; moreover the competent authority of the institute can dismiss a novice.

§2. When the novitiate is completed, a novice, if judged suitable, is to be admitted to temporary profession; otherwise the novice is to be dismissed. If there is a doubt about the novice's suitability, the time of probation can be extended by the major superior according to the norm of proper law, but not more than six months.

This canon lists the options that an institute and novice have during the course of and at the end of the novitiate. A novice can leave or be dismissed from the novitiate, be admitted to profession, or have the time of the novitiate extended.

§1

During the course of and at the completion of the novitiate, a novice can freely leave the institute or the competent authority can dismiss the novice.

CIC 571, §1 was more explicit regarding dismissal, stating it was to be according to the constitutions by superiors or chapters for any justifiable reason, and the reason need not be revealed to the novice.

Whether a novice leaves freely or is dismissed, both should be preceded by proper discernment. A summary of the discernment should be written in case the novice should apply again to the same institute, another institute, or a diocese, so that an accurate report can be made.

Proper law should determine the competent authority in cases of dismissal and could also include some internal procedure for the institute to follow for a dismissal.

This section does not enumerate the causes for dismissal, and these would likewise be a matter for proper law. The former law in providing that a novice need not be given the reason for dismissal did not prevent the institute from revealing the reason for dismissal. Revealing the reason has been the common practice of institutes, and it is difficult to imagine circumstances in which it would be just to withhold the reason for dismissal from a novice.

§2

At the end of the novitiate, there are three options for the institute and the novice: (1) admission to vows, (2) dismissal, and (3) extend the time of novitiate, presuming the novice does not freely leave at the end of the novitiate.

Profession is the subject of CC 654–658 and dismissal is covered by C 653, §1.

If there is doubt concerning suitability, the novitiate can be extended by the major superior according to the norm of proper law, but not more than six months. Extension may occur at the request of the institute or the novice. This six-month extension is not the same as the requirement for days to be made up. It applies only after days have been made up and the novitiate completed.

Prolongation should not be granted if there is no real hope that suitability can be established during the extended period. A novice who was sick during the time of novitiate and completed the canonical requirement of twelve months but was unable to fully participate in the program, or a novice who was occupied with some problem of vocation or personal growth for much of the time of the novitiate so as to impair participation in the novitiate program but has sufficiently resolved the problem, or other similar situations would be appropriate causes for extension.

Since the novitiate has been completed the rules governing interruption of the novitiate do not apply, however, long absences during the extension may not permit the institute to arrive at an appropriate decision.

The six-month extension is applicable at the end of the novitiate whether the novitiate be twelve, eighteen, or twenty-four months. Thus, if proper law provided for a novitiate of twenty-four months, a superior could extend the time six months, making the total time thirty months.

RELIGIOUS PROFESSION

CC 654–658 cover both temporary profession and perpetual profession. Regarding temporary profession, the canons define the length of time, the requirements for validity, and the option of renewal. Additional qualifications are added for perpetual profession. The law no longer provides for the profession of solemn vows; however, an institute can determine whether its perpetual vows will have the effect that formerly belonged to solemn vows in its proper law. It can also describe its vows as solemn in proper law. This would be especially suitable for those institutes that have always professed solemn vows.

C 654

By religious profession members assume by public vow the observance of the three evangelical counsels, are consecrated to God through the ministry of the Church, and are incorporated into the institute with rights and duties defined by law.

By religious profession a novice: (1) publicly vows to observe the three evangelical counsels, (2) is consecrated to God through the ministry of the Church, and (3) is incorporated into the institute with the rights and duties defined by law.

The first two results of profession emphasize the continuing themes of living the gospel[15] and the connection between the divine calling and the living body of Christ, the Church. The vows themselves obligate a member to their observance as determined by the law of the Church and the law of the institute. There is also the explicit recognition that religious enjoy a special calling in the life of the Church.[16]

The third result has a more direct juridic importance, since by professing vows a member is incorporated into the institute and has the rights and duties defined by law, which refers to both universal and proper law.

The express use of the term "vows" in this canon makes vows the norm and changes the practice of the use of promises or other sacred bonds which was permitted by RC 34. Although C 573, §2 uses the language "vows or other sacred bonds," that terminology is meant to apply to all the institutes governed by the common norms. The sole use of "vows" in this canon represents the choice that applies to religious institutes.[17]

C 655

Temporary profession is made for the time defined in proper law, which may not be less than three years and no longer than six.

The length of time for temporary profession is to be stated in proper law, but it is to be for a minimum of three years and a maximum of six years (see C 657, §2 regarding extensions).

CIC 574, §1 and §2 provided that temporary profession would be for three years or longer if the member would not reach the required age for perpetual profession within three years unless the constitutions stipulated otherwise. *RC* 4 introduced the principle that the time of formation should be extended over a longer period of time. *RC* 37 provided that the time should not be less than three nor more than nine years, but without allowing for an extension. The present law is a combination of the former Code and *RC* in making the norm three to six years, while allowing an extension of three years.

The purpose of the time of temporary profession is to further discern and test the call of the member. Since it is much longer than the novitiate, a greater variety of studies and experiences can be planned. Moreover, this whole article on profession places no conditions on the formative experiences that may be included in this period of time. The flexibility of granting from three to six years is to allow each institute to determine the length of time it needs to complete its program. Some institutes adopt a regulation similar in wording to this canon and then establish by policy an internal norm such as four or five years, while others set no internal norm except the readiness of the member, which is the most important qualification regardless of internal policy. The limit of six years is meant to prevent a member of the institute from putting off a decision which might otherwise needlessly waste the life and time of the member and the institute.

The present practice of professing vows for a time period of one or two years and renewing them at appropriate intervals to fulfill the time of temporary profession is not barred by this section. In addition, if an institute permits perpetual profession after three years and a member has been in temporary vows for three years and renews for one year, the institute may admit the member to perpetual profession at any time during the fourth year of vows and need not require the member to complete the fourth year, since the established time limit has been fulfilled.

C 656

For the validity of temporary profession, it is required that:

1⁰ the person who is about to make the profession shall have completed at least the eighteenth year of age;

2⁰ the novitiate has been validly completed;

3⁰ admission has been freely given by the competent superior with the vote of the council in accord with the norm of law;

4⁰ the profession be expressed and made without force, grave fear or fraud;

5⁰ the profession be received by the legitimate superior personally or through another.

The five requirements for the validity of temporary profession are the subject of this canon. The five requirements are similar to those contained in CIC 572.

The further requirement of CIC 576 regarding the rite of profession whether temporary or perpetual is now covered by the rite[18] published by the Sacred Congregation for Divine Worship which directs institutes to submit their formula to SCRIS for approval. Normally, this formula is stated in the proper law of the institute. According to SCRIS the essential elements are vows made to God comprised of poverty, chastity, and obedience;[19] intent to assume the obligations of the institute according to the rule and constitutions; declaration of the name and office of the person who receives the profession in the name of the Church; and specification of the time for which the vows are pronounced. If the above essentials are contained in the formula of profession, each institute may adapt the formula in accord with its own spirituality. In addition, individuals with the consent of the superior may add their own words at the beginning or the end of the formula provided they are moderate, clear, and totally consonant with the seriousness and solemnity of the act of profession.[20]

The commentary on the following parts of this canon will use the term "formation director" rather than "novice director," since some of the provisions apply to perpetual profession as well as temporary profession.

1°

The novice must have completed his or her eighteenth year of age. This is a change from CIC 573, which established the minimum age at sixteen. The raising of the age is consistent with the older age requirement of seventeen for being admitted to the novitiate. As with all the age requirements in the canons on formation the institute is free to have a higher minimum age in its proper law.

2°

The novitiate must be validly completed in accord with CC 647, 648, and 649 and any other requirements in the proper law of the institute.

3°

Admission to temporary profession is by the competent superior with the vote of the council. The competent superior should be designated in the proper law as well as the style of votation, which may be either consultative or deliberative. A petition for vows should be written and signed by the candidate for vows. The petition and the report of the formation director should be forwarded to the superior and council. In addition, some institutes follow the practice of having the formation director present at the council meeting when admission is on the agenda allowing for discussion and explanation of material contained in the report.

4°

There are two requirements contained in this part, first, the profession must be expressed, and second, it must be pronounced without force or fear. Regarding force and fear see C 643, 4°. The idea that a vow is expressed means that the person must use some word or sign to indicate profession is being made. One is not automatically or passively admitted to profession. If a person is mute, a sign such as signing the vow formula would fulfill the condition of the canon.

5°

The profession is to be received by a legitimate superior personally or by delegate. The legitimate superior may be any superior and should be determined by the proper law. It is the legitimately designated superior who has the authority to delegate another to receive the profession.

According to SCRIS the correct interpretation of superior in this canon refers to the internal superior. SCRIS states further that even in institutes of diocesan right, which are subject according to law to the local Ordinary, it is not the bishop or his delegate who is to receive the profession but the designated superior of the institute. The above norm applies even if a bishop or priest is the celebrant of the liturgy at which profession takes place. The superior is still to receive the profession.[21]

C 657

§1. When the time for which the profession has been made has elapsed the religious who freely requests it and is judged suitable is to be admitted to a renewal of profession or to perpetual profession; otherwise the religious is to leave.

§2. If it seems opportune the period of temporary profession can be extended by the competent superior, according to proper law, but in such a way that the entire time in which the member is bound by temporary vows does not exceed nine years.

§3. Perpetual profession can be anticipated for a just cause, but not by more than three months.

This canon describes the options available to the institute when the time for temporary profession has elapsed. The options are: (1) to renew temporary vows, (2) to profess perpetual vows, (3) to extend the time of temporary vows, or (4) to leave the institute. The third section covers anticipation of perpetual vows.

§1

This section covers three of the options. The first is that of renewal. The object of renewal would be to complete the time of temporary profession preceding perpetual profession. Institutes should adopt norms to govern the qualifications and procedures for a member to be admitted to the renewal of vows. In fact these may be the same as or very similar to those used for admittance to first profession. Institutes which use the system of annual renewal sometimes permit the supreme moderator or major superior to approve a member for renewal without requiring any kind of votation. This is permissible since it is not barred by universal law. One of the objects of a program of periodic renewal for the time of temporary vows is to provide periodic reviews of the progress of the member and to allow the member to review the state of his or her calling at specified times. Periodic reviews can and should be a part of the program whether there is renewal or not. Some institutes prefer a longer period of temporary profession to provide stability and a chance to grow freely without the threat of dismissal or being advised to leave before having the opportunity to grow.

The second option is to profess perpetual vows. This is an important step, since it means a life commitment. The member and the institute must be certain of his or her calling to religious life and to the institute. The requirements for perpetual profession are to follow the norms for the training of religious outlined in CC 657–661 and to assure the fulfillment of the conditions for validity contained in CC 656 and 658.

The third option is to leave the institute. This section would apply to leaving freely or being denied renewal or perpetual profession of vows.

The canon leaves it to the institute to adopt any necessary process to cover cases of denial of renewal or perpetual profession. The wording here is different than C 653, §2, which refers to the dismissal of a novice at the end of the novitiate. If a member questions the reasons or the process for the denial of renewal or perpetual profession, an institute may wish to provide a special review process to satisfy the questions of the member. If an institute refuses a petition to renew vows or profess perpetual vows, it seems just to give the reason(s) to the person. The reason does not need to be some specific fault or negative quality. A member must be positively considered to have a calling and a vocation to the life of the institute as well as being capable of living the life. Thus, it is sufficient to say the member is not suitable for life in the institute and to give the reasons that led to the decision. The formulation of reasons for refusing renewal or perpetual vows emphasizes the importance of establishing objective criteria for admission to vows that are communicated to members so they have notice and awareness of the criteria which will be used in reviewing their petition for vows.

§2

In appropriate cases the period of temporary profession can be extended; however, the maximum time a member may be in temporary vows is nine years. The extension is to be accomplished by the competent superior according to the proper law.

This section is like CIC 574, §2, which provided for a prolongation of vows of up to three years. The difference is the former law permitted a maximum of six years in temporary vows, while the present maximum is nine years. This is closer to the change made by *RC* 37.

RC 6 offers helpful considerations in regard to the extension of temporary vows. It notes the whole purpose of the time of temporary vows is to bring the person to that level of spiritual maturity so that a perpetual commitment can be made. In some cases lengthening the period of probation can foster such maturity, while in other cases it may not. If a member remains too long in a state of uncertainty, maturity may not be fostered. Rather, it may aggravate a tendency toward procrastination or indecision. In addition, if a person is not admitted to perpetual vows, to return to the lay state or determining if a religious vocation is elsewhere requires adjustments which may be more burdensome and difficult in proportion to the time spent in the present institute under temporary vows. Superiors thus have a serious responsibility not to delay too long in making their decision because of the effect it can have on the future of the member.

§3

Perpetual profession can be anticipated for a just cause, but not by more than three months. This is a change from CIC 577, §2, which allowed anticipation of renewal by up to a month but prohibited anticipation of perpetual profession under penalty of invalidity.

Since the law does not cover anticipation of renewal of vows, it seems in keeping with the sense of this section that it be permitted but also not in excess of three months. Anticipation in regard to renewal in the previous law was understood to be effective from the date when the previous profession expired. This is reasonable but it also seems a formula for renewal could state it is effective, for example, for one year from the date of renewal and thereby terminate the previous vows and establish the length of the period of renewal as beginning on the date of profession.

The anticipation is to be for just cause. This is different from C 641, §2, which allows anticipation but does not state the gravity of the reason. Mere reasons of convenience would not appear to meet the standard of this section; however, just cause would include danger of death or departure for an important assignment such as the missions. It should be noted that in cases in which the minimum of three years in vows has been completed a case of anticipation is no longer present; thus, a member who has completed three years in temporary vows and has renewed for one year may be admitted to perpetual profession at any time after the completion of the three years.

C 658

Besides the conditions mentioned in can. 656, 3⁰, 4⁰ and 5⁰ and others attached by proper law, for the validity of perpetual profession the following are required:
1⁰ the completion of at least the twenty-first year of age;
2⁰ previous temporary profession for at least three years, with due regard for the prescription of can. 657, §3.

In order to validly make perpetual profession, this canon adds two requirements beyond those mentioned in C 656, §3, §4, and §5.

1°

A member must have completed the twenty-first year. It can be seen that the age of twenty-one years is set by adding the minimum time of temporary vows, which is three years, to the minimum age requirement of eighteen. This would normally not be a problem unless a person were exactly eighteen at profession of temporary vows and wanted to anticipate the time of perpetual vows. Anticipation could not be allowed until the member is twenty-one. If this case arose, a dispensation could be requested from SCRIS for pontifical institutes or the local Ordinary for diocesan institutes.

2°

A member must have been temporarily professed for at least three years, without prejudice to C 657, §3 regarding anticipation. Proper law can of course provide for a longer minimum period. Some institutes provide a norm from which exceptions can be easily made by the appropriate authority.

TRAINING OF RELIGIOUS

Article IV on the training of religious consists of three canons that cover the purpose and spirit of formation from the time of first profession throughout the entire life of the member. The provisions are general, indicating directions rather than offering specific regulations. Since this period of training is longer and more varied than novitiate it will require a more extensive study and development of proper law and policy than the time of novitiate.

C 659

§1. In individual institutes after first profession the formation of all members is to be continued so that they may lead more fully the proper life of the institute and carry out its mission more suitably.

§2. Therefore, proper law must define the program of this formation and its duration, keeping in mind the needs of the Church and the circumstances of human persons and times to the extent this is required by the purpose and character of the institute.

§3. The formation of members who are preparing to receive holy orders is regulated by universal law and by the program of studies proper to the institute.

This canon offers the general principle that training should be directed toward living the life of the institute while giving the institute the responsibility of determining the nature and extent of the program in accord with its mission and needs. The final section regulates the training of members preparing for holy orders.

§1

After first profession, the training of members should be carried out for the twofold purpose of (1) to lead more fully the life of the institute and (2) to carry out its mission more suitably. These two purposes are the foundation on which the program of training is to be built. All the studies, and spiritual and apostolic experiences, are to be developed in light of these purposes and their effectiveness and usefulness measured against these purposes.

As *RC* 7 pointed out, the program of training is meant to prepare a member to faithfully live out a life commitment to God in the institute. The time of temporary profession is both a time of testing and discernment. It is an extended period when the member and the members of the institute come to know each other better. This allows those in temporary profession to decide if the institute is offering the life they believe they are called to and whether in fact the members of the institute live out their commitment. At the same time, the institute in arranging its program is able to structure it so they can come to know and understand the member's character, personality, gifts, and imperfections so that each can make a well-considered decision regarding each other.

§2

It is up to the institute to define its program of formation in proper law. In doing so the institute is to keep in mind the needs of the Church, the people, and the times as they relate to the purpose and character of the institute.

The main principles and the general structure of the program can be defined in the constitutions. The changeable parts of the program, especially those which are related to the needs of the Church, people, and times, may be more changeable and can be in the directory or policy statements of the institute.

The inclusion of the factor of the duration of the program received special attention in *RC* 4. In promulgating new guidelines for formation, one of the observations of SCRIS, based on its experience and the experience of the institutes it serves, was that formation "must be extended over a longer period of time." Later in *RC* 6, the question is raised whether the period of profession before perpetual vows should be prolonged. *RC* did not answer the question but offered guidelines which may be helpful in fulfilling the intent of this canon.

The duration of a program is to be a means to assure the program offers ample opportunity for a member to reach the certainty of calling and the spiritual and personal maturity that will enable the member to embrace the life and mission of the institute. It is clear that the increased minimum ages and the lengthened time options for temporary profession are making room for slower maturation in a society or culture and the greater challenges that confront the person who is called to serve God and his people in a religious institute. In addition, the accepting of new ministries by religious institutes may require additional spiritual or apostolic training that would be cause to lengthen the time of the formation program.

Such flexibility in the law is an attempt to recognize the operation of grace in each person and thus to offer each institute wide enough parameters to allow the grace to operate, to observe the development and growth in each person, all within the flexible structure of a common program that leads to a member being able to make a life commitment.

§3

Members of institutes that are preparing for holy orders are governed by the universal law and the law of the institute in regard to studies. The universal law, based on the Vatican II Decree on the Formation of Priests, is found in CC 242–264. *ES* II, 34 implemented the decree by stating the training of priests should be adapted according to the particular character of each institute. [22] Thus, religious priests are to receive training that forms them for the specific pastoral needs of their locale and the spirit and purpose of their institute. The charism of an institute may require special training or experiences that prepare a priest for work in home or foreign missions, evangelization, ministry to the poor, education, or communications. All such ministries require special training to fulfill the purpose of the institute.

C 660

§1. The formation is to be systematic, adapted to the capacity of the members, spiritual and apostolic, doctrinal and at the same time practical, and when it seems opportune, leading to appropriate degrees both ecclesiastical and civil.

§2. During the time of this formation duties and jobs which would impede the formation are not to be assigned to members.

The characteristics and the areas of training of members are outlined in a positive manner in the first section of this canon, while the second section is a caution against anything that would interfere with the training.

§1

The characteristics of the training are that it should be systematic, adapted to the capacity of members, and practical. While the terms spiritual, apostolic, and doctrinal can refer to the characteristics of training, they also refer to areas of training.

The spirit of the section is to place before institutes their responsibility to provide a balanced and integrated program of training for each member of an institute. Since each member is a gift of God to the institute and entrusted to the institute for the growth and development of a divine calling, the gifts and capacities of each person are to be given the opportunity to grow and develop. The training is not only to be helpful for ministry and enable a member to faithfully live the life of the institute but should also provide a measure of self-worth and esteem. In cases in which degrees and certificates are helpful, they should be obtained whether they are for professions or trades.

Many institutes have always had and continue to have a certain number of members who serve the members of the institute by applying themselves to tasks without which a community could not function such as cooking, cleaning, hospitality, care of guests, transportation, etc. The spiritual and doctrinal training of those preparing to serve in such ministries should not be overlooked while providing training or education in these skills.

§2

Members in formation are not to be given jobs or assignments which would interfere with their formation. The intent of this section is to protect members who are in formation. Sometimes the pressure of the apostolic needs of an institute may lead it to look to members in formation to help in the apostolate. This section points out that such assignments should not interfere with formation, since a short-range need may have a long-range negative effect on the life of the member in the institute. There are times when a talented, well-educated, or highly experienced member may have all the professional qualifications and natural talent it takes to fulfill an assignment. Yet, the person is very young in the life of the institute and to make such a decision based primarily on professional qualifications and experience is a disservice to the member. It is even worse if the member is unprepared for such an assignment, but there is pressure on the superior to fill an opening. This section is a directive to superiors not to do so if it impedes the primary purpose of formation.

This section, of course, would not apply to apostolic missions or assignments planned as a regular part of the program of formation. However, the caution mentioned above would still apply, since such assignments are primarily for the purpose of formation and not to fill apostolic personnel openings. *PC* 18 states that members "should not be assigned to apostolic works immediately after the novitiate. In stable residences and in a fitting manner let them continue in their training in the religious life and the apostolate, in doctrine and technical matters, even to the extent of winning appropriate degrees." The emphasis is clearly on formation regardless of the training the member is undertaking. Even if the training is experience or work oriented, it is still to be conducted in the manner of training so that a member receives instruction, counsel, and evaluation rather than being left on his or her own without caring and appropriate supervision.

C 661

Throughout their entire life religious are to continue carefully their own spiritual, doctrinal, and practical formation, and superiors are to provide them with the resources and time to do this.

This canon is a restatement of *PC* 18 noting that "throughout their lives religious should labor earnestly to perfect their spiritual, doctrinal and professional development. As far as possible, superiors should provide them with the opportunity, the resources, and the time to do so."

This canon recognizes that formation is a lifelong project. The profession of perpetual vows is not the end of formation but a commitment to be formed throughout the whole of one's life.

The on-going formation is to foster spiritual, doctrinal, and practical renewal. Regardless of the apostolate of the religious, each member needs further formation in these three areas, first for personal growth and development and second to serve others well in ministry.

In one sense practical or professional formation may be the easiest of the three because many assignments provide the time and the budget to undertake such training. In addition, the pressure from co-workers and the needs of those to be served are important motivating factors in receiving practical or professional updating.

Doctrinal formation may be the next easiest, since most dioceses, institutes, and educational institutions frequently hold conferences that aid members in understanding theological development, pastoral practice, or Church teaching.

The most difficult but perhaps the most important is on-going spiritual formation. Although there is a revival of interest in spiritual renewal, religious will often relegate this to last place, since it is the most personal area of renewal; thus, it is fitted in when nothing else interferes. Both *PC* and this section mention it first. This is a clue to the fact that spiritual renewal is of primary importance. Both the life of a member and the institute is built on a shallow foundation if members are not spiritually renewed.

The last clause of the canon highlights the importance of on-going formation. Superiors are given the responsibility to provide members with the time and means to do so. This is not a passive responsibility that superiors are to pass on to members by communicating to them they should undertake such renewal or even providing opportunities. Although many members seek out such means of renewal, many do not. The failure of those who do not often provides a gap in understanding that can be divisive in an institute. Thus, superiors should actively motivate members to receive continuing formation to keep their institute revitalized. To ensure on-going formation is a reality in the institute a superior may review the extent to which members have taken advantage of opportunities for on-going formation.

In order to provide time both major and local superiors should be aware of the schedule demands of their members so as to help them plan time to undertake on-going formation. The pressure of apostolic commitments may require the intervention of the superior in order to adjust them so that a person can free a period of time for on-going formation. This may require long-range planning such as a year ahead of time to insure that time is available to the member, since the member's commitments may require a substitute while the member is absent.

The means include financial means. While certain assignments provide both the time and finances for on-going formation or a particular area of it, this is not true in all cases. In cases in which it is not true, it is up to the superior to provide such means according to the available resources of the institute. Thus, budgetary planning at the general, provincial, and local level should provide financial resources for on-going formation. If it is not in the budget, it is unlikely that on-going formation will be a reality. The sense of the canon is that on-going formation is not an option but an important responsibility.

Some institutes provide for on-going formation in proper law by requiring each member to undertake an aspect of such formation annually, biannually, or with a stated frequency, while at the same time providing for a specific budget request for ongoing formation. The means to accomplish on-going formation are varied and need to be accommodated to the needs of each institute.

NOTES

1. The former canons on dowry, and studies in clerical institutes were included in the total. Even if they are omitted, the reduction is more than 50 percent (from 42 to 20).

2. The omitted impediments apply to those who belonged to a non-Catholic sect, those who can or have been accused of a serious crime, and a bishop or a cleric who is bound to service by the disposition of the Holy See. CIC 542, §1.

3. For religious who are contemplating priesthood, the simple impediment of "having a wife," C 1042, 1° (formerly CIC 987, 2°) would not require a dispensation if the party had received a decree of nullity. However, the SCCE has required that the sentences of the tribunal of first and second instances be forwarded to them to determine that there would be no scandal should the man in question be advanced to ordination to diaconate and priesthood. RR (1982) 41.

4. In 1979 SCRIS replied in a similar case that it did not have the faculties to grant such a dispensation and forwarded the case to the Secretary of State who did not grant the petition. The most recent response in 1980 was granted by SCRIS by reason of special faculties conceded by the Holy Father. RR (1982) 28-29. In the case of a similar petition, which was made to SCDF because the petitioner was not baptized at the time of her marriage, the Holy Father granted the dispensation with the condition that "before the petitioner makes perpetual profession, she is to contact the Sacred Congregation for the Doctrine of the Faith. If, however, she leaves the religious life and wishes to enter a new marriage, she is to contact the same Sacred Congregation for the dissolution of the bond of her marriage." *Ibid*. 28.

5. The requirement of evidence of some infidelity to prove that the former spouse has forfeited his or her marital rights seems stringent. Beyond a divorce or a spouse presenting no objection, there seems to be little room to prove forfeiting of marital rights. It is suggested that a simple written statement by the former spouse that there is no intent to resume marital rights or if a statement cannot be obtained the individual circumstances of the case such as length of separation, cause of separation, and the refusal of the former spouse to respond be accepted as appropriate evidence in such cases.

6. The following discussion of force and grave fear relies on Wrenn, Lawrence, G., *Annulments*, 3rd ed., CLSA, 1972.

7. NCCB Guidelines, January 24, 1979.

8. Bankruptcy discharge does not relieve the following obligations:
   1. Claims not provable, such as certain tort claims, fines, and penalties;
   2. Taxes—generally federal, state, or local, owing within three years preceding bankruptcy;
   3. Liability for obtaining money or property by false pretenses or representations;
   4. Liability for willful and malicious injuries to the person or property of another;
   5. Alimony and support payments;
   6. Liability for seduction;
   7. Debts not scheduled (listed as owed);
   8. Fraud or embezzlement by the bankrupt while acting as a fiduciary;
   9. Wages earned within three months prior to bankruptcy;
   10. Sums due employee by bankrupt employer under a contract authorizing retention of sums to secure faithful performance of an employment contract. *Lawyers Desk Book*, 5th ed., IBP (1978) 21-22.

9. See comment on C 643, §1, 2°.

10. The novitiate no longer begins with the reception of the habit or some other manner

prescribed by the constitutions. However, it is necessary for the institute to designate the date the novitiate begins.

11. See C 651, §1 requiring that the novice director be a member of the institute.

12. C 201, §1 defines continuous time as that which is subjected to no interruption, and C 202 §2 states that if time is continuous, a month and a year are always to be taken as they appear in the calendar.

13. Abbo, John A., and Hannan, Jerome D., *The Sacred Canons*, Herder (1952) 579.

14. *Ibid.* 582.

15. See C 574, §1 and C 575.

16. See C 574, §2.

17. See *RC* 6, 7, and 34 for a dicsussion of the rationale for allowing the use of promises or other bonds rather than temporary vows.

18. *CLD* (7) 515; *CLD* (8) 365.

19. Traditionally some institutes do not explicitly mention the three vows.

20. *CLD* (8) 365–366.

21. *CLD* (8) 361–364.

22. In addition to the adaption necessary for priestly life in an institute, each country is to have its own norms for the training of priests. See "The Program of Priestly Formation" for the United States approved by SCCE, January 18, 1971, published in a booklet bearing the name of the program by the NCCB.

BIBLIOGRAPHY

Gambari, E., "The Updating of Religious Formation," Boston: Daughters of St. Paul, 1969.

RC, "The Formation of the Modern Religious," *Supplement to the Way*, vol. 7, 1969.

RC II, "Preparing for Religious Life," *Supplement to the Way*, vol. 8, 1969.

SCRIS, The Contemplative Dimension of Religious Life, no. 17, 19, 1982.

Obligations and Rights
Canons 662–672, 277, 285–287, 289, 279, §2

DAVID F. O'CONNOR, S.T.

There is no intention here to treat all of the obligations and rights of institutes or their members. Certainly, all of the obligations and rights of the Christian faithful (CC 208–223) apply to religious. Many of the specific obligations of religious are treated elsewhere in the Code. Those associated with the profession of the vows are also contained in CC 599-601 and in the proper law of each institute. The same can be stated concerning those matters which have to do with some aspects of the common life in CC 602 and 607, §2. The implications of an appropriate separation from the world (C 607, §3) are also left to the further determination of the proper law of the institute. The obligations of superiors are broadly stated in CC 619 and 628–630. Those for treasurers are contained in C 636. There are implied obligations about a simple life-style contained in C 634, §2. Therefore, this chapter makes no pretense at enumerating all of the obligations and rights of religious, but is limited to statements about only some of the more traditional, obvious, or common obligations.

There are some changes in the revised Code which make it different from the former one. For example, C 672, concerning activities prohibited to religious, does not mention the practice of medicine as did the 1917 Code in CIC 592 and 139, §2, but there is a somewhat stricter prohibition against involvement in partisan politics and public civil offices. No longer is there any canon concerning the correspondence of religious as in the 1917 Code (CIC 611). Moreover, the former Code (CIC 595) made it the obligation of the proper religious superior to see to it that subjects performed religious exercises and that they frequented the sacraments. The 1983 Code places such obligations on the religious members themselves and not on the superiors. These are some examples of welcome changes.

C 662

Religious are to have as their highest rule of life the following of Christ as proposed in the gospel and expressed in the constitutions of their institute.

THE FOLLOWING OF CHRIST

The consecrated life of religious is a specific, ecclesial style of evangelical witness. *PC* 1 asserts that the very purpose of religious life is the pursuit of perfect charity by means of the evangelical counsels, which are founded on the teachings and example of Jesus Christ. He is the supreme model of the Christian life and, therefore, of the religious life. All who respond generously to a vocation to the religious life seek only to follow Christ with greater freedom and to imitate him. With their fellow Christians, they search the Scriptures in prayer and meditation in order to encounter the Word Made Flesh. "The evangelical witness of the religious life clearly manifests . . . the primacy of the love of God . . . of a constant seeking for God, of an undivided love for Christ alone, and an absolute dedication to the growth of his kingdom."[1]

ROLE OF THE CONSTITUTIONS

ES II, 12–14 stated that the constitutions must contain the necessary spiritual and juridic elements in order that they have a particularly stable foundation. It stated that a text which was only juridic or one that was merely exhortatory should be avoided. It was clear that the ascetical-doctrinal-inspirational aspects of constitutions are meant to specify gospel values for the members, to particularize the call to conversion, to reconciliation, and to the paschal mystery in the lives of members of a religious family. The juridic-canonical-practical aspects of constitutions are a manifestation that the institute is an ecclesial reality, an organized and stable community within the Church. Juridic norms set up minimal expectations and regulations for accountability. They are meant to protect the members and the institute, to promote justice and good order. They take relationships seriously, relationships within the institute, and the relationship of the institute to outside figures such as bishops or other institutes.[2]

Therefore, the constitutions are the basic book of the institute outlining and describing the character and identity of the institute in the ordering of its life and activity corresponding to its own traditions and identity (CC 578, 587). They are a code of life in a spiritual and normative sense, so as to inform and characterize the way of life and activity of the institute and its members. Constitutions are limited to what is fundamental, substantial, and characteristic, leaving to other books the determination of those elements which must be adapted to diverse times and places. These complementary or supplementary books are, by their nature, subject to periodic revision.

Members of a religious institute live an evangelical life and follow Christ in a specific manner by observance of the constitutions. The approbation of the constitutions by the proper ecclesiastical authority is an ecclesial guarantee that the counsels are being correctly interpreted and lived; that by their observance the members are truly following Christ. [3]

C 663

§1. Contemplation of divine things and assiduous union with God in prayer is to be the first and foremost duty of all religious.

§2. Members are to participate in the Eucharistic Sacrifice daily if possible, receive the Most Sacred Body of Christ and adore this same Lord present in the Sacrament.

§3. They should apply themselves to the reading of Sacred Scripture and to mental prayer; they are to celebrate the liturgy of the hours worthily according to the prescriptions of proper law, with due regard for the obligation of clerics in can. 276, §2, 3⁰, and they are to perform other exercises of piety.

§4. They are to cultivate a special devotion to the Virgin Mother of God, model and protector of all consecrated life, including the Marian rosary.

§5. They are faithfully to observe an annual period of spiritual retreat.

§1

All forms of work, especially the ministry and involvement in the apostolate, can be made prayerful. However, if these activities are not accompanied habitually and regularly with periods of personal and communal prayer, the non-praying person will find it impossible, eventually, to find God in his or her work or apostolate because that person does not experience the Lord in prayer-communication. Intimacy with God, the necessity to adore him, the need to intercede for others, and the experiences of the Christian life all manifest the importance of prayer in which God can reveal himself to his servants. Indeed, faithfulness to prayer or its abandonment is the test of the vitality or the decadence of religious life. [4] Religious in apostolic institutes must integrate interiority and activity. The first duty of all religious is to be with Christ. An ever-present danger is that religious can become so involved with their work for the Lord that they forget the Lord of good works. [5] Therefore, this canon simply reiterates, in an exhortatory manner, the great value and importance of a deep prayer life.

§2

The Eucharist is the center of the entire life of the Church. All other sacraments, apostolic works, and ministries are linked to the Eucharist and directed toward it. The Eucharist contains the entire good of the Church, Christ himself, our Passover and Living Bread. Its celebration is the supreme means by which the faithful come to express in their lives the mystery of Christ and the true nature of the Church.[6] Therefore, this great emphasis on daily participation in the Eucharistic liturgy is presented as the ideal norm and expectation for those consecrated to the Lord. Although particular circumstances and missionary endeavors may make this impossible in given instances, they do not invalidate the norm.

Pope John Paul II has stated:

> The commitment to take part daily in the Eucharistic Sacrifice will help religious renew their self-offering to the Lord every day. Gathered in the Lord's name, religious communities have the Eucharist as their natural center. It is normal, therefore, that they should be visibly assembled in their chapel, in which the presence of the Blessed Sacrament expresses and realizes what must be the principal mission of every religious family.[7]

§3

The reading of sacred Scripture and periods of mental prayer and meditation are all part of the Christian patrimony, especially for those who are committed to a life in service of the Word. Time for spiritual reading, prayerful silence, and reflection are necessary for promoting intimacy with God, especially for those who must find God in the midst of the noise and the confusion of a busy apostolate.[8]

The liturgy of the hours is the public prayer of the Church that is designed to sanctify the whole day. It is left to the proper law of each institute to determine whether or not it is obligatory for its members, since it has not been part of the tradition of every institute. However, it is the obligation of all clerics and remains an obligation even if the institute does not impose it (C 276, §2, 3°). The divine praises are a source of inspiration and nourishment. Those in the consecrated life are encouraged to pray them as an important aspect of participating intimately in the life of the Church.[9] All other exercises of piety are left entirely to the determination of each institute in accordance with its own patrimony and spiritual traditions.

§4

The Virgin Mary is preeminent among the saints because of her divine Motherhood. She has been presented as the model of all consecrated in the Church because she is characterized as listening to the Word of God; standing courageously by the cross of Jesus, teaching us to contemplate the passion; and as a woman of prayer, she is the model of faith, hope and charity. Therefore, Pope John Paul II has stated:

> The contemplative life of religious would be incomplete if it were not directed in filial love towards her who is the Mother of the Church and of consecrated souls. This love for the virgin will be manifested with the celebration of her feasts and, in particular, with daily prayer in her honor, especially the Rosary. The daily recitation of the rosary is a centuries-old-tradition for religious, and so it is not out of place to recall the suitability, beauty and efficacy of this prayer, which proposes for our meditation the mysteries of the Lord's life.[10]

§5

As in the 1917 Code (CIC 595, §1), the length of an annual retreat and all other specifics are left to the determination of the proper law of the institute. However, many institutes have the practice of requiring a minimum of five consecutive days.

It should be noted that none of the practices contained in C 663 are juridically imposed by the Code, with the exception of the liturgy of the hours for those in orders (C 276, §2, 3°). However, all of them are quite traditional and are recommended in the Vatican II documents. *ES* II, 21, which implemented the conciliar documents, insisted that devotional exercises traditional in the Church should not be dropped. A great number of religious continue to find them rewarding and they should be fittingly fostered.

C 664

Religious are to apply themselves to conversion of heart to God, examine their conscience even daily, and frequently approach the sacrament of penance.

Traditionally, the religious life has been presented as a vocation which demands a conversion of life and morals. Each institute, in its own way, invites its members to embrace an ascetical life-style. The constitutions or rule of an institute contain customs and practices which foster the spiritual life. One of the most common and proven practices has been the daily examination of conscience, usually entered into for a brief period at the end of the day. It remains as a part of the preparation for night prayer in the divine office. The present canon is an exhortatory one and does not impose any juridic obligation. It simply calls attention to the value that this time-tested ascetical practice continues to enjoy in the spiritual life and urges that it be done daily.

THE SACRAMENT OF PENANCE

The Church is a Church of sinners. We recognize our sinfulness and our need for conversion and for healing when we approach the sacrament of penance. While religious may not need reconciliation because of the awareness of grave sin in their lives, they have had the practice of making devotional confessions with some frequency. Such devotional confessions are the occasion for a more intense review of our spiritual health. They force us to specify our sinfulness and offer us the opportunity to receive the advice of a confessor-spiritual director, and to receive the grace of the sacrament. The present canon exhorts religious to approach the sacrament frequently. How frequently? In 1970, SCRIS suggested twice a month.[11] However, there is no specific time stated in the universal law. Even if the proper law of the institute states that members are to approach at certain times or on certain occasions, these are exhortations and not juridic or moral obligations. All the faithful enjoy freedom in this matter. This includes those in the consecrated life. The universal law simply states that the faithful are obliged to receive the sacrament of penance once a year if they are conscious of grave sin (C 989). However, the strong commendation given to the reception of the sacrament in the Code is but one indication of the important place it holds in the life of the Church. All religious who are solicitous for fostering their union with God will be careful to approach the sacrament of penance with an appropriate regularity and frequency. Also, the latest documents not only urge a personal reception but a community rite which evidences the ecclesial and fraternal dimensions of this sacrament.[12]

It might be noted that the present Code no longer has detailed designations of confessors for religious as did the 1917 Code in CIC 518–530. These canons tended to reflect an even more ancient practice when members of religious institutes had little freedom to approach the confessor they wished. There was a time when some institutes required members to confess only to a priest of the institute approved for such a ministry. The 1917 Code guaranteed that religious would enjoy a greater degree of freedom to approach confessors. Moreover, it is only in recent decades that religious have greater options to go out to select their own confessors. Today, superiors should be solicitous to provide confessors at appropriate times for their religious who are confined to the house. Likewise, an ordinary confessor should be requested for houses of formation, large houses with concentrations of religious, cloistered communities and those that care for the aged, infirm, or handicapped religious (C 630, §2, §3).

C 665

§1. Observing a common life, religious are to live in their own religious house and not be absent from it without the permission of their superior. However, if it is a question of a lengthy absence from the house the major superior for a just cause and with the consent of the council can permit the member to live outside a house of the institute, but not for more than a year, except for the purpose of caring for poor health, for the purpose of studies or undertaking an apostolate in the name of the institute.

§2. Members unlawfully absent from the religious house with the intention of withdrawing from the power of their superiors are to be solicitously sought after by them and aided to return and persevere in their vocation.

§1

C 602 has already addressed the obligation of religious to develop a community life proper to each institute and through which the members are united as a special family in Christ, support one another in living their vocation, and offer an example of Christian life built upon love and reconciliation. C 665 seems to imply that an experience of community grows out of and requires some form of common life. That is, in ordinary circumstances, religious of the same institute are to live habitually with each other in a house of their own institute subject to a superior. Absences from their house require permission. For short absences the local superior grants permission. For lengthy absences the proper major superior, usually of the province, may give permission with the consent of the council.

Permission to be absent need not always be explicit. It may be implied in the very nature of the assignment given to a religious. For example, if a priest is assigned to a mission band that travels about preaching in parishes throughout the country, permission to be absent is included in the assignment itself. If a religious institute staffs small mission churches where there can be no community of religious and this work requires extended periods of time living apart from a house of the institute (if not most of one's time), then this is of the nature of the ministry and apostolate of the institute. Each institute must look at its own established practices and recognized ways of operating in its efforts to promote a common life. Those institutes which permit their members periods of vacation, recreation, spiritual retreat, or encourage them to participate in special pastoral or continuing education programs, are granting them permission to be absent for these things. In such instances, good communication, courtesy, and consideration are necessary between superiors and members so that all are aware of the expectations and procedures regarding absences for these activities.

What is a "lengthy" absence? This must be left to each institute to determine. Generally, an absence of a few weeks would seem to qualify as a lengthy period. Each institute develops its own practices and customs which determine these things for the members. The discretion of the local superior and the circumstances of the absence will often indicate whether this is something which must be referred to a major superior or not. The major superior can grant permission to be away from a house of the institute up to one year with the consent of the council. If the members of the council do not give their consent, the major superior can not grant the permission.

If permission is sought to be away from a house of the institute for more than one year, again, the major superior with the consent of the council may grant this but only for (1) reasons of health (mental or physical), (2) reasons of study, and (3) for exercising an apostolate or ministry in the name of the institute. This appears to be a taxative enumeration so that the major superior cannot grant it for other reasons. Moreover, it should be noted that the expression "leave of absence" is not used in the canon because it may imply something that is not intended. Someone who is away for the above reasons is not on a "leave of absence."

When the canon addresses the fact of an absence for reasons of exercising the apostolate in the name of the institute, the specific apostolate should be in accord with the purpose and the nature of the institute. Therefore, it would not be proper for a member of an institute wholly dedicated to contemplation to be permitted to be absent for a pastoral ministry never envisioned in the nature of the institute (C 674), for example, to give a cloistered nun permission to be a missionary or a cloistered monk to be a military chaplain. Religious are not free to undertake any form of the apostolate, but only those forms recognized by the nature of the institute and its proper law.[13]

If the reasons for being absent for more than a year are not because of health, studies, or apostolate, then the major superior might consider whether or not an indult of exclaustration (C 686) is justifiable. If the reasons do not justify the absence, and an exclaustration is granted, the canonical effects differ from those of C 665. Permission to be absent in no way places the religious in a special category or implies an absence from the institute, as does an exclaustration. Absence does not take away active or passive voice, but exclaustration does. Also, exclaustration may not be given to a religious in temporary vows, but only to those in perpetual vows. Permission to be absent may be given to religious in temporary vows.

§2

If a religious unlawfully leaves the religious house with the intention of effectively being removed from obedience to the religious superior, the superior is obliged to attempt to get the member to return. Hence, the first reaction of a superior should not be a punitive one but the pastoral act of attempting reconciliation. If there is a vocation crisis involved, possibly the proper superior might grant permission for a temporary absence for an extended spiritual retreat. Therefore, the immediate response of superiors is to help the religious resolve whatever problem may be present. However, if there is no response or the absent religious has rejected all such solicitude, the major superior can move toward formal dismissal of the religious after he or she is illegitimately absent for six months (C 696).

While the present Code has dropped the terms "fugitive" and "apostate," as contained in CIC 644 of the 1917 Code, superiors can have recourse to appropriate penalties for those religious who persist in disobedience and do not give any indication of returning to the expected norm of religious life. Repeated violations of one's vows or pertinacious disobedience to lawful commands in serious matters given by the proper religious superior are grounds for dismissal after warning (C 696). Note that the intention to remove oneself effectively from obedience to one's superiors is required as well as the fact of absence. This intention may become clear as the result of rejecting the solicitude of the religious superior along with the fact of a continued absence. C 1371, §2, states that persistent disobedience after warning, even without an absence, can be legitimately and appropriately punished.

C 666

Necessary discretion is to be observed in the use of media of communication, and whatever is harmful to one's vocation and dangerous to the chastity of a consecrated person is to be avoided.

This canon is exhortatory and in accordance with traditional ascetical admonitions to religious concerning the need to maintain a recollected spirit and avoid unnecessary distractions or occasions of sin. [14] With the pervasiveness of the media (newspapers, magazines, radio, television, films, etc.) in modern society, it is increasingly difficult even in religious houses to maintain a modicum of religious recollection. While there have been instructions directed at strictly contemplative monasteries regulating the use of these things for religious observing a papal cloister,[15] there is no attempt to impose such restrictions on all religious. C 666 simply calls attention to the need for discretion to be exercised in the use of these instruments and that, in some cases, they can be abused and occasion harm to religious. For example, it would seem to be quite out of order and to be offensive to the sensibilities of religious to keep a television set habitually playing in the dining room during meals. This undermines the social aspect of the community table and destroys any conversation or sharing. This is detrimental to community life. Likewise, to have radios and stereos constantly playing in the house during the day so that all are forced to listen to them is an unnecessary distraction. Certainly, when it comes to determining guidelines or norms for the use of these things, a great deal of latitude must be left to mature religious to use them with prudence and discretion. They should never be permitted to be a source of unnecessary disturbance.

C 667

§1. In all houses cloister adapted to the character and mission of the institute is to be observed according to the determinations of proper law, with some part of the religious house always being reserved to the members alone.

§2. A stricter discipline of cloister is to be observed in monasteries ordered to the contemplative life.

§3. Monasteries of nuns which are totally ordered to the contemplative life must observe *papal* cloister, namely according to norms given by the Apostolic See. Other monasteries of nuns are to observe cloister adapted to their own character and defined in the constitutions.

§4. For a just cause the diocesan bishop has the faculty of entering the cloister of monasteries of nuns which are in his diocese, and, for a grave cause and with the consent of the superior, of permitting others to enter the cloister and nuns to leave the cloister for a truly necessary period of time.

§1

This canon is a simplification of CIC 597–606 of the 1917 Code. In the 1983 Code there are no details concerning the cloister and all is left to the proper law of each institute to determine. In this paragraph "cloister" is synonymous with the statement that "some part of the house always be reserved to the members alone." What part should be reserved? Since the cloister never included the chapel, sacristy, guest quarters, parlors, and public offices, none of these should be in the reserved part of the house. Certainly, the private rooms or sleeping quarters should be reserved. Also, recreation rooms where the community meets to relax ought to be reserved habitually for the exclusive use of the members. While communities with spacious buildings will find no major problem in determining the area reserved to the members, smaller houses may well find it difficult to do so. Nevertheless, while the requirements of Christian hospitality are most important, they must be balanced by the equally important needs of the religious who have a right to be "at home" in their own houses and enjoy some privacy. [16] Respecting and safeguarding this right seems especially necessary for active religious in a busy and demanding apostolate. They, possibly more than others, need time and a place for silence, quiet prayer, study, and relaxation with their brothers and sisters in religion in order to foster their own spiritual, mental and physical well-being.

§2

Traditionally, the cloister, in its proper sense, is a monastic practice. The *clausura* or enclosure has always been that area of the monastery, including the gardens, which was reserved for the monks or the nuns as necessary in order to preserve and foster the monastic concept of withdrawal (physical and mental) from the secular society. It prohibits egress from the monastery on the part of the religious and entrance to everyone else, with certain exceptions. It is quite proper, therefore, that all religious men or women who live in monasteries and convents ordered to the contemplative life should observe a stricter cloister.

Again, it is reserved to the proper law of each institute, based on their traditions and purposes, to determine the implications of a cloister. *ES* 32 suppressed the minor or episcopal cloister. Since then, all nuns who are engaged in any form of the active apostolate which requires external activities, if not part of their original purpose at the time of their foundation, have had to make a choice. They have had to choose whether to continue with these activities and define a cloister in their constitutions or abandon these activities and adopt a papal cloister. In some cases it has been necessary that the Apostolic See approve these determinations.

§3

This paragraph is concerned with the enforcement of the papal cloister as stated in *PC* 16 and *ES* II 30–32. It is called "papal cloister" because the norms which govern it are sanctioned by the Apostolic See. They are contained in the instruction *Venite Seorsum*, August 15, 1969. [17] This is an instance where the revised Code does not treat in the same way monks and nuns who are totally ordered to the contemplative life. Nuns are bound by the papal cloister. Monks are not bound and can determine for themselves the particulars of the cloister. In this matter the drafters of the Code were simply following the instructions given them in March 1980 at the *plenaria* of SCRIS. [18] This special treatment of nuns is also evident in the fact that the permission of the Apostolic See is required to erect a monastery of nuns (C 609, §2) or suppress an autonomous monastery of nuns (C 616, §4). *VS* demands a strict cloister that obliges all postulants, novices, and nuns so that they can not leave it except in special cases prescribed in the instruction. Those nuns not obligated by the papal cloister determine the extent of their cloister in their own proper law.

§4

This right of the bishop is not restricted. It is applicable to all monasteries of nuns, including those with a papal cloister. This paragraph is taken from *PM* 34 and now becomes part of the universal law. Moreover, the right of the diocesan bishop does not take away the right of others to enter the papal cloister. *VS* 8 permits, for example, cardinals and their attendants, apostolic delegates and nuncios in their own jurisdiction, heads of state and their wives and retinue, priests and their servers to administer the sacraments or visit the seriously ill, doctors and others whose skill is necessary to provide a service to the monastery, and others mentioned in the instruction, to enter the monastery. In general, the papal cloister prohibits anyone of whatever condition, age, or sex from entering the monastery cloister unless they have proper permission granted to them. Nuns may not leave the monastery except under the conditions stated in *VS* 7. It should be noted, however, that there is no specific penalty stated in the general law for violation of the cloister.

C 668

§1. Members are to cede the administration of their goods to whomever they prefer before first profession, and unless the constitutions state otherwise, they are freely to make disposition for their use and their revenues. Moreover, they are to draw up a will, which is also valid in civil law, at least before perpetual profession.

§2. In order to change these dispositions for a just cause and to place any act whatsoever in matters of temporal goods they need the permission of the superior who is competent according to the norm of proper law.

§3. Whatever a religious acquires through personal work or by reason of the institute is acquired for the institute. Unless it is otherwise stated in proper law those things which accrue to a religious by way of pension, subsidy or insurance in any way whatever are acquired for the institute.

§4. Those who must renounce their goods completely because of the nature of the institute are to make a renunciation before perpetual profession in a form which, if possible, is also valid in civil law and takes effect from the day of profession. Religious in perpetual vows who wish to renounce their goods either in part or totally according to the norm of proper law and with permission of the supreme moderator are to do the same thing.

§5. Professed religious who have fully renounced all their goods because of the nature of the institute lose the capacity of acquiring and possessing, and therefore invalidly place acts contrary to the vow of poverty. Moreover, those things which accrue to them after the act of renunciation belong to the institute, according to the norm of proper law.

C 668 is concerned with some of the practical implications of the vow of poverty. The vow requires that religious be essentially dependent upon their institute in regard to the use of all material and temporal goods. This canon aims to foster the common life and to regulate this basic dependency of religious upon their institute. However, because of the differences in the nature of religious institutes and the requirements of their proper law, there will be some differences in regard to the implications of the vow for members of various institutes beyond this basic dependency, which is the same for all religious.

§1

Generally, there are three things which are to be done by a novice about to make first profession of vows: (1) cede the administration of his or her possessions to another, (2) dispose of the use and revenue from these possessions, and (3) make a legal will. These requirements are not new and were contained in CIC 569.

CESSION OF ADMINISTRATION

To cede the administration of one's possessions means to select whomever one wishes to choose (and who, in turn, is willing to perform this office) and transfer to that person the duty of overseeing these possessions. The person selected may be a relative, a trusted friend, a lawyer, or the religious institute itself, which can perform this service through an agent, usually the provincial treasurer. This cession can be done informally or it can be drawn up so that it is a civilly legal document. It must be done for the period of temporary profession. For those who belong to an institute with a simple-vow tradition, it must be continued throughout the period of perpetual profession, unless the religious makes a total renunciation (C 668, §5). The purpose of the cession is to detach effectively and practically the religious from involvement with such possessions so that he or she is dependent upon the religious institute.

DISPOSITION OF INCOME

To dispose of the use and revenue means that arrangements are to be made about the income that the possessions may produce, for example, interest from investments or rent from property that is owned. The novice can give the administrator whatever instructions are desirable. They can be detailed or the whole matter can be left to the good judgment of the person fulfilling this obligation. Again, the purpose is to distance religious from their possessions and keep them from involvement with such things so that they are dependent upon their institute. It is left to the proper law of the institute to lay down any other regulations about this matter. If this restricts the right to dispose of the use and revenue, it will not be altered by the present canon.[19] Also, while the present law does not forbid a novice to renounce one's possessions before first profession, as did CIC 568 of the 1917 Code, the proper superiors ought to instruct and exhort novices not to do anything imprudent in a moment of initial fervor in the religious life.

LAST WILL

To make a last will and testament that is valid under civil law means to make a determination of one's property which becomes effective after one's death. It would be wise to have some professional legal advice about this when drafting a will. The various civil jurisdictions have different regulations about this matter. If a novice actually does have possessions, then it would be better to have a will drawn up before first profession. If the novice does not, then a will may be made at a later time. Nevertheless, one must be made before perpetual profession.

CHANGING THE DISPOSITIONS

§2

The 1917 Code in CIC 580, §3 forbid making a change in favor of giving a notable part of the property to the institute. This does not appear in the new Code. Any changes in the disposition of one's possessions or the last will and testament may be made only with the permission of the proper superior, usually the major superior. The religious may not give away, loan, invest, or alter in any way the disposition of his or her temporal goods without proper permission. Any reasonable request made by the member should be sufficient reason for the superior to grant permission. However, frequent requests for changes in the disposition of these things would appear to violate the spirit of detachment which should characterize those trying to live evangelical poverty.

COMMON GOODS

§3

Everything a religious acquires by way of gift, offering, stipend, fee, salary, pension, insurance settlement, or similar manner, belongs to the religious institute and not the individual member. This is true even if it may not be recognized by civil law. Hence, the canonical presumption will always favor the institute if there is a doubt in a particular case. Therefore, if a nursing sister is left a bequest in the will of a former patient, or if the parents of a student give a hundred-dollar gift certificate to a teaching brother, or a parishioner presents a chalice to a religious priest, these things are canonically given to the religious institute.

GIFTS OR INHERITANCES

Doubts about whether gifts are given to the individual religious or the institute will never arise concerning a religious who has perpetual vows in an institute with a solemn-vow tradition. Such religious renounce their capacity to acquire. This is not so regarding religious who are in temporary vows or belong to an institute with a simple-vow tradition who do not make a complete renunciation. Their constitutions permit them to retain the right to acquire, even though they do not have the right to the use or usufruct without the proper permission. In these cases administrators are also retained to oversee the personal property or patrimony. This patrimony can be added to by bequests of relatives and in those unusual situations where they are given gifts *intuitu personae*, that is, to them personally because of some special relationship of blood or friendship and not to them as religious. Therefore, unless the proper law of an institute states otherwise, an inheritance from a relative is presumed to be given to the individual and becomes part of that member's patrimony. Again, where there is serious doubt about the facts or the intention of the benefactor, the canonical presumption is that the gift or inheritance is given to the institute.

SMALL GIFTS

Many people offer gifts to friends in religion with the understanding that this is "just for you." However, the religious should know that the well-meant intention of such gifts does not alter the fact that these gifts belong to the community. Permission can always be requested to have the use of a gift which is given to a religious. Although each institute has its own recognized customs when it comes to the reception of small gifts on such occasions as Christmas, profession, or jubilee celebrations, it must be remembered that these gifts do belong to the institute and that the individual may be given permission only to use them. Therefore, radios or television sets used by religious, indeed the very clothing on their backs, belong to the institute and the individual member has only the use of them, even though it may be an exclusive use in some instances.

PENSIONS AND OTHER BENEFITS

In regard to pensions, social security benefits, medicaid or medicare, insurance settlements and the like, unless the proper law of the particular institute states otherwise, all belong to the institute and not the individual religious. Even though the civil law may not recognize this in certain cases, it is, nevertheless, the law of the Church and the consequence of the obligations assumed by professing public vows in a religious institute. Obviously, if religious are dispensed from their vows and leave religious life, social security benefits and the like will go directly to them and no longer to the institute. [20]

RENUNCIATION OF OWNERSHIP

§4

The first part of this paragraph refers to religious in an institute with a solemn-vow tradition. Although the canon law does not use these distinctive terms any longer, the practical implications do remain and are determined by the proper law of each institute in fidelity to its own tradition. Moreover, there is no reason why the terms can not be used in popular parlance if one chooses to do so. So when perpetual or final vows are made in an institute which requires the complete renunciation of all personal possessions and the right to acquire, this is what has been referred to as professing solemn vows. When this renunciation is made, it should be made in such a way that the civil law recognizes it. In the United States this is usually impossible. The civil law will not permit anyone to give away what is not yet possessed. Nevertheless, this fact does not alter the canonical consequences of the profession of vows in the institute.

The second part of this paragraph is concerned with religious in institutes with a simple-vow tradition. In these institutes members retain radical ownership and do not give up the right to acquire. However, if the proper law of the institute permits it, the religious may give away a part or all of his or her patrimony (the personal possessions which are overseen by the administrator) by an act of renunciation. The proper law, the constitutions or directory, may stipulate that such an act of renunciation may not be made until a certain number of years after perpetual profession. However, if the relatives of a religious are in financial need and he or she wishes to help them by giving them part of his or her patrimony, this should be permitted by the proper superior. The canon states that the supreme moderator is the proper superior. While much should be left to the discretion of the particular member desiring to make a partial or total renunciation of his or her property, and reasonable requests to do so honored, the superior should be prudent in granting these permissions.

CONSEQUENCES OF A RENUNCIATION

§5

After perpetual profession, a religious in an institute with a solemn-vow tradition loses his or her canonical capacity to own or acquire anything personally. If an attempt is made to exercise ownership, this has no standing in canon law, even though the civil law may recognize it. It would be a violation of the vow of poverty by the religious. Again, whatever a religious acquires in any manner and under any title as a member of an institute where complete renunciation is made at perpetual profession, is acquired for the institute.

In institutes with a simple-vow tradition, a religious who is permitted to make a partial or a total renunciation of his or her patrimony with the permission of the proper superior does not give up the right to own and acquire. This act of total renunciation could not be made under the stipulations of CIC 583, 1° of the 1917 Code, but is now permitted if the proper law of an institute grants this right to the members.

C 669

§1. Religious are to wear the habit of the institute made according to the norm of proper law as a sign of their consecration and as a testimony of poverty.

§2. Clerical religious of an institute which does not have its own habit are to wear clerical dress according to the norm of can. 284.

§1

Unlike CIC 596 of the 1917 Code, this canon states nothing about when a habit is to be worn. In fact, it leaves this and all other matters about the habit to be determined by the proper law of each institute. Not every institute has a habit as part of its tradition. Many have never had a habit or an identifiable garb. Some institutes were founded during periods of persecution of the Church and purposely never adopted a distinctive style of dress. Others, such as the Society of Jesus, have from their foundation simply adopted the customary clerical garb of the particular locale where they live and minister.

While the Latin term *habitus* has a long and venerable tradition, it is more accurately associated with monastic and conventual institutes than it is with the many apostolic institutes of men and women which have developed in the last two centuries.[21] These latter institutes often adopted the contemporary clerical dress if they were institutes of priests. If lay people, they chose the garb of the common folk, peasant's dress, or widow's weeds. In any case, many did not adopt a habit in the monastic sense, but a style of dress that only became uniform with the passage of time because it was not changed or adapted. During his pontificate Pope Pius XII exhorted women religious to modernize their garb. These exhortations went unheeded for the most part. It was only in the post-Vatican II years that great change took place. So much change, in fact, that the Apostolic See was concerned that institutes which had a habit as part of their patrimony were abandoning it rather than adapting it.[22]

It might be recalled that the concept of a habit does not necessarily include the wearing of a veil by women religious. It is possible to have a habit and not a veil. Some institutes of women religious wore a garb from their very foundation but never a veil. Also, the Apostolic See has stated that purely secular dress, without any recognizable sign, can be permitted by the competent superior when the habit is an impediment or obstacle in the normal exercise of activities which should be undertaken by the religious.[23] All of these issues might be resolved by considering the proper law of each institute, the expectations of the local church, the requirements of the particular culture, and the demands of the apostolate.

REASONS FOR A DISTINCTIVE GARB

The canon gives the purpose of a religious habit as (1) a sign of consecration and (2) a testimony to poverty. There is no doubt that the intent of the canon and its underlying presupposition is that religious, at least in the apostolate, ought to be identifiable and to dress simply. *PC* 17 stated that "since they are signs of a consecrated life, religious habits should be simple and modest, at once poor and becoming. They should meet the requirements of health and be suited to the circumstances of time and place as well as to the service required by those who wear them."

Experience has showed how difficult it is to dress appropriately for every occasion. This often requires an extensive wardrobe which must be frequently changed as styles change. To do this is expensive and time-consuming. Adopting a simple garb that is modest and dignified can resolve a multitude of practical problems for religious who are called to witness detachment and a spirit of poverty. Again, this does not imply that it must be worn all of the time.

Religious life has a public dimension to it, and some form of distinctive dress has a value from this perspective. Generally people in service roles wear some distinctive dress in that capacity so that they can be recognized by the public. It is interesting to note that there was a suggestion made to change this canon to read: "Religious should wear a specific sign of their institute. . . ." but this was rejected by the Secretary of the Pontifical Commission for the Revision of the Code, referring to the conciliar quote above as well as to *ET* 22, the *Notification* of February 24, 1972 and the *circular letter* of SCRIS, July 10, 1972. [24] Since the debate over this issue is not very intense in many parts of the world, this made it difficult to alter the canon and the customary expectations in this regard.

§2

This reference to C 284 addresses the compliance which is expected of clergy with respect to clerical attire as stipulated by the episcopal conference and local custom. (It is noteworthy that the Latin expression in C 284 is that clerics wear a *decentem habitum ecclesiasticum. Habitus* is not translated as habit, but as garb or dress.) The clerical members of a religious institute which does not have its own garb, such as the Society of Jesus, are expected to adopt the recognized style of clerical dress in the local church where they live and minister. Again, while the clergy are expected to wear the cassock, clerical collar, and suit, or whatever is stipulated or customary, they are not expected to wear it all of the time. There will be occasions, such as periods of recreation, where it may be inappropriate or unreasonable to expect it to be worn. The instruction given the clergy and religious of the Diocese of Rome addresses this issue and makes it clear that appropriate clerical dress should be worn for liturgical celebrations, administration of the sacraments, for preaching, and in the ambit of the pastoral ministry.[25]

C 670

An institute must furnish for its members all those things which are necessary according to the norm of the constitutions for achieving the purpose of their vocation.

Many canons are concerned with the obligations of religious and their essential dependence upon their institute. For example, religious should observe a common life as understood and practiced in the institute (CC 608 and 665, §1). Religious must obey their superiors according to the proper law of the institute (CC 601 and 671). They may not have the use of things without proper permission because their vow of poverty makes them dependent upon their institute and its superiors in the disposition of material things (C 600). Whatever they acquire as religious, they acquire for the institute (C 668, §3). The present canon, therefore, expresses the reciprocal obligation of the institute to care for its members.

Since religious are completely dependent upon their institutes, the proper authorities within the institute are obliged to see that the individual members are adequately cared for, especially regarding the necessities of life. Certainly this includes food, clothing, and a roof over their heads. Religious are to receive proper medical attention when required. Wise provision should be made by the institute to care for the sick, the elderly, and the incapacitated members. The proper law of the institute will determine the type of intellectual and spiritual formation for the members, as well as the training and formal education which will prepare them for the life and apostolate in which they will engage. Generally, there is the well-established practice of institutes to provide periods of relaxation and vacation for the members, even though there is no right in universal law to have an annual vacation. However, it would seem, if this is a recognized practice in an institute, every member should have the opportunity to do so. The common life would require that the same be stated about jubilee trips and similarly recognized customs and practices in the institute. All the members should be given the same opportunities and receive the same reasonable consideration.

It must be remembered that Church law, community regulations, and practices cannot take the place of charity, reasonableness, and common sense. While there may be no canonical right for religious to select their own physicians, dentists, and professional help, a certain amount of mature freedom and discretion should be recognized in this matter, unless in individual cases there is evident abuse. Sometimes it will be the obligation of the proper superiors to intervene and obtain the professional care that may be necessary for the religious, as may be the case in helping a member who is addicted or evidencing emotional problems.

It is the responsibility of the institute to care for these members. It is not the responsibility or obligation of their relatives or friends. Religious superiors should be sensitive to the human dimensions in such situations when they have to consider the feelings of relatives and friends of a sick religious as well as the individual religious.

Conversely, there are occasions when a member will feel obligated to help care for a sick, elderly, or incapacitated relative. These delicate issues are not covered by canon law but by charity and reasonableness. Although the religious has no canonical right to demand to be given time for this purpose, permission should be granted for such reasonable requests. Almost always, institutes have manifested charity, magnanimity, and sensitivity when it came to caring for the relatives of its members.

C 671

A religious is not to accept duties and offices outside the institute without the permission of the legitimate superior.

Membership in a religious institute tends by its nature to be an all-encompassing style of Christian life. Celibate religious must build new relationships with their brothers or sisters in a common life. Vowed evangelical poverty means ultimate material dependence upon the institute. The nature and purpose of the institute defines the perimeters of the activities in which the individual may engage. The private and public lives of religious will converge, more or less, because the religious life involves the whole person. It is impossible to think that a religious can give only part of him or herself and be faithful to the demands of this consecrated life. Religious give up the freedom to make choices independently of the institute concerning what they will do or not do, what they have or won't have, where they will live or not live. Ascetically, religious abandon themselves to the Lord in their response to an ecclesial vocation.

Most institutes have made radical changes in the manner in which assignments are made for individual religious since the reforms of Vatican II. Cultural and ecclesial alterations have allowed institutes to manifest a greater sensitivity toward the individual members and to recognize their personal talents and gifts. This rediscovery has promoted individual and corporate discernment practices in the approach to the specification of duties, responsibilities, and assignments. A one-sided and authoritarian approach to government and obedience, to a significant extent, has been discarded in most religious institutes. Today, religious superiors attempt to implement processes by which appropriate attention is given to the desires, charisms, and talents of the individual, as well as to the needs of the institute and the demands of the apostolate. Less and less frequently do religious find themselves forced to be square pegs in round holes.

OPENNESS TO "BEING SENT"

However, any process through which religious have a mature and responsible role to play in their own assignments, duties and offices—in or outside of the institute—must recognize that the final decision belongs to the religious superior in accordance with the proper law of the institute. Religious must leave themselves open to the experience of "being sent." When this is impossible in an institute, then one may question whether the vow of obedience is possible in that institute.[26]

Therefore, every institute has the right to expect the availability of its members and to control essentially the commitment which individual members wish to make of their time and talent. This is not intended to inhibit the generosity of the members nor the movement of the Spirit. But it is meant to channel talents within the context of the institute and its own charisms and purposes and to recognize and confirm the movements of the Spirit. It is within this context that a religious professes to live his or her dedicated life of prayer and service. Therefore, a member is not free to accept duties and offices outside the institute. All commitments of one's time and talent must be made under the aegis of religious obedience. The proper religious superior has the right and duty to pass judgment on these. Good communication between members and the superior is necessary so that reasonableness and sensitivity are promoted in making these determinations.

C 672

Religious are bound by the prescriptions of cann. 277, 285, 286, 287 and 289, and, moreover, religious clerics are bound by the prescriptions of can. 279, §2; in lay institutes of pontifical right, the permission mentioned in can. 285, §4 can be granted by the proper major superior.

This canon specifies certain obligations which bind both the clergy and religious. These have to do with activities which are prohibited, for the most part, to both religious and clergy because of the public nature of their commitment and service in the Church. Religious life has a close link with the hierarchical apostolate and there is a special relationship which binds religious life to the pastoral responsibilities of the Church. [27] Therefore, throughout the history of the Church there has been a certain consistency in the tenor of these prohibitions, although the particular culture, time, and place have helped determine them. They have been manifested in the exhortations and instructions of popes, bishops, and councils, as well as in the regulations, decrees, and laws of the Church, that religious and clergy are to refrain from engagement in certain activities that are considered to be generally inappropriate, unbecoming or foreign to the gospel ministry.

The 1917 Code treated this matter in CIC 592, 139, 141, and 142. Some of the specific activities are no longer in the present law. For example, there is no mention about engaging in clamorous hunting with hounds, which always seemed quaint and foreign to our culture, but was not so if considered in the text of a late nineteenth century European situation. Also, no longer is there any prohibition concerning medicine and surgery as prohibited activities. Again, times have changed and the missionary endeavors of the Church have often required such expertise.

PROTECTING A CELIBATE COMMITMENT

C 277 is concerned with the implications of a chaste and celibate commitment. Religious are required to be prudent and to avoid associations with persons which would endanger their chastity or occasion scandal for the faithful. The diocesan bishop does have the legal right to enact specific regulations for his diocese which would oblige the religious there as well as the clergy. Also, he has the right to pass judgment on particular cases. If these concern a religious, it would be expected that the bishop would fully involve the appropriate religious superior.

ACTIVITIES ALIEN TO THE RELIGIOUS LIFE

C 285, §1 and §2 states that religious are also obliged to avoid those things which are unbecoming to their state and observe the particular laws that determine such activities. Even if not unbecoming, they are to be avoided if they are alien to the religious life. Again, much will be determined by the particular time, place, and culture. The classical example of an unbecoming activity for clergy and religious was that of being a tavern keeper or bartender. [28] However, there are many activities which are perfectly legitimate but would seem to be out of place for a religious, for example, a religious being an officer of the law, a flight attendant, an employee of the sanitation department, a salesperson in a department store, etc. Much has to be left to the good judgment, common sense, and prudence of people. Certainly, in particular cases, a religious is obliged to follow the directives of religious and ecclesiastical superiors.

PUBLIC CIVIL OFFICE

C 285, §3 forbids religious to assume any public office which involves the exercise of civil authority. Examples of such offices would be those of an attorney general, a mayor, a governor, or similar positions. It should be noted that the canon has been changed since the 1980 draft which indicated who could grant permission. It appears that in doing this the intent is to tighten the canon and make exceptions to it more extraordinary. Religious are to undertake an apostolate that is in accordance with their constitutions and the charism of their institute. Generally, this will exclude public civil positions because religious are at the service of people as heralds of the gospel in the name of the Church.

SECULAR FINANCIAL RESPONSIBILITIES

According to C 285, §4, religious are not to undertake, without the proper permission, the management of property owned by laity or assume secular offices which require financial accountability. Permission may be granted when necessary by the major superiors of pontifical institutes. In the case of diocesan right institutes, both the major superior and the local ordinary of the generalate need to grant permission. This canon is a protection for religious who should avoid such involvement unless necessary. For · example, a religious may be obliged to manage the affairs of an elderly or incapacitated parent, or a specific apostolate may demand that a religious assume such responsibilities for a time. Each case should be examined on its own merits and the proper superior should be aware of the civil and legal implications before granting the permission, especially if a considerable amount of money is involved. Also, without consulting the proper authority, religious must not assume the obligation of acting as surety or paying debts in case a debtor fails to do so. They should not sign promissory notes by which they assume the obligation of paying a certain amount of money for an undetermined reason. This, especially, presents a problem for religious because of their vow of poverty. Great prudence must be exercised in these matters.

BUSINESS AND TRADE

C 286 prohibits religious from engaging in business and trade, personally or through others, for their own benefit or that of others, without permission of the ecclesiastical authorities. This means that permission is required of the major superior and the appropriate ecclesiastical authority. Necessity may require a religious who inherits a large business to make sure it is properly administered until disposition can be made of it. Or a poor school may have to sell products produced by the students to maintain itself. Certainly, cloistered and contemplative religious have supported themselves customarily by selling products made by the monks or nuns such as wine, bread, altar furnishings, cheese, etc. Such traditional activity is not proscribed by this canon. Nor is the presence of a religious book or goods store at a shrine or religious house prohibited. Moreover, there would seem to be many exceptions to the general prohibition. In fact, this canon states expressly that permission can be given to engage in some form of trade or business, unlike CIC 142 or the 1917 Code. Care should be taken so that the civil law regulations are observed and that taxes are paid to the government on unrelated income.

POLITICAL AND TRADE UNION INVOLVEMENT

C 287 states that religious are greatly obliged to foster peace and concord based on justice among people. They are forbidden to take an active role in political parties or in the management of labor unions, unless in the judgment of the proper ecclesiastical authorities this is required for the protection of the Church or the promotion of the common good. It would seem that the prophetic dimension of religious life demands that they stand apart and be critical of the limitations of all political movements. [29] They are not to be "of a party." They are to be concerned with fostering peace and justice as agents of reconciliation, not division. This will preclude, ordinarily, their direct involvement in partisan politics where divisions are inevitable. When permission is requested, it is given not only by the proper religious superior, but also by ecclesiastical authority. This could be not only the local Ordinary but the SCRIS as well. The Church has discouraged all such involvement because priests and religious are not social or political figures or officials of a temporal power. They should be recognized as servants of Christ and stewards of the mysteries of God. [30]

MILITARY SERVICE AND CIVIL EXEMPTIONS

C 289 states that religious are not to volunteer for military service and that they should take advantage of all exemptions granted by the civil authorities so that they be freed from such service and any other public or civil duty that is foreign to the religious life. In particular cases the proper religious superior and the ecclesiastical authority can decide otherwise. While this canon is not concerned with the ministry of religious as chaplains, it is concerned with all other forms of military service. Also, the canon urges religious to take advantage of civil exemptions for such things as serving as a juror in criminal trials or litigations because it is inappropriate that they be in a position of condemning people or deciding upon their civil guilt.[31]

POST-ORDINATION STUDIES

Religious priests are obligated by C 279, §2, which requires them to follow the prescriptions of particular law concerning post-ordination studies. Priests are to attend pastoral lectures, theological meetings, and conferences which give them the opportunity to acquire a deeper knowledge of the sacred sciences and pastoral methods. Therefore, diocesan regulations concerning these matters bind religious as well as diocesan priests. These would apply especially to those engaged in pastoral activities in the local church.

NOTES

1. *ET* 1–2.
2. Miriam Cerletty, "Some Practical Helps for the Development of Constitutions," *StudCan* 14 (1980) 155–70; David F. O'Connor, "Some Observations on Revised Constitutions," *RfR* 39 (1979) 771–79, and "Constitutions and the Revised Code of Canon Law," 42 (1983) 506–13.
3. *LG* 43; C 576.
4. *ET* 42–45.
5. SCRIS, *CDR* (March 1980) 4.
6. *SC* 10; *LG* 11; *PC* 6; *ET* 47–48.
7. Message of John Paul II to SCRIS, March 7, 1980, *ConLife* 5 (1982) 8–9.
8. *ET* 45–46; *CDR* 13.
9. *CDR* 12.
10. *CDR* 13.
11. SCRIS, *DC* (December 8, 1970) *AAS* 63, 318.
12. *CDR* 10.

13. *ConLife* 2 (1978) 166.

14. *ET* 31–41.

15. *VS* 10–11.

16. *ET* 35.

17. See *CLD* 7 (1975) 538–41.

18. *ConLife* 6 (1982) 5–124.

19. *CLD* 1 (1934) 304.

20. *ConLife* 2 (1978) 152–53; 170–73; 5 (1982) 104.

21. Jean-Claude Guy, "Religious Costume Yesterday and Today," *Supplement to The Way* 4 (1967) 66–77.

22. *CLD* 7 (1975) 534–35.

23. Dinn, M. J., Tessier, L., Courneene, E., *Canonical Documents on Consecrated Life 1963-1976*, Ottawa: St. Paul University (1977) 367–68.

24. John A. Alesandro, "Religious in the Church: A Look at the New Code of Canon Law," *Proceedings, Sixteenth National Assembly of Vicars for Religious*, Wheeling, W. V. (March 29–April 1, 1982) 57.

25. Directive from Cardinal Ugo Poletti, Vicar General of the Diocese of Rome, October 1, 1982, *Crux of the News*, (November 1, 1982).

26. George Aschenbrenner, "Prayer, Mission, Obedience," *Supplement to The Way* (1980) 50–61.

27. SCRIS, "Religious and Human Promotion," *CLD* 9 (1983) 379–410.

28. See Bouscaren, Ellis, Korth *Canon Law* (1963) 118.

29. SCRIS, "The Prophetic Role of Religious in the Promotion of Human Progress," *ConLife* 4 (1980) 416–29.

30. See Address of John Paul II, *OssRomEng*, February 17, 1981, 6; David F. O'Connor, "Religious in Politics," *RfR* 41 (1982) 834–48.

31. Joseph Betz, "A Sister in the Jury Box," *RfR* 41 (1982) 849–52.

BIBLIOGRAPHY

Alesandro, J. "Religious in the Church: A Look at the New Code of Canon Law," *Proceedings: Sixteenth National Assembly of Vicars for Religious* (March 29-April 1982) Wheeling, W.V., 23–60.

Aschenbrenner, G. "Prayer, Mission and Obedience," *Supplement to The Way* (1980) 50–61.

Betz, J. "A Sister in the Jury Box," *RfR* 41 (1980) 849–52.

Cerletty, M. "Some Practical Helps for the Development of Constitutions," *StudCan* 14 (1980) 155–70.

Guy, J-C. "Religious Costume Yesterday and Today," *Supplement to The Way* (1967) 66–77.

O'Connor, D. "Some Observations on Revised Constitutions," *RfR* 39 (1979) 771–79.

O'Connor, D. "Religious in Politics,"*RfR* 41 (1982) 834–48.

O'Connor, D. "Constitutions and the Revised Code of Canon Law," *RfR* 42 (1983) 506–13.
O'Connor, D. "What Does a Religious Institute Owe Its Members?" *RfR* 43 (1984) 558–66.
Pennington, G. "Venite Seorsum—An Evaluation," *StudCan* 5 (1971) 245–57.
Said, M. "Particular Law of Institutes in the Renewal of Consecrated Life," *RfR* 36 (1977) 313–35.
SCRIS "The Prophetic Role of Religious in Promotion of Human Progress," *ConLife* 4 (1980) 416–29.

The Apostolate of Institutes
Canons 673–683

RICHARD A. HILL, S.J.

This chapter, as a distinct section or grouping of norms, is entirely new in the Code of Canon Law and did not appear in the 1917 Code as a distinct section.[1] It deserves, therefore, some comment in its own right. The 1917 Code never employed the terms apostolate or apostolic works, but spoke instead of ministry or sacred ministry, which were applicable only to those who had been ordained, and works *(opera)* or pious works, which were applicable to both lay persons and clergy.

Prior to the mid-nineteenth century the expression "apostolate" was reserved in ecclesiastical terminology to the hierarchy and by participation extended to presbyters. As lay persons, however, especially the members of the newly founded and canonically recognized lay congregations, were increasingly clearly seen as sharing in the task of building up the Body of Christ and spreading the Kingdom of God, they began to be said to participate in or assist with the hierarchical apostolate. But widespread use of these expressions and their recognition by use in official ecclesiastical documents did not emerge until after the 1917 Code was promulgated. It was Pope Pius XI who first began to speak of lay apostolic works, but he tended to identify this with Catholic Action, which was always viewed, at least popularly, with considerable suspicion, especially outside Italy. The struggle between the Church and the fascist government of Italy preoccupied the final decade of Pius XI's pontificate. It remained for Pope Pius XII, beginning with the encyclical *Mystici Corporis Christi* in 1943 and concluding with his addresses to the First and Second World Congress of the Lay Apostolate in 1951 and 1957, to broaden the meaning of apostolate when predicated of laity, to recognize it as deriving from baptism and confirmation and not solely from a mandate of and in close dependence upon the hierarchy, and to liberate it from the popular ideas which tended to obscure it.

Vatican Council II definitively embraced the expression "apostolate" as fully applicable and belonging to laity as well as clergy by promulgating the Decree on the Apostolate of the Laity and by employing the expression in practically all of its other documents. The council described the apostolate as all activity of the Mystical Body directed to the attainment of the goal of spreading the Kingdom of Christ everywhere. [2] This apostolate should be carried forward by every member of the Church because the vocation to be a Christian is itself the vocation to the apostolate. [3] Religious, therefore, must also share in the apostolate of the Church by reason of their own commitment in baptism and confirmation, which is not lost or stifled by their religious profession.

The 1983 Code appears, however, precisely at a time when the word "apostolate" seems to be fading from Catholic vocabulary, at least in North America, if not everywhere in the English-speaking world, and to be in the process of replacement by the word "ministry," which, as it is being presently used by many, seems to connote the same reality as "apostolate," but appears to add the notion of a more stable and official role or function in the Church. There is a growing corpus of literature on this subject and it may eventuate that, similar to the expression "apostolate," ministry will find acceptance in official Catholic vocabulary. If and when this is perceived as a reality throughout the Church, it should find its way into official documents and thus appear in the canonical lexicon.

This has not yet happened, and consequently the Council and the Code do not substitute ministry for apostolate. Only in the case of lay men does the Code recognize a formal and stable commission of ministry, that of lector and that of acolyte. [4] In Catholic teaching the ministers of the sacrament of matrimony are the bride and groom, although the law does not speak that way. To be sure, other lay persons, in the absence of the appropriate minister, can be and are deputed to fulfill some of the functions of ministers by exercising the ministry of the Word, by presiding at liturgical prayers, by administering baptism and by distributing Holy Communion. [5] The difficulty of canonical language and its meaning when speaking of extraordinary ministers exceeds the scope of the present commentary, touching, as it does, on the distinction between possessing a ministry and exercising it either in extraordinary circumstances or by special mandate. Extraordinary ministers cannot be called upon unless ordinary ministers are absent or impeded.

None of this, however, implies that the increasingly popular use of the expression "ministry" is mistaken or inappropriate. Patience may be needed now and again until the meaning becomes clear.

Turning now to the apostolate of religious institutes, it may first be noted that this chapter addresses only institutes as such, with two exceptions which will be noted in the relevant places, and not apostolic works of individual religious apart from the corporate apostolic works of their institutes. The apostolate in question here is corporate. The law is aware of the need and the fact that individual religious engage in apostolic works other than those which are proper to or committed to their institutes. [6]

This chapter offers a good example of the use of conciliar language and principles in articulating the law and of the incorporation of post-conciliar implementational norms into the codified law. Of its eleven canons only one, which will be noted below, does not derive in whole or at least in significant part from the conciliar documents. For this reason those who study or consult these canons should also be familiar with the sources from which they principally derive and which provide a more ample context for them. [7]

Finally, before discussing the individual canons of chapter V, it is worthwhile to call to mind certain provisions incorporated elsewhere in the Code which are part of the context within which these canons should be interpreted and applied. They are:

1) the just autonomy of life, especially of governance, which every institute enjoys in the Church (C 586).
2) the subjection of every institute to the highest authority in the Church (C 590), which also extends to internal governance and discipline (C 593).
3) the much more extensive role of the diocesan bishop with respect to institutes of diocesan right and autonomous houses (CC 594, 595, 615, and *passim*).
4) the right which religious have to carry on the apostolic works proper to their respective institutes (CC 611, §2, 2° and 612).

C 673

The apostolate of all religious consists first in their witness of a consecrated life which they are bound to foster by prayer and penance.

The statement made in this introductory canon highlights the doctrinal position of Vatican Council II that the principal or foundational ecclesial role of religious is their witness or testimony to the holiness of the Church and that consequently their primary obligation is to cultivate this holiness in themselves by prayer and penance. [8] By offering a broad, general statement of that which primarily constitutes apostolate for religious as such, it contextualizes the norms which follow, especially in the next two canons.

C 674

Institutes which are wholly ordered to contemplation always retain a distinguished position in the mystical Body of Christ: for they offer an extraordinary sacrifice of praise to God, they illuminate the people of God with the richest fruits of their sanctity, they move it by their example, and extend it through their hidden apostolic fruitfulness. For this reason, however much the needs of the active apostolate demand it, members of these institutes cannot be summoned to aid in various pastoral ministries.

After enunciating the general principle in the first canon of this chapter, that all religious share in the apostolate of the Church primarily by the testimony of their lives, the Code here distinguishes between institutes which are wholly ordered to contemplation in this canon and those committed to the works of the apostolate in the next canon. Contemplative institutes are said, in the language of the Council,[9] to occupy a conspicuous place in the mystical body and that in four ways: by offering a preeminent sacrifice of praise to God; by enriching the People of God with the choicest blessings of holiness; by inspiring the Church by their example of prayer, penance, silence and sacrifice; and by contributing to the growth of the Church by their hidden apostolic fruitfulness. In this way these institutes can properly be said to share in the apostolate of the whole Church and of a particular church in a unique and indispensable way, so much so that their members cannot in any circumstances be pressed into service in the pastoral ministry.[10]

The second sentence of the canon, which provides the specifically juridic element which should be found in every statute, is a conclusion from the first. The subject of this normative provision is the members of exclusively contemplative institutes rather than the institutes themselves, thus affirming the right of these religious to pursue their vocation without any diversion to external works of the apostolate even within their own monasteries. It also precludes any diversion of the institute itself, e.g., this monastery or convent, to apostolic activity, whether by bishops or by the religious themselves, because this would imply a permanent or very long-term modification of the purpose and nature of the institute. Even the most pressing need of the pastoral office, therefore, does not constitute the truly necessary reason for a member to leave the cloister, as mentioned in C 667, §4.

This canon is not addressed to those institutes which by rule or by healthy tradition combine the contemplative life and at least its principal choral observances with apostolic work, e.g., schools or hospitals; they are addressed in the following canon.[11] There are, however, some monasteries, especially of nuns, which, because of circumstances beyond their control, such as persecution or critical economic necessity, have been compelled to take up apostolic work in order to survive, e.g., teaching, nursing, retreats. Neither by rule nor by long tradition has apostolic endeavor of this kind become integral to their way of life. The challenge of renewal for them and for the ecclesial community in which they find themselves is either to find a way to return to the exclusively contemplative life or to integrate the changed circumstances harmoniously with their life of prayer and penance. In the latter case they have to reduce the tension which they experience as a result of the effort to combine truly disparate elements; in the former case the Church will have to come to their assistance.

C 675

§1. In institutes dedicated to works of the apostolate, apostolic action pertains to their very nature. Hence, the whole life of members is to be imbued with an apostolic spirit, indeed the whole apostolic action is to be informed by a religious spirit.

§2. Apostolic action is always to proceed from an intimate union with God, and it is to confirm and foster that union.

§3. Apostolic action, to be exercised in the name and by the mandate of the Church, is to be carried out in its communion.

This canon of three paragraphs turns to the only other generic form of religious life presently known in the Church, institutes committed to the works of the apostolate. It seems good to begin by referring to the first draft of the canons on institutes of consecrated life. As is well known that document was concerned to distinguish different kinds of religious institutes and to describe them in detail. Of all the aspects of that draft it was this which was most universally criticized. The promulgated Code addresses religious institutes as such and minimizes the differences among them.

This canon introduces the legislation of the remainder of the chapter by underscoring the bipolar nature of apostolic institutes, their essentially religious character, and their relationship to the hierarchical structure of the Church precisely by reason of their apostolic nature. §1 is taken almost verbatim from *PC* 8, stressing that apostolic work is an essential, not incidental, dimension of the nature of such institutes.

This conciliar statement is by no means new; it is deeply rooted in the tradition of the Church and has always been viewed as foundational in institutes founded for apostolic purposes. In practice, however, it has never been easy to maintain the equilibrium and mutuality of apostolic action and the observance of the evangelical counsels, serious and persevering prayer and genuine community life: the whole way of living and working which has been traditionally identified as specifically religious. The two poles have to exist and interact in creative tension.

§2 and §3 are also derived from *PC* 8. §2 identifies union with God as the source and root of apostolic effectiveness and it is for this reason that it should be nurtured and strengthened. Growing union with God is discerned precisely in a deeper faith which sheds its own light on the circumstances within which apostolic enterprises are carried out, in a more energetic hope and confidence that the Spirit of God is at work, and in a stronger love of God and of every human person in God which sustains and energizes what the members of apostolic institutes undertake in order to build the Kingdom of the Father. Without the conscious and consistent cultivation of union with the Lord, the religious becomes a technician, perhaps an excellent technician, relying more and more exclusively on personality and skills in what is of its nature a mysterious undertaking.

§3 states a broad, general principle and reflects the conciliar teaching in a summary manner. [12] It introduces the remainder of this chapter. The apostolic activity of religious institutes is of necessity ecclesial activity. In order to be such it has to be carried on in the name of the Church, which means that it is explicitly Catholic and constitutes part of the broader apostolic effort of the Church. It must also be exercised with the mandate of the Church, which implies that it is approved by competent ecclesial authority and is not a purely private initiative, and throughout the course of an apostolic enterprise communion with the Church must be maintained.

Communion with the Church is defined in C 205 as being joined with Christ in the visible organization of his Church by the bonds of faith, the sacraments, and ecclesiastical governance. As the Council says, "Union with those whom the Holy Spirit has assigned to rule the Church of God is an essential element of Christian apostolate." [13] This clearly implies that any apostolic work should be coordinated with the other apostolic undertakings within the particular church under the guidance of the bishop. [14]

The mandate of the Church to engage in various apostolic works, however, derives from more than one source. The canonical erection of a particular religious institute through the approval of its constitutions provides the original mandate given to it to engage in the kinds of activities which constitute its very purpose. The permission of a diocesan bishop to establish a house within the diocese carries with it the right to engage in the works which are proper to the institute. [15] Any subsequent change in the apostolic works of a house, which requires the consent of the bishop, implies a new charge or permission to engage in the new work.[16] Finally, the approval of the appropriate religious superiors of the community is certainly part of the mandate of the Church.

C 676

Lay institutes, whether of men or women, share in the pastoral office of the Church through spiritual and corporal works of mercy and offer the most diverse services to men and women; therefore they are to persevere faithfully in the grace of their vocation.

This canon speaks of lay institutes as such, whether they be of men or of women, and is essentially a paraphrase of *LG* 46 and of *PC* 10. These institutes as a whole have as their special apostolate the spiritual and corporal works of mercy and, because the Church is always in need of such apostolic efforts, they are directed to continue to provide the People of God with these various services.[17]

There is no parallel canon in this chapter concerning clerical institutes because by definition clerical institutes are those which assume the exercise of sacred orders and an additional canon in this chapter would have been redundant because of C 588, §2.

C 677

§1. Superiors and members are faithfully to retain the mission and works proper to the institute; nevertheless they are to accommodate these prudently to the needs of times and places, including the use of new and appropriate means.

§2. Moreover, if they have associations of the Christian faithful related to them, institutes are to assist them with special care so that they are imbued with a genuine spirit of their family.

§1

The principal conciliar source of §1 is *PC* 20. Whereas the Council addressed institutes themselves, the present text addresses the superiors and the members as being responsible to maintain or continue the works proper to each religious institute. This is a specific application of the frequently cited C 578 concerning the patrimony of each community which must be preserved intact. The conciliar source, however, makes it clear that apostolic works which today are less compatible with the spirit and authentic character of the institute should be set aside. For example, if a congregation of women were to have among its proper apostolic works, determined by the founder herself, the education of the daughters of the aristocracy, it might prudently judge that this is no longer an appropriate apostolate for its own sake, but that it should be changed to the education of youth in general. Similarly a community of brothers might judge that training chefs is no longer compatible with its spirit as this has developed during the past century.

The paragraph calls for basic fidelity to the kinds of apostolic work elected by the founders or introduced in the course of time by way of sound traditions, but it also requires on-going critical assessment of the forms and the means of carrying them out. The founders and their original companions were obviously concerned about the needs of the Church and of society which actually confronted them and these decisively conditioned their choices and the way they expressed them. This was especially the case when religious communities were born out of widespread crises in the Church or came into existence as a result of very specific and even localized needs. What has to be done is to discern within the specific choices of the founders or of subsequent modifications the apostolic motivation or intent and then to translate that core value into contemporary forms to meet contemporary needs. This is especially necessary for communities which were established to meet social needs which have since become the primary concern of civil agencies or have even ceased to exist.

An important distinction is made in *ES* I 29.1 and .2 and in this paragraph[18] between works which are proper to an institute and those apostolic works which are entrusted to it by ecclesiastical authority, usually by a diocesan bishop. The canonical norms for these two kinds of apostolic activity are somewhat different.

An apostolic work is proper to or belongs to an institute if it was undertaken by the founder and the original members or was subsequently introduced for special reasons and eventually came to be part of the patrimony of the institute. In either case the kind of work is found in the constitutions. These are the works which religious have the right to engage in according to C 611, 2°, unless limiting conditions have been agreed upon at the time the institute established a house in a specific place, and are mentioned in the document of consent signed by the diocesan bishop or by his delegate.

Thus, when a religious community has been invited into a diocese by a bishop to establish a secondary school, presuming that education is an apostolic enterprise proper to it, the authority or power of the bishop with respect to that school is subject to certain limitations. This is what is meant by an apostolic work proper to the institute; it belongs to the community (even if it does not own the property or the buildings). If, however, the same religious institute is also asked to staff a parochial elementary school or a diocesan high school, every aspect of this apostolic work is subject to the authority of the diocesan bishop normally exercised through departments of his curia or office. This work is said to be committed to, not proper to, the religious institute.

This paragraph, furthermore, cannot be interpreted to mean that there is an obligation on the part of the institute to maintain faithfully each and every specific institutional embodiment of apostolic works proper to it. C 616 makes that clear. It addresses rather the continuing inclusion within its foundational or traditional patrimony of certain kinds of enterprises as corporate apostolates. Attention to employing new and apt means may very well indicate that this or that institutional commitment should be abandoned in order to take up more needed and more effective efforts.

§2

§2 addresses a special relationship which exists between some religious institutes and associations of the faithful who are not themselves religious, which provide their members the opportunity of living more intense spiritual lives molded by the spirituality characteristic of the religious institutes. The third orders affiliated with the mendicant orders are examples of such associations and there are many others as well. [19] It is an important aspect of the apostolic outreach of the religious communities to provide formation and spiritual direction in their own spirituality for these associations, not only for the benefit of their members but also to extend their own apostolic effectiveness through the members of the associations to the society in which they live and work. This paragraph pertains to the purpose of this canon because this concern for related associations is a traditional dimension of the apostolate of these religious institutes which the Church values and wishes to nurture. [20]

C 678

§1. Religious are subject to the authority of bishops, whom they are obliged to follow with devoted humility and respect, in those matters which involve the care of souls, the public exercise of divine worship and other works of the apostolate.

§2. In exercising an external apostolate, religious are also subject to their own superiors and must remain faithful to the discipline of the institute, which obligation bishops themselves should not fail to insist upon in cases which warrant it.

§3. In organizing the works of the apostolate of religious, it is necessary that diocesan bishops and religious superiors proceed after consultation with each other.

With this canon the chapter turns away from what might be called the internal concerns of apostolic institutes to their relationship to the Church as a whole. It treats of the dual ecclesial authority involved when members of these institutes engage in the apostolic undertakings of the Church, the bishops, and the religious superiors, concluding with the relationship which should exist between bishops and superiors. It is conciliar in origin [21] and is best understood in light of the Council's position regarding the preeminent role of the bishop in the diocese, especially in coordinating all apostolic initiatives with a view to unity and effectiveness.

§1

§1 derives substantially from CD 35.4, the obligation of religious to show deference and respect for bishops occurring in 35.1. [22] The care of souls *(cura animarum)* is a classic canonical expression, describing in a general way the parochial office, that is, the multiple ways in which the pastor and those who assist him minister to the community of the Christian faithful, which is a parish. [23] This is the pastoral care spoken of throughout the norms for parishes, pastors, and parochial vicars (CC 515–552), which is also ascribed to certain kinds of chaplains (CC 564–572). [24] The expression care of souls is not technically applied to persons other than priests, although deacons and lay persons can participate in its exercise, [25] and it is not used of the spiritual and temporal works of mercy. Schools, hospitals, centers of social apostolate, etc. are not included in this concept.

The public exercise of divine worship requires some explanation. Divine worship will include, but reach beyond, strictly liturgical worship to embrace what is commonly called paraliturgical worship. Liturgical worship, including the celebration of the sacraments, funerals, the liturgy of the hours, blessings, religious profession, is of its nature an action of Christ and his Church regardless of the circumstances in which it is carried out. For this reason the Council states that "liturgical actions are not private actions." [26] This paragraph deliberately employs the much broader concept of divine worship.

It also implicitly distinguishes between the public exercise of worship and the non-public or private exercise of worship. Of its nature private, individual, or small-group worship does not pertain to the external forum of Church governance and for this reason is not said to be subject to the power of the bishops. To the extent, however, to which worship involves many people, is open indiscriminately to all, or is known by many, it is public and is the object of regulation and supervision by the bishops, either individually or through their conferences.

While it is clear that strictly liturgical celebrations, such as the celebration of the sacraments, fall under the authority of the bishops if they are carried out in a public manner, questions can be raised regarding worship which is not technically liturgical, for example, a penance service which does not include the celebration of the sacrament, a wake service, or the recitation of a modified liturgy of the hours apart from the canonical choral celebration. In such cases, provided that they are public, the authority of the bishop would not extend beyond a requirement that the celebration conform to Catholic teaching and be reverently carried out.

What has just been said implicitly includes the private, i.e., non-public, celebration of the liturgy itself, and this too requires further explanation. The bishops, especially the conferences of bishops, have an important role to play in the actual design of the liturgy and the conferences have been especially active in this regard during the past fifteen years and can be in the future. Individual bishops have little practical discretion in actually shaping the liturgical rites themselves; their principal function is to promote good liturgy in their dioceses and to supervise its celebration. Religious, like all other Christian faithful, are obligated to celebrate the liturgy in conformity with its laws, whether they be universal, regional (national), or local. This obligation exists on the part of all regardless of whether the celebration is actually public or private or is, in the case of the celebration of the Eucharist, completely individual with no other person present. In this sense every celebration of the liturgy is subject to the authority of the bishops, but only in this sense.

A bishop, however, has no way of exercising his authority when the celebration of divine worship, even of liturgical worship, is in fact private without violating the legitimate autonomy and privacy of a religious community,[27] since this would of necessity imply an unwarranted intrusion into its internal governance.

The expression "other works of the apostolate" is deliberately general and avoids the unsatisfactory, because incomplete, listing of specific kinds of apostolic works found in *CD* 35.4. Any external enterprise undertaken by a religious institute which is directed to building up the Body of Christ is subject to the authority of the bishops. This authority is limited with respect to elementary and secondary schools established and directed by religious (those which are said to be proper to them) as well as with respect to Catholic colleges.[28]

§2

§2 turns to the authority which religious superiors possess with respect to apostolic works undertaken by their institute. These are said to be external in the sense that they reach out to persons who are not members of the institute itself. The law does not wish to deny that there exists an internal mission which is truly apostolic, for example, formation of younger members, care of the infirm and aged, governance, and the like. Indeed, bearing in mind the apostolic fruitfulness of contemplative religious (C 674), they are said to exercise a very important apostolate which would not normally be characterized as truly external.

The text is derived, with some modifications, from *CD* 35.2. Religious who engage in an apostolic enterprise are not by that fact or to that extent freed from the obligation arising from the vow of obedience to their superiors and their general obligation to observe the discipline and rules of their own institute. The authority of superiors in this case mainly, but not exclusively, looks to the specifically religious well-being of the members who have been missioned by them for a specific apostolic commitment. Superiors, as well as bishops, should do what they can to see to it that the enterprise is successful.

Tensions can obviously arise from this dual authority, which should not be allowed to result in the need to choose one over the other. Apostolic life is not to stifle religious life because it pertains to the very nature of an apostolic institute. For example, a religious institute or a province or a local community will usually have and should have policies or covenants regarding communal prayer, meals and recreation. These should be observed and harmonized with the requirements of the specific work and the work itself should be, to the extent possible, structured with a view to such important religious practices. The demands of directing and staffing a good Catholic school will differ notably from those of a parish or retreat center, none of which should be permitted to harm religious life itself.

The concluding statement of §2 is itself derived from the Council.[29] It is useful because it exhorts bishops to be aware of and sensitive to the special needs of religious life and to insist upon them, not in an intrusive manner, but when the situation warrants it. This safeguards the appropriate internal autonomy of C 586 and is notably parallel to §2 of that canon.

§3

The authority of the bishop, which principally concerns the apostolic enterprise itself, and that of the religious superior, which mainly looks to the personal and community welfare of the religious who carry on the apostolate, obviously require that their respective functions be harmoniously coordinated. §3 calls for this. Its conciliar source is *CD* 35.5, and *MR* treats at length and in a constructive way the appropriate interaction of bishops and religious. It may be noted that C 681, §1 speaks of this mutual consultation as a right of the religious superiors by referring to C 678, §2 and §3.

The regular and structured consultation of bishops and superiors can and sometimes does create a special burden for major superiors. It is understandable that bishops will want to dialogue with those superiors who are ultimately responsible for the placement of personnel and for the expenditure of funds. For major superiors, especially those whose religious are missioned in many dioceses, such regularly scheduled consultation with the various bishops can be very time-consuming. Some kind of joint gatherings in such cases will probably have to be devised in which all the major superiors can meet with the bishop or in which several diocesan bishops can meet with these superiors. *MR* 59 speaks about a similar structure but clearly has in mind mainly local superiors; it acknowledges the need for relationships and negotiations between individual bishops and individual communities, which usually entail the direct involvement of the appropriate major superior.

C 679

When a most serious reason demands it a diocesan bishop can prohibit a member of a religious institute from living in his diocese; if the major superior of that religious has been advised and neglects to act, the matter is to be referred to the Holy See immediately.

At least in its present form this canon is new and was found neither in the 1917 Code nor in the first draft on institutes of consecrated life; there is no conciliar source for it. This matter undoubtedly arose in response to the consultations on the first draft. It first appeared in the 1980 draft as C 521, §4, which is now C 593. After this draft had been circulated to the members of the revision commission in preparation for the final plenary meeting in October 1981, the report *(relatio)* of written amendments proposed by members relocated this paragraph, now as a distinct canon, to its present position. It is not clearly germane to the subject of the present chapter.

The norm refers to a situation in which a religious has placed an action which the bishop judges to be a most serious offense *(gravissima causa)*, warranting immediate remedy. While it is not possible to identify a specific action of this nature, because there will always exist some relativity, such a most serious cause might be a published statement directly contradicting the teaching of the magisterium on abortion or publicly impugning the character or motives of someone in a serious matter, or it might be a public indecent or criminal act. In some cases such a most serious offense would be constituted by repeated acts over a sufficient period of time and joined with clear warnings about the consequences.

It does not suffice, however, that the action be simply most serious. The bishop cannot act on his own authority unless he has notified the appropriate religious superior of his intention to expel the religious from his diocese if the superior does not take effective action. The canon does not specify what action the superior should take, but it clearly would have to be such that the harm done, e.g., scandal, loss of reputation, would thereby be adequately compensated for or remedied. The bishop is the judge of this.

Only in the event that the superior fails to act in a reasonable period of time and in an adequate manner may the bishop formally prohibit the religious from continued residence in the diocese. In this event he must immediately notify the Holy See of his judgment about the extreme gravity of what has occurred, his notification and warning communicated to the religious superior, the failure of the superior to respond adequately, and his order to leave the diocese communicated to the religious.

In the case of a religious priest, he could revoke the faculty to hear confessions in his diocese (C 974) and could impose ecclesiastical sanctions on any religious if the offense occurred in a matter in which religious are subject to the authority of the diocesan bishop (C 1320), but only by observing the process prescribed for imposing ecclesiastical penalties (CC 1341–1353).

C 680

Among the various institutes and also between them and the secular clergy, orderly cooperation as well as a coordination of all apostolic works and activities, under the direction of the diocesan bishop, with due regard for the character and purpose of individual institutes and the laws of the foundation, is to be promoted.

The conciliar source for this canon is CD 35.5, although the role of the bishop as ultimately responsible for the coordination of all apostolic works in the diocese is thematic throughout the council documents, especially in CD 17. MR, especially in 36–43 and 52–59, addresses this subject in considerable detail.

This canon establishes the principle underlying the final three canons of this chapter. Two issues are addressed: first, orderly cooperation among religious institutes themselves and between them and the diocesan clergy; second, coordination of all apostolic works and activities in the diocese under the direction of the bishop. Cooperation is contrasted to rivalry or to indifference, either of which is ultimately destructive in the apostolate of the Church. It implies mutual understanding and respect which alone will make effective coordination of efforts possible. Diocesan councils of religious can be very helpful in creating the climate of cooperation, although if they always segregate men and women religious or clerical and lay religious, whether men or women, from each other, they will be less effective than they could be.

Elsewhere in the Code provision is made for representation of religious priests on the presbyteral council or senate of priests (C 498) and for representation of religious women and men in the diocesan synod (C 463) and on the diocesan pastoral council (C 512). In these ways, as well as in many others which may be established, e.g., diocesan boards and commissions, a structured cooperation can be nurtured and the bishop can be effectively assisted in fulfilling his responsibility as chief coordinator of the apostolate.

C 681

§1. Works which are entrusted to religious by the diocesan bishop are subject to the authority and direction of this same bishop, with due regard for the right of religious superiors according to the norm of can. 678, §§2 and 3.

§2. In these cases a written agreement is to be drawn up between the diocesan bishop and the competent superior of the institute, which, among other things, expressly and accurately defines what pertains to the work to be carried out, the members to be devoted to this, and economic matters.

§1

As has been noted in the commentary on C 677, §1, apostolic works are distinguished as those belonging to the patrimony of each religious institute and called proper to it and those entrusted to religious by an ecclesiastical authority. In this canon there is question of the latter and specifically of works entrusted or committed to religious by a diocesan bishop, even when the work is of a kind which is also proper to the institute. In no event can it be contrary to its nature or character. In this case, as has been noted, the authority of the bishop extends to every aspect of the work in question, for example, a diocesan or parochial school, a diocesan retreat center or house of prayer, and most obviously a parish.

§2

§2 repeats *ES* 30.1 virtually verbatim. This contract or agreement is of the utmost importance and should never be neglected. Like *ES*, this paragraph requires that the contract, which must always be signed by the appropriate persons representing the diocese and the religious community, must deal with at least three subjects: a description of the work and how it is to be carried out, personnel issues, and financial arrangements. These should be as detailed as is seen to be necessary by either party to forestall, to the extent that this is ever possible, future misunderstandings and disputes.

It should be noted that the paragraph uses the expression "among other things" *(inter alia)*. This is not accidental. Broadly understanding the three indicated areas which such a contract should attend to, it is difficult to imagine what such other matters might be. The phrase, however, serves to alert the parties to the agreement that the list given in the canon may not be taxative or exhaustive, that there may be other, somewhat tangential or unique issues which should be included in its terms.

The mission and goals of the work in question should be clearly stated and the lines of authority and responsibility expressly agreed upon. Accountability is always important, as are evaluation and planning. Any special conditions or circumstances should be found in the signed text.

Personnel issues are probably the most difficult to cover adequately, but they usually are the issues which occasion the most difficult and serious disagreements. The qualifications and the number of religious to be assigned to the enterprise, their rights and duties, hours of service, holidays, vacations, and periods of retreat should be spelled out. Any obligatory or expected service to the parish or diocese or to the institute over and above the normal duties of the apostolic work itself should be adequately indicated. Most important, this contract must detail the process of appointment and promotion, as well as the causes and process of dismissal.

Finally, financial arrangements should include, in addition to salary or its equivalent, housing or housing allowance, travel and transportation, equipment and furnishings, health and retirement benefits, and continuing education and sabbatical provisions, whenever appropriate. It should be made clear to whom and at what intervals such compensation will be made.

Commonly there exist standardized contracts, the result of long experience, especially for various well-established apostolic works, such as schools and parishes, but this should not inhibit the institute from insisting upon added details which it perceives as needed or useful. If the apostolic project is new or untested, such as a counseling service for battered women, a peace institute, a community organizing team, a refugee center, a free clinic, and the like, the contract should be drawn to fit what is in fact anticipated and be easily reviewed and amended in the light of experience.

Such a contract should not be entered into in perpetuity, but should be subject to periodic review, providing for the right of either party to terminate it for stated causes and with timely notice. What needs to be stressed here is the importance of a properly drawn contract. Contracts belong to the arena of justice, a forum of clearly defined rights and obligations. When justice has been served, however difficult the process, harmony and cooperation can best be assured.

It is worthy of note that there is not here a question of contracts between ecclesiastical institutions and individual religious. What is dealt with here is a contract between two ecclesiastical juridic persons, a diocese (or a parish) and a religious institute as such, each represented by a person who legally speaks for the juridic person. [30] This is not to imply that contracts between institutions and individual religious are seen as improper; sometimes they are necessary. The law is simply silent on this point. It is not silent, however, about the conferral of an ecclesiastical office upon an individual religious, which is the burden of the next canon.

C 682

§1. If there is a question of conferring an ecclesiastical office in the diocese upon a certain religious, the religious is appointed by the diocesan bishop, following presentation by or at least assent of the competent superior.

§2. A religious can be removed from the office entrusted to him or her either at the discretion of the authority who entrusted it, after having notified the religious superior, or at the discretion of the superior, having notified the authority; and neither requires the consent of the other.

This canon addresses the conferral of an ecclesiastical office upon an individual religious, a matter altogether distinct from the corporate commitment of an apostolic work to an institute as such. This is the only place in chapter V, with the exception of C 679 (which may be misplaced by way of a compromise) where a canon directly concerns an individual religious.

Ecclesiastical office is the subject of a lengthy title of Book I, CC 145–196, and is not appropriately treated here in any but a summary manner. Certain points have to be attended to, however, in order to understand adequately what is at issue in this canon. Until the council the expression "ecclesiastical office" was used both in a broad sense and in a strict sense. Office in the broad sense meant any function or role *(munus)* legitimately performed for a spiritual purpose. In the strict sense, however, office was any function or role, established by law and conferred in a stable manner, which carried with it some degree of participation in ecclesiastical power whether of orders or of jurisdiction. By the law itself ecclesiastical office was always to be understood in the strict sense unless the context required otherwise.[31] Since only a cleric could hold an office in the strict sense, because only a cleric could participate in the power of orders or of jurisdiction, ecclesiastical office was treated in Book II of CIC under the general rubric of clergy.

The Council changed this by deciding that "from now on [an ecclesiastical] office should be understood as any function (*munus*) which has been conferred with stability for a spiritual purpose," [32] i.e., in the broad sense of CIC, omitting any reference to the power of orders or of jurisdiction. There is now only one sense of the expression "ecclesiastical office," and the subject was transferred to Book I, General Norms. Lay persons can and do hold ecclesiastical offices, although some such offices, e.g., pastor, vicar general, and others, can be conferred only on priests.

§1

§1 regulates the conferral of office upon a religious and is taken almost verbatim from *ES* I 31–32, although it omits what is found there about the need for a written agreement or employment contract. This is a very significant omission and will be discussed below in the context of removal from office.

Presentation is one of the four ways in which an ecclesiastical office can be conferred, but here there is only a question of presentation in a broad sense.[33] This is the normal and more appropriate way, for example, in which the pastor of a parish, which itself has been confided to a religious province, is appointed. The major superior indicates or nominates the priest whom he recommends be appointed pastor and the bishop, if he finds the candidate suited, makes the appointment. The same procedure should be followed in presenting a religious for any office.

Frequently enough, however, a particular religious will be known by the bishop or have come to his attention as a candidate for an ecclesiastical office, e.g., superintendent of schools, judicial vicar (*officialis*), director of religious education, episcopal vicar for the Spanish-speaking. While he may request the assignment of this religious to his curia, he cannot appoint him or her without the consent of the major superior.

§2

Presumably the reasons for removal from office would be given in the notification, but there is no canonical requirement of justification, much less proof, of the reasons. The canonical principle operative here is found in C 193, §3, according to which a person can be removed from office for a just cause provided the office had been conferred "at the prudent discretion of the competent authority." Here the canon states that the religious can be removed "at the discretion *(ad nutum)*" of the bishop or of the religious superior—an even stronger formula. This constitutes an important departure from *ES* I 32, which required that there exist a grave or serious cause for this removal.

Evidently, especially given the relationship of cooperation and mutual trust which is expected to exist between religious superiors and bishops, the sudden removal of a religious by either authority should not occur except in the most unusual circumstances, e.g., serious misconduct or scandal or overriding need elsewhere, and removal by either without explanation of the reasons should be even more rare. Extraordinary circumstances, nevertheless, can and sometimes do occur. For example, a religious who is the diocesan superintendent of schools is elected superior general or is appointed superior of a seriously troubled house in a distant diocese.

Can there be a contract of employment which specifies a term of office and the causes and procedures of termination prior to the expiration of that term, which would prevent sudden or summary removal of a religious from a diocesan office? A bishop, as well as a major superior, could limit the discretion granted to them by this paragraph. Some consequences, however, should be noted.

First, neither the bishop nor the major superior can bind his or her successor in office beyond the provisions of the law. If such an employment contract were to exist, it would have to be renewed or renegotiated by the successors of the bishop and of the religious superior. Second, the contract in question is not between the diocese and the religious officeholder, but between the diocese and the institute, because it is the major superior who is accepting a limitation on his or her freedom to act in the future. Third, both the religious who is being appointed and the major superior would have to realize that the passive voice of the religious is being curtailed and this would require at least the approval of the superior general, since this actually restricts the freedom of the general chapter to elect members of the institute to internal offices such as superior general or general counselors. If the province chapter, moreover, has the power to elect its superiors and counselors, the same restraint would apply. Indeed, these limitations on chapters would probably be unconstitutional without prior approval by them. The same limitation would arise with respect to the appointment of a religious to an internal office of the institute and with respect to the freedom of the major superior to appoint a religious to an apostolic work of the institute.

Hence, it would seem at least problematic that a contract of employment would in fact provide the security of tenure which appears to many to be desirable for the diocese, the religious officeholder, and the religious community, unless it could be written in such a way that the foregoing difficulties would be obviated.

Nothing is said in the Code about the appointment of religious to positions other than diocesan offices, e.g., within a parish. There are two ways of looking at this situation. One is to say that the diocesan officials and pastors are in fact acting as the agents of the diocese in making such appointments and that what is said in the canon is applicable to its agents. Another is to say that there is a lacuna in the law which calls for the application of parallel canonical provisions and this canon would certainly be the parallel. The result is the same in either explanation. The pastor for example, in appointing a religious as director of religious education for the parish has the same rights and obligations as are established in this canon with respect to the bishop.

C 683

§1. At the time of the pastoral visitation and also in case of necessity the diocesan bishop, either in person or through someone else, can make a visitation of the churches of religious or of their oratories, which the Christian faithful habitually attend, schools and other works of religion or charity, whether temporal or spiritual, entrusted to religious; however he may not visit schools which are open only to students belonging to the institute.

§2. But if by chance he discovers abuses and has advised the religious superior in vain, he himself can provide for it on his own authority.

This is the concluding canon of chapter V and concerns the episcopal visitation of institutions in the hands of religious, whether their own proper works or works entrusted to them by the diocesan bishop. [34] There is question here of a formal visitation made by the bishop or his agent, e.g., the superintendent of schools, the vicar for the social apostolate, in order to familiarize himself with the apostolic enterprises in his diocese and to evaluate them precisely as elements of the diocesan apostolate in general, which he is supposed to promote and supervise. [35] Visitation is an important means of supervision. Two distinct kinds of visitation are mentioned, the ordinary, at least quinquennial, pastoral visitation of the entire diocese [36] or an extraordinary visitation occasioned by serious concern aroused by reports reaching the bishop from usually reliable sources.

There are three categories mentioned: the churches and chapels of religious, schools, and other apostolic works. In North America there are very few churches in the strict sense[37] which belong to religious and are not parish churches. The oratories or chapels (*oratoria*)[38] of religious are distinguished as those which are habitually used by the Christian faithful in general and implicitly as those chapels not so used. Chapels which are habitually open to anyone who wishes to come there for divine worship are, like churches and the now-suppressed public oratories,[39] looked upon as places for exercising divine worship in a public manner and are subject to the bishop's supervision.[40] As such the bishop can, although he is not obliged to, make an official visitation.

The scope of such a visitation is not limited in any way. It may include inspection of the physical plant and of the arrangement of furnishings for the liturgy; examination of the security of the building, of the tabernacle and of places where sacred objects are stored; observation of the liturgical celebrations themselves; interviews with staff and others.

The bishop, however, does not have the right to conduct a formal visitation of the chapels of religious to which the faithful do not have habitual access, even if they do come there for a special occasion or if a few people regularly assist at the liturgy there. The reason for this is that it would imply an unwarranted intrusion upon the legitimate privacy of the religious community.[41] Superiors are to be presumed to be conscientious about seeing to it that their chapels are properly arranged and maintained and that the liturgy is correctly celebrated there.

Schools are a special kind of apostolic work and are addressed at some length in Book III, CC 796–806, because they are a unique instrument of the teaching office of the Church. In general, it can be said here that schools, like other apostolic works, are distinguished as those which pertain to the institute, in the sense that they have been established and are operated by them (usually called private schools in the United States), and those which belong to the diocese or parish and are merely staffed by religious. In the latter case the right of the bishop to conduct a formal visitation is unlimited. In the case of the former kind of schools, the right of the bishop to make a visitation is secured by the present canon, but its scope is somewhat limited. The bishop has the right to establish general policies for all Catholic schools (C 806, §1), to supervise religious formation and education imparted in schools (C 804, §1), to approve the appointment of those who are to teach religion and to require their removal if he judges this necessary for reasons of religion or morals (C 805), but the right of the religious to direct or manage these schools remains intact (C 806, §1). Excluded from such a visitation are schools open only to members of the religious institute, e.g., juniorates, seminaries, and the like.

With respect to the other apostolic works, here called works of religion or charity, the scope of an episcopal visitation is not qualified.

§2 extends what *ES* I 38 says about places of worship to schools and other apostolic works. If in the course of the visitation abuses come to light the bishop is to notify the appropriate religious superior and require that the situation be corrected. Only if this action proves ineffective can he take remedial action on his own authority. There is no mention made of his having to notify the Holy See at all, as in the case of C 679.

The abuses which are considered here have to be related to the apostolic work as apostolic, i.e., related to the mission of the Church itself. They have to concern actions or lack of action which are truly and certainly harmful and which are not trivial or the subject of legitimate differences of informed opinion. This has to be the case especially with regard to schools founded and operated by religious with the approval of the diocesan bishop or one of his predecessors and with regard to liturgical matters. Otherwise the long-term cooperation and mutual trust between the diocese and religious communities will be seriously eroded.

NOTES

1. Much of the subject matter of this chapter can be found, although in significantly different contexts, in CIC 497, §2; 512, §2, 2°; 608; 615; 617.

2. *AA* 2. Cf. *PC* 8, *CD* 35, *AG* 40.

3. Cf. *AA* 3, *PO* 2, *LG* 44.

4. C 230, §1. Cf. Paul VI, *Motu proprio, Ministeria quaedam*, August 15, 1972. *AAS* 64 (1972) 529–34.

5. C 230, §3. Cf. CC 766, 861, §2; 910, §2.

6. Cf. CC 665, §1; 671; 682.

7. The two conciliar documents which underlie chapter V are *PC*, esp. 7, 8, 10, and 20, and *CD* 35. The most important post-conciliar sources are *ES* I 22–40 and *MR, passim*.

8. Cf. *LG* 31, 39, 44; *AG* 18; *ET, passim*.

9. *PC* 7; *VS* III.

10. Although she would never have employed the word "apostolate," St. Teresa of Avila, Doctor of the Church, considered herself to be an effective sharer by her prayers and penance in the work of preachers and theologians engaged in the effort to recall Protestants to orthodox Catholic teaching (*Life*, ch. XXXII; *Spiritual Relations*, III; *Way of*

Perfection, chs. I-III, in *Complete Works*, trans. and ed. E. Allison Peers. London: Sheed and Ward, 1946). Similarly St. Thérèse of Lisieux, co-patron of the missions, who engaged in a voluminous correspondence with missionaries, described herself as their partner by her prayers *(Collected Letters*, ed. Abbe Combes, trans. F. J. Sheed. New York: Sheed and Ward, 1949, 291–92, 352–54).

11. *PC* 9. Such institutes, sometimes improperly called semi-cloistered, have traditionally minimized their direct contact with people in general and have limited their apostolic enterprises to those which they could engage in within their own houses, e.g., schools, retreat houses, hostels.

12. Cf. *CD* 17, 33–35; *ES* I 22–40; *AA* 23–24.

13. *AA* 23; *MR* 9 (a).

14. Cf. C 394, §1 and *MR* ch. II.

15. C 611, 2°. It is evident that any limitations upon the scope of apostolic enterprises of the institute accepted by it at the time of the canonical erection of a house must be respected. This, however, underscores the caution and foresight which superiors should exercise in agreeing to limitations which in the future may hamper the apostolic flexibility and effectiveness of the community.

16. C 612.

17. A medieval expression which became traditional in ecclesiastical language, the "corporal works" of mercy were derived from Matt 25:35–36 with the addition of burying the dead from Tob 12:12. The "spiritual works" of mercy were traditionally listed as converting sinners, instructing the ignorant, counseling the doubtful, consoling the afflicted, bearing wrongs patiently, forgiving injuries and praying for the living and the dead. In brief, any ministry to the needs of others.

18. Cf. C 681.

19. Associations of the Christian faithful are the subject of CC 298–329. C 303 makes clear the obligation of a religious institute with respect to any lay association organically related to it.

20. Cf. C 303.

21. Cf. *CD* 35.1, .2 and .4.

22. Cf. *LG* 45.

23. Cf. CC 515, §1; 519; 528–530.

24. The English word "curate," derives from this expression, as does the French *cure*. The classic English phrase "cure of souls" is still in use among Anglicans.

25. Cf. C 517, §2.

26. *SC* 26, which is incorporated into the Code as C 837, §1.

27. Cf. C 586, §1.

28. Cf. CC 806, §1; 810; 812.

29. *CD* 35.2.

30. Juridic persons are addressed in CC 113–123.

31. CIC 145.

32. *PO* 20. Cf. *LG* 33 and 37.

33. Cf. CC 158–163.

34. There is a serious difficulty with the text, and therefore with the meaning, of §1, specifically with the phrase "committed to religious" *(religiosis commissa)*. The source of this canon is *ES* I 38 and 39.2, where the right of the local Ordinary to make a formal visitation of the churches of religious, even the exempt, and their semi-public oratories (chapels), which the faithful ordinarily frequent, is explicitly affirmed in 38, while 39.2 affirms his right to make such a visitation "of all schools, colleges, chapels, recreation centers,

protectorates, hospitals, orphanages and other similar institutions of religious institutes devoted to works of religion or to the temporal or spiritual works of charity, except those schools of an institute which are open exclusively to the institute's own students."

No mention of this was made in the first draft on institutes of consecrated life. C 609, §1 of the 1980 draft, however, was identical with the text of the present paragraph with one important change. The draft retained the language of *ES*, while eliminating the rather long list of specific kinds of apostolic works other than schools, and spoke of them as "the churches, chapels, schools and other works of religious *(religiosorum)*." No change was then introduced by the 1981 *relatio* or by the final plenary session of the revision commission itself. The change, which appears in the promulgated text of §1, occurred after the commission approved the final draft of the Code.

As has been noted the apostolic works of religious are consistently distinguished as those proper to their institutes and those committed to religious by some ecclesiastical authority. There is a corresponding difference of relationship to the diocesan bishop, as has been noted in the commentary on CC 677, §1 and 681. A credible case can be made that the final wording of C 683, §1 intentionally introduces a sweeping and substantive change from *ES* and the draft of the Code unanimously approved by the revision commission by restricting the institutions which are subject to formal episcopal visitation to those which have been entrusted or committed to religious.

It is difficult to reconcile this interpretation with the evident effort to retain in the codification the provisions of *ES*, with some amendments, and of the final draft, with the tenor of the present chapter and especially regarding schools with the explicit provision of C 806, §1. There appears rather to have been an infelicitous and probably precipitate amendment of the canon as drafted.

35. Cf. C 394, §1.
36. Cf. C 396, §1.
37. Cf. C 1214.
38. Cf. C 1223.
39. Cf. CIC 1188, §2, 1°.
40. Cf. supra, C 678, §1.
41. Cf. CC 586 and 608 and supra, C 678, §1.

Separation of Members from the Institute
Canons 684–709

Elizabeth McDonough, O.P.

INTRODUCTION

Following logically in the sequence of other titles of the canons on consecrated life are the canons on separation from the institute. These include (1) transfer, CC 684–685, (2) departure, CC 686–693, and (3) dismissal, CC 694–704. The first two categories are often referred to as "voluntary" separation and the third as "involuntary" separation to indicate generally the source from which the separation action is initiated. These divisions are not mutually exclusive, however, since the "imposed exclaustration" of C 686, §3 and the "exclusion" from subsequent profession of C 689, §1 and §2, are not exactly "voluntary" on the part of the member or members involved. In addition, the "readmittance" of C 690 and the "expulsion from the religious house" of C 703 do not constitute separation from the institute as such.

Since in consecrated life a commitment is made to God by vow or other sacred bond through the mediation of institutes legitimately established in the Church, the possibilities of changing the locus of one's commitment (i.e., transfer) or of seeking legitimate dispensation from the consequences legally recognized by the Church as the result of this commitment (i.e., departure) or, when necessitated for the sake of the individual or common good of the institute, the temporary (i.e., exclaustration) or permanent (i.e., dismissal) alteration of status with respect to the institute must be acknowledged and properly provided for in the law. Most of these canons deal with procedural law and some touch upon the matter of sanctions. As such, the processes indicated in these canons may not be dispensed, and those concerning sanctions must be strictly interpreted as required by the Code itself in CC 87 and 18, respectively.

221

For facility in dealing with the material contained in these canons—even though the Code does not divide them in these categories—the following commentary on the separation canons uses the topical division of: transfer (CC 684–685), exclaustration (CC 686–687), legitimate departure prior to perpetual profession and readmittance after profession (CC 688–690), voluntary departure for those in perpetual profession (CC 691–693), and dismissal (CC 694–704). Also for facility of treatment, each of these divisions is subdivided to outline the notions and history of the concept, to analyze the specific canons, to indicate major differences between the 1917 and 1983 Codes, to outline procedures (where applicable), and to raise common actual and anticipated questions regarding the canons in each division. Wherever necessary terms are defined or the reader is referred to other portions of the commentary which deal more specifically with matters related to these canons. It is especially important to note that this material is in no way intended to substitute for sound, on-going, expert advice of qualified persons when matters concerned in these canons do arise in particular institutes. These comments are merely intended as an informational guide for members of institutes to initially identify fundamental rights, obligations, and procedures in the title on separation.

TRANSFER: NOTION AND HISTORY

Transfer consists in simultaneous departure from and entrance into an institute of consecrated life legitimately established by ecclesiastical authority and following the general and proper law that is pertinent.

In the early centuries of monastic life, there were no restrictions placed on such movement. Eventually, in order to safeguard stability and to avoid transfers made merely from fickleness on the part of the individual or with a desire to escape the obligations already undertaken, a juridic bond between the member and the institute was recognized and transfers were restricted on the bases of motivation, of types of institutes involved, and of the authority competent to grant them. By the Middle Ages transfers to groups of less strict observance or those requested without serious cause were generally denied. In order to curtail numerous transfers and the concomitant wanderings of those in transit, Trent imposed certain ecclesiastical disqualifications on those who had transferred for any reason, and by the eighteenth century the Holy See reserved most transfers to itself in a further attempt to curtail the practice. The 1917 Code generally incorporated the legislation and practice flourishing at the turn of the twentieth century.

After Vatican II the number of transfers increased sharply as the response or non-response of religious institutes to the call for renewal made it more or less difficult for religious who sincerely wished to remain such to live out their commitment in the communities in which they had made profession. Consequently the prayerful and sincere desire to transfer to another institute accompanied by sufficiently serious reasons and fulfilling the requirements of universal and proper law has become a more common phenomenon in the last two decades. [1]

TRANSFER: CC 684 AND 685

C 684

§1. A member in perpetual vows cannot transfer from one religious institute to another without the permission of the supreme moderator of each institute given with the consent of their respective councils.

§2. After completing a probationary period which is to last at least three years, the member can be admitted to perpetual profession in the new institute. However, if the member refuses to make this profession or is not admitted to making it by competent superiors, the member is to return to the former institute, unless an indult of secularization has been obtained.

§3. For a religious to transfer from an autonomous monastery to another of the same institute or federation or confederation, it is required and is sufficient to have the consent of the major superior of both monasteries and the chapter of the receiving monastery, with due regard for the other requirements determined in proper law; a new profession is not required.

§4. Proper law is to determine the time and mode of probation which is to precede the profession of a member in the new institute.

§5. For one to transfer to a secular institute or a society of apostolic life or from them to a religious institute permission of the Holy See is required, and its mandates are to be observed.

§1

The canon concerns transfer to another religious institute for those who are perpetually professed or otherwise definitively incorporated into a religious institute. The canon does not deal with those in temporary profession or with transfers to or from institutes of consecrated life which are not classified as religious institutes. [2] The canon makes clear that the approval of each supreme moderator and the consent of each respective council are required for validity of the act of transfer. Supreme moderators of institutes, diocesan or pontifical, are those indicated by their proper law. Those in charge of provinces of an institute are major superiors but are not supreme moderators. [3]

To initiate the process of transfer the member would petition both supreme moderators in writing clearly stating his or her reasons for desiring to transfer out of or into the institute concerned. A brief outline of the process by which the person has come to his or her decision is not required but certainly may be helpful in obtaining the desired response.

The canon gives no specification of a time limit for a response to such a petition. It would seem appropriate that acknowledgment of the petition by the supreme moderator with an indication of when it will be considered by the council should be communicated to the petitioner as soon as possible. It would also seem appropriate that any reasonable requests for additional information to be supplied by the petitioner be complied with as soon as possible. Unreasonable delays in either acknowledging or in responding positively or negatively to the petition could, in effect, block the transfer process, as could non-response on the part of the petitioner.

What is unreasonable delay depends in part on the organization of the institute and the location of the persons involved if direct contact is desired. For acknowledgment of such a petition one month might be quite reasonable for a small diocesan institute whereas three months might be quite reasonable for a large international institute. What are reasonable or unreasonable requests made by either supreme moderator and council on the petitioner and vice versa depend in part on the nature of the institutes involved and on the actual disposition and condition of the petitioner. In general, requests for information concerning one's basic physical and emotional state and curriculum vitae are not unreasonable, but requests involving violation of personal rights or requiring manifestation of conscience are unreasonable.

Conditions on permission to transfer should not be such that they preclude the possibility of pursuing what is sought. Although the canon is phrased in the negative indicating transfers are viewed as the exception and not as the rule, if no action is forthcoming the matter could be referred to the local vicar for religious for mediation if necessary or, ultimately, to the Sacred Congregation.

§2

The transfer process is officially initiated by the mutual exchange of approvals and consents. The time of probation begins after this and extends for as long as is required by the proper law of the institute, but not less than three years computed in the standard canonical manner. A new novitiate is not required. The member in transfer remains a religious under vow. During the period of probation, the religious lacks active and passive voice in both institutes because the rights in the former institute have been suspended and he or she does not yet enjoy the rights of those professed in the new institute.

Admission to perpetual profession following the period of probation is by the competent superior with the vote of his or her council according to the proper law of the institute. If the member is not admitted to profession in the new institute he or she has the right and obligation to return to the former institute. If the member does not wish to return or if the former institute, although legally obliged to do so, is unwilling to allow the member to return, he or she may seek one of the options described below in Special Question, 6.

Any dowry or patrimony owned by the member while in the former institute is transferred to the new institute at the time of profession in that institute. The will which the member made in the former institute should be returned to him or her and, likewise, the document of cession of administration. If these were drawn up in such a manner as to be rendered void upon leaving the original institute, then a new will and document of cession should be drawn up at the time of profession in the new institute. If they are still valid and require alteration, this can be done with the permission of the competent superior of the new institute. [4]

§3

Monasteries of the same institute or federation or confederation are those which have the same rule and have some major superior at a level between that monastery and the Holy See who has some actual power over the self-governing monastery. [5]

To initiate the transfer the member should submit a request (as described for C 684, §1) to the major superior of both monasteries. In addition to the consent of both major superiors, the chapter of the receiving monastery must consent to accept the new member. Any additional requirements of the proper law of both monasteries must be observed.

Since a new profession is not required by the general law, by analogy the three-year probation period required prior to the new profession for transfers as indicated in §2 of this canon does not apply as such. The transfer is effected upon the receipt of the required consents. The law of each institute may very well, and perhaps should, indicate an appropriate time and manner in which the new monastery may become familiar with the one requesting transfer prior to giving the required consent. Absence from monasteries of nuns of papal cloister as treated in C 667, §3 can be granted for this purpose by the diocesan bishop according to C 667, §4. Absence from monasteries of monks for this purpose can be granted by their superiors and councils following the norm of proper law.

§4

This canon leaves the time and manner of probation, retaining the required three years of §2 prior to the new perpetual profession, entirely to the proper law of the institute. The time of probation should not be unduly extended, however, since a perpetually professed member would already have spent a minimum of a one-year novitiate and three years temporary profession in the former institute.[6]

Proper law may cover this obligation by using the duration of general law and by specifying who is responsible for the manner of probation in any particular transfer situation.

Although not specified in the canon, some mutual agreement regarding financial maintenance of the person in the process of transfer should be decided by the respective major superiors for the duration of probation. Any such arrangements should be in writing and duly authorized for the protection of both groups and of the member involved.

§5

This canon restricts transfers as dealt with in §§1-4 to those between institutes that qualify as religious only. The same restriction is placed on transfer in secular institutes and in societies of apostolic life.[7] Since a monastery is a religious institute, as such, the restriction of this canon does not apply to transfers to or from a monastic and non-monastic religious institute, although the period of probation and new profession mentioned in §1 would be required in such a case.

For consistency, the procedure of §1, although not required for the transfers of §5, could be followed with the approval of both competent superiors and their respective councils being forwarded to the Sacred Congregation. It would seem, however, that the present practice of the originating community petitioning the Sacred Congregation for transfer, notifying the new community upon receipt of the rescript, with subsequent acknowledgment of the rescript and acceptance of the transferring member for probation could also be followed.

C 685

§1. Until the religious makes profession in the new institute, while the vows remain, the rights and obligations which the member had in the former institute are suspended; however, the religious is obligated to observe the proper law of the new institute from the beginning of the probationary period.

§2. By profession in the new institute the member is incorporated into it, while the preceding vows, rights and obligations cease.

§*1*

As mentioned under C 684, §2, the member in the process of transfer remains a religious under vow and during the time of probation is still a professed member of the original institute. Also as previously mentioned their active and passive voice are lost in the former institute and, likewise, have not yet been acquired in the new institute during the time of probation. Rights and obligations in the prior institute are suspended and the member is required to observe the proper law of the new institute because, obviously, he or she in the process of transfer is living as if he or she were a member of the latter institute rather than of the former. This mutual suspension and new obligation of observance begins when the transfer probation time begins, either by the dual exchange of the required consents or at the time specified therein.

§2

Profession of vows in the new institute following due probation and admission to profession establishes a juridic bond between the member and the new institute. The juridic bond of profession in the former institute simultaneously ceases. Recall that a person in the process of transfer remains throughout the duration of the process a religious under vow by law and the completion of transfer merely changes the juridic bond from one institute to another.

TRANSFER: MAJOR DIFFERENCES IN 1983 CODE

1. The supreme moderators and respective councils are the competent authorities for transfer from one religious institute to another, whereas from the 1917 Code to present either the Sacred Congregation or the diocesan bishop was competent depending on the type of institute.

2. The approval of the supreme moderators and consent of the respective councils are required for validity of transfer, whereas the opinion of the originating institute and the willingness to accept of the new institute was previously all that was required because the transfer itself depended on the decision of the Holy See.

3. Only transfers between religious institutes and non-religious institutes are reserved to the competence of the Holy See, whereas before all were.

4. The transfer to monasteries of the same order is extended in the 1983 Code to monasteries of the same institute, federation, or confederation without probation or new profession being required.

5. A period of probation as defined by the institute with a minimum duration of three years is required for the person transferring, whereas before a new novitiate was required.

6. The 1983 Code does not mention alteration of the type of vows (e.g., solemn or simple) because these vow distinctions are no longer in the general law with respect to consecrated life as such.

7. The 1983 Code does not mention directly the transfer of dowry or patrimony or the arrangements for sustenance during time of transfer as the 1917 Code did, which does not mean, however, that these should be neglected.

8. The 1983 Code does not mention possible transfer of those in temporary profession, whereas the 1917 Code made an indirect reference to the possibility of such transfer by not using the adjective "perpetual" for professed who wished to transfer and by inserting a special canon for those perpetually professed who did transfer.

TRANSFER: BASIC PROCEDURE FOR RELIGIOUS INSTITUTE TO RELIGIOUS INSTITUTE

1. The one desiring transfer submits a written request to both supreme moderators and councils indicating the desire to and reasons for transfer.

2. With the approval of each supreme moderator and council (both required for validity) the probation period may begin.

3. A mutually agreeable financial arrangement between the two institutes for the duration of probation should be formulated with the expected time of probation (should it be other than the required three years) clearly specified.

4. After probation fulfilled according to the manner specified in the new institute, the person is admitted to perpetual profession by the competent authority or returns to the original institute.

5. At profession in the new institute the dowry and patrimony (if any) are transferred to the institute and the person, with a new will and cession of administration being made if necessary.

TRANSFER: SPECIAL QUESTIONS

1. *What if either institute requires a psychological evaluation of the person desiring transfer as a condition for granting the request?*

If the present emotional state of the person requesting transfer objectively warrants such a request it would not be unreasonable, however the assertion of C 630, §5 forbidding superiors to induce a manifestation of conscience on the part of their subjects would limit the right of the originating institute somewhat in this regard. The new institute could reasonably require of the person desiring transfer whatever testing and certifications it requires of any person seeking admittance.

2. *What if the person desiring transfer wants to live with the other community for a period before officially initiating transfer?*

The option for living outside a house of the institute as provided for by C 665, §1 would apply in non-monastic institutes. For monks the requirements of universal and proper law should be followed. This would include use of the habitual faculty of abbots president of monastic congregations to allow subjects to be absent from the house for up to one year (*Cum Admotae* 15, November 6, 1964). For nuns the requirement of universal and proper law should be followed and, if proper law makes no provisions, the faculty of the diocesan bishop in C 667, §4 could be used, since this is not one of the categories included in *VS* 7 for leaving papal cloister but would seem to constitute a just cause for doing so.

3. *What if the originating community refuses the request for transfer and insists that the person seek exclaustration?*

Objectively speaking the rights of the religious are being violated, since transfer without exclaustration is provided for by the universal law and should be available as legislated unless proper law provides otherwise. The matter could be referred by mutual agreement to a board of arbitration if one is available for the institutes concerned and if either side becomes intransigent the matter should be referred to the Sacred Congregation.

4. *What if the person transferring is not admitted to profession in the new institute and does not wish to or feels unable to return to the original institute?*

Since the person is obliged by law to return to the institute in which he or she is still professed, he or she must seek an indult of departure as required by C 684, §2. Though not mentioned in the canon it would seem that an indult of exclaustration could also be requested following the prescriptions of CC 686 and 687 in order to provide the person with some time of transition prior to secularization.

5. *What if the person wishes to return to the original institute, but the institute demonstrates unwillingness to receive him or her back?*

Objectively speaking the person's right to live religious life in the community of profession is being violated because the original institute has the obligation of accepting back such persons. Subjectively speaking if a person is not wanted in an institute, other options could be pursued including temporary absence from the house (C 665) or another transfer

(CC 684 and 685) or exclaustration (CC 686 and 687). Ultimately refusal to accept a member back after a period of probation in transfer amounts to dismissal and the procedures for dismissal would have to be followed.

6. *What if a member wishes to transfer from a religious institute to the eremitical life or to consecrated virginity?*

Strictly speaking transfer does not apply because neither the eremitical life nor consecrated virginity, recognized as forms of consecrated life (CC 603 and 604), qualify as religious institutes as such (CC 607–609). Such a request could be handled by seeking an indult of exclaustration (C 686) or by permission for absence from the house (C 665) for a period of time in order to live the consecrated life desired under the authority of a willing diocesan bishop and then an indult of departure could be requested of the Holy See so that it would take effect at the moment of the new consecration to the eremitical life or to consecrated virginity.

7. *What if someone in temporary profession desires to transfer to another institute?*

Generally speaking the principle that what is not forbidden is permitted would apply, however the omission of reference to transfer of those in temporary profession was deliberate.[8] Likewise, the requirements of probation coupled with the ordinary requirements for temporary profession (CC 655 and 657) make it very likely that temporary profession would expire during the time of probation. In such a case it is not very reasonable to expect to be admitted to renewal of vows in a community from which one is seeking transfer, and it is not legally possible to pronounce vows before completion of probation in the community to which one is seeking transfer. Release from temporary profession or allowing the vows to expire (C 688) and then seeking regular admission to the other institute seems to be the only legally viable option in this case.

EXCLAUSTRATION: NOTION AND HISTORY

Exclaustration consists in the permission granted by legitimate authority for a member to remain outside the cloister, i.e., outside the religious institute, for a definite or indefinite period of time during which the person so exclaustrated remains a religious but some effects of the juridic bond with the institute are mitigated with respect to the rights and obligations of the religious. It is not to be confused with absence from the house as treated in C 665 or with permanent departure as treated in CC 691–693, even though a religious on exclaustration is absent from the house and exclaustration has been referred to in the past as temporary secularization.

Imposed exclaustration as contained in this Code was first evidenced in 1953 in order to protect the rights of institutes from religious whose vested right by profession to life in the institute was well protected by the law and whose behavior was disruptive but not such as to warrant dismissal.

EXCLAUSTRATION: CC 686 AND 687

C 686

§1. With the consent of the council the supreme moderator for a grave reason can grant an indult of exclaustration to a member professed of perpetual vows, but not for more than three years, and with the prior consent of the local ordinary where he must remain if this concerns a cleric. Extending the indult or granting it for more than three years is reserved to the Holy See or, if there is question of institutes of diocesan right, to the diocesan bishop.

§2. It belongs to the Apostolic See alone to grant an indult of exclaustration for nuns.

§3. If a supreme moderator with the consent of the council petitions, exclaustration can be imposed by the Holy See on a member of an institute of pontifical right or by a diocesan bishop on a member of an institute of diocesan right for grave reasons, with equity and charity being observed.

§1

The supreme moderator of the institute is the person designated according to proper law who fulfills the requirements of C 622. Since consent is required, he or she must act with and according to the deliberative vote of his or her council. No higher authority need be approached for approval of the exclaustration unless the exclaustration extends beyond the three-year maximum, or unless the one exclaustrated is a cleric, or unless §2 of this canon applies.

A perpetually professed member of a religious institute who has received diaconate ordination is incardinated as a cleric in that institute by C 266, §2. Clerics so incardinated do not lose this incardination by exclaustration, but such exclaustration may not be granted without the consent of the Ordinary where the cleric is to live. Consent must be given before the exclaustration is given and, although the canon makes clear that the requirement is not invalidating, the cleric so exclaustrated cannot function in clerical ministry in the diocese without it.

The grave cause required for granting the indult of exclaustration is not for validity but for liceity, and the judge of the gravity with respect to the request would be the supreme moderator and council competent to grant it.

Should the person so exclaustrated be a member of an institute of pontifical right, an extension beyond the three year maximum must be requested of the Holy See. Should the person be a member of an institute of diocesan right, the diocesan bishop can grant the extension. The canon does not indicate whether the diocesan bishop of the principal house of the institute or the diocesan bishop of the house of assignation is competent, thus theoretically either would be competent. By analogy with C 691, §2, however, where the bishop of the house of assignation is competent to grant an indult of secularization for the member of an institute of diocesan right, it would be appropriate that exclaustration be done by this same bishop, and a 1939 interpretation of the Code Commission indicated this right belongs exclusively to the Ordinary of the place where the religious is assigned.[9]

§2

This canon applies only to nuns (*moniales*) as described in C 667, §3 who observe papal cloister and are governed by the norms of the Apostolic See. This canon leaves intact departures from the monastery as treated in *VS* 7 and C 667, §4, since these are not exclaustration.

A religious exclaustrated according to C 686 may return prior to the time stipulated in the indult and must return at the expiration of that time or whenever the indult is revoked by a competent authority during that time.

§3

Imposed exclaustration is initiated not by the member but by the supreme moderator and his or her council. The Holy See is competent to act for institutes of pontifical right, and the diocesan bishop, with the same comments as applied to the diocesan bishop in §1, is competent in institutes of diocesan right. It is an administrative act which may be initiated when a member who has been on exclaustration or in transfer cannot feasibly return to his or her institute or when a cleric seeking exclaustration cannot find the consenting bishop required in §1, or when a member's attitudes and behavior are so extremely difficult to handle that common life of the institute cannot be peacefully lived or the goals of the institute cannot be attained but the attitudes and behavior are not such as to constitute the legal requirements for dismissal. Sometimes imposed exclaustration is granted when dismissal might be warranted objectively speaking, but the advanced age of the religious involved suggests the use of this procedure instead.

As is indicated by the reasons for imposed exclaustration, the action is not necessarily penal in nature and should be for the mutual benefit of the community and the person involved. Usually no period of time is given, with the imposed exclaustration effective as long as the cause prevails and ceasing only by revocation of the original decree. Imposed exclaustration ought not to become perpetual or it amounts to a type of effective dismissal in practice. Since imposed exclaustration according to present practice appears to have the intent of being more or less perpetual however—that is, while the conditions perdure and usually revoked only for reasons of advanced age and necessity—those responsible only for initiating the process should be direct and honest with the religious concerned regarding the institute's legal and moral intentions and obligations.

The procedure to be followed for imposed exclaustration is similar to that for dismissal but applied with less rigor. [10] When erratic or disruptive or seriously irresponsible behavior on the part of the religious is the cause of initiating the procedure, every effort should be made on the part of the institute to use whatever means of reconciliation and arbitration are available to alleviate the situation if possible and to safeguard the rights of both the individual and the institute throughout the process.

The process of seeking exclaustration for any professed member of a religious institute should include such basic information as the person's complete curriculum vitae, reasons for requesting the indult, efforts that have been made to alleviate the difficulty or difficulties motivating the request, and the period of time for which exclaustration is desired. In voluntary exclaustration the request would be submitted by the religious to the supreme moderator. In imposed exclaustration the request would be submitted by the supreme moderator to the Sacred Congregation. Careful documentation must accompany requests for cases in which the religious presently exclaustrated or in the process of transfer cannot feasibly return to the institute or when a cleric desiring exclaustration cannot find a welcoming diocesan bishop. In addition, in cases involving religious whose attitudes and behavior are difficult and disruptive requests for imposed exclaustration must be accompanied by careful documentation of the process closely parallel to that required for dismissal as treated in CC 697–700.

C 687

Exclaustrated members are free from obligations which are incompatible with their new condition of life and at the same time remain dependent on and subject to the care of their superiors and also the local ordinary, especially if the member is a cleric. The members may wear the habit of the institute unless it is determined otherwise in the indult. However, they lack active and passive voice.

The effects of exclaustration are identical whether it is voluntary or imposed. The person is still considered a religious and the juridic bond with the institute remains. Observance of the vow of chastity is not altered. Obligations entailed under the vow of obedience are partially transferred to the Ordinary of the place in which the religious resides. The vow of poverty is mitigated so that the exclaustrated religious may administer his or her own goods and may maintain a standard of living in keeping with particular circumstances.

An exclaustrated religious may not vote or be elected in elections of the institute, and, for protection of the institute, he or she should be asked to sign a waiver of agency with respect to the institute. The obligations relating to common life are suspended, but personal obligations entailed in the constitutions or in the objective status of religious should be observed insofar as possible and obligations of clerics, as such, remain intact. So, for example, an exclaustrated religious is not bound to live in community but, depending on one's constitutions, may be bound insofar as possible to daily Liturgy of the Hours, and is certainly so bound by C 276, §2, 3° if a cleric.

The canon makes clear that an exclaustrated religious may wear the habit of his or her institute unless the indult provides otherwise. Exclaustrated religious clerics would still be bound to clerical attire as indicated in C 284.

CC 686 and 687 refer only to exclaustration for religious in perpetual profession. As in the case of transfer, what is not forbidden is theoretically permitted, but the circumstances warranting exclaustration coupled with the options of C 688 for departure of those in temporary profession as well as the specific wording of the exclaustration canons clearly indicate the intent of their application only to those perpetually professed.

EXCLAUSTRATION: GENERAL PROCEDURE

A. Voluntary Exclaustration

1. The religious desiring such an indult should submit a written request to the supreme moderator indicating his or her (a) curriculum vitae, (b) reasons for requesting the indult, (c) efforts made to resolve difficulties (by spiritual direction, counseling, etc.), (d) the desired duration of exclaustration. In monasteries of nuns the request must be directed to the Sacred Congregation, whose practice it has been not to grant such re-

quests without the opinion of the supreme moderator regarding the relationship of the religious with the institute and the desired duration of exclaustration. If the request is from a religious cleric, the consent of the Ordinary of the place where he is to live must be included.

2. The decision regarding the requested exclaustration following the deliberative vote of the supreme moderator and council should be communicated to the religious as soon as possible and takes effect when communicated or as otherwise stipulated in the indult.

3. Any exclaustrated religious should sign a document, duly witnessed, indicating (a) that he or she clearly understands the obligations of the vows as they are to be observed according to the law of exclaustration, (b) that he or she lacks active and passive voice (and may not act as an agent of the institute) during the period of exclaustration, (c) that he or she may wear the habit of the institute unless otherwise specified in the indult, and (d) that either the religious or the institute will notify the diocesan bishop of his or her presence and exclaustrated status.

B. Imposed Exclaustration[11]

1. The supreme moderator submits to the competent authority (the Sacred Congregation for pontifical institutes, and the diocesan bishop for diocesan institutes) the same basic information as in (1) above.

2. If exclaustration is sought because of difficult and disruptive attitudes and behavior, prior to submitting the material in (1) the competent authority of the institute must first (a) have clearly warned the religious at least twice, either in writing or in the presence of two witnesses, about the behavior and attitudes in question indicating expected amendment and possible imposed exclaustration, (b) have allowed at least fifteen days between warnings, (c) have permitted the religious ample opportunity to respond to the warnings and to justly defend one's self, (d) have obtained the deliberative vote of his or her council with regard to requesting imposed exclaustration after fifteen days from the last warning have elapsed.

3. The decision of the Sacred Congregation is communicated to the religious and is effective as indicated in the rescript.

4. Any religious so exclaustrated should be made aware of his or her status relative to the vows, communal obligations, wearing of the habit, active and passive voice, and communication with the Ordinary of the place where he or she resides. It is advisable, if possible, that a duly witnessed document as indicated in (3) of (A) above be used for this purpose, and the requirement that he or she may not act as a legal agent of the institute should be included.

EXCLAUSTRATION: MAJOR DIFFERENCES IN THE 1983 CODE

1. Exclaustration may now be granted for up to three years by the supreme moderator with the deliberative vote of his or her council, whereas previously it could be granted only by the Holy See or Apostolic Delegate (for pontifical institutes) or by diocesan bishops (for diocesan institutes).

2. A three-year maximum is specified for the exclaustration granted by the competent internal authority of the institute, whereas no time was specified in the canons of the 1917 Code, although the common practice was to limit its duration to three years in ordinary circumstances.

3. A specific canon provides for imposed exclaustration which did not appear in the 1917 Code and has developed from the practice of the Sacred Congregation in cases as they have occurred in the last few decades.

EXCLAUSTRATION: SPECIAL QUESTIONS

1. *What if a religious in temporary profession desires exclaustration?*

Since the canon deals specifically with those in perpetual profession, the options of C 688 should be pursued.

2. *What if a religious at the end of the time of probation in the process of transfer does not wish to return to the original institute or the original institute is unwilling to allow the member to return?*

The religious in the process of transfer has a right to return to the original institute and could refer the matter to the competent authority (i.e., local Ordinary or Sacred Congregation) or, recognizing the unwillingness of the original institute, could seek exclaustration from its supreme moderator. If the religious does not wish to return, he or she must seek exclaustration or an indult of departure according to the norm of law.

3. *What if an exclaustrated religious desires to transfer to another institute?*

The religious may return to his or her community and initiate the process of transfer or may initiate the process of transfer while exclaustrated so that exclaustration ceases upon beginning of probation in the new institute.

4. *What if a cleric desiring exclaustration cannot find a bishop who will consent to having the exclaustrated cleric live in his diocese?*

The cleric should refer the matter to the Sacred Congregation.

5. *What if an exclaustrated religious refuses to return to the common life and obligations of the institute at the expiration of the time of exclaustration?*

The competent superior should seek out the religious offering whatever help is needed for him or her to return and persevere in the religious life according to C 665, §2. If the religious demonstrates no intention of returning the process for imposed exclaustration or for dismissal could be initiated according to the norm of law.

6. *What if a religious thinks his or her rights are being violated by the imposition of exclaustration or in the process of voluntary exclaustration?*

In the earlier stages of the process conciliation and arbitration by a mutually acceptable board of arbitration, if any is available for the institutes concerned, can and should be utilized. In a diocesan institute the matter could be referred to the diocesan bishop and eventually to the Sacred Congregation. In a pontifical institute it could be referred directly to the Sacred Congregation. In imposed exclaustration, since it is an administrative precept, recourse would not suspend the effect of the indult.

LEGITIMATE DEPARTURE PRIOR TO PERPETUAL PROFESSION AND READMISSION AFTER PROFESSION: NOTION AND HISTORY

Departure from an institute prior to profession, that is during the time of prenovitiate (if such existed) or during the novitiate has always been recognized. Since the recognition of temporary profession and the requirement of such prior to perpetual profession in any religious institute, the freedom to depart from the institute at the expiration of these vows has also been recognized. The temporary nature of such vows is with respect to their juridic duration as governed by the norms of law. The perpetual nature of regularly renewed temporary profession as mentioned in C 607, §2, which is equivalent to perpetual commitment excludes such vows from the considerations of CC 688 and 689 once they are beyond the requirements of universal and proper law for temporary profession.

Readmission to a religious institute, the same one to which a person formerly belonged or to another, is possible but entails different procedures depending on the type of departure and the institutes involved. Readmission has undergone considerable alteration since the 1917 Code, and the canons of the 1983 Code are slightly altered from the immediately previous extant legislation.

LEGITIMATE DEPARTURE PRIOR TO PERPETUAL PROFESSION AND READMISSION AFTER PROFESSION: CC 688–690

C 688

§1. Whoever wishes to leave an institute when the time of profession has expired can depart from it.

§2. During the time of temporary profession whoever asks to leave the institute for a grave reason can be granted an indult to leave by the supreme moderator in an institute of pontifical right with the consent of the council; in institutes of diocesan right and in monasteries mentioned in can. 615, the indult, in order to be valid, must be confirmed by the bishop of the house of assignment.

§1

Freedom to depart at the completion of the time of temporary profession is recognized both juridically and morally. Such departure is legitimate and would qualify for readmission according to C 690. Strictly speaking completion of the time of profession is on the anniversary date. Anyone wishing to depart prior to that time should use the norm of §2.

At such departure all rights and obligations entailed by profession cease, and the will and cession of administrative documents and dowry (if any) are returned to the person departing. The former religious in keeping with C 702 may not claim remuneration for any works while a member of the institute, but the institute must observe equity and charity in dealing with the former member.

§2

The request for an indult to leave should be presented in writing to the supreme moderator who must act on it with the deliberative vote of his or her council. Such departure is legitimate and would qualify the person for readmission according to C 690. No additional act is needed in the case of institutes of pontifical right, but diocesan institutes and those self-governing monasteries with no superior having actual power between them and the Holy See must submit the approved request to the bishop of the place where the religious is assigned for his confirmation, without which the act is invalid.

The request with affirmative response, or request with affirmative response followed by required confirmation, constitutes an indult of departure as mentioned in C 692 and would be subject to the specifications and consequences of that norm. This canon would never apply to religious clerics, since C 266, §2 restricts reception of diaconate until after perpetual profession.

C 689

§1. If just causes are present, when temporary profession has expired a member can be excluded from making a subsequent profession by the competent major superior after listening to the council.

§2. Even if it is contracted after profession, physical or psychic illness which in the judgment of experts renders the member mentioned in §1 unsuited to lead the life of the institute, constitutes a reason for not admitting such a person to a renewal of profession or to making perpetual profession, unless the infirmity had been incurred through the institute's negligence or through work performed in the institute.

§3. A religious, however, who becomes insane during temporary vows, even though unable to make a new profession, cannot be dismissed from the institute.

§1

Major superiors as indicated in C 620 need not necessarily be, but can be, the supreme moderator as mentioned in C 622. The superior competent to admit to profession should be clearly indicated in the proper law of the institute. C 689, §1 indicates that the major superior must act having heard his or her council, which in itself requires only a consultative vote. If, however, the proper law of the institute requires a deliberative vote of the council to admit to renewal of profession or to perpetual profession, then exclusion from either—as the decision not to admit—would have to fulfill the same requirements of the proper law of the institute.

Note that exclusion requires just causes (plural) which might include obvious lack of religious spirit or clear incapacity to effectively live the life of the institute. There is no special process indicated for exclusion from profession, but justice and charity would dictate that reasons for such exclusion be clearly communicated to the person involved, with the possible extension of C 657, §2 being utilized if necessary.

Generally speaking the longer the time already under temporary profession, the greater is the gravity of the causes required for exclusion, and exclusion from perpetual profession after a number of years in temporary profession should be only for very grave reasons usually related to the good of the institute. [12] A religious so excluded could have recourse to the Holy See with the decision for exclusion not being thereby suspended but with actual exclusion from the institute not effective until so confirmed by the Holy See.

Exclusion from renewal of profession or from perpetual profession constitutes legitimate departure from the institute and qualifies the person for readmission according to C 690. Such exclusion is not equivalent to dismissal.

§2

The decision that one may be unfit to lead a life in the institute belongs to the authority competent to admit with the vote of his or her council given according to the norm of general and particular law as in §1. The experts referred to would have to qualify according to C 1574 where it states that their examinations and opinions, rooted in the principles of the arts and sciences, should be used for ascertaining some fact or for better understanding the true nature of something. The language of the canon does not as such require their opinion for validity, but acting without the advice of such experts could easily result in recourse by the religious resulting in reversal of the exclusion decision.

It does not matter whether the infirmity is physical or mental, whether it was acquired before or after profession (with the qualification of the last clause remaining, however), or whether it concerns renewal of temporary profession or making of perpetual profession.

A member may not be excluded from renewal of profession or from perpetual profession if the physical or mental infirmity has been contracted because of the negligence of the institute or because of work done in the institute. The canon makes clear that the clause regarding the cause of the infirmity is invalidating, meaning that such exclusion when either of the causes mentioned is present would be null and void. Thus, in utilizing this exclusion the burden of proof rests with the institute should this clause of the canon be applicable to the situation. Non-negligence, such as provision for ordinarily available medical services for known and treatable illnesses in their incipient stages and with appropriate follow-through, would have to be documented by the institute. If work done in the institute may be related to the reasons for the illness leading to exclusion, the etiology of the illness would have to be ascertained and would have to date from before first profession in the institute. Work done in the institute refers to work of any kind done once one is legally a member of the institute.

Obviously a degree of charity and justice which is not subject to legislation should be observed in the exclusion of any religious who is ill from making further profession in the institute. By C 643, §1, 4° admission to the novitiate under fraud is invalid, and by CC 656, 4° and 658, temporary or perpetual profession made under fraud is likewise invalid. Knowing concealment of an illness, physical or mental, that would render one unfit for life in the institute would certainly constitute fraud and render the admission or professions invalid. Non-knowledge would not do so but could bring this canon into use at the time of renewal or perpetual profession. Superiors on the other hand should not admit persons to the novitiate or to profession conditionally or experimentally, that is, with the stipulation that he or she will be admitted or not admitted to future profession depending on the future improvement or non-improvement of one's physical or mental health as presently known.

Exclusion from profession by C 689, §2 constitutes legitimate departure and qualifies the person for readmission according to C 690. Such exclusion is not equivalent to dismissal, and the consequences of departure are the same as mentioned under C 688, §1. A religious so excluded from profession could have recourse to the Holy See as mentioned in §1.

§3

The canon refers only to those already in temporary profession. Mental derangement or insanity would have to be ascertained by experts competent in the field, although this is not directly mentioned in the canon. Since a new profession is not validly possible, the member remains perpetually in the institute in the same condition as when the illness became manifest.[13] Such a situation is not, strictly speaking, departure from the institute even though it is treated in this section of canons. Should the family of the religious wish to accept responsibility for the religious so afflicted such could be mutually arranged and legal steps required for separation from the institute could possibly be pursued.

C 690

§1. A religious who after completing the novitiate or after profession has left the institute legitimately, can be readmitted by the supreme moderator with the consent of the council without the burden of repeating the novitiate; it is up to the same moderator to determine a suitable probationary period before temporary profession and a time in such vows prior to perpetual profession according to the norm of cann. 655 and 657.

§2. With the consent of the council, the superior of an autonomous monastery enjoys this same faculty.

§1

Completion of the novitiate is completion according to universal and proper law. General law requires twelve months but proper law of the institute may require a longer period according to C 648. The phrase "after profession" is not qualified by either temporary or perpetual, thus the canon applies to any religious who has legitimately left after profession.

Legitimate departure includes departure (a) at the completion of the novitiate according to C 653, §2, (b) at the expiration of temporary profession according to C 688, §1, (c) by an indult granted to a religious in temporary profession according to C 688, §2, (d) by exclusion from subsequent profession according to C 689, §1 and §2, (e) by an indult granted to a perpetually professed religious according to C 691, and (f) by dismissal according to the various categories and procedures of CC 694–703. Whether or not a person who had legitimately departed in these various categories would actually be admitted again to the institute depends on the type of departure, the present condition of the person involved, and the judgment of the competent authority of the institute, but all those who fulfill the requirements for any legitimate departure listed fall under the norm of C 690.

The admission referred to in this canon is to the same institute to which one previously belonged or in which the novitiate was made.[14] The right to readmit according to this canon is reserved to the supreme moderator with the consent of his or her council, whereas admission originally to the novitiate is by the major superior according to proper law (C 641), and admission originally to profession is by the competent superior with his or her council acting according to proper law (C 656).

The same supreme moderator determines the suitable probation. Repetition of the novitiate could be required as the suitable probation, but the intention of the canon is certainly that the supreme moderator may judge a new novitiate as not necessary upon reentrance. There is no time specification for the duration of probation prior to temporary profession. The time in temporary profession prior to perpetual profession must be within the limits specified in CC 655 and 657.

§2

The comments of C 690, §1 apply to those treated in C 613. The superior of such a monastery is the supreme moderator.

PROCEDURES FOR DEPARTURE AND READMITTANCE: CC 688-690

1. For departure initiated by the religious, he or she should submit a request in writing to the competent superior giving appropriate reason for the request.

2. If such a request comes at the termination of a period of temporary profession, it is actually a declaration of intent which becomes fact upon expiration of the person's profession and no further action is necessary.

3. If it is a request made by one temporarily professed in a pontifical institute, the supreme moderator with the consent of his or her council may grant the indult as requested. If the request is not granted or there is unusual delay, the religious may have recourse to the Holy See or may wait until his or her vows expire.

4. If the request is made by one temporarily professed in a diocesan institute or in a monastery which has no superior having actual authority between it and the Holy See, the bishop of the house of assignation must confirm the request after it has been granted by the supreme moderator with deliberative vote of his or her council.

5. Granting, or granting with subsequent confirmation, of the requests in §3 and §4 results in the consequences of an indult of departure as mentioned in C 692.

6. The cession of administration and will (if one has been made) and dowry (if there is any) should be returned to the person.

7. Since exclusion from profession (C 689) is initiated on the part of the institute, those responsible for formation and those involved in the decision and others whose services may be helpful should, in justice, communicate the possibility of such exclusion to the religious prior to the actual decision, even though this is not required by the law as such. Since just causes are required in §1 and, since the judgment of experts is mentioned in §2, the initiating authority is responsible for manifesting these to the religious in question and, it would seem in justice, of giving the person time to amend if possible.

8. Since readmission to an institute refers to the same institute, all original admission and departure records should be available to the institute in question. Additional information could be requested of the applicant in keeping with the current admission procedures of the institute.

LEGITIMATE DEPARTURE PRIOR TO PERPETUAL
PROFESSION AND READMISSION AFTER PROFESSION:
MAJOR CHANGES IN 1983 CODE

1. The grant of an indult of departure for those in temporary profession may be granted at the level of supreme moderator with consent of council (and for diocesan institutes or *sui iuris* monasteries must, for validity, be confirmed by the diocesan bishop). The 1917 Code restricted such indults to the Holy See for pontifical institutes, although legislation in the mid-1960s extended the faculty to those mentioned in C 688.

2. A qualifying clause is added to the requirements for non-admission to further profession in C 689, §2, whereas the legislation of *Dum Canonicarum* (December 8, 1970) apparently allowed such exclusion for illness however and whenever contracted. The 1917 Code had no canon on exclusion for illness except that which was concealed at the time of admission.

3. There is an addition to the canon on exclusion from profession incorporating a 1925 interpretation of SCR (AAS 17 (1925): 107) regarding those in temporary profession who may have become mentally deranged and may not be dismissed from the institute.

4. Return to the same institute after legitimate departure does not necessitate a new novitiate. In the 1917 Code any such departure and return required a new novitiate, and the interim legislation (*RC* January 6, 1969) applied only to those in temporary profession.

5. Time and manner of probation for those readmitted by C 690 is decided by the supreme moderator, and duration of temporary profession must follow the general law minimum and maximum (CC 655 and 657), whereas those readmitted by the interim legislation (only those who had been in temporary profession) were required a minimum of one year temporary profession or the time that had been remaining at the time of their departure. There is no such canon in the 1917 Code.

6. There is no mention of apostates and fugitives from religion as there was in the comparable section of the 1917 Code. There is a reference to the responsibility of superiors towards those illegitimately absent from the house in C 665, §2.

LEGITIMATE DEPARTURE PRIOR TO PERPETUAL PROFESSION AND READMISSION AFTER PROFESSION: SPECIAL QUESTIONS

1. *What if after the request for such an indult by one in temporary profession, the religious changes his or her mind?*

An indult of departure takes effect as indicated in C 692 unless otherwise specified in the indult itself. Thus, the religious can refuse it in the act of notification and thereby remain in the institute under his or her present vows.

2. *What if a religious in temporary profession who is on exclaustration comes under the exclusion of C 689 or requests an indult of departure as in C 688?*

Strictly speaking the canons on exclaustration do not consider this possibility, since they refer to religious who are perpetually professed. Should such a case happen to occur, however, the religious would be automatically released from his or her vows upon their expiration or at the time of exclusion from renewed profession. Should there be a notable delay before either occurs, the religious should seek an indult of departure for one in temporary profession according to C 688, §2.

3. What if someone after legitimate departure after profession (temporary or perpetual) wants to be admitted to an institute different from the original one?

He or she must follow the procedure of universal and proper law for initial admission to the institute. C 643, §1, 5° invalidates such admission to a new novitiate if the previous admission has been concealed by the former religious.

VOLUNTARY DEPARTURE FOR THOSE IN PERPETUAL PROFESSION AND EFFECTS OF AN INDULT OF DEPARTURE: NOTION AND HISTORY

Departure from religious life for those in perpetual profession has always been considered a serious step taken only for the most grave reasons. Prior to the Code, departure of those with solemn vows was referred to as secularization (either temporary or perpetual) and allowed the religious to return to life outside the cloister but did not necessarily include a dispensation from one's vows. At the time of the 1917 Code, temporary secularization became known as exclaustration. Perpetual secularization for pontifical institutes was reserved to the Holy See and for diocesan institutes, to the local Ordinary of the house of assignation. Prior to the 1917 Code, dispensation from the vows of religion was reserved to the Holy See, but a 1922 interpretation of the Code Commission indicated that local Ordinaries had this faculty for members of institutes of diocesan right. [15]

The primary effect of a legitimately granted and nonrejected indult of departure is cessation of the rights and obligations that arose from the contract of profession in the institute. The person is no longer considered legally as a "religious" and is either a lay person or a cleric depending on whether or not orders have been received. Clerics who receive such an indult must find a benevolent bishop who will accept them, either immediately or conditionally, for incardination.

VOLUNTARY DEPARTURE FOR THOSE IN PERPETUAL PROFESSION AND EFFECTS OF AN INDULT OF DEPARTURE: CC 691-693

C 691

§1. One who is professed in perpetual vows is not to seek an indult to leave the institute without very grave reasons weighed before the Lord; such a petition is to be presented to the supreme moderator of the institute, who is to transmit it to the competent authority with a personal opinion and that of the council.

§2. An indult of this kind in institutes of pontifical right is reserved to the Apostolic See; but in institutes of diocesan right the diocesan bishop of the house of assignment can also grant it.

§1

This canon applies only to those who are perpetually professed. The wording is phrased in the negative and uses superlatives in order to communicate the seriousness of the matter at hand.[16] The request for such an indult should be addressed to the competent authority as indicated in §2 but must be directed through the mediation of the supreme moderator whose opinion (and that of his or her council) with respect to the request should be expressed. The request should contain (a) brief and concrete reasons for motivating the request, (b) specific spiritual, psychological, and medical resources that have been used in an attempt to resolve the difficulties motivating the request, (c) a curriculum vitae of the religious. The supreme moderator and council should add an objective evaluation of the circumstances of the request as well as their approval or disapproval.

§2

The canon clearly indicates what authority is competent to act for each type of institute. Obviously for large institutes divided into provinces the request would first be channeled through the provincial superior and his or her council. The indult should be requested by the religious desiring to depart and must fulfill the minimum requirements for obtaining a valid rescript as enumerated in CC 59–75 in addition to following the policies for such requests as established by the Sacred Congregation.

C 692

Unless it has been rejected by the member in the act of notification, an indult legitimately granted and made known to the member brings with it, by the law itself, a dispensation from vows and from all obligations arising from profession.

Permission to permanently depart from an institute of consecrated life is granted through an indulgence (to which one, strictly speaking, does not have a right) by the competent authority who responds to the petition in the form of a written reply or rescript. Rescripts constitute administrative acts granting some favor to one who has requested it and was not impeded by law from making the request (CC 59–60). Ordinarily they take effect without acceptance on the part of the petitioner whenever the response is given or is communicated to the person concerned (CC 61–62). At least what is required in standard canonical practice must be true in the request or the single motivating cause of the request must be true for it to be validly granted (C 63). Minor errors do not invalidate rescripts as long as the matter of the content is clear, and when in doubt rescripts are considered valid and recourse to the grantor should be had for clarification (CC 66–77). Rescripts which have no definite time or conditions can be executed at the time and in the manner decided by those responsible provided there is no fraud involved (CC 69–70). No one is obliged to use a rescript unless there is some other obligation to do so, and rescripts should be in writing in order to have effect in both the internal and external form.

An indult of departure as treated in this canon is legitimately granted if it basically fulfills the general requirements for rescripts, but there are some notable differences. The indult takes effect upon notification which means that its content is inoperative prior to communication of the rescript to the person who has made the request. The religious must refuse the indult in the act of notification in order to render the indult subsequently inoperative. [17] Notification and rejection, if the indult is rejected, should be in writing although the immediate oral communication of rejection at the time of notification suffices to suspend the effect of the indult until refusal can be formally written. If a supreme moderator wishes that the option of rejection not be available to the religious seeking the indult, then he or she should make the reasons for this known in the opinion required when the request is originally submitted to the competent authority in accord with C 691, §1. Then, according to the judgment of the competent granting authority, specifications concerning the nonpossibility of rejection could be included in the rescript containing the indult of departure. [18]

Upon notification without rejection of the indult of departure, the member is automatically dispensed from the vows of poverty, chastity, and obedience as mentioned in C 654 and from all legal consequences of them as indicated in CC 599–601 and in the proper law of the institute. The juridic bond between the member and the institute ceases and with it all the mutual rights and obligations of the member and of the institute however contained in universal or proper law as arising from profession.

C 693

If the member is a cleric, the indult is not granted before he finds a bishop who will incardinate him into a diocese or at least receive him experimentally. If he is received experimentally, he is incardinated into the diocese by the law itself after five years have passed, unless the bishop has refused him.

One becomes a cleric by ordination to the diaconate (C 1009). Perpetually professed members of religious institutes or definitively incorporated members of societies of apostolic life are incardinated into their respective institutes by diaconal ordination (C 266, §2). Members of secular institutes are incardinated into the diocese for which they have been promoted to orders upon reception of diaconal ordination unless incardinated into the institute itself by special grant of the Apostolic See (C 266, §3). Clerics can receive an indult of departure which severs the juridic bond with the institute and the rights and obligations arising from profession, but such indults are not granted in practice until the conditions of this canon are fulfilled.

A willing or benevolent bishop may accept the cleric for incardination effective immediately upon execution of the rescript containing the indult of departure. If unwilling to do so, he may accept the cleric conditionally in which case it is the practice of the Apostolic See to grant the cleric an indult of exclaustration for the duration of the time of conditional acceptance. At the completion of the time for conditional acceptance, or before that time, the receiving bishop is usually granted the faculty of issuing the indult of departure which simultaneously incardinates the cleric into his diocese.[19]

This canon limits the duration of conditional acceptance to five years, which does not imply that five full years are required for conditional acceptance into the diocese. However, should the five-year limit expire without a formal refusal by the bishop of the cleric conditionally admitted to the diocese, he becomes automatically incardinated into the diocese and excardinated from the institute. Since the canon does not mention that an indult of departure would also be required at this point and, since only exclaustration is granted in practice for clerics who are received conditionally by a benevolent bishop, the documentation for the original exclaustration should attend to the required details of this possibility of automatic incardination.

PROCEDURES FOR VOLUNTARY DEPARTURE FOR THOSE IN PERPETUAL PROFESSION

1. Requests for indults of departure are addressed to the pope or to the diocesan bishop depending on who is competent according to C 691, §2. They are directed through the supreme moderator of the institute who may involve other major superiors of the institute more directly concerned with the member in question. The supreme moderator should add an opinion regarding the request having first consulted his or her council.

In practice, such requests are not granted by the Apostolic See without the explicit approval of the supreme moderator.

2. The one requesting the indult must relate in brief and concrete detail the specific, not merely generic or vague, reasons motivating the request. Mere declarations of fact about the intent to depart are not acceptable and explanations of motives are required.

3. The request should indicate what spiritual, psychological, or medical means have been used to resolve his or her present difficulties. It should also contain a curriculum vitae of the member's employments, occupations, and community experiences, as well as an evaluation of these. The request need not be profuse but should clearly identify all those concerned (institute, member, etc.) as well as those items required for its successful processing.

4. Should the member be a cleric and have a receiving bishop, appropriate documentation indicating his intent should be included. Should the member be a cleric and not have a receiving bishop, the request might include that some special provision be made by the Apostolic See.

5. Upon receipt of the indult it should be communicated to the member without delay with any qualifications contained therein, as well as the member's right of rejection, being clearly indicated to him or her at the time of notification.

VOLUNTARY DEPARTURE FOR THOSE IN PERPETUAL PROFESSION AND EFFECTS OF AN INDULT OF DEPARTURE: MAJOR CHANGES IN 1983 CODE

1. The 1917 Code used the term secularization to refer to those who had obtained such an indult, whereas the 1983 Code does not use that term and speaks of this severing of the juridic bond with an institute as an "indult of departure" in contrast to the "indult of exclaustration" mentioned in CC 686 and 687.

2. The 1917 Code had three canons limiting the activities of "secularized" religious clerics with respect to certain ecclesiastical offices and functions. These disqualifications were abrogated by interim legislation (*Experimenta Circa*, February 2, 1972) and have not been included in the 1983 Code.

3. The time limit for automatic incardination of a cleric accepted conditionally by a benevolent bishop is now five years, whereas in the 1917 Code it was articulated as for three years with possible renewal for an additional three years at the discretion of the bishop.

4. The indult of departure according to the 1983 Code must be rejected in the act of notification or it automatically takes effect. Although this was the case in the 1917 Code following the general norms for rescripts, it has been the practice of the Sacred Congregation since 1953 to require acceptance of the indult within ten days of notification in order for it to take effect.

VOLUNTARY DEPARTURE FOR THOSE IN PERPETUAL PROFESSION AND EFFECTS OF AN INDULT OF DEPARTURE: SPECIAL QUESTIONS

1. *What if a member in temporary profession desires an indult of departure?*

Follow the prescriptions of C 688, §2.

2. *What if the supreme moderator will not process the request as required by C 691, §1?*

The member could have recourse to an arbitration board within the institute if any exists or could submit the collected material to the competent authority with an indication of the supreme moderator's unwillingness to process the request in the required manner.

3. *What if the competent authority denies the request for an indult of departure on the basis of insufficient reasons?*

The member should resubmit the request with more specific, detailed, and directly related motivating causes for the request. If this is still insufficient, he or she might ask the competent authority to indicate precisely what additional information is required.

4. *What if the competent authority denies the request for an indult of departure because the approval of the supreme moderator was lacking?*

If the approval was simply not included in the request by an oversight in procedure, the request should be resubmitted with the required approval included. If the approval was withheld by the supreme moderator because he or she simply disapproved of the request, then the matter should be dealt with by the member in direct consultation with the supreme moderator and his or her council whose opinion is also required before the supreme moderator acts according to C 691, §1. Should the parties to the misunderstanding become intransigent, the matter should be referred to the Sacred Congregation.

5. *What if the motivating reasons for the request are not true and the minimum requirements for validity of rescripts are not present according to the practice of the curia?*

If the rescript is *motu proprio,* that is, issued on the initiative of the pope himself, then it is valid nonetheless according to C 63, §1. If the rescript is not *motu proprio* and the conditions required for validity are not met due to actions on the part of the one seeking it, the invalidity will probably never be known and the rescript will be executed with the indult taking effect.

6. *What if a cleric is unable to find a benevolent bishop as required before the indult can be granted as indicated in C 693?*

If the problem is not with respect to the merits of the request but merely with respect to the lack of a benevolent bishop for at least conditional acceptance, the cleric could change his request to one for exclaustration which could be done following the norm of CC 686 and 687. In this case the cleric is under the special care of the bishop where he resides and must have his permission in order to function in any ministerial capacity but the possibility of incardination under the five-year statute of limitations would not apply. During this period of exclaustration the cleric might seek a benevolent bishop for the purpose of possible incardination as required by C 693. Should he have no success whatever, he should refer the matter, carefully documenting the problem, to the Sacred Congregation.

7. *What if a member rejects the indult in the process of notification and then changes his or her mind?*

Rejection of the indult upon notification renders it inoperative. Such rejection should be communicated to competent authority as soon as possible and the rescript should then be revoked by the granting authority. If this is not done and the rescript were to be considered as dependent on the member's subsequent acceptance or rejection it would be both contrary to the notion of the indult and would leave the member potentially on the verge of perpetual departure at any time subsequent to the rejection. Once the rescript has been rejected, the member should resubmit a request if he or she has a change of mind or heart.

8. *What if the member does not reject the indult in the act of notification and subsequently changes his or her mind wishing to remain in the institute?*

If the rescript is not rejected it is thereby accepted with the legal consequences taking effect according to C 693. Should there be a doubt on the part of the member at the time of notification, he or she should reject the indult and reprocess it again as mentioned in (7) if necessary. If the member does not reject the indult in the act of notification, subsequent changing of one's mind does not alter the legal consequences of the completed juridic act. Such legal consequences and the significance of rejection or nonrejection of the indult should be clearly and carefully explained to the member in the early stages of the process of requesting the indult of departure.

9. *What if the member who has obtained an indult of departure wishes to return to the institute or to another institute of consecrated life?*

One who wishes to return to the same institute can do so following the requirements of C 690, §1 and need not make a new novitiate. One who wishes to enter another institute of consecrated life must fulfill the requirements of universal and proper law for admission to the institute concerned unless some special provision is made for mitigation or waiving of any of these requirements by competent authority. No one who conceals incorporation in an institute of consecrated life or society of apostolic life may be validly admitted to another institute according to C 643, §1.

DISMISSAL: NOTION AND HISTORY

Dismissal of a professed member of an institute of consecrated life is a serious action taken by competent ecclesiastical authority through which permanent departure is imposed on a member concomitant with dispensation from one's vows and from all the rights and obligations arising from profession. Prior to the 1917 Code there was a distinction between "dismissal," which was used in reference to those who had professed simple vows, and "expulsion," which was used in reference to those who professed solemn vows. The 1917 Code had several categories for dismissal: (1) automatic dismissal for certain specified transgressions, (2) an administrative procedure for those in temporary vows, (3) an administrative procedure for those in perpetual vows in clerical exempt or lay institutes of men, (4) a slightly different administrative procedure for those in perpetual vows in institutes of women, and (5) a judicial procedure for any professed members of clerical exempt institutes. As of 1974 the judicial process for clerical exempt institutes was abrogated (*Processus Iudicialis*, March 2, 1974, SCRIS) and since the mid-1970s it has been the practice of SCRIS to require the same procedure for dismissal of both men and women in perpetual vows.[20] The 1983 Code has only three categories for dismissal: (1) automatic dismissal for certain specified transgressions, (2) instances in which the dismissal is not automatic but ought to be initiated by competent authority for certain transgressions, and (3) a single administrative process for all other instances.

It is important to note that dismissal procedures relate to penal legislation and thereby are subject to strict interpretation according to the norms of the Code itself, C 18, and that dismissal as such is to be distinguished from non-admission to profession or non-admission to renewal of vows which in themselves are not penal procedures.

DISMISSAL: CC 694–704

C 694

§1. A member is to be held to be ipso facto dismissed from the institute who:

1⁰ has notoriously abandoned the Catholic faith;

2⁰ has contracted marriage or has attempted it, even only civilly.

§2. In these instances the major superior with the council without any delay and after having collected proofs should issue a declaration of the fact so that the dismissal is established juridically.

§1

Automatic or *ipso facto* dismissal is an extraordinary penalty whose use is for the protection of the institute itself against the actions of members whose behavior is directly and publicly contrary to the nature of consecrated life. Neither defection nor what constitutes notorious defection from the Catholic faith are defined in the Code. Clearly in the context of the canons on consecrated life the person concerned would have to be someone who is a practicing juridically verifiable member of the Catholic Church (because such is required for admission to an institute) who subsequently abandons this position—in a practicing and/or juridically verifiable manner—in favor of some non-Catholic belief. Notorious defection must be at least public, that is from a juridic point of view already divulged or such that it will be or should be divulged. Since penal legislation must be strictly interpreted, that is within the narrowest meaning of the words without doing violence to the actual meaning, mere disagreement with or objection to or questioning of certain matters of faith or pronouncements of the magisterium would not constitute matter for *ipso facto* dismissal even though such might be related to other circumstances which collectively suggest initiating the dismissal process according to C 696.

The wording of the canon with respect to marriage distinguishes contracted and attempted marriages. C 1088 of the 1983 Code renders invalid any marriage by one who is bound by the public perpetual vow of chastity in a religious institute. Thus exchange of marriage vows by such a person is considered as "attempted" because there is no juridically recognized effect of the act. Those not bound by public perpetual vow would "contract" marriage by exchange of marriage vows but would do so illegally. A civil bond of marriage is that which is recognized in civil law as such. Again, since this concerns penal legislation, the canon must be strictly interpreted and the action brought to completion with full deliberation and consent.

§2

Note that the major superior, who may or may not happen to be the supreme moderator depending on the organization of the institute, is competent to act in declaring automatic dismissal already incurred. The major superior must act with the council, but the canon does not state whether deliberative or consultative action of the council is required. Proper law of the institute may indicate one or the other manner of acting, but in the absence of proper law specification, only consultation would be required by the wording of the canon. Such action on the part of the major superior does not constitute dismissal of the member because this has already automatically been incurred, but the declaration of fact of the already incurred dismissal brings with it the full effect of the law regarding future consequences such as the observance and remission of it and related penalties. [21] For protection of the institute automatically incurred penalties ought to be declared by the competent authority acting in accord with this canon.

C 695

§1. A member must be dismissed for the offenses in cann. 1397, 1398 and 1395, unless in the delicts mentioned in can. 1395, §2, the superior judges that dismissal is not entirely necessary and that the correction of the member and restitution of justice and reparation of scandal can be sufficiently assured in some other way.

§2. In these cases the major superior, having collected proofs about the facts and imputability, is to make known the accusation and the proofs to the member who is about to be dismissed, giving the member the opportunity of self-defense. All the acts, signed by the major superior and a notary, along with the written and signed responses of the member, are to be transmitted to the supreme moderator.

§1

A delict was defined in the 1917 Code as an external, morally imputable violation of a law to which at least an indeterminate canonical sanction was attached. [22] The 1983 Code uses the word without defining it, but indicates that no one is liable to an ecclesiastical penalty unless there has been an external violation of a law or precept which is gravely imputable to someone through *dolus* (the intent to do wrong) and *culpa* (blameworthiness by fault or defect). [23]

C 1397 concerns homicide, abduction, detention, mutilation, and gravely wounding someone. C 1398 concerns the procurement of an abortion. C 1395 concerns clerical concubinage and transgressions of the sixth commandment. §1 of C 1395 deals with external transgressions in which the person persists after appropriate warnings, and §2 deals with lesser transgressions which may be more or less public or may involve persons under sixteen. In the matter of §2, as C 695, §1 indicates, the superior judges whether or not dismissal is necessary and whether or not other means of amendment, restitution, and reparation can be made by the culpable party. Since the previous canon and C 695, §2 both refer to the major superior as the competent authority, he or she would be the competent authority for the action of this canon also. Since laws regarding sanctions are involved, the "must be dismissed" of this canon would apply only when the strict meaning of the words are fulfilled. Even though imputability is presumed by external violation of a law, the canons on those who are liable to ecclesiastical penalties indicate a variety of morally mitigating circumstances in which either the penalty does not apply or may be adjusted according to the judgment of competent authority. Given the seriousness of the matter and the complexity of penal law, qualified experts should be consulted before any action is taken regarding the dismissal indicated in this canon. [24]

§2

Should the major superior judge the facts and imputability required for §1 of the canon to be operative, he or she must collect the information regarding both facts and imputability. The accusation as well as the evidence supporting the facts and imputability must be made known to the member concerned, and this member must be given the opportunity of self defense. Defense made by the member should be in writing, and should he or she wish to give it orally it can be subsequently written and attested to by the notary. Telephone communication does not suffice for notifying the member concerned, since it does not constitute juridic proof of contact. Registered mail with return receipt addressed to the party concerned or to the party's next of kin would suffice. Although this canon is not dealing with strict canonical monitions (as in C 697), comparable procedures regarding notification and opportunity for defense could be responsibly used. If the member concerned is unable to be contacted, notification of impending dismissal action could be made through the institute's official channel of communication or by posting in the house to which the member is assigned. Refusal to accept notification or preventing notification from reaching him or her on the part of the member would be considered equivalent to notification. [25]

This canon does not require the major superior to act in consultation with his or her council, but all the acts of the case must be signed by a notary in addition to the major superior. As indicated in C 698 below, the member always retains the right of communicating directly with the supreme moderator. The acts as collected by the major superior are transmitted to the supreme moderator who then acts in accord with CC 699 and 700 as indicated below.

C 696

§1. A member can also be dismissed for other causes, provided that they are grave, external, imputable and juridically proven, such as: habitual neglect of the obligations of consecrated life; repeated violations of the sacred bonds; pertinacious disobedience to lawful prescriptions of superiors in a serious matter; grave scandal arising from the culpable behavior of the member; pertinacious upholding or spreading of doctrines condemned by the magisterium of the Church; public adherence to ideologies infected by materialism or atheism; unlawful absence mentioned in can. 665, §2 lasting six months; other causes of similar seriousness which may be determined by the proper law of the institute.

§2. Even causes of lesser seriousness determined in proper law suffice for the dismissal of a member in temporary vows.

§1

This canon does not refer to a "delict" directly as mentioned in C 695, whence the requirements of penal law do not strictly apply to the interpretation of this canon. Nevertheless, the procedure and consequences are penal in nature and have been treated as such by SCRIS when dealing with dismissals as has previously been noted in the introductory remarks for these canons on dismissal. The four elements usually required of delicts are mentioned: grave, external, imputable, and juridically proven. Legal imputability involves *dolus* and *culpa* (1983 CIC 1321) and juridically proven acts require all the formalities indicated in procedural and penal legislation. The examples indicated, which do not constitute a taxative or exhaustive listing of possible reasons for dismissal, are generic in nature (with the exception of the six-months absence contrary to C 665, §2) but are directed against matter fundamental to the obligations of consecrated life in the Church.

The terminology of the canon clearly indicates that the violations envisioned are not occasional or out of context behavior on the part of the member but rather habitual or repeated or pertinacious or public behavior that can fulfill the four requirements of the canon. Habitual or repeated violations may be in the same matter or different matters protracted over an extended period of time. The matter involved for disobedience or scandal must be grave. Should an institute wish to include other matter in its proper law that might warrant dismissal action, this should be clearly articulated and must, according to the canon, be of the same gravity as those already indicated.

§2

This paragraph is the only reference the 1983 Code makes to a difference in treatment for any professed member of any institute with respect to vows. Note that a temporarily professed member also qualifies for the dismissal indicated in §1 of this canon as well as the dismissals possible in CC 694 and 695. Since a member in temporary profession may be granted an indult of departure by C 688, §2, or leave at the expiration of profession by C 688, §1, or be refused subsequent profession by C 689, §1, this present canon would probably only be operative if a grave matter, albeit less grave than required for §1, were concerned. The requirements of external, imputable, and juridically proven would still hold, however, and the canon also requires such less grave causes to be articulated in the proper law of the institute. It would not be advisable to include such in an institute's proper law unless there are matters which clearly apply only to those temporarily professed and which have been specific difficulties for the institute.

C 697

In the cases mentioned in can. 696, if the major superior, after having heard the council, believes the process of dismissal is to be begun:

1⁰ the major superior is to collect or complete proofs;

2⁰ the major superior is to warn the member in writing or before two witnesses with an explicit threat of subsequent dismissal unless the member reforms, the cause of the dismissal is to be clearly indicated and the member is to be given the full opportunity of self-defense; but if the warning is in vain the superior is to proceed to a second warning, after an intervening time of at least fifteen days;

3⁰ if this warning also has been in vain and the major superior with the council believes that there is sufficient proof of incorrigibility and that the defenses of the member are insufficient, and fifteen days have elapsed since the last warning without any effect, the major superior is to transmit to the supreme moderator all acts, signed by the major superior and a notary, along with the signed response of the member.

This right to act given to the major superior, who as previously noted may or may not be the supreme moderator depending on the organization of the institute, is facultative and not preceptive. The major superior is not bound to initiate a process of dismissal, and before he or she acts the council must be heard which means the advice given is not binding although the canons on consultation indicate that such advice should not be disregarded without good reason (C 127, §2, 2°). Once the decision is made to initiate the process of dismissal, the prescriptions of this and the following three canons must be carefully observed or, upon recourse, the dismissal may be nullified for lack of proper procedure. [26]

To "collect and complete proofs" means that the alleged transgressions must be documented regarding their gravity, their external nature, their being properly attributed to the person in question, and their juridic value. Civilly recognized documents as well as sworn statements attested to by witnesses suffice in these matters, whereas conjectures, hearsay information, or things for which a person cannot be held morally responsible do not suffice. Record of having warned a member in writing is had if done by direct delivery or by registered mail with return receipt, and as noted under C 695, §2 the member who prevents notification from reaching himself or herself can be considered as having been notified. Such attempts and the nonacceptance of the member concerned should be carefully noted in the acts. If the warning to the member is given orally with two witnesses this should be subsequently recorded and signed by the major superior and witnesses and included in the acts.

The warning to the member *must* contain *specific* mention of (1) the action or actions of the member which gave rise to initiation of the process, (2) the action or actions expected of the member that would constitute amendment or at least are being required of the member by the major superior, and (3) the threat of subsequent dismissal if the member does not act according to the actions imposed.

The member must also be given the opportunity of presenting a defense of his or her actions, and this should be in writing or transcribed if given orally and included in the acts of the case. If fifteen days have elapsed from the receipt of the warning by the member and the presentation of defense notwithstanding, he or she has not altered behavior as requested, another warning containing the same specific information as in the first should be given in the same manner. If, after another fifteen days have elapsed from receipt of this warning by the member and the presentation of another defense notwithstanding, the major superior and council decide that the member is incorrigible—that is, not willing or not able to alter his or her behavior—and that the defenses presented do not suffice to negate this judgment, then all the acts and responses signed by those indicated are sent to the supreme moderator or, if the major superior is the supreme moderator of the institute, to the competent authority as indicated in CC 699 and 700.

C 698

In all cases mentioned in cann. 695 and 696, the right of a member to communicate with and offer a defense directly to the supreme moderator always remains intact.

Obviously, if the major superior and the supreme moderator are the same person, the requirements of this canon are met by the communications and presentations of defense as indicated in C 697. This canon protects the right of the member to communicate directly with the person who, according to the next canon, is responsible for issuing the actual decree of dismissal.

C 699

§1. With the council, which must have at least four members for validity, the supreme moderator is to proceed collegially to the careful weighing of the proofs, arguments and defenses; if it has been so decided by a secret ballot, the supreme moderator is to issue the decree of dismissal, with the motives in law and in fact expressed at least in summary fashion for validity.

§2. In autonomous monasteries mentioned in can. 615 the decision on dismissal pertains to the diocesan bishop, to whom the superior is to submit the acts examined by the council.

§1

The supreme moderator with a council of not less than four members weighs the merits of the acts of the entire case. If the council of a particular institute should consist of less than four members, the supreme moderator with the approval of the other members of the council may appoint the additional member or members needed or these may be indicated in the proper law of the institute for such circumstances. [27] By majority vote of a secret ballot, the supreme moderator and council decide whether or not to issue a decree of dismissal. The supreme moderator must act according to the decisive vote. The decree which is subsequently issued must contain references to the law that pertains to the case at hand as well as the circumstances substantiated by the acts which prompted the issuance of the decree. These need not be profuse but should clearly delineate the pertinent matter of the case in summary fashion at least. The decree so issued has no force until confirmed as required by C 700, which also indicates additional requirements for the validity of the decree.

§2

Upon completion of the requirements indicated in C 697, since the monastery mentioned in C 615 has no major superior beyond its own moderator and is not associated with any other institute of religious so that its superior has true power over this monastery and, since the requirements of C 698 are automatically fulfilled, the acts of the case should be submitted directly to the diocesan bishop. The diocesan bishop decides whether or not to issue a decree of dismissal based on the information and opinions submitted by the major superior, council, and member concerned as required by C 697. The decree so issued has no force until confirmed as required by C 700.

This canon does not mention a procedure for monasteries of any other category such as those in federations or confederations where there is a supreme moderator (other than the major superior) who has actual power over the monastery as delineated by the constitutions. In these cases the norms of proper law in addition to the directives of CC 697, 698, and 699, §1 must be followed. In any case the decree so issued has no force until confirmed as required by C 700.

C 700

A decree of dismissal does not take effect unless it has been confirmed by the Holy See to whom the decree and all the acts are to be transmitted; if it is a question of an institute of diocesan right, the confirmation belongs to the bishop of the diocese where the house to which the religious is assigned is situated. The decree, for validity, must indicate the right which the dismissed religious enjoys to have recourse to competent authority within ten days from receiving the notification. The recourse has a suspensive effect.

For an institute of diocesan right, the decree of dismissal issued according to C 699, §1 is confirmed by the bishop of the diocese where the house to which the member in question is assigned. His confirmation of the decree gives it legal force. For an institute of pontifical right the decree of dismissal issued according to C 699, §1 is confirmed by SCRIS. SCRIS confirmation of the decree gives it legal force. Since only the decree of dismissal in diocesan institutes comes under the competence of the diocesan bishop according to this canon, the decree issued by the bishop for autonomous monasteries as indicated in C 699, §2 must also be confirmed by SCRIS before it has legal force.

For validity, in addition to expressing at least in summary fashion the motives in law and in fact for dismissal as required by C 699, §1, the decree must indicate that the member being dismissed has the right of recourse to the competent authority within ten days of receiving notification of the dismissal. SCRIS is the competent authority for recourse against any decree of dismissal.[28] Recourse may be placed directly by the person being dismissed or through the person who communicated the decree. It should be done in writing but verbal indication of the desire to have recourse communicated to the person executing the decree suffices because that person should pursue the request as indicated in writing to SCRIS.

That the recourse against a decree of dismissal has suspensive effect means, simply, that the member still belongs to the institute with all the rights and obligations arising from profession unless these have been restricted or lost in some other manner indicated in general or proper law. Since any decree except that for a diocesan institute has legal force subsequent to SCRIS confirmation, such confirmation contains the explicit approval of SCRIS for the dismissal action after having carefully considered the behavior, procedure, and decision of the supreme moderator and council. However, upon recourse the case is reinvestigated and this may result in the presentation of new information, the discovery of an injustice, the perception of biased or subjective judgments at various stages of the process, or even a procedural formality that might warrant reversal of the original decree. If a dismissal is reconfirmed upon recourse to SCRIS, the only other recourse for the dismissed member would be to the Apostolic Signatura, which has competence only if violation of procedure, and not the merit of the case itself, is being questioned.[29]

If recourse is made to SCRIS against confirmation of a decree of a diocesan bishop for an institute of diocesan right, SCRIS could—being the higher ecclesiastical authority—reverse the confirmed decree, but certainly would not do so without careful investigation of the case and consultation with those involved. Recourse from reconfirmation of the decree by SCRIS could be referred to the Apostolic Signatura but only on the same basis as mentioned above.

C 701

Vows, rights and obligations derived from profession cease ipso facto by legitimate dismissal. However, if the member is a cleric, he cannot exercise sacred orders until he finds a bishop who receives him after a suitable probationary period in the diocese according to can. 693 or at least allows him to exercise sacred orders.

The wording of the canon makes it clear that all rights and obligations arising from profession as well as the obligations of the vows cease by reason of legitimate dismissal. This effect does not take place during the process of recourse as noted in C 700. Definitive dismissal from an institute results in complete severing of the juridic bond between the member and the institute.

In the same manner as mentioned for the canons concerning exclaustration (C 687) and for the canons concerning an indult of departure (C 693), clerics cannot function in any diocese except in union with the diocesan bishop and under his authority. For an indult of departure or for dismissal the incardination of the cleric in the institute ceases, and he must find a bishop who is willing to incardinate him permanently or accept him experimentally or at least let him function in the diocese. In practice those things warranting dismissal often also warrant the imposition of other ecclesiastical sanctions when clerics are involved depending on the specifics of each case. If in any case a benevolent bishop cannot be found recourse should be had to the Holy See as indicated for C 693.

C 702

§1. Those who have legitimately left a religious institute or have been legitimately dismissed from one can request nothing from it for any work done in it.

§2. The institute however is to observe equity and evangelical charity toward the member who is separated from it.

§1

The canon excludes the possibility in law of the former member requesting or obtaining compensation for any and all work done while in the institute. Those automatically dismissed according to C 694, §1 are included in this canon whether or not the declaration of C 694, §2 has been made (although the declaration should not on that account be omitted). Those who have illegitimately left the institute should be dismissed according to the procedure of CC 696–700 if it is ascertained that they have no intention or desire to return and regularize their status.

§2

Whereas §1 legally excludes the right of the former member to compensation for his or her work while in the institute, §2 legally requires the institute to treat the former member with equity and charity. In context the canon appears to refer to monetary compensation although this is not specifically mentioned in either paragraph. If the member retained ownership of his or her goods by profession, these obviously still belong to him or her and the cession of administration, disposition of use and usufruct, as well as the will mentioned in C 668, §1 should be returned to the person who should alter them as needed. If the member renounced ownership by profession or by choice as indicated in C 668, §4, this renunciation would no longer hold with respect to future acquisition of goods.

If a member may have brought a dowry as formerly required by the 1917 Code or may even now be required by proper law, the principal should be returned in full to the former member. Strictly speaking the former member has no right to income from the investment of any dowry while he or she was a member of the institute, since in its origin dowry income was the means of support for the members of institutes without other means of fixed income. If, however, the income from any dowry may be judged proportionately greater than any expenses which might have been incurred while the religious was a member of the institute, it seems this should be taken into consideration when observing the equity and charity mentioned by the canon.

Equity and evangelical charity are not defined by the canon and obviously admit of different degrees of assessment and application in particular cases. In any case they are not fundamentally restricted to monetary matters and a recent decree of SCRIS (*Deserunt praebendo,* January 25, 1974) notes that institutes should provide for the spiritual, moral, social and economic welfare of former members and that institutes should likewise investigate programs whereby these provisions can be made available.

C 703

In the case of serious exterior scandal or very grave imminent harm to the institute a member can be immediately expelled from the religious house by the major superior, or, if there is a danger in delay, by the local superior with the consent of the council. If it is necessary the major superior should see that the process of dismissal is begun according to the norm of law or refer the matter to the Apostolic See.

The canon clearly refers to immediate expulsion from the house and not dismissal from the institute. The competent authority is the major superior or the local superior with the consent of the council. The canon does not require the major superior to consult the council but, since either the dismissal process may be initiated or the matter may be referred to the Apostolic See, some consultation by the major superior is prudently indicated if time and circumstances permit. The reasons for expulsion from the house are two only: (1) serious exterior scandal or (2) very grave imminent harm to the institute. For the first, the matter would have to be objectively serious, known outside the religious house, and actually causing scandal. For the second, the harm must be very grave, actually about to happen, and be a real threat to the good of the institute. In order to act in either case, the competent superior must judge that the scandal or harm cannot be otherwise avoided, that it is morally certain to occur unless some action is taken, and that the scandal or harm pertains to the institute and not to one or a few persons only.

The canon gives no indication as to where the religious so expelled from the house should be sent, but common sense dictates that he or she should be sent to a clearly specified place (preferably another house of the institute if at all possible) with clearly specified expectations articulated and that the competent superior if necessary should then proceed with one of the two options indicated in the canon. Note also that the canon does not give any indication regarding the number in reference to the scandal or harm, since the wording itself is so strong as to indicate that one instance truly fulfilling these requirements would suffice for such expulsion from the house. Recall however that the process of dismissal requires much more than this in order to be pursued to conclusion thus indicating that referring the matter to the Apostolic See might in some cases be the better choice. If the scandal or harm is duly averted by the action permitted in this canon, the major superior should initiate the process of dismissal or contact the Apostolic See only if either is judged necessary, since the canon does not require this step.

C 704

The report to be sent to the Apostolic See referred to in canon 592, §1 is to mention members separated from the institute in any way whatsoever.

Members in any stage of any process included in CC 684–703 should be mentioned. Thus those in transfer, those on voluntary or imposed exclaustration, those with profession of temporary vows who have requested and received an indult of departure, those who have not been admitted to first or subsequent profession, those for whom dismissal has been initiated or completed, and those expelled from the house are part of this report. Once a process of separation has been completed and the member has been duly mentioned in the report, he or she need not be mentioned in subsequent ones. Thus, for example, a member on voluntary exclaustration should be mentioned in each report submitted for the time which encompasses any portion of the exclaustration but need not be mentioned in subsequent reports as having in the past been on exclaustration.

DISMISSAL: STANDARD PROCEDURE

Since the procedures for dismissal are clearly indicated in the respective canons (automatic dismissal in C 694; required dismissal for certain delicts in C 695; and possible dismissal for the causes in CC 696–700), the procedure will not be repeated here for each of these. The process of CC 697–700 is the most common and includes:

1. the major superior having heard the council initiating the process,
2. collecting and completing the proofs,
3. warning the member in writing or in the presence of two witnesses about the cause of concern, the desired amendment, and the possibility of dismissal,
4. allowing the member full faculty of defense communicating directly with the supreme moderator if so desired,
5. warning the member again in the same manner with the same right of defense after fifteen days have passed since communication of the first warning,
6. the major superior deciding with the council after fifteen days have passed since communication of the second warning that incorrigibility is sufficiently manifest and the member's defenses are inadequate,
7. transmitting all the acts including the member's defense to the supreme moderator who, with the decisive vote of at least a four-member council, issues a decree of dismissal (unless it involves an autonomous monastery as in C 615),
8. the decree, expressing the summary motives in fact and in law and indicating the right of recourse with suspensive effect, confirmed by the competent authority as indicated in C 700.

DISMISSAL: CHANGES IN THE 1983 CODE

1. The reasons for automatic dismissal have been limited to two, dropping that of dismissal for running away with a person of the opposite sex which was included in the 1917 Code.

2. There is no distinction made between the effects of departure or dismissal for those in temporary profession and those in perpetual profession. After dismissal those in temporary profession under the 1917 Code were automatically dispensed from vows while those in perpetual profession were still under vow unless otherwise indicated. The 1983 Code frees all those dismissed from the vows and the rights and obligations of profession.

3. There are no longer distinct procedures for persons of different religious status, clerical status, and sex as were contained in the 1917 Code.

4. There are no automatically incurred sanctions for clerics by reason of dismissal itself.

5. Since the vows, rights and obligations of profession cease with dismissal under the 1983 Code, there are no requirements for subsequent

amendment and return to the institute for those who had been perpetually professed at the time of dismissal.

6. There is no distinction based on sex as to whom should be treated with charity and equity after departure, whereas the 1917 Code in C 643, §2 gave preference to women in this regard and did not mention men at all.

DISMISSAL: SPECIAL QUESTIONS

1. *What if the major superior is not certain whether the requirements of CC 694, §1; 695, §1, and 696, §1 are sufficiently fulfilled to warrant declaration of or initiating the process of dismissal?*

In cases of uncertainty, and even in cases where the major superior is rather certain regarding these requirements, a competent canonist should be consulted so that precipitous or erroneous actions are not taken.

2. *What if the member refuses to receive the required warnings by returning unopened letters, not appearing when summoned, not answering the phone, etc.?*

Should any of these be the case attempts might be made to contact the member through family or friends. Since legally one who has never been properly warned cannot be dismissed, a legally knowledgeable member might use these means to avoid this action. After repeated and carefully documented attempts to contact and warn the member, the entire acts of the case should be referred to the Apostolic See.

3. *What if a member refuses to offer any defense in response to the warnings?*

The law requires that the right of defense be afforded the member. If the member chooses not to exercise that right, it should be carefully noted in the acts.

RELIGIOUS RAISED TO THE EPISCOPATE: NOTION AND HISTORY

The question of whether or not those who were monks (the only form of "religious" at the time) could be chosen as bishops was decided in the early centuries by Pope Siricius, who in 385 decreed that bishops could be *aut ex monachis aut ex clericis.* [30]

Pope Innocent I in 404 made it clear that monks who became bishops were still monks, however; and Gregory I in 506 stated that a monk ought not to accept any office outside the monastery without the approval of his abbot. [31] Hadrian II in 870 required that monks who were bishops retain the style and color of their religious garb. This regulation was maintained with various alterations until 1969 when the rules for dress, titles, and coats-of-arms of cardinals, bishops, and other prelates were simplified and unified after Vatican II by Paul VI.[32]

Legislation and practice regarding religious who are bishops is eclectic and gradual stemming from the tenth-century Council of Altheim (916), which legislated regarding garb, property, and permissions, from Sixtus V, who in 1586 indicated that at least some bishops and cardinals should be named from among regulars or mendicants, from Paul IV, who in 1559 negated active and passive voice in their institutes for bishops who were religious, from Clement XIV, who in 1716 reaffirmed the Council of Altheim's decision that the goods coming to a "religious" bishop were acquired for the Church or diocese unless specifically given to his person or to his institute, and from Benedict XIII, who in 1726 decreed that former "religious"bishops and cardinals could choose a place to live even outside a house of the institute after retiring from active service as bishops.[33] The 1917 Code incorporated the extant legislation at the time and included canons regarding religious priests who were pastors in the same section. The 1983 Code is highly simplified in this regard dealing only with religious who are bishops, including regulations on "religious" pastors in the canons treating pastors, and leaving decisions regarding active or passive voice in the institute to the proper law of the institute.[34]

Since these canons concern only a small number of persons in very specific circumstances, and since these persons usually are highly qualified canonically, the following comments will be appropriately brief and primarily informational for those who are not numbered among this group of persons.

RELIGIOUS RAISED TO THE EPISCOPATE: CC 705–707

C 705

A religious raised to the episcopate remains a member of his own institute but is subject to the Roman Pontiff alone in virtue of his vow of obedience and is not bound by obligations which he himself prudently judges cannot be reconciled with his position.

The canon makes clear that a bishop who belongs to any religious institute remains a member of the institute but is removed from the power of the superiors of the institute with respect to the vow of obedience. He is the judge of which obligations can or cannot be reconciled with his position as bishop, but obviously this would not include such matter as the constitutive elements of the vows. The principle operative here is that the religious who is a bishop has at least as much dispensing power with respect to his obligations in the institute as the supreme moderator of the institute and also has the dispensing powers of a bishop according to law.

C 706

As regards the above-mentioned religious:

1° if through profession he has lost the ownership of goods, he has the use of goods which come to him as well as their revenues and administration; however the diocesan bishop and those mentioned in can. 381, §2 acquire the ownership for the particular church; all others, for the institute or the Holy See depending on whether the institute is capable of ownership or not;

2° if through profession he has not lost the ownership of goods, he regains the use, revenues and administration of the goods which he had; he fully acquires for himself those which come to him afterwards;

3° in either case, however, he must distribute goods coming to him according to the will of the donors when they do not come to him for personal reasons.

By C 668, §1 all religious cede the administration of their goods and dispose of their use and revenues prior to first profession. By C 668, §4 and §5 and the proper law of any institute, the individual religious may also have renounced ownership of goods. If ownership has been renounced by the religious as a consequence of the vow of poverty, the "religious" bishop may now acquire goods either for the institute or for the Holy See if the institute itself cannot acquire goods (as, for example, Capuchins or Carmelites). If, however, he is a diocesan bishop or is in charge of a community of the faithful equivalent to a particular church so that he is equivalent to a diocesan bishop (as, for example, an apostolic vicar or apostolic prefect), he acquires goods for the particular church instead of for the institute or for the Holy See. In any case he has the use, administration, and revenues of the goods which come to him as bishop.[35]

If the "religious" bishop has not renounced ownership by profession in his institute, he can still acquire goods as a bishop and also regains the use, revenues, and administration of the goods he had. Thus the cession and disposition of C 668, §1 are nullified by the prescriptions of this canon for those religious who become bishops. Nevertheless, any goods acquired must be distributed according to the desires articulated by the donor whenever there are any stipulations for their use or whenever the goods are not intended specifically for the person as such.

C 707

§1. A retired religious bishop may choose a place to live for himself even outside the houses of his institute unless something else has been provided by the Apostolic See.

§2. If he has served a certain diocese, suitable and worthy sustenance is to be his according to can. 402, §2 unless his own institute wishes to provide that sustenance; otherwise the Apostolic See is to provide.

This canon makes clear that residence for a retired bishop is entirely at the discretion of the retired bishop unless the Apostolic See indicates otherwise. Likewise it makes clear that for a bishop who has served a diocese, the diocese has the primary responsibility to provide suitable and worthy sustenance for the retired bishop. The institute may wish to provide that sustenance even though the diocese has the primary responsibility according to this canon. C 402, §2 also mentions the episcopal conference as providing sustenance for retired bishops. If the "religious" bishop has not served a diocese (and even if he has), the institute has some responsibility for providing sustenance by reason of his membership in the institute as such. Since C 402, §2 mentions the responsibility of the episcopal conference with respect to any (that is, not just diocesan) bishops who are retired, the episcopal conference would have some responsibility also in this regard. Nevertheless, the final portion of this canon and of C 402, §1 indicate clearly that the Apostolic See should ultimately provide for any retired bishop who has not served a diocese or for whom certain other conditions or circumstances apply.

CONFERENCES OF MAJOR SUPERIORS: NOTION AND HISTORY

At the initiative of Pope Pius XII, and for the purpose of providing a forum to share experiences, visions, and similar problems, the First International Congress of the States of Perfection was held in Rome from November 26 to December 8, 1950. This and additional similar meetings, including the International Congress of General Superiors held in Rome from September 11–13, 1952 and the Second General Congress of the States of Perfection held in Rome from December 8–14, 1957, resulted in the formation of approximately twenty-five conferences of major superiors by 1957 and foreshadowed the articulations regarding conferences of major superiors as contained in *PC* 23, *CD* 35, *AG* 33, and *ES* II 21, 42, 43.[36]

The statutes for the International Union of Superioresses General were first approved on December 6, 1965 and revised on June 8, 1967. The statutes of the International Union of Superiors General were first approved on May 29, 1967 and revised on June 28, 1972.[37] Presently in the

Western Hemisphere the Conference of Latin American Religious (CLAR), the Canadian Religious Conference (CRC), the Leadership Conference of Women Religious (LCWR), and the Conference of Major Superiors of Men (CMSM) are established and operate to promote unity and interdependence in matters of mutual concern and to provide a practical and effective means for religious and hierarchy to dialogue and collaborate for the good of the Church.[38]

There is no parallel in the 1917 Code for these canons on conferences of major superiors because such entities did not exist at that time.

CONFERENCES OF MAJOR SUPERIORS: CC 708-709

C 708

Major superiors can usefully associate in conferences or councils so that joining forces they can work toward the achievement of the purpose of their individual institutes more fully, always with due regard for their autonomy, character and particular spirit, transact common business and foster suitable coordination and cooperation with conferences of bishops and also with individual bishops.

Note that the canon is very general allowing wide possibility for implementation. The purpose of such conferences is to foster cooperation and coordination with both episcopal conferences and individual bishops.[39] Such associations should help care for common concerns while maintaining the autonomy of the institutes involved. The canon does not mandate conferences or councils of major superiors but the Apostolic See is clearly in favor of them in light of their historical development which was initiated by Pius XII over thirty years ago.[40]

C 709

Conferences of major superiors are to have their own statutes approved by the Holy See, by which alone they can be erected, even as a juridic person, and under whose supreme governance they remain.

The canon makes clear that only the Holy See can approve the statutes of conferences of major superiors and only the Holy See can formally erect such a conference. Such organizations may or may not be juridic persons depending on the manner in which they are formally approved. If a conference is a juridic person (comparable in the Church to a corporation in the civil sector) it has the rights of such an institute including owning and administering property and is likewise bound by the obligations of juridic persons as contained in CC 113-123.

NOTES

1. Anne Fulwiler, *Transfer and Readmittance in Non-Clerical Institutes of Simple Vows* (unpublished license thesis, Washington: Catholic University of America, 1980) 6–10; T. Schaefer, *De Religiosis* (Rome: Vatican Polyglot Press, 1947) 885–87; F. X. Wernz and P. Vidal, *Ius Canonicum*, vol. III: *De Religiosis* (Rome: Gregorian University, 1933) 449–52.

2. C 607, §2 indicates the qualities of a religious institute as such. CC 603 and 604 mention hermits and consecrated virgins as canonically recognized forms of consecrated life. C 684, §5 deals with transfers to or from secular institutes or societies of apostolic life.

3. See CC 620 and 622, respectively, for those who qualify as major superiors and supreme moderators by general law.

4. C 668, §1 and §2.

5. Houses of canons regular (not ordinarily found in the United States) and of monks *(monachorum)* are described in C 613, §1 as self-governing. Self-governing monasteries of nuns *(monialium)* are mentioned in C 616, §4. The monasteries which would not qualify for the transfer of members as mentioned in C 684, §3 are those described in C 615.

6. CC 648, §1 and 655. The ordinary maximum for noviciate and temporary profession are two years and six years, respectively (CC 648, §3 and 655), meaning the person transferring could easily have spent up to eight years in formation prior to probation in the new institute.

7. CC 730 and 744, §2, respectively.

8. Acta Commissionis, *Comm* 13 (1981) 326, 328.

9. *AAS* 31 (1939) 321.

10. CC 697–700. The usual procedure for imposed exclaustration, also known as exclaustration *ad nutum Sanctae Sedis*, is known only from the practice of the Sacred Congregation as it has been utilized since 1953.

11. *CLD*, 1978 Supplement, C 639.

12. Schaefer, 906; Acta Commissionis, *Comm* 13 (1981) 335.

13. SCRIS, February 5, 1925, *AAS* 17 (1925) 107.

14. The Latin of the 1980 Schema canon 616 was *readmitti* but was changed to *rursus admitti* possibly to clarify that the admission was to the same institute (i.e., *again*) and not to another. A similar clarification was made by the Sacred Congregation in 1973 regarding the readmission mentioned in *RC* 38 as referring to readmission to the same institute, *CLD* 8:359.

15. Schaefer, 909–10, 916–18.

16. Acta Commissionis, *Comm* 13 (1981) 334.

17. In keeping with the universal law regarding rescripts, they can be refused and need not be used unless some other requirement of law so obliges (CC 62, 71). This was the case for such indults under the 1917 Code, but the practice of the Sacred Congregations since 1953 has been to add a clause indicating that such indults were void unless accepted by the petitioner within ten days of notification. Although this practice could have been continued a clear choice was made to include the requirement for this formal act at the time of notification. *CLD* IV:239 and Acta Commissionis, *Comm* 13 (1981) 338.

18. Rescripts in response to requests for indults of departure may refuse the request, suggest other possibilities (such as exclaustration) to alleviate the situation, grant the request as submitted, or grant it with imposition of certain qualifications (such as the non-possibility of rejection).

19. Schaefer, 920–22; *CLD* 4:244.

20. *AAS* 66 (1974) 215 and *Informationes* (1976) 83–86.

21. By C 1364 apostates, heretics, and schismatics (who are not specifically the subject of C 694) also incur automatic excommunication and, if they are clerics, are subject to additional penalties. CC 1335, 1342, 1355, and 1356 indicate different consequences for declared and non-declared automatically incurred penalties according to circumstances and competent authority.

22. 1917 CIC 2195, §1.

23. 1983 CIC 1313, §1 and 1321, §1.

24. C 1323 indicates instances in which penalties simply do not apply, and C 1324 indicates instances in which penalties do apply but may be tempered or other penances may be utilized instead. Important to remember is that penalties are not incurred by persons who act unknowingly or unwillingly or imperfectly and that the general principles of law dictate restriction rather than extension in harmful matters. The rights and dignity of individuals in these cases must be carefully balanced with the rights of the institute and the seriousness of the matter concerned.

25. Schaefer, 971, 974. The manner of notification is adapted from 1917 CIC 2143 and 2309, which are comparable to 1983 CIC 1509 and 1510. Proof of notification or attempts thereof are required, since the canon requires the member to be afforded to the possibility of defense, which right is clearly not respected if the person is not notified of the impending action.

26. For actual examples in which dismissals have been reversed after recourse to the Holy See because of finding irregularities in procedure, see *CLD* 8:430–37 and *CLD* 1979 Supplement, C 651.

27. This parallels the manner of supplying for necessary councillors in similar actions in collegiate tribunals in the 1917 Code CC 655, §1 and 516, §1. The 1983 Code does not specify the manner for supplying the required number of councillors.

28. Schaefer, 953–55.

29. The Apostolic Signatura is competent to pass judgment on the admissibility of recourse or on the illegality of an impugned act after a decision has been made by any other department of the Roman Curia within its respective area of competence, *(Reqimini Ecclesiae Universae*, August 15, 1967).

30. Joseph J. Marositz, *Obligations and Privileges of Religious Promoted to the Episcopal and Cardinalitial Dignities* (Washington: Catholic University of America, 1948) 11–12.

31. Marositz, 13–14.

32. Martin V in 1420 excommunicated some exempt mendicants who were titular bishops in foreign lands for not complying with the wearing of religious garb. Benedict XIII in 1726 reiterated the requirement of religious garb—adjusted only with respect to type of material—for regulars and mendicants who were bishops. Eventually more and more of the "episcopal" attire was granted to this category of bishops, and Paul VI (*Ut sive sollicite*, March 31, 1969) required the use of the same attire for all bishops. Marositz, 15, 28, 40, and *AAS* 61 (1969) 334.

33. Marositz, 16–21, 37, 46, 53–54.

34. Acta Commissionis, *Comm* 13 (1982) 362–64.

35. CC 381, §2 and 368 indicate the equivalencies of various particular churches according to the new Code.

36. For a comprehensive history of the evolution of such conferences with special reference to LCWR, see Margaret Mary Modde, *A Canonical Study of the Leadership Conference of Women Religious of the United States of America* (Washington: Catholic University of America, 1977) from the first few chapters of which this historical information has been culled, especially 1, 49–56, 63–67, 74, 78, 100, 102.

37. *CLD* 6:448–55 and 472–76; *CLD* 462–67 and 472–77.

38. Modde, 107, 152, 170.

39. In the United States the NCCB has commissions for both men and women religious. The LCWR and CMSM are associations related to the USCC.

40. Modde, 110–11. In fact, the then Sacred Congregation for Religious indicated to the April 9, 1956 meeting of the executive committee of the National Congress of Mothers General in the United States that it favored the formation of such a conference while the executive committee objected that such an organization would merely duplicate the work being done by other groups such as the National Catholic Welfare Conference and the Sisters' Formation Conference.

BIBLIOGRAPHY

Abbo, J., and Hannan, J. *The Sacred Canons.* 2 vols. Rev. ed. St. Louis: Herder Book Co., 1957.

AAS. Rome: Typis Polyglottis Vaticanis, 1909–.

Bouscaren, T., Ellis, A., and Korth, F. *Canon Law.* 4th rev. ed. Milwaukee: Bruce Publishing Co., 1966.

Bouscaren, T., and O'Connor, J. I. *CLD.* 8 vols. Milwaukee: Bruce Publishing Co., 1917–1969. Chicago: Chicago Province S.J., 1974, 1978.

Commentarium pro Religiosis et Missionariis. Rome: Claretian Institute, 1920–.

Comm. Pontifical Commission for the Revision of the Code of Canon Law, 1969–.

Conciliorum Oecumenicorum Decreta. 3rd ed. Joseph Alberigo, ed. Bologna: Instituto per le Scienze Religiose, 1972.

Creusen, J., and Ellis, A. *Religious Men and Women in Church Law.* Milwaukee: Bruce Publishing Co., 1957.

Dinn, M. J., Tessier, L., and Courneene, E. *Canonical Documentation on Consecrated Life (1963–1976).* Ottawa: Saint Paul University, 1977. Private distribution.

Fulwiler, Anne. *Transfer and Readmittance in Non-Clerical Institutes of Simple Vows.* Washington: Catholic University of America, 1980. Unpublished license thesis.

Informationes. Sacred Congregation for Religious and Secular Institutes, 1967–.

Marositz, Joseph J. *Obligations and Privileges of Religious Promoted to the Episcopal and Cardinalitial Dignities.* Washington: Catholic University of America, 1948.

McDonough, Elizabeth. *Ready Reference for the 1980 Schema of Canons on Consecrated Life (with 1983 UPDATE).* Columbus: Springs Press, 1983. Private distribution.

Modde, Margaret Mary. *A Canonical Study of the Leadership Conference of Women Religious of the United States of America.* Washington: Catholic University of America, 1977.

Schaefer, Timotheus. *De Religiosis.* 4th ed. Rome: Typis Polyglottis Vaticanis, 1947.

Wernz, F. X., and Vidal, P. *Ius Canonicum.* VIII vols. vol. III: *De Religiosis.* Rome: Gregorian University, 1933.

Secular Institutes
Canons 710–730

Thomas E. Molloy

INTRODUCTION

One of the great innovations of the revised Code is the presence of secular institutes. It is to be hoped that their treatment in an organic way in a text defining the institutions of the Church will draw attention to secular institutes and make them better known and better understood.

Up to now, these institutes were ruled by three legislative texts: the Constitution *Provida Mater Ecclesia* (February 2, 1947), the *motu proprio Primo Feliciter* (March 12, 1948), and the Instruction *Cum Sanctissimus* (March 19, 1948). Although these texts are abrogated by the new Code, they are necessary background references and sources of the new legislation whenever newer legislation is not contrary to their provisions. The conciliar decree *PC* and the discourses of Paul VI and John Paul II on secular institutes remain important.

Secular institutes are located in the Code under Institutes of Consecrated Life. They are, therefore, identified as one of two kinds of consecrated life, the other being Religious. It was after much discussion that the generic term "consecrated life" was decided upon which, despite its drawbacks, permits a clear demarcation between secular institutes and religious institutes, while safeguarding their common characteristic commitment to the evangelical counsels.

Obviously secular institutes are treated in other parts of the Code, particularly the canonical condition of physical persons (CC 96–112), juridic persons (CC 113–123), elections (CC 164–189), the faithful in general (CC 204–231; 265–289), the administration of temporal goods, etc.

It is fortunate that the Code has abandoned the vocabulary of "states of perfection" and the vocabulary of *Provida Mater* which could lead people to believe in a hierarchy in the institutes of perfection, the secular institutes being a category of a third order behind religious. The generic name of consecrated life permits the avoidance of all recourse to religious vocabulary; even the decree *Primo Feliciter* still spoke of a life "substantially religious." The terminology and the location of secular institutes in the revised Code indicate the equal dignity of religious and secular institutes.

The canons affirm positively what the fundamental law of 1947 said negatively, that is, that members of secular institutes are not religious and the law of the religious cannot be applied to them. Positive expression is found in C 711 which repeats affirmations repeated many times by Pope Paul VI and by Cardinal Antoniutti, that is, that the members of secular institutes do not change their canonical condition in the Church by reason of membership. Lay members remain lay people and diocesan priests remain diocesan priests. It follows then that in the new understanding of consecrated life in the revised Code that religious having special canonical condition in the Church is not by virtue of their consecration, but rather because of their common life which is a specific character and which puts them apart from other Christian people.

Because of this, the Code will emphasize that members of secular institutes live in the ordinary conditions of other people in the world. The Code, therefore, proposes a more secular formulation than previous legislation. Houses are no longer imposed on the general government of a secular institute or for formation. In the entire manner and style of life lay people are to live as lay people in the world, either alone or with their families, and diocesan priests are to live as priests of their diocese. As for the apostolate, for lay members the Code proposes two forms. The first is to participate in the world and within the world by the witness of a Christian life and especially by fidelity to a consecrated life while pursuing a secular profession, living as a lay person in the world. Second, by cooperating in the world of a secular Church which wishes to order the temporal realities according to God. A distinctly subsidiary manner of apostolate is that the members offer their collaboration in the service of the Church. The Code insists more on the insertion of the lay person in temporal reality in order to transform it in an evangelical manner. The institute as such cannot take charge of ecclesial works. The members may, individually, and in a personal way, collaborate in an official ecclesiastical apostolate. At the same time, they must be careful to remain lay and remain secular and to avoid specifically religious works that might lead to a common life or diminish the secular character of the institute.

The canons which follow then are for secular institutes a breath of fresh air and a new recognition of their unique place in the life of the Church.

C 710

A secular institute is an institute of consecrated life in which the Christian faithful living in the world strive for the perfection of charity and work for the sanctification of the world especially from within.

This canon locates secular institutes within the framework of consecrated life. It recognizes secular institutes as an equal and distinct form of consecrated life along with religious institutes, institutes of apostolic life, the eremetical life, and consecrated virginity. They are distinguished from religious institutes by the different characteristics the defining canons give them. Religious institutes *are* characterized by community life, an external sign of consecration, and a certain separation from the world. In contrast, the secular institutes *are* characterized by a consecration that is lived *in the world*. There is no characteristic of separation from the world, but rather members contribute to the sanctification of the world *from within*. Likewise, as a general rule, there is no community life or community of goods and no external sign of consecration. The member lives as a person in the world and shares the life-style of his or her fellow lay persons, or priests.

C 711

The consecration of a member of a secular institute does not alter the member's proper canonical condition among the people of God, whether lay or clerical, with due regard for the prescriptions of law affecting institutes of consecrated life.

The canons have already specified this about consecrated life in general. Consecrated life does not pertain to the hierarchical structure of the church, but rather to its life and its holiness. Consecrated life, likewise, is by its nature neither clerical nor lay, but arises from among both groups, as a special gift of the Holy Spirit to the People of God.

This is especially true of a secular institute. In the past, when the canons tended to make religious part of the structure of the Church, members of secular institutes were put in a very ambiguous position and many times felt they were forced to be religious although they did not want to be. A lay person who consecrates him or herself to God with sacred bonds in a secular institute does not become less a lay person. In a sense, it could be said that this person is more a lay person because precisely as a lay person living in the world, he or she is consecrated to God.

The consecration is done within the physiognomy of the lay person living in the world or of a diocesan priest living as a part of the presbyterate of the diocese. Likewise, the secular priest who is consecrated in a secular institute is not in the least separated from the rest of the presbyterate of his diocese nor is he less a secular priest. By assuming the sacred bonds and evangelical counsels as a secular priest, he consecrates himself precisely as what he is, a secular priest of a certain diocese, and he strives to live a consecrated life under the precise conditions and circumstances of the vocation to the diocesan priesthood in his particular diocese.

A diocesan priest who is a member of such an institute would avoid requesting his bishop to assign him to live or work with other members of his institute, since this would approximate the life-style of members of a religious institute. He lives with other priests of his diocese precisely as other diocesan priests and strives to live out his consecration.

C 712

With due regard for the prescriptions of cann. 598–601, the constitutions are to determine the sacred bonds by which the evangelical counsels are taken in the institute and are to define the obligations flowing from these same bonds, while always preserving, however, in its way of life the distinctive secularity of the institute.

The task given secular institutes in this canon is the same given to all institutes of consecrated life. The rule of life must specify exactly what the consecration entails and the sacred bonds and the way of living the evangelical counsels must be specified. In another affirmation of the value of a secular institute as a distinct form of consecrated life and not as a watered down version of religious life, the canons direct these institutes to preserve the distinctive secularity of the institute. They should be careful, therefore, to avoid falling into patterns of life that more approximate the religious form of consecrated life, for instance, community life, community property, a religious-type habit, or other external sign of consecration or a preference for an apostolate under the auspices of the church rather than a "secular" profession in the world. The same is true for institutes of secular priests. Members should avoid any external insignia of consecration and avoid the temptation to want to live and work together.

C 713

§1. The members of these institutes express and exercise their own consecration in their apostolic activity and like a leaven they strive to imbue all things with the spirit of the gospel for the strengthening and growth of the Body of Christ.

§2. Lay members share in the Church's evangelizing task in the world and of the world through their witness of a Christian life and fidelity toward their consecration, and through their efforts to order temporal things according to God and inform the world by the power of the gospel. Also, they cooperate in serving the ecclesial community, according to their particular secular way of life.

§3. Clerical members through the witness of their consecrated life, especially in the presbyterate, help their brothers by their special apostolic charity and in their sacred ministry among people of God they bring about the sanctification of the world.

This canon emphasizes the lack of separation from the world which is a characteristic of a secular institute as opposed to a religious institute. Members live in the world in the same condition as other lay people or secular priests and for their consecration strive to be "like a leaven" imbuing all things in the spirit of the gospel. This is particularly true of the way in which they exercise a secular profession.

The particular apostolate of the members of a secular institute is the sanctification of the world from within. Some have objected that the word "world" is ambiguous; whether it means humanity, human history, or the physical cosmos, has been open to some discussion. If we understand the word to mean all of humanity, then the canon is an adequate expression of the particular call of members of a secular institute.

One might have wished for a richer section on clerical members of these institutes. It directs them to only two things: to help their brethren in the priesthood by a particular apostolic charity and to contribute to the sanctification of the world by their ministry. These rather vague formulas might have been enriched by the words of Paul VI and John Paul II. Paul VI had spoken of "a specifically priestly responsibility for the just arrangement of the temporal order which the priest exercises principally through his ministerial action and in his role as an educator in the faith." John Paul II has said that a priest in a secular institute can bring to other priests three things: an experience of evangelical life, fraternal help, and a particular sensitivity to the relationship of the Church to the world.

C 714

Members are to lead their life according to the norm of the constitutions, in the ordinary conditions of the world, either alone or each in their respective families, or in a group of brothers or sisters.

This canon again emphasizes the specifically secular style of life of members of secular institutes. Presumably they live alone, or with their own family. The third possibility of living in a group is a concession to those secular institutes which have adopted a more religious style of life and practice some form of community life.

C 715

§1. Clerical members incardinated in a diocese depend on the diocesan bishop, with due regard for those things which pertain to consecrated life in their particular institute.

§2. If those who are incardinated in an institute according to the norm of can. 266, §3, are appointed to particular works of the institute or to the governance of the institute, they depend on the bishop in a way comparable to religious.

This canon reiterates for clerical members of secular institutes what the prior canon specified for lay members. A diocesan priest continues to be a diocesan priest and depends in all things on his bishop. In extraordinary circumstances the bishop might release such a priest for a particular work of the institute, but this would be quite rare. More commonly, if the priest is elected to the government of the institute, he could be released by his bishop for a short period of time to engage in this apostolate.

C 716

§1. All members are to share actively in the life of the institute according to proper law.

§2. Members of the same institute are to maintain communion among themselves, carefully fostering unity of spirit and genuine relationship as brothers or sisters.

This canon states something which, to a religious, would seem obvious and self-evident. Secular institutes, however, because of the nature of the life, sometimes experience a particular difficulty in maintaining the bonds among the members which should be present in any family of consecrated life. This is because there is no community life or community property and because members move and sometimes find themselves geographically isolated. These factors require a particular effort on the part of the moderators and members to maintain that spirit of unity which seems to come more spontaneously in a religious institute.

C 717

§1. The constitutions are to prescribe a particular manner of governance and define the time during which moderators hold their office and the way in which they are chosen.

§2. No one is to be chosen supreme moderator who is not definitively incorporated.

§3. Those who are put in charge of the governance of the institute are to take care that the unity of its spirit is kept and that active participation of the members is encouraged.

The norms for the selection and term of office of the moderator are basically the same as for other institutes. We note again the emphasis that the law puts on the obligation of the moderators to foster the unity of the institutes and to keep in contact with all of the members, especially those who are scattered and isolated.

C 718

The administration of the goods of the institute, which should express and foster evangelical poverty, is ruled by the norms of Book V, *The Temporal Goods of the Church*, and by the proper law of the institute. Likewise the proper law is to define especially the financial obligations of the institute toward members who carry on work for it.

The law and the administration of property is substantially the same as for other juridic persons in the Church. There is emphasis on the obligations toward anyone who is employed by the institute; this might be neglected in some institutes because of the scattered membership and the lack of common life.

C 719

§1. In order that members may respond faithfully to their vocation and that their apostolic action may proceed from their union with Christ they are to be diligent in prayer, concentrate in a fitting manner on the reading of Sacred Scripture, make an annual retreat and carry out other spiritual exercises according to proper law.

§2. The celebration of the Eucharist, daily if possible, is to be the source and strength of the whole of their consecrated life.

§3. They are freely to approach the sacrament of penance, which they should receive frequently.

§4. They are freely to obtain necessary guidance of conscience and should seek counsel of this kind even from their moderators, if they wish.

The Church, in this canon, lays out in a very general way the means of sanctification for all the members of God's People. They are particularly commended to members of secular institutes as they strive to live their consecration without the support system which is present in the religious life.

C 720

The right of admission into the institute, whether for probation or for the assumption of sacred bonds, whether temporary or perpetual or definitive, pertains to the major moderators with their council according to the norm of the constitutions.

C 721

§1. One is invalidly admitted to the initial probation:

1° who has not yet reached the age of majority;

2° who is still bound by a sacred bond in some institute of consecrated life or who is incorporated in a society of apostolic life;

3° who is married while the marriage lasts.

§2. The constitutions can establish other impediments, even for the validity of admission, or place certain conditions.

§3. Moreover, for one to be received it is necessary to have the maturity to lead the life proper to the institute.

C 722

§1. The initial probation is to be so arranged that the candidates may understand more fittingly their divine vocation and indeed the vocation proper to the institute and may be trained in the spirit and way of life of the institute.

§2. The candidates are to be properly formed in living according to the evangelical counsels and taught to translate this life completely into the apostolate, using those forms of spreading the gospel which better respond to the purpose, spirit and character of the institute.

§3. The manner and time of this probation before first undertaking sacred bonds in the institute are to be defined in the constitutions; yet it is to be no less than two years.

C 723

§1. After the time of the initial probation has passed, the candidate who is judged worthy is either to take on the three evangelical counsels strengthened by a sacred bond or to depart from the institute.

§2. This first incorporation, no shorter than five years, is to be temporary according to the norm of the constitutions.

§3. When the time of this incorporation has passed, the member who is judged worthy is to be admitted to perpetual or definitive incorporation, that is, with temporary bonds always to be renewed.

§4. Definitive incorporation is equivalent to perpetual incorporation as far as certain juridic effects are concerned, to be determined in the constitutions.

C 724

§1. After the sacred bonds are first taken formation is to be continued according to the constitutions.

§2. Members are to be formed in divine and human matters equally; the moderators of the institute are to take seriously the continuing spiritual formation of members.

The whole program of formation is a very difficult problem for secular institutes because of the secular style in which the consecration is lived. Members applying to a secular institute presumably remain in the world in a secular profession and are living by themselves. The formation program, therefore, is very "part-time" compared to that required for entrance into a religious institute. The periods of probation are consequently longer than required for admission to first profession and final profession in a religious institute. Because of the nature of a secular institute and the kind of life that the members are being formed for, it obviously would be inappropriate to have a novitiate house and a period of time living in community with other novices away from one's own home or family or secular profession. Because of this, secular institutes sometimes have a very difficult time establishing adequate formation programs for their members.

C 725

The institute can associate to itself, by some bond determined in the constitutions, other members of the Christian faithful who strive toward evangelical perfection according to the spirit of the institute and share its mission.

The canon looks toward the association of other members of the faithful, both married and single, with a secular institute according to the pattern of "Third Order" with religious institutes. A number of secular institutes have experienced great difficulty and conflict because of this association. Some institutes have moved toward allowing married people to enter them as full members taking a vow of "charity." Other institutes have allowed married people to come in as associate members, to participate fully in the group meetings and in the general assemblies of the institute. Some members feel that this is entirely inappropriate and threatens to turn the secular institute into a movement like the Focolare or something similar.

From the general law on consecrated life, it is obvious that a married person cannot be a member of a secular institute strictly speaking and that if an institute of men wants to accept women or vice versa there should be a separate branch for the members of that sex. Likewise if a secular institute of diocesan priests wishes to accept laymen, a separate branch of the institute should also be founded and another rule of life written, since the secularity of the diocesan priest and the secularity of the layman living in the world are entirely different contexts in which to live out a consecrated life.

C 726

§1. When the time of temporary incorporation has elapsed, the member can leave the institute freely or be excluded from renewal of the sacred bonds for a just cause by the major moderator after hearing the council.

§2. For a serious reason the temporarily incorporated member can freely petition and obtain from the supreme moderator with the consent of the council an indult to leave.

C 727

§1. The perpetually incorporated member who wishes to leave the institute, having thought seriously about this before God, may seek an indult to leave from the Apostolic See through the supreme moderator if it is an institute of pontifical right; otherwise from the diocesan bishop as it is defined in the constitutions.

§2. If it is a question of a cleric incardinated in the institute, the prescription of can. 693 is to be observed.

C 728

When the indult to leave has been legitimately granted, all bonds, rights and obligations emanating from incorporation cease.

C 729

A member is dismissed from the institute according to the norm established in cann. 694 and 695; furthermore, the constitutions may determine other causes of dismissal, provided they are proportionately serious, external, imputable, and juridically proven and the procedure determined in cann. 697–700 shall be observed. The prescription of can. 701 applies to the dismissed member.

C 730

In order that a member of a secular institute may transfer to another secular institute, the prescriptions of cann. 684, §§1, 2, and 4, and 685 are to be observed. In order that a transfer be made to another or from another institute of consecrated life, the permission of the Apostolic See is required and its mandates are to be obeyed.

The final canons deal with separation from the institute or transfer to another institute and are basically the same as those for religious institutes (see commentary above on CC 688–704 and 684–685).

BIBLIOGRAPHY

Beyer, Jean. "Religious Life or Secular Institute." *The Way Supplement* 7 (June 1969) 112–32.

Muller, Hubert. "Secular Institutes for Priests." *The Way Supplement* 12 (Spring 1971) 81–89.

Pius XII, Pope. "Primo feliciter." *AAS* 40 (1948) 283–86.

Pius XII, Pope. "Provida Mater Ecclesia." *AAS* 39 (1947) 114–24.

"Secular Institutes." *The Way Supplement* 12 (Spring 1971).

Secular Institutes in the Magisterium of the Church. CMIS. Rome, 1974.

Secular Institutes: The Official Documents. CMIS. Rome, 1981.

Tresalti, Emilio. "The Identity of the Secular Institute." *The Way Supplement* 33 (Spring 1978) 133–40.

Societies of Apostolic Life
Canons 731–746

CECIL L. PARRES, C.M.

Societies in the Church now designated as societies of apostolic life were commonly referred to from their descriptive title in the 1917 Code as societies of common life or societies without vows. The new title, actually Section II of Part III, Book II "The People of God," is thought to express better the nature and purpose of these societies as eminently apostolic in purpose and in way of life.

INTRODUCTION

Societies of apostolic life existing in the Church today took their origin from foundations of secular communities or congregations of men and women in the sixteenth and through the seventeenth centuries, such as the Oratory of St. Philip Neri, founded in 1575; the Oratory of France (Pierre de Berulle, 1611); the Congregation of the Mission of St. Vincent de Paul (1625); the Daughters of Charity (St. Vincent de Paul and St. Louise de Marillac, 1633); the Society of St. Sulpice (Jean Jacques Olier, 1642); the Congregation of Jesus and Mary (St. John Eudes, 1643); and the Paris Foreign Mission Society (1660). These societies through the subsequent centuries have persisted in maintaining their secular character of non-religious institutes.

Whereas most congregations founded in the eighteenth and nineteenth centuries were patterned after religious orders, though with simple rather than solemn vows, and did in fact become religious congregations under the 1917 Code, there were others which maintained their secular character, such as the Congregation of the Most Precious Blood (St. Gaspar del Bufalo, 1815), and the Society of the Catholic Apostolate (St. Vincent Palotti, 1835). These, with more recent societies, such as, the Society of Missionary Priests of St. Paul the Apostle (Isaac Hecker, 1858), and numerous missionary societies, came to be recognized in the 1917 Code as Societies of Common Life or Societies without (public) Vows.

More positively than a secularity as opposed to the religious life and state, there was present the idea of being within the Church in the world with an apostolate or mission, while preserving a way of fraternal common life, a distinct spiritual life, a certain communality of goods, and a quest for Christian perfection and sacerdotal holiness, in keeping with the specific apostolate and mission. For some this also involved the assumption of the evangelical counsels by some bond other than public vow.

These societies always seemed to defy, perhaps rightly so, attempts at a common categorization. Purposes were varied, internal organization was often distinct, concepts of membership and ways of incorporation differed from society to society. With the 1917 Code there was introduced a greater legislative assimilation of these societies to religious institutes. There was a stated imitation of religious by living in common under the governance of superiors. Negatively, it was stated that members were not bound by the usual public vows and that the societies were not properly speaking religious institutes and the members not properly speaking religious. This gave rise to use among some commentators of terms such as "quasi-religious societies" and to the inclusion of societies of common life under a common denomination of institutes of perfection, of which they were said to be a species along with religious institutes and secular institutes.

The Apostolic Constitution of Pius XII *Provida Mater Ecclesiae* (February 2, 1947) on secular institutes, declared that the Church (in the Code of Canon Law) wished to assimilate societies of common life to the canonical state of perfection (of religious).[1] It is interesting that a noted canonist, Fr. Jean Beyer, S.J., offered the following comment concerning the passing reference in *Provida Mater* to societies of common life:

Whoever knows the history of these societies easily sees that this interpretation deforms the facts and expounds an opinion which does not correspond with the intentions of all these societies. The text says clearly that the Church wished to assimilate these societies to the canonical state of perfection. Must one conclude that such was the intention of the founders, and of the present members of these societies? This cannot be affirmed.[2]

The 1917 Code, *Provida Mater*, and much of commentaries written on societies of common life are now matters of history, since the present Code takes a new approach to these societies. Further, C 6 abrogates the 1917 Code and other laws, universal or particular, contrary to its prescriptions, unless it provides otherwise for particular laws.

The theory on which the first completed schema of the new Code (published for consultation, February 2, 1977) was based, retained a common classification of societies of apostolic life along with religious institutes and secular institutes. Life, state, and institute constituted by profession of the evangelical counsels was to include all three. The theory, based on an excessively juridic interpretation of documents of Vatican Council II, especially the Dogmatic Constitution on the Church and the Apostolic Constitution on the Renewal of Religious Life, remained constant throughout the years of the development of the schema. There was only a change of terminology of interest to societies of apostolic life from the general rubric of *De Religiosis* (to include religious in the strict sense and religious in the wide sense), to institutes of perfection, and finally to institutes of consecrated life by profession of the evangelical counsels.

During the two years of labor of the commission for revision of the schema on institutes of consecrated life from June 1978 to the publication of the schema of 1980, the position came finally to be adopted that the societies of apostolic life should not be considered institutes of consecrated life. Rather, they should have their own section of law in Book II of the People of God, though they share in some ways a law in common with the institutes.

The canons on societies of apostolic life in the 1983 Code indicate the existence in the Church of a way of apostolic life for the Christian faithful, which is distinct from the form of life of institutes of consecrated life, whether religious or secular. These societies are also distinct from associations of the faithful, which do not of themselves include a fraternal life in common. The apostolic identity of the societies of apostolic life embraces life as well as mission and includes an apostolic end or purpose, a fraternal life in common, and the pursuit of the perfection of charity. Both the clear exclusion of societies of apostolic life from the category of institutes of consecrated life and the recognition of a position of their own right in the Church should be an encouragement for these societies to develop more their own identity and mission in the Church. Much is left to the proper law of each society in the organization of its life and mission. All are, by their nature, for an apostolate within the mission of the whole Church. Each should in turn be characterized by its own manner of participation in that mission, by its own common way of life and quest for the perfection of charity in relation to its share in the mission of the Church.

THE CONCEPT OF SOCIETY OF APOSTOLIC LIFE

C 731

§1. Comparable to institutes of consecrated life are societies of apostolic life whose members without religious vows pursue the particular apostolic purpose of the society, and leading a life as brothers or sisters in common according to a particular manner of life, strive for the perfection of charity through the observance of the constitutions.

§2. Among these there are societies in which the members embrace the evangelical counsels by some bond defined in the constitutions.

The first canon wisely deals more with a concept than with a neat definition. The title and name given indicate apostolicity as the key to understanding the nature, end, manner of life, and spirituality of societies of apostolic life. There is a factual statement of the components which are proper to the notion of such societies: apostolic end, life in common, and the pursuit of the perfection of charity. These components are common to all societies of apostolic life and at the same time proper to each, as expressed in the purpose, way of life, and constitutions of each. The relationship of each to the other and their coordination pertain to the patrimony of each society. The assumption from the title is rather that the apostolic spirit should pervade the entirety and that the end and *raison d'etre* of each society is precisely apostolic and participative of the mission of the Church through apostolic activity. With this, life in common and personal perfection are harmonized, as also is the practice of the evangelical counsels assumed by some bond in certain societies.

While the canon views the objectives of societies of apostolic life from the standpoint of personal commitment and involvement of members, neither the apostolic end, the manner of life, nor the quest for holiness of life are purely personal and individual. They are undertaken in community and fraternal communion in a visibly organized and structured society within the Church and according to the proper law of each society.

However the initial words of C 731, *Institutis vitae Consecratae accedunt* may be interpreted in translation "approaching, similar to, or in addition to," the notion of imitation in manner of life and governance as stated in CIC 673 is absent. Actually, in context and as a juridic expression, *accedunt* can refer only to those general norms for institutes which are applicable to societies of apostolic life according to the following C 732.[3] In that canon the similarity is explicitated and the applicability of the norms stated, so that both the resemblance and the application are always according to the nature of each society. The expression should not cause anxiety to societies in the revision of constitutions and other texts of proper law, and, it is to be hoped, should not give rise to doctrinal or juridical impositions contrary to the nature and spirit of these societies. The priority of the proper law of each society is most clearly built into this entire section of the law.

That an apostolic way of life which includes the practice of the evangelical counsels of chastity, poverty, and obedience assumed by some bond is compatible with the basic concept of a society of apostolic life as approved by the Church is shown in C 731, §2. This statement of the canon is also a factual one, namely, that the proper law for some societies does include for members the assumption of the evangelical counsels by some kind of bond. The kind of bond, whether vow, oath, promise, intention, or good purpose, is not mentioned. Only religious vows are excluded, that is, the public vow whereby the observance of the evangelical counsels is assumed in religious profession. However, even for these societies there is clearly not a profession of the evangelical counsels in the sense in which the Church understands and regulates profession for institutes of consecrated life.

Societies whose members do assume one or more of the evangelical counsels by vow or some other bond should be conscious of their own foundations and traditions and avoid terminology of religious profession or that of the more recent secular institutes. The evangelical counsels are seen as integral to the apostolic nature of these societies but not as constitutive of their canonical position in the Church, even if the personal act required of members according to the constitutions as a special commitment to obedience, chastity, and the form of poverty proper to the society, should be one or more of the vows. Such vows do not have the canonical effects of the public vows of religion and, though they may be reserved and have juridic effects according to the proper law of the society, they remain essentially private vows if not received by a superior in the name of the Church. It should be noted that the legislator continues to distinguish public from private vows by this sole criterion in C 1192.[4]

Societies whose members do not assume the evangelical counsels by some bond will direct obedience to superiors in keeping with the nature of the society, chastity proper to the celibate state of life, whether clerical or lay, and the acquisition, use, and disposition of community and personal property in keeping with the manner of life proper to the nature and apostolic end of the society. This should not be construed as an implicit bond, which is not willed or admitted by these societies.

GENERAL NORMS

C 732

Whatever is determined in cann. 578–597 and 606 is applicable to societies of apostolic life, with due regard for the nature of each society; in addition, cann. 598–602 are applicable to the societies mentioned in can. 731, §2.

The sharing of many of the general norms of Part III, Section I, Title I, with institutes of consecrated life is shown in the specific and enumerated application of these norms to societies of apostolic life. The norms excluded in C 732 are not applicable. Also the priority of the proper law of each society is implicit in the phrase which safeguards the nature of each society, so that legitimate diversity found among the societies from their foundations and approved traditions may be preserved.

In general, it can be noted here that societies are established, divided into parts, suppressed, etc., in the same manner as institutes. They are to have a fundamental code, or constitutions, approved by the competent ecclesiastical authority, which may be changed only with the consent of the same authority. Other norms enacted by the competent authority of the society and which form part of the proper law are changed, adapted, etc., by the same authority of the society.

Societies are either clerical or lay according to the description given in C 588. The position of lay members, or brothers, in clerical societies is not directly addressed in the canon. A society is clerical by reason of its purpose in the Church as derived from its founder or from its traditions and from recognition as clerical by the authority of the Church. Although the total mission of the Church requires the ministerial priesthood and the exercise of sacred orders, the mission of the Church is accomplished also by the apostolic and missionary activity of those not ordained.

The apostolic or missionary role of the lay member of a clerical society parallels this concept of total ecclesial mission in relation to the specific apostolic and missionary objectives of a clerical society. The question of the participation of lay members of clerical societies in the governance of the society needs to be approached from the principles of law on the power of ecclesiastical governance, or jurisdiction, and ecclesiastical office, especially CC 129 and 150. In clerical societies of pontifical law, there is an institutional sharing through offices of internal governance in the teaching, sanctifying, and governing of the Church as these pertain to ordained ministry in union with the pope and the bishops. The laity may cooperate in the exercise of jurisdiction according to the norm of law. This will be according to the universal law and the proper law of the society. Offices which carry with them the full care of souls (*cura animarum*) and require the exercise of priestly order are reserved to priests.

Societies of apostolic life are of diocesan or pontifical law, according to the general norms, and may also be exempt according to the norm of C 591. Superiors and chapters have the authority defined in universal and proper law. In clerical societies of pontifical law, they have the power of ecclesiastical government, or jurisdiction, for both the external and internal forum.

Societies whose members assume the evangelical counsels by some bond are also to apply the general norms of CC 598–602 in keeping with the nature of each society. These norms regard the basic meaning and obligations of the evangelical counsels, not the juridic effects of religious profession.

Finally, the brief norm of C 606 means that the Code is equally valid for societies of men and societies of women, unless otherwise evident from the context or the nature of the matter.

HOUSES AND COMMUNITIES

C 733

§1. A house is erected and a local community is established by the competent authority of the society with the prior written consent of the diocesan bishop, who must also be consulted for its suppression.

§2. Consent to erect a house entails the right of having at least an oratory in which the Most Holy Eucharist is celebrated and reserved.

In keeping with fraternal life in common proper to societies of apostolic life, houses and local communities are to be erected or constituted by the competent authority of the society. The proper law of each society determines the competent authority, e.g., the supreme moderator or the major superior. Previous consent of the diocesan bishop in writing is required, and he must be consulted for the suppression of a house or community.

Houses or local communities in which fraternal life in common is lived form the basic units of societies of apostolic life. Local communities may be established apart from canonically erected houses, according to the proper law of a society, which should also determine the governance, the manner of life in common of members, and their relationship to houses or other parts of the society. The law should be seen as having a flexibility for structure on the local level in view of the apostolic end of the society.

§2 states the right of houses to have an oratory. The law no longer distinguishes between public and semi-public oratories. There are only churches, oratories, and private chapels.[5] An oratory is for the convenience of a community or group of the faithful, as designated by permission of the Ordinary, to which others may have access with the consent of the competent superior.[6] Further permission of the diocesan bishop is required for a church.[7] The competent Ordinary for the erection of an oratory is the major superior of a clerical society of pontifical law. For other societies he is the diocesan bishop or his vicar.[8]

GOVERNMENT

C 734

The governance of a society is determined by the constitutions, with due regard for cann. 617–633, according to the nature of each society.

The constitutions of societies of apostolic life are the primary expression of the structure and reality of government. The canons (617–633) for religious institutes on superiors, councils, and chapters apply to societies according to the nature of each society. Thus, traditional terminology and structures expressive of the particular nature of each society should be preserved in the constitutions.

Added to the canons on superiors is C 630, which reorders the law on the sacrament of penance, the direction and manifestation of conscience, and confessors. Of note for societies is the requirement of ordinary confessors for lay societies in houses of formation and in large communities. This canon is intended to provide ample opportunity for the sacrament, while not limiting due freedom.

ADMISSION, MEMBERSHIP, AND FORMATION

C 735

§1. The admission, probation, incorporation and training of members are determined by the proper law of each society.

§2. In respect to admission into the society, the conditions established in cann. 642–645 are to be observed.

§3. Proper law must determine especially the doctrinal, spiritual and apostolic method of probation and training suited to the purpose and character of the society, in such a way that the members, recognizing their divine vocation, may be fittingly prepared for the mission and life of the society.

The general canons referred to in the commentary on C 732 as applicable to societies of apostolic life contain one norm which concerns admission to a society. C 597 in application to societies of apostolic life means that only Catholics, with the right intention, duly qualified according to universal law and the proper law of each society, and bound by no canonical impediment, may be admitted. Moreover, no one is to be admitted without suitable preparation. These with the requirements for valid admission and other conditions mentioned in CC 642–645, complete the universal law for societies regarding admission. For the rest, admission, probation, incorporation, and formation are governed by the proper law of each society.

The suitable preparation mentioned in C 597, §2 should not be construed as requiring a formal postulancy of specific duration or program, or even a group program. Negatively it means one should not be admitted to probation in a society without some assessment of right intention and proper attitudes. Positively it means a guided direction of vocation which takes into consideration qualifications of the candidate in relation to the purpose, nature, manner of life, and apostolate of the society.

Although the canons cited (642–645) speak in the context of admission to the novitiate of a religious institute, it should be noted that a novitiate is not required for societies. The conditions of these canons are required for admission to the first or probatory stage of membership in societies before incorporation, whatever may be the terminology used by a particular society and the rights and obligations of those admitted as well as the program of initial formation, according to the proper law of each society. No other canons on novitiate or religious profession are applied by universal law to societies of apostolic life. The traditions and proper law of each society in the initial and other stages of formation are respected and should be maintained.

For the changes from the law of the 1917 Code on admission and for the interpretation of the canons, readers are referred to the commentary of this handbook on CC 642–645.

C 735 does not specify the competent superior of a society for admission and incorporation and does not legislate details of the programs of probation and further formation. These matters are referred to the proper law of each society. Both admission to a society and incorporation therein are essentially actions of the society through a proper superior in response to one requesting admission or incorporation. The manner of effecting this should result in a juridically provable acceptance of a candidate at a definite time, at which the initial or probatory stage of formation is begun. The duration of this stage is not specified in the Code and is left to the proper law of a society. Incorporation likewise should be juridically provable and have a definite beginning. Incorporation is said to be definitive or nondefinitive in relation to the subsequent canons on departure and dismissal. Nondefinitive incorporation is always temporary. Definitive incorporation is perpetual or temporary but always renewable. These are matters calling for exact specification in the proper law of each society, that is, in the constitutions according to the application of C 587.

The relationship to incorporation of oath, vow, promise, good purpose, or any other bond by which obedience to superiors or dedication to the end of a society, or by which one or more of the evangelical counsels may be assumed, should also be made explicit in the constitutions.

C 735, §3 indicates a general content and purpose of probation and further formation, rather than a detailed and time-conditioned plan or program. Plan and details are left to the proper law of each society. The plan should include doctrinal, spiritual, and apostolic formation, as basic to the notion of apostolic society. This should be accommodated and added to, according to the purpose and character of each society. The purpose of probation and formation is preparation for the mission and life of the society, as the member acknowledges in response the divine call to that mission and life.

CLERICAL SOCIETIES

C 736

§1. In clerical societies the clerics are incardinated in the society itself, unless the constitutions provide otherwise.

§2. In those matters which pertain to the course of studies and the reception of orders the norms for secular clerics are to be observed with due regard however for §1.

The previous canons have not distinguished between clerical and lay societies, except in the reference to C 588 in C 732, which has already been commented on. The law applies equally to societies of men or women, and, for the most part to lay as well as to clerical societies.

In clerical societies incardination into a society is effected by reception of the diaconate by a definitively incorporated member according to the norm of C 266, §2, unless the constitutions of a society provide otherwise, that is, for incardination into a diocese. However, the universal law, according to the norm of C 1019, gives the right of granting dimissorial letters for ordinations of definitively incorporated members only to major superiors of societies of apostolic life which are of pontifical law. Ordination of members not definitively incorporated and of members of societies of diocesan law are governed entirely, in this matter, by the law for ordination of secular clerics.

The constitutions of a society of apostolic life may provide for incardination into a diocese. The dual alliance thus effected by incorporation into a society and incardination into a diocese is governed by the constitutions of a society or by particular agreements between the society and the proper bishop.

A diocesan cleric entering a society of apostolic life loses incardination in his own particular church only when he becomes definitively incorporated into the society,[9] unless, of course, the constitutions provide for incardination into a diocese according to the exception mentioned in C 736, §1.

A cleric incardinated into a society of apostolic life loses incardination after departure or dismissal in the same manner as a religious cleric, that is, when incardinated into a diocese according to the prescriptions of CC 693 and 701.

C 736, §2 states the principle of clerical studies and reception of orders, aside from the previous prescription on incardination, in terms of norms for secular clergy. The logic of this position follows from the secularity of societies of apostolic life and the close identity of clerics of these societies with the particular church where they serve and the secular clergy of the diocese. Besides the requisites for clerical studies and the principles of clerical and sacerdotal formation as found in CC 232–264, clerical societies are certainly able to have their own programs in keeping with their mission and apostolic activities.

OBLIGATIONS AND RIGHTS

C 737

Incorporation entails obligations and rights for the members defined in the constitutions as well as a concern on the part of the society to lead the members to the end of their particular vocation, according to the constitutions.

C 738

§1. All the members are subject to their particular moderators according to the norm of the constitutions in those matters which affect the internal life and discipline of the society.

§2. They are subject also to the diocesan bishop in those matters which affect public worship, the care of souls and other works of the apostolate, with due regard for cann. 679–683.

§3. The relations of a member incardinated in a diocese with his proper bishop are defined by the constitutions or particular agreements.

C 739

Besides the obligations which they have as members according to the constitutions the members are bound by the common obligations of clerics, unless something else is evident from the nature of the matter or from the context.

C 740

Members must live in a house or community legitimately established and observe common life according to the norm of proper law, by which absences from a house or community are also governed.

Obligations and rights of members and of societies with respect to members flow from incorporation and are defined in the constitutions of each society. Rights and obligations will, of course, be different for definitive and nondefinitive membership. It should be noted that CC 662–672, which concern the obligations and rights of religious institutes and members, are not applied to societies of apostolic life. In keeping with its apostolic nature, its own character, and sound traditions, each society should express its own spirituality, its own manner of life, and the mutual relations and rights and obligations of members and the society.

C 737 is careful to highlight a basic obligation of societies of apostolic life, namely, that of caring for the vocation of each member and its fulfillment according to the constitutions of the society. This does not mean fulfillment in a way that is individualistic or whimsical and detrimental to the common purpose of the society. However, the special talents and aptitudes of an individual in relation to vocation within a society should be developed and channeled, so that each finds fulfillment of vocation in the gift of self in response to divine call within the mission and works of the society.

C 738 approaches the subject of mutual relations between societies and the diocesan bishop. This is stated in terms of members' obedience to moderators of a society in matters of internal life and discipline according to the norm of the constitutions of a society. As a statement of principle, it is valid for all societies and is one without which a society could not effectively function and fulfill its purpose within the Church. As a principle, it must apply to societies of diocesan as well as of pontifical law.

§2 of the same canon implies subjection to the proper moderators of a society in matters pertaining to public worship, the care of souls, and other works of the apostolate. The statement of a canon also looks directly to subjection to the diocesan bishop in these matters, while calling attention to the canons cited (679–683), which deal with the mutual relations between religious superiors and the diocesan bishop in the matters mentioned. Societies of apostolic life function within the mission of the universal Church and within the mission of the particular church, of which the diocesan bishop is the head. Close cooperation with and obedience to the bishop in the three areas mentioned are vital to the unity of the particular church and should flow also from the very nature of societies of apostolic life in the pursuit of apostolic and missionary objectives.

Particular attention should be called to CC 681 and 682. The importance of written agreements between diocesan bishops and the competent superiors of societies for works committed by the bishop to members of a society is stressed in C 681. The wisdom of this provision of law is obvious. Of particular application is the parallel provision of C 520 on parishes entrusted to a clerical society of apostolic life, even if the parish is erected in a church belonging to the society.

A member of a society of apostolic life is appointed to an ecclesiastical office in a diocese by the diocesan bishop, following the presentation by or at least the assent of the competent superior of the society. The one appointed may be removed by either the bishop or the superior, with observance of the terms of C 682, §2. The same law is applied specifically to the appointment and removal of pastors and parochial vicars, according to CC 523, 538, §2, 547, and 552.

C 738, §3 indicates a special relationship with the proper bishop for societies whose members are incardinated into a diocese. The constitutions of the society and particular agreements with the bishop of incardination take precedence over the universal law as stated in the above paragraphs on mutual relations.

At the beginning of the commentary on CC 737–740, which was entitled "Obligations and Rights," it was stated that rights and obligations on the part of both member and society flow from incorporation. More radically, they flow from divine vocation, response to a divine vocation by the member, and recognition of this vocation and response by the society. Incorporation is the visible expression and continuance by member and society of this reality within the Church and the society. The constitutions, as approved by the Church, express the basic accordance of member and society concerning mission and life and the mutual rights and obligations flowing from the nature of the society and membership therein.

C 739 stresses the obligations of members within the above context as coexistent with the common obligations of clerics as stated in CC 273–289. Clerical members of societies are, of course, bound by the obligations of these canons as priests or deacons of the society to which they belong. All members of societies, whether clerical or lay, are held to the prescriptions of the stated canons which, from the purpose of the law or the nature of the matter, are equally applicable to the lay or clerical condition of members. These canons are particularly 277, 285, 286, 287, and 289.

Finally, in C 740 the obligation of common life proper to societies according to the law of each society is stated as requiring living in a house or in a legitimately constituted community. The proper law of each society also determines legitimate absence from a house or community. The demands of fraternal life in common and the apostolic nature of a society, together with a secularity which excludes application of the law of religious on houses (CC 606–616) and the canons (662–672) on the obligations and rights of religious institutes and members, should find their coordination in the proper law of a society. Living apart from a house or community to which a member belongs, for reasons determined by proper law, while exceptional, should not be seen as living outside the society. The latter involves a temporary separation from a society, which is provided for in C 745.

TEMPORAL GOODS

C 741

§1. Societies and, unless the constitutions state otherwise, their parts and houses are juridic persons, and, as such, capable of acquiring, possessing, administering and alienating temporal goods according to the norm of the prescriptions of Book V, *The Temporal Goods of the Church*, cann. 636, 638, and 639 and the norm of proper law.

§2. According to the norm of proper law the members are also capable of acquiring, possessing, administering and disposing of temporal goods, but whatever comes to them in consideration of the society belongs to the society.

Temporal goods of the Church form the subject of Book V of the Code. Ecclesiastical goods are those in ownership of some public juridic person in the Church. Societies of common life are public juridic persons in the Church and as such, capable of acquiring, possessing, administering, and alienating temporal goods. Other parts of a society, such as provinces or the equivalent, and houses are juridic persons, unless the constitutions of a society provide otherwise and are also, as such, capable of the same acts in relation to temporal goods. These actions by the juridic person of the society or other juridic persons within the society are governed by the norms of Book V, by the three specific canons mentioned (636, 638, and 639), and the proper law of each society.

Commentary on Book V of the Code is beyond the limited scope of our commentary. One notation of importance for clerical societies is that the term Ordinary, used frequently in Book V, means the major superior of clerical societies of pontifical law, unless specified as Ordinary of the place. Another is that for alienations below the sum fixed for a region by the Holy See, permission is granted by the competent superior with consent of the council according to the proper law of a society. The sum set by an episcopal conference is not controlling for pontifical religious institutes and societies of apostolic life. Only societies of diocesan law need additional permission of the Ordinary of the place.

C 741, §2 does not pretend to regulate the question of ownership of goods by individual members of societies, their acquisition, possession, administration, or disposition. Goods belonging to individual members are not ecclesiastical goods and, as such, are not subject to the prescriptions of canon law on ecclesiastical goods. The proper law of each society should contain norms governing the capacity and actions of individual members in relation to personal temporal goods. Basic norms pertaining to rights of individual members and of the society should be incorporated into the constitutions, so that what pertains to the society and what pertains to the individual in acquisition is clearly evident. The norm of the canon that what comes to members in view of the society, i.e., for the society, belongs to the society, should be made more explicit in the law of the society.

C 741 deals with the ecclesiastical goods of a society and the personal goods of members. It is not in itself directive of the apostolic poverty of societies or of the evangelical counsel of poverty embraced by members of societies referred to in C 731, §2. Community of goods and communal and personal poverty in keeping with the apostolic nature and end should find apt expression, direction, and regulation in the law of each society.

DEPARTURE, TRANSFER, AND DISMISSAL

C 742

The departure and dismissal of a member not yet definitively incorporated is governed by the constitutions of each society.

C 743

A member definitively incorporated can obtain an indult of departure from the society from the supreme moderator with the consent of the council, unless it is reserved to the Holy See by the constitutions; the rights and obligations flowing from incorporation cease, with due regard for the prescription of can. 693.

C 744

§1. It is reserved to the supreme moderator also with the consent of the council to grant permission to a member definitively incorporated to transfer to another society of apostolic life; in the meantime the rights and obligations associated with the prior society are suspended, and the member has the right to return before definitive incorporation into the new society.

§2. In order to transfer to an institute of consecrated life or from that to a society of apostolic life, the permission of the Holy See is required and its mandates must be observed.

C 745

The supreme moderator with the consent of the council can grant to a definitively incorporated member an indult of living outside the society, not however beyond three years, with the rights and obligations which are not suitable for the new condition being suspended; the member remains however under the care of the moderators. If it is a question of a cleric there is required in addition the permission of the ordinary of the place in which he must dwell, under whose care and dependency he also remains.

C 746

For the dismissal of a member definitively incorporated, cann. 694–704 are to be observed with due adaptations being made.

Nondefinitive Members

The departure and the dismissal of members who are not definitively incorporated into a society are governed entirely by the constitutions of each society. C 742 enters into no details, and a commentary should follow the wise absence of prescription of the canon. The constitutions should include clear statements on the departure and dismissal of those admitted to probation. Reasons for and the competency of superiors to grant departure or to effect dismissal of nondefinitively incorporated members, procedure of dismissal, dissolution of mutual rights and obligations of incorporation and of any bond relating to the evangelical counsels or other oath or promise, should be clearly addressed in the constitutions.

The law of the Code likewise does not legislate concerning transfers of nondefinitive members to another society of apostolic life or to an institute of consecrated life. The supposition of the law would favor definitive departure before admission to another society or admission to an institute. Absent likewise are regulations on possible indults for living outside the society, with rights and obligations suspended, and return to life in the society. Readmission of nondefinitively incorporated members after departure or dismissal is also not regulated by the canons.

DEFINITIVE MEMBERS

Departure

The granting of an indult for departure to a definitively incorporated member is reserved to the supreme moderator with the consent of the council, or it may be reserved to the Holy See by the constitutions of a society. The indult carries with it cessation of all rights and obligations had from incorporation. Reservation of the granting of the indult to the Holy See may be seen as important for some societies whose members assume the evangelical counsels by some bond. However, there is nothing in the nature of such a bond, even a vow, which would require its dispensation being reserved to the Holy See. If the granting of the indult is not reserved in approved constitutions, dispensation from bonds is implicit from the law granting authority for the indult, whether in clerical or in lay institutes.

The application of C 693, mentioned in C 743, means that a cleric incardinated into a society cannot be granted an indult of departure until he finds a bishop to incardinate him into a diocese or at least who will receive him into a diocese on an experimental basis. In the latter case, incardination into the diocese becomes effective from the law after five years, unless the bishop has refused him. Obviously, the bishop receiving a cleric experimentally may incardinate him before the expiration of the five-year period. C 693 is not applicable to clerics who are not incardinated into their society but into a diocese. They have a proper bishop from incardination.

It may seem strange that there is no canon on readmission of members after lawful departure. Just as admission, probation, and incorporation are matters regulated by the proper law of a society according to C 735, so too will the proper law regulate readmission, probation, and reincorporation.

TRANSFER

C 744 considers two possibilities of transfer: (1) transfer to another society of apostolic life, and (2) transfer to an institute of consecrated life or from such an institute to a society. The latter is reserved to the Holy See to grant and determine the conditions.

Permission to transfer to another society of apostolic life is granted by the supreme moderator of the society of the member requesting a transfer, with the consent of the council. Obligations and rights in the society from which one transfers are suspended and the right to return to the society remains until definitive incorporation into the second society.

Nothing is said about admission into the society to which transfer is made. Admission must be effected by the competent superior and according to the law of the society, which should also determine time and conditions of probation before incorporation.

INDULT TO LIVE OUTSIDE A SOCIETY

The terms of C 745 concerning an indult to live outside a society of apostolic life are rather comprehensive. The granting of the indult is reserved to the supreme moderator with the consent of the council. It cannot be granted beyond three years. Rights and obligations not compatible with the new condition, i.e., living outside the society, are suspended. The one to whom the indult is granted remains under the care of moderators of the society. For a cleric, priest or deacon, permission of the Ordinary of the place where he must live and under whose care and dependence he remains, is also required.

What obligations and rights are suspended should be delineated in the proper law of a society and incorporated into the text of the indult. Further terms of the permission to live outside the society could be specified in a written agreement signed by the major superior and the member.

For a lay member of a society, the indult will generally mean living in the ordinary lay and secular condition of life of one who is not a member of an institute of consecrated life or of a society of apostolic life, responsible for his or her own decisions and financial affairs. The obligations of chastity in an unmarried condition of life remain, and, for a cleric or one under vow or some other bond relating to the evangelical counsel of chastity, the obligations of clerical celibacy and of the bond remain. Moreover, a cleric will depend on the Ordinary of the place mentioned for the exercise of orders and the manner of life of his new condition.

DISMISSAL

Dismissal of a definitively incorporated member is governed by the same causes, procedures, and canonical effects of CC 694–704 for the dismissal of perpetually professed religious, with congruous application.

The congruous application of these canons to societies of apostolic life will mean adapting the law to the structures and terminology peculiar to each society. The first two reasons for dismissal enumerated in C 696, that is, habitual neglect of the obligations of consecrated life and repeated violations of sacred bonds, will apply to similar violations according to the nature of each society as embodied in the constitutions. Other reasons of similar gravity to those mentioned in C 696 may be determined in the proper law of a society. Unlawful absence from a house or community, as a reason for dismissal, should be specified in the proper law of a society according to C 740.

C 701, in application to societies of apostolic life, means that all bonds with the society and any bond whereby the evangelical counsels are assumed, together with all rights and obligations arising from incorporation, cease when dismissal becomes effective according to the law. A dismissed cleric may not exercise sacred orders until he finds a bishop who will receive him into a diocese after suitable trial according to the norm of C 693 or at least permit him to exercise orders. The latter part of C 701 is, of course, not applicable to clerics who are not incardinated into their society but into a diocese. Such clerics have a proper bishop with incardination.

NOTES

1. *AAS* 39 (1947) 117; *CLD* 3, 138. A more accurate post-Vatican Council II statement, though not completely embracing all societies, on the nature, mode of life, and juridic relationship of societies to religious institutes is found in *RC*, an "Instruction on the renewal and adaptation of formation for living the religious life," 1, 3. *AAS* 61 (1969) 103: *CLD* 7, 493–94.

2. *Gregorianum* 48 (1947) 754. English translation from French by the author.

3. *Comm* 13, 2 (1981) 383–84. The opinion expressed was also that of Archbishop Lara, then secretary of the Commission, who stated that the reference intended by *"accedunt"* was not to the first canon of the schema (now C 573 of the Code) but to the common norms of institutes of consecrated life, some of which were applicable to the societies and others not.

4. C 1192 *Votum est publicum, si nomine ecclesiae a legitimo superiore acceptetur; secus privatum.* Various attempts to find a name for vows taken in societies of apostolic life, such as, recognized vows, social vows, secular but public vows, have not in the opinion of the author been successful and were not adopted in the terminology of the Code. That the object of the vows is determined by the constitutions, that the taking of vows is with

the permission of the competent superior, that vows are taken in the presence of the community, or that the dispensation from the vows is reserved and granted for the external forum, may be viewed as giving a certain "public" or social character but does not make the vows juridically public in the meaning and intent of the law.

5. CC 1214, 1223, 1226.

6. C 1223.

7. C 1215.

8. CC 1223, 134.

9. CC 268, §2; 266, §2. The relationship of definitive incorporation to incardination is not based on the distinction between societies of pontifical law and societies of diocesan law. Clerics of societies of both pontifical and diocesan law will be incardinated into the society, unless the constitutions provide otherwise. This change was made in the final wording of C 736, whereas the schema of 1980 provided for incardination only into societies of pontifical law.

BIBLIOGRAPHY

Bouscaren-Ellis-Korth, *Canon Law, a Text and Commentary*, 4th ed. Milwaukee: Bruce Publishing Company, 1963.

Fernandez, J. *Sociedades O Asociaciones de Apostolado Consociado*, 2nd ed. Salamanca: extracted from *Revista Espanola de Derecho Canonico*, vol. 33 (1977) 296–394.

Nugent, J. *Ordination in Societies of Common Life*. Washington: Catholic University of America Press, *CanLawStud* 341, 1958.

Ristuccia, J. *Quasi-Religious Societies*. Washington: Catholic University of America Press, *CanLawStud* 261, 1949.

Scanlan, K. *Ordination and the Canonical Status of Clerics in Societies without Vows*. Rome: Pontificium Athenaeum "Angelicum," 1960.

Stanton, W. *De Societatibus sive virorum sive Mulierum in Communi Viventium sine Votis*, 2nd ed. Halifax: 1936.

Monastic Life Under the Rule of St. Benedict and the New Code

DANIEL J. WARD, O.S.B.

INTRODUCTION

In the formative years of the revised Code of Canon Law, it was proposed that there be a special section entitled *De Ordine Monastico*.[1] The charism, governance, and tradition of monasticism seemed to necessitate special legislation, particularly because of the autonomy of most monastic communities. Although the Code has not adopted a special section on monastic life as such, it does include various canons and references to monastic communities,[2] which indicate that the Code does distinguish in some ways the monastic life from other forms of the consecrated life.

This special commentary is based on the premise that the charism of monastic life does differ from other forms of the consecrated life and that this difference must be accorded recognition in the interpretation and application of the Code to monastic life, in keeping with the canonical tradition that a law must be understood in its text and context.[3] The context is obviously the consecrated life as lived in a monastic community. Further, the Code specifically states that when a canon refers to the old law, it is to be assessed in accord with canonical tradition.[4] Certainly the section on the consecrated life refers to and must be understood in light of past legislation and development. It could not be a section devoid of enfleshment in the canonical tradition of religious life in general and, in the instance of monasticism, in the canonical tradition of monastic life.

It should be noted that this commentary is written in the context of monasticism as lived under the *Rule of St. Benedict* and similar monastic

307

institutes marked by the important characteristic of autonomy. The autonomy of these monastic communities determines the relationship between the various governing structures. It establishes a system of governance which for the most part rests with the local community rather than with a hierarchical, multi-level structure. Certain canonical terms and phrases have a different reference point and understanding in autonomous monastic communities than they may have in most other institutes. Such difference dictates a different understanding of the Code as applied to monastic communities because for the most part the Code is written in light of more hierarchically structured institutes.

The basic structure of most monastic communities is an autonomous monastery (abbey or priory) under the leadership of a person (abbot, abbess, prior, or prioress) directly elected by all the finally professed members of the community (members of the chapter or capitulars). Such a community is most often united to other autonomous communities through a federation or congregation. Because of varying histories, the relationship between federations or congregations and individual communities may vary greatly. Generally "congregation" refers to a more structured association of communities which has canonical authority over the individual communities, while "federation" refers to a loose association which has no canonical authority over the individual communities. Federation has typically described the unions of small, autonomous monasteries of women scattered throughout Europe. However, the North American monastic associations have adopted the term, not in the European sense, but in the sense that in English federation describes more accurately the reality of the associations. The North American communities are highly autonomous with minimum authority given to the federation. It is the individual communities as corporate entities which belong to the federation, not the individual monastics of each monastery. Within the North American religious culture, federation is used to distinguish the monastic associations from the more centralized, hierarchical apostolic congregations of other religious. Federation also seems more appropriate in English, since the international association of Benedictine groups is called the confederation. Nevertheless, federation in the North American usage is equivalent to congregation as used in the Code when referring to monastic groupings.

Throughout this commentary, "federation" will be used, since this is the term used by the North American associations of monastic communities, and it is hoped that the Apostolic See will understand and permit the continued use of this word as descriptive of the North American view of monastic associations with some canonical authority.

The male communities following the *Rule of St. Benedict* are united in the International Confederation of Benedictines. having its origins in the desire of Pope Leo XIII to centralize monks under a single head, like other institutes. Although Pope Leo founded the Collegio di Sant' Anselmo in Rome and placed at its head an "abbot primate," the latter is without Ordinary jurisdiction over any federation and its members. In 1964 Pope Paul VI confirmed the confederation's charter, which leaves intact the independence of federations and their respective communities.[5]

The female communities following the *Rule of St. Benedict* are considered to be "associated" with the confederation, although the meaning of being "associated" is not fully agreed upon, nor, for that matter, accepted by all Benedictine women. Nevertheless, when the Code refers to confederation, this commentary will consider Benedictine women as within the confederation because such association has advantages within the structure of the Code.[6]

Although the issue is discussed later,[7] the issue of who is the supreme moderator within monastic organization is very unclear in the Code. The 1917 Code, in CIC 488, distinguished the president of a monastic federation from the head of other religious institutes and applied supreme moderator only to the latter. In the legislation resulting from Vatican Council II, certain faculties were granted to the heads of various religious orders and congregations. The law would then state that the president of a monastic federation would have the faculty within the monastic organization.[8] The law was careful not to state that the president was the same as the head of a religious order or congregation. The new Code is not so careful. It refers to the head of a religious institute as the supreme moderator,[9] but nowhere defines the term nor identifies the supreme moderator within the monastic context. However, in three canons in Book VII on canonical processes, the Code does distinguish between the president of a monastic federation and the supreme moderator of other religious institutes.[10] C 620, which states that superiors of monastic congregations do not have all the power attributed to a major superior by universal law, definitely indicates that the supreme moderator automatically cannot be identified with the president of a federation.

When the Code, therefore, refers to the supreme moderator, the text must be interpreted in reference to canonical tradition, since it is referring to functions exercised in the old law.[11] Under the old law, the authority accorded to supreme moderator in the new Code at times belonged to the president of a federation and at times to the head of the autonomous community. Therefore, supreme moderator in the new Code must be interpreted accordingly, since there exists a *dubium*. This position is strengthened by two canonical principles. First, custom, which is the best interpreter of the law,[12] clearly stands on the side that the president of the federation would not be considered as a person with supreme authority and responsibility. Second, a doubt as to the meaning of a law should be interpreted to the benefit of the subject. In the present issue, to interpret supreme moderator as the president of the federation would be detrimental to many monastic groupings, since it would destroy their spirit and nature, which would be contrary to C 576. The doubt, therefore, must be given to the tradition of the monastic federation, that is, the president is not the supreme moderator.

The solution to this issue is that each federation must define in its proper law who will have the authority of the supreme moderator. Reference may be made to the old law, but since there is doubt, the federation could realign the authority in a way different from the old law. Therefore, the head of the local community could be given the authority previously given in the old law to the president and vice versa.

The issue will eventually be solved by negotiations with the Apostolic See, especially as federations are required to submit their proper law to the Apostolic See. But monastic federations must be careful not to accept *carte blanche* curial interpretations of this issue, especially if such interpretations erode the federation's structure or the autonomy of individual communities and the traditional role and authority of the head of the autonomous community.

COMMENTARY

C 582

Mergers and unions of institutes of consecrated life are reserved to the Apostolic See alone; confederations and federations are also reserved to it.

In one sense the Code considers that those religious called "Benedictines" constitute one institute.[13] Yet this "one" monastic institute is not the same as other institutes. For example, C 581 states that the jurisdictional division of an institute is left to the competent authority of the institute. However, if different institutes merge—that is, if separate "religious orders" join together, such a merger requires the approval of the Apostolic See. However, C 582 requires that a merger of two Benedictine federations requires the approval of the Apostolic See, even though the two federations belong to the same confederation. Thus, the canon recognizes that a monastic "order" such as the Benedictines does not constitute an institute in the strict canonical usage applied to other orders and congregations. A monastic order is not an internationally governed community; rather, an order such as the Benedictines comprises a number of groupings, each somewhat analogous to a religious institute. Yet the order is not a religious institute *per se*, as is evidenced by C 620, which states that the head of a monastic confederation—i.e., "order"—is a major superior but does not have all the jurisdictional authority which the universal law attributes to a major superior.

C 582 recognizes a basic structural anomaly in monastic groupings. Even though there may be an international grouping such as the Benedictine Confederation, such a grouping is not strictly speaking an institute. On the other hand, a smaller grouping, that is, a federation, is to be treated in many instances as a religious institute. Yet it is not a religious institute in the strict sense, as is seen in C 620, which states that the president of a monastic congregation[14] does not have all the jurisdictional authority of a major superior.

C 587

§1. In order to protect more faithfully the particular vocation and identity of each institute, its fundamental code or constitutions must contain, besides what must be observed according to can. 578, fundamental norms about the governance of the institute and the discipline of members, the incorporation and formation of members, and the proper object of sacred bonds.

§2. A code of this kind is approved by the competent authority of the Church and can be changed only with its consent.

§3. In this code spiritual and juridical elements are to be suitably joined together; however norms are not to be multiplied unless it is necessary.

§4. Other norms established by the competent authority of the institute are to be suitably collected in other codes, which can moreover be fittingly reviewed and adapted according to the needs of places and times.

An issue which presents special concerns for monastic federations is the requirement of a fundamental code or constitution. A constitution is required of each institute, it is to contain the basic norms of the institute, and it must be approved by the competent authority, either the Apostolic See for pontifical institutes or the diocesan bishop for diocesan institutes. The constitution distinguishes the institute from other institutes.

For monasticism it is difficult to determine on what level such a fundamental code should exist. As stated in the Introduction, Pope Paul VI approved in 1964 a charter for the male International Confederation of Benedictines. But this certainly is not a constitution in the strict sense. The practice has been to require the federation, which is approved by the Apostolic See, to submit a constitution, a practice apparently to be continued after the new Code, even though nothing is specifically stated in the Code which would make a federation equivalent to an institute. The practice of a federation submitting a constitution is in keeping with C 6, §2, which requires looking to tradition if the new Code refers to the old law. However, in certain instances one autonomous monastery may be considered an institute and thus required to submit its own individual constitution. [15]

The problem is that in many loosely organized federations there generally is only one governing document which contains organizational principles of the federation, the relationships of the federation to the member communities, enabling legislation required by the universal law, and other provisions; and although this document generally contains some fundamental norms, it also contains other norms which under C 587 do not require the approval of the Apostolic See. The federation document generally is not viewed as constitutional—that is, the fundamental code—for two reasons. First, the fundamental code is the *Rule;* any other document is secondary. Second, the federation is not viewed as an institute like other religious institutes; it is at most a quasi-institute. Its major function is to aid the autonomous monasteries in their seeking God. The monasteries as corporate entities, not the individual monastics, belong to the federation.

Nevertheless, since the practice of the Apostolic See is to require a monastic federation to submit a constitution rather than the *Rule,* the constitution should contain only those elements of organization which pertain to the basic organization of the federation and to general or protective norms applicable to the individual monasteries. The latter are such elements as the consent required of the monastic chapter, the general conduct of the election of the monastic superior, and the canonical effect of the vow of poverty. Other more detailed norms, such as the conduct of a visitation, the establishment of a dependent priory, requirements for a leave of absence, and financial matters, should be contained in other documents which need not be submitted to the Apostolic See.

Since the Code refers to "fundamental code or constitutions," the title for this basic document need not be the "constitutions," a term used by most other institutes. A federation should use another term, such as basic articles or juridic elements, in order to prevent an identification of this basic document with a canonical institute's constitutions and thus the identification of the federation as an institute in the strict canonical sense of the word.

C 608

A religious community must live in a house legitimately constituted under the authority of the superior designated according to the norm of law; each house is to have at least an oratory in which the Eucharist is celebrated and reserved so that it truly is the center of the community.

A monastic house may be called an abbey, an independent priory, a dependent priory or a mission, depending upon its status and purpose. Except in a few federations, an abbey or an independent priory is an autonomous community with its own major superior. It is the basic unit of monastic life. Such a community may wish to start a foundation which is called a dependent priory, a community of persons who still are subject to and remain part of the autonomous community. Usually the goal of a dependent priory is to become an independent community. Except for a few highly centralized monastic federations with numerous dependent houses, an autonomous monastic community establishes a "new child," a dependent priory, in the hope that such a priory will thrive, become financially independent, and become a new autonomous community.

Mission is a traditional term for a small community established without any intention of becoming autonomous. Rather, the community has been established away from the main community to carry on some work of the community. The term's origin seems to be rooted in the principle that a small group's being sent from the monastic cloister "to the world" is permissible when the members are needed outside the cloister for the mission of the Church.

C 609

§1. Houses of a religious institute are erected by the competent authority according to the constitutions with the previous written consent of the diocesan bishop.

§2. In order to erect a monastery of nuns the permission of the Apostolic See is also required.

Generally speaking, a dependent priory is established by an independent community. Both the monastic chapter of the founding monastery and the diocesan bishop of the place where the priory is to be located must consent to the foundation and there must be a sufficient number of persons to celebrate communally the Liturgy of the Hours and to live the common life. After a dependent priory has a stable number of members, realistic hope of new members, and financial security, it may become an autonomous community.

Under the 1917 Code independence for a community of pontifical right belonging to a federation required not only the consent of the founding community's chapter, the diocesan bishop, and the federation, but a decree from the Apostolic See. Besides establishing the autonomy of the new community, the decree in the case of a community of men or a cloistered community of women determined whether the title of the new community would be an independent priory or an abbey. Usually the title of abbey was not granted immediately, but only after the community had been an independent priory for a few years. If the community was to affiliate with a federation, the decree so stated. Once the title and the affiliation had been established by the Apostolic See, their change required permission of the Apostolic See.

C 609 of the revised Code no longer requires the approval of the Apostolic See for the establishment of an autonomous community; CIC 497 required the consent of the Apostolic See in the establishment of all canonical houses of an institute. C 609 leaves such permission to the competent authority according to the constitutions, providing that the diocesan bishop comments in writing. No difference is made between the types of houses, and C 609 replaces entirely the older canon. There is no reason to interpret C 609 differently for a monastic community, especially since C 616, §3 requires only the consent of the general chapter of the federation to suppress an autonomous monastery unless the constitutions state otherwise. Nevertheless, there still remains the question of title, of which the Code does not speak. A decree of title still might be required from the Apostolic See if a community is to receive the title of abbey. It seems prudent, therefore, to clarify explicitly the granting of independence and title in the fundamental law which must be approved by the Apostolic See.

The canon still requires the consent of the Apostolic See to establish a monastery of nuns *(monialium)*, that is, a cloistered community of women monastics. Since the canon does not distinguish between dependent and independent houses, both require this permission. Thus, it is clear that the Apostolic See also would establish whether the house would be a priory or an abbey.

In North America, with very few exceptions, such as the Abbey of Regina Laudis in Bethlehem, Connecticut, Benedictine communities of women are not strictly cloistered. The historical reason for this is that papal cloister was lifted so that the nuns could engage in apostolic work alongside the monks. It should be noted, however, that because of the elimination of cloister to become apostolic, the women lost many of the traditional monastic rights and, in fact, were treated as if they had become modern apostolic congregations of sisters with simple vows. [16] On the other hand, the apostolic-oriented monks lost no traditional rights. A male monastery could be an abbey with an abbot, while a female monastery only could be a priory with a prioress. The men enjoyed a great deal of autonomy, while the women were subject to the bishop. In many instances the women's communities had to be established as diocesan, rather than be established as members of an independent federation.

Today the situation has changed somewhat. The women's communities, for the most part, are autonomous and belong to independent federations. Yet differences such as abbot versus prioress, abbey versus priory or convent still exist. Since the Code does not refer to these matters, the old practices still govern, but they need to be reexamined in light of monastic history, modern circumstances, and the principles of equality enunciated in CC 208 and 606. The Code, itself, would not prevent a community of women without strict papal cloister from being called an abbey with an abbess as its monastic superior.

In a particular instance, the Apostolic See may erect an autonomous community of pontifical right which is not affiliated with any federation. Such an autonomous community, referred to in the Code as an autonomous monastery of C 615, besides being governed by the canons applicable to all institutes, is governed by particular canons, which are discussed under C 615.

Besides communities of pontifical right, a monastic community may be established as a community of diocesan right. In such an instance the new community is not affiliated with a federation nor has it likely been a dependent community of an autonomous community. The reasons for such a community may vary; for instance, a group of persons not affiliated with any monastery may wish to begin a monastic group or members from one or several monasteries may not be able to receive the requisite support from an autonomous community or federation. Whatever the reason, the diocesan bishop, following C 579 for the erection of any diocesan institute, may establish such a monastic community. The diocesan monastic community, which would not belong to any federation, would be subject to the diocesan bishop and would follow the canons referring to diocesan institutes. [17]

C 613

§1. A religious house of canons regular and monks under the governance and care of its own moderator is autonomous unless the constitutions state otherwise.

§2. A moderator of an autonomous house is by law a major superior.

While this canon states the general principle of autonomy for monastic communities, it is unique, since it is the only canon which uses the word "monks" and refers to a religious house of monks as autonomous. Does the canon mean that a community of women monastics cannot be autonomous? If the present autonomous women's communities are no longer autonomous, have they again become subject to a bishop or to an abbot? If this canon reflects the idea that nonordained persons cannot have jurisdiction, it is not very apparent. The meaning of the canon as referring to males only is very unclear.

Therefore, the principle of C 606, which requires the application of the law equally to either sex unless the contrary is apparent, applies to this canon. There is no apparent reason that men's communities are to be autonomous, while women's communities are not. Under the old law, women's communities also have been autonomous. Therefore, despite the unfortunate use of "monk," the canon must be understood to apply to all monastics.

C 615

An autonomous monastery which has no other major superior beyond its own moderator and is not associated with any other institute of religious in such a way that the superior of the latter enjoys true power over such a monastery determined by the constitutions is committed to the special vigilance of the diocesan bishop according to the norm of law.

As noted under the commentary to C 609, the Apostolic See may establish an autonomous monastery of pontifical right which does not belong to a federation. Since such a community is not subject to the general supervision of a federation, especially to visitation, the law establishes the norm that the diocesan bishop should take special interest in the community to be exercised according to law. Besides the general relations between a monastic community and the diocesan bishop established by law, the Code sets down special rights and responsibilities of the diocesan bishop toward this particular type of monastic community. C 625, §2 provides that the diocesan bishop preside at the election of the superior. C 628, §2, 1° establishes the right and duty of the diocesan bishop to conduct a visitation of the community, including review of monastic discipline. However, the canon does not give the bishop authority to legislate for or govern the community if he finds problems in the community. The community is autonomous and of pontifical right, so it must be treated like an autonomous monastery belonging to a federation. For instance, a federation can exhort and strongly try to persuade a community to act upon a recommendation, but if the community refuses, the federation under traditional law could only resort to the Apostolic See to seek the removal of the superior. However, the removal of a superior is a rare event, since the federation respects the individual spirit and style of the community, while the community realizes that the federation is trying to offer positive assistance to enable the community to respond authentically to the monastic charism. A diocesan bishop is to act similarly to a C 615 type monastery, since his visitation rights are no greater than a federation's, and his purpose is to act as a substitute for a federation.

C 637 requires that the unfederated community provide a report of administration to the diocesan bishop. Under the canon this report seems to include more than a financial report, since the canon uses the phrase *rationem administrationis* for the autonomous monastery, but the phrase *rationibus oeconomicis* for diocesan institutes. It would seem that the "report of administration" is broader than a financial report, and would include the latter. Since visitation of the community would take place only every three-to-five years, as is the custom in a federation, the annual report would provide the bishop with a summary picture of the community and might provide useful information for a future visitation or give indication of the need for a special visitation. The requirement of a financial report is in keeping with modern federation practices, which require such annual reports. In some federations the report must be audited by a certified public accountant. The report is meant to protect against financial irresponsibility. The bishop, like the head of a federation, receives the reports and can use persuasive guidance if there appear to be difficulties, but he has no direct authority over the community. His direct action must be to the Apostolic See.

C 638, §4 requires the consent of the diocesan bishop for extraordinary administration of property, such as alienation and exceeding the debt limitation established by the Apostolic See. It also includes items specified in the fundamental code of the community.

According to C 688, §2, the diocesan bishop grants a dispensation from temporary vows for a member of an autonomous community governed by C 615.

C 699, §2, which concerns dismissal of a member, states that the diocesan bishop decides on the dismissal. Since the monastery is of pontifical right, the dismissal must then be transmitted to the Apostolic See for confirmation.

C 616, §3

The suppression of an autonomous house, such as that described in can. 613, belongs to the general chapter, unless the constitutions state otherwise.

As mentioned under C 609, the Code changes the old law regarding the suppression of an autonomous monastic community. The old law required a decree from the Apostolic See to suppress an autonomous community, that is, to abolish the community or to reduce its status to a dependent priory. Under the Code, only the consent of the general chapter of the federation is required, unless the fundamental code states otherwise. Therefore, the fundamental code should establish procedures for suppression, empower the president with the consent of counsel to establish a timetable for the suppression, and provide for the distribution of the assets of the community in the event that a community is abolished. Such provisions must keep in mind that the abolition of an autonomous house differs from the suppression of a province of other religious institutes.

The assets of the autonomous house are in no way assets of the federation, and the federation as a whole has no claim on the assets. It would seem that the distribution should be governed by the principle that the assets be given in some proportion to communities which accept members from the suppressed house. The fundamental code also should make special provision, differing from the ordinary transfer process, for the transfer of the vow of stability, because, when the monastery is abolished or changed to a dependent priory, there is no canonical entity to which the vow attaches. Although a waiting period before transfer takes place may not be possible, this generally should not present a problem if the community members are transferring back to their original community of profession. [18]

C 620

Major superiors are those who govern a whole institute, a province of an institute, some part equivalent to a province, or an autonomous house, as well as their vicars. Comparable to these are the abbot primate and superior of a monastic congregation, who nonetheless do not have all the power which universal law grants major superiors.

As noted under C 613, a superior of an autonomous house is by law a major superior. The abbot primate of a monastic confederation and the president of a monastic federation[19] are also deemed major superiors, but do not have the authority granted major superiors by the universal law. The authority of an abbot primate and a head of a federation is found in the proper law.

C 622

The supreme moderator holds power over all provinces, houses and members of the institute, which is to be exercised according to proper law; other superiors enjoy power within the limits of their office.

The head of an institute generally is termed the supreme moderator. This person exercises authority over all members and subdivisions of the institute. In a very real sense, the supreme moderator is the chief superior of the institute and possesses the authority given by the universal law.

In a monastic federation the term "supreme moderator" presents difficulties. Except in the highly centralized monastic federations, the president is not given extensive jurisdictional power over autonomous communities, and is not the chief superior of the communities. C 620 clearly states this. The president of a monastic grouping does not have all the power which universal law grants a major superior. Nonetheless, the universal law of the Code does equate the president as a supreme moderator in some instances[20] and at times leaves in doubt who is to exercise the authority of the supreme moderator within the monastic context.

There seems to be a definite trend in the Code to treat a monastic federation as an institute of the consecrated life with the president holding the position of the supreme moderator. Such legislation is contrary to much monastic tradition, especially within North America, and to the spirit of many federations. The Code, itself, calls for religious life to grow and flourish "according to the spirit of the founders and wholesome tradition."[21] The spirit of many monastic communities is autonomy within a loosely knit federation. To consider the federation as the institute or the president as the supreme moderator is a violation of that spirit. Monastic groupings must consider the issues of institute and supreme moderator. In writing the laws of the federation, care in vocabulary should be used. Words, such as constitutions, supreme moderator, even general chapter, all of which have specific meanings in canonical language and reference to an institute, may require alternate wording in a monastic federation so as to avoid in the Church at large identification of the federation as an institute. The fundamental code could specify which of those powers attributed in the universal law to a supreme moderator are to be exercised by the president and which by the head of the community.

C 624

§1. Superiors are to be constituted for a certain and appropriate amount of time according to the nature and needs of the institute, unless the constitutions state otherwise for the supreme moderator and for superiors of autonomous houses.

§2. Proper law is to provide in suitable norms that superiors constituted for a definite time do not remain too long in offices of governance without an interruption.

§3. Nevertheless they can be removed from office during their term or transferred to another office for reasons determined in proper law.

The ancient tradition of monasticism has been life-time superiors of autonomous communities. This ancient tradition has been modified in certain federations, such as the male English Benedictine Congregation, which has an eight-year term for an abbot with no limit on reelection. Most North American federations of women have followed the old general law for religious institutes and have short terms of office with limitations on reelection due to the historical difficulties and treatment encountered when cloister was lifted. [22]

The Code now recognizes the monastic tradition under this canon, and so an autonomous community's term of office for the head of the community need not be a definite period or subject to limitations on reelection. Monastic federations may adopt life-time tenure, age limitations, or terms for the superior of a community. By tradition, subordinate superiors within the monastic community do not have terms of office but serve at the discretion of the head of the community, since these superiors are the personal representatives of the head of the community and are freely chosen by the head of the community.

By tradition the head of an autonomous monastic community can be removed only by a decree of the Apostolic See. The Code does not seem to change this practice. In certain federations with less autonomy for individual houses, the superior of a local community may be removed without approval of the Apostolic See. Nevertheless, since the Code does not prevent a change in the tradition, the issue of removal of the head of an autonomous community should be studied in light of chapter 64 of the *Rule* and the principle of subsidiarity, that is, would it be better to have the federation, which is nearer to the difficulty, intervene rather than the Apostolic See, which may interfere more extensively in the life of the community than is desired. However, if the head of a community can be removed by the federation, the federation must establish procedures which protect both the rights of the superior and the community.

C 625

§1. The supreme moderator of an institute is to be designated by canonical election according to the norm of the constitutions.

§2. The bishop of the principal seat presides at elections of the superior of an autonomous monastery, mentioned in can. 615, and of the supreme moderator of an institute of diocesan right.

§3. Other superiors are to be constituted according to the norm of the constitutions, but in such a way that if they are elected they need the confirmation of the competent major superior; if they are appointed by the superior, a suitable consultation is to precede.

An election of the head of an autonomous monastic community generally differs significantly from elections in other religious institutes. In the monastic community all finally professed members (capitulars) have the right and duty to participate directly in the election unless impeded by law. Until recently, monastic federations, at least of men, have provided only for nominations during the election chapter, in keeping with monastic tradition and with the old law, which was interpreted as forbidding the election process of a life-time superior to begin until the office was actually vacant. Under C 153 the election process may now begin prior to the vacancy of the office, since the canon prohibits only conferral of a life-time office before the office is vacant.

After the completion of the nomination process and other preliminary requirements, the chapter for the actual election is held. In keeping with monastic tradition, which has the force of law, each chapter member has the right and duty to speak about the candidates. This process is based upon the right of a chapter member to speak on the issue before the chapter, a right which cannot be denied except in accordance with law. The election itself is a direct election by all those present and voting, although some federations may provide for voting by absent members through proxy, or through another method, such as phone contact, if the absent members can be in direct contact with the election chapter so as to cast a new vote on each ballot.

The president of the federation or delegate confirms the election, except for an abbot nullius, who must be confirmed by the Apostolic See. For an autonomous community of pontifical right which belongs to no federation, the head of the community must be confirmed by the diocesan bishop. For a diocesan monastic community, the diocesan bishop confirms the election.

C 631

§1. The general chapter, which holds supreme authority in the institute according to the norm of the constitutions, is to be so formed that, representing the entire institute, it should be a true sign of its unity in love. Its foremost duty is this: to protect the patrimony of the institute mentioned in can. 578, and promote suitable renewal in accord with this patrimony, to elect the supreme moderator, to treat major business matters and to publish norms which all are bound to obey.

§2. The composition and the extent of the power of the chapter is to be defined in the constitutions; proper law is to determine further the order to be observed in the celebration of the chapter, especially regarding elections and procedures for handling various matters.

§3. According to norms determined in proper law, not only provinces and local communities but also any member at all can freely send his or her wishes and suggestions to the general chapter.

In most monastic federations the general chapter does not enjoy the status nor fulfill the function of a general chapter in other religious institutes because the federation itself is not the equivalent of a religious institute. The general chapter is not considered the fundamental monastic body; it is secondary to the autonomous community. Federations, after all, are an outgrowth of the eleventh-century Cistercian reform and were not universally mandated for monastic communities until the Fourth Lateran Council in 1215. In many instances this universal mandate was not immediately implemented. In fact, it was refuted. Further, the reason for the federation was either to provide a system of corrections for individual communities or to protect individual communities from abuses such as commendam abbots.

In monastic terminology the chapter is the finally professed members of the autonomous community. This chapter, in conjunction with the head of the community, is the basic governing body of the community. Monastic tradition and particular law, both of the federation and of the local house, govern the chapter. By tradition, which has the force of law, the chapter must consent to admission to the novitiate and to first and final vows, to the alienation of property, and to the expenditure of large sums of money. A chapter member, called a capitular, has the right to speak on the issue before the chapter and cannot be limited in this right except in accordance with law.

In many communities, the method of voting, the nonrequirement of a quorum, the effect of neutral votes, and the numerical requirement for an affirmative vote have been governed more by tradition than by federation or universal law. Books I and V affect these traditions, since they establish certain new procedures and requirements for collegial bodies.[23] These monastic traditions and customs will have to be examined in light of CC 5 and 6 to determine whether they are abrogated. The laws of a federation will need adaptation to the Code's new requirements.

C 641

The right of admitting candidates to the novitiate pertains to major superiors according to the norm of proper law.

The admission of persons to the novitiate in an autonomous monastic community usually requires the consent of the chapter. The consent does not force the head of the community to admit the person but the absence of the chapter's consent invalidates admission to the novitiate.

C 647, §1

The erection, transfer and suppression of a novitiate house are to take place through a written decree of the supreme moderator of the institute with the consent of his or her council.

The very existence of an autonomous community includes the right to have a novitiate. A novitiate anywhere but at the monastery has not been part of the general monastic tradition. An exception is a dependent priory which may want to have its own novitiate. The old law required the consent of the president of the federation and council to establish a novitiate in a dependent priory. If the supreme moderator is identified with the president, then C 647 continues the old requirement. However, since such identification is a *dubium*, the fundamental code must define the required consent.

C 654

By religious profession members assume by public vow the observance of the three evangelical counsels, are consecrated to God through the ministry of the Church, and are incorporated into the institute with rights and duties defined by law.

In most instances monastic vows incorporate a person to a particular autonomous community rather than to a federation.[24] The legal consequences of this are important. The person has the right to be a member of his or her monastic community of profession and not to be forced to become part of another community even within the same federation. On the other hand, the person does not have the right to transfer freely to another community, but must comply with C 685, §3 and the federation requirements. Benedictine monastics by tradition do not profess the three evangelical counsels in the vow formula, but rather in keeping with chapter 58 of the *Rule* profess stability, *conversatio morum,* and obedience. Monastic life does include a life of chastity and poverty or common ownership. Since this canon only requires the assumption of the evangelical counsels, not their inclusion in a vow formula, there is no need to change the present monastic vow formula to specifically state the evangelical counsels.

C 667

§1. In all houses cloister adapted to the character and mission of the institute is to be observed according to the determinations of proper law, with some part of the religious house always being reserved to the members alone.

§2. A stricter discipline of cloister is to be observed in monasteries ordered to the contemplative life.

§3. Monasteries of nuns which are totally ordered to the contemplative life must observe *papal* cloister, namely according to norms given by the Apostolic See. Other monasteries of nuns are to observe cloister adapted to their own character and defined in the constitutions.

§4. For a just cause the diocesan bishop has the faculty of entering the cloister of monasteries of nuns which are in his diocese, and, for a grave cause and with the consent of the superior, of permitting others to enter the cloister and nuns to leave the cloister for a truly necessary period of time.

The Code changes the law of cloister. The old law permitted institutes to determine the privacy of their houses; except monastics were obligated to retain cloister.[25] The Code now treats cloister as privacy and leaves its determination to each institute. The canon recognizes three types of cloister: a limited cloister to be observed by most communities; a stricter cloister to be observed by monasteries ordered to the contemplative life; and papal cloister to be observed by nuns totally ordered to the contemplative life. The second type of cloister appears to be the proper cloister for Benedictine communities. This second type of cloister, which has been the actual practice, undoes the historical wrong done to women's communities when papal cloister was lifted. A community of women need not be under papal cloister to be monastic. This was never the canonical requirement for men. Yet women's communities were treated as late-nineteenth-century apostolic congregations rather than as monastics when papal cloister was lifted, even though the "lifted cloister" was no different from the cloister of the men's communities, which were allowed to maintain their monastic identity, heritage, and autonomy.[26]

C 684, §3

For a religious to transfer from an autonomous monastery to another of the same institute or federation or confederation, it is required and is sufficient to have the consent of the major superior of both monasteries and the chapter of the receiving monastery, with due regard for other requirements determined in proper law; a new profession is not required.

As discussed under C 654, profession of vows in most instances incorporates a member into a particular autonomous community; profession is made to the particular community and not to the federation. Generally, under the old law transfer to another monastery within the same federation was treated like transfer of a religious from one institute to another institute, except that the probationary period might have been less than three years and a new profession was not required. Transfer to a community belonging to another federation required more formalities, since the abbot primate had to issue a decree of transfer in the case of a monk. A transfer of a sister or nun from a cloistered monastic community to a more active monastic community, even if within the same "order," e.g., Benedictine, required an indult of exclaustration, a new novitiate, and a new profession of vows.

The Code now simplifies the process, although proper law may require more formalities. Under the Code, if a member transfers from one community to another within the same federation or confederation, only the consent of the two superiors and the chapter of the receiving community is required; no waiting period nor new profession is required. Since transfer now is permitted within a confederation, it is important, particularly for women's federations, to define "confederation."[27]

C 686

§1. With the consent of the council the supreme moderator for a grave reason can grant an indult of exclaustration to a member professed of perpetual vows, but not for more than three years, and with the prior consent of the local ordinary where he must remain if this concerns a cleric. Extending the indult or granting it for more than three years is reserved to the Holy See or, if there is question of institutes of diocesan right, to the diocesan bishop.

§2. It belongs to the Apostolic See alone to grant an indult of exclaustration for nuns.

§3. If a supreme moderator with the consent of the council petitions, exclaustration can be imposed by the Holy See on a member of an institute of pontifical right or by a diocesan bishop on a member of an institute of diocesan right for grave reasons, with equity and charity being observed.

The entire section on "Departure from the Institute" presents a particular problem for monastic communities. Under the Code the various procedures for permanent or temporary departure require the consent of the supreme moderator of the institute, but as discussed above,[28] most monastic federations do not have a supreme moderator. If the president is to be considered the supreme moderator for cases of departure, then the present monastic practice for departures is changed, and the federation is interposed in this personal decision between the member and the head of the autonomous community.

The authority to grant the indult of exclaustration needs to be addressed in the proper law of the federation.

C 688

§1. Whoever wishes to leave an institute when the time of profession has expired can depart from it.

§2. During the time of temporary profession whoever asks to leave the institute for a grave reason can be granted an indult to leave by the supreme moderator in an institute of pontifical right with the consent of the council; in institutes of diocesan right and in monasteries mentioned in can. 615, the indult, in order to be valid, must be confirmed by the bishop of the house of assignment.

Under the old law, a dispensation from temporary vows was granted by the president of the federation. The Code states that the supreme moderator grants the indult to leave. By virtue of C 6, §2, the president seemingly would continue to grant the indult, since C 688 merely reflects the old law. The president would be the equivalent in this instance of the supreme moderator. However, since the concept of supreme moderator presents a *dubium* in the case of monastic federations, it would seem that the head of an autonomous monastery could grant the indult to leave. This would be more proper in the light of the concept of "abbot" within the *Rule*. The proper law of the federation should specify who grants the indult to leave.

C 690

§1. A religious who after completing the novitiate or after profession has left the institute legitimately, can be readmitted by the supreme moderator with the consent of the council without the burden of repeating the novitiate; it is up to the same moderator to determine a suitable probationary period before temporary profession and a time in such vows prior to perpetual profession according to the norm of cann. 655 and 657.

§2. With the consent of the council, the superior of an autonomous monastery enjoys this same faculty.

The old law required the consent of the president of the federation for a person to return to a community after dispensation from temporary vows without the necessity of completing a new novitiate and three-year temporary vow period before final profession. The Code now grants this faculty to the head of the autonomous community without reference to the president.

C 691

§1. One who is professed in perpetual vows is not to seek an indult to leave the institute without very grave reasons weighed before the Lord; such a petition is to be presented to the supreme moderator of the institute, who is to transmit it to the competent authority with a personal opinion and that of the council.

§2. An indult of this kind in institutes of pontifical right is reserved to the Apostolic See; but in institutes of diocesan right the diocesan bishop of the house of assignment can also grant it.

This canon, concerning the petitioning for an indult of dispensation from final vows, would seem to change the present procedure and offers great difficulties to autonomous monastic communities. The recent practice has been that the head of the autonomous community submitted the petition directly to the Apostolic See along with his or her *votum*.

The Code states that the petition is to be sent by the supreme moderator with his or her *votum* and that of the council. In this instance, if the president of the federation is the equivalent of the supreme moderator, the process no longer requires the involvement of the head of the autonomous community; rather, the professed member submits the petition directly to the president. To bypass the head of the autonomous community seems inappropriate and to involve the president seems unnecessary. The involvement of the president's council is almost impossible, since the council members belong to various monasteries, usually at great distances from one another. A council meets infrequently. To require more frequent meetings either in person or by phone would greatly enhance expenses and inconvenience members. To wait for a regularly scheduled council meeting would delay unnecessarily a petition for dispensation. Profession of vows is not made to the federation nor is the president involved in admission or profession. Further, the president in no sense is the superior of the petitioner; neither the federation president nor his council generally knows the member. The head of the autonomous community is the superior of the member and knows the situation.

Monastic federations will need to seek a clarification of this canon and a change by indult if necessary. If the Apostolic See requires the involvement of the federation president and council, federation procedures should be established to involve the head of the autonomous community in the process. These procedures, however, do not belong in the fundamental code, but in other documents such as the bylaws, which do not require approbation of the Apostolic See.

C 695

§1. A member must be dismissed for the offenses in cann. 1397, 1398 and 1395, unless in the delicts mentioned in can. 1395, §2, the superior judges that dismissal is not entirely necessary and that the correction of the member and restitution of justice and reparation of scandal can be sufficiently assured in some other way.

§2. In these cases the major superior, having collected proofs about the facts and imputability, is to make known the accusation and the proofs to the member who is about to be dismissed, giving the member the opportunity of self-defense. All the acts, signed by the major superior and a notary, along with the written and signed responses of the member, are to be transmitted to the supreme moderator.

Under the old law, the head of an autonomous community sent decrees of dismissal directly to the Apostolic See for confirmation. The Code seems to alter this procedure. Under this canon the major superior collects the required proofs, or issues the canonical warnings required by C 697, and forwards the acts to the supreme moderator and council for a decisive vote. The acts are then forwarded to Rome.

Just as it is inappropriate for the president and council to be involved in the dispensation from final vows, it is similarly inappropriate in the dismissal procedure. If the concern is the protection of rights, these are provided for because the person has the right to counsel and defense, and the acts must be sent to the Apostolic See for an objective review and decision.

Nonetheless, the Code seems to require the involvement of the president and council if the principle of looking to parallel places in the Code is used. [29] C 699, §2 requires that the head of an unfederated autonomous community of pontifical right[30] submit the acts of dismissal to the diocesan bishop, who judges the issue and, if he believes dismissal is warranted, forwards the acts to the Apostolic See for decision. The diocesan bishop acts as a substitute for a federation president. Since the intervention of the bishop is specifically required, it seems that the intervention of the president and council also is required.

C 707, §1

§1. A retired religious bishop may choose a place to live for himself even outside the houses of his institute unless something else has been provided by the Apostolic See.

By monastic tradition, a retired bishop who is a monk may choose to live at any monastery and is not obligated to return to the monastery of his profession. The Code does not change this tradition.

ABBOTS

CIC 625 of the former Code stated the privileges of abbots, namely, to confer tonsure and minor orders[31] and to enjoy episcopal privileges of dignity, such as the use of crosier, miter, and pectoral cross. These privileges are no longer mentioned in the Code. Nonetheless, abbots retain these privileges by virtue of C 5, which recognizes the continuance of such customs.

NOTES

1. Cf. "A Monastic Proposal for the Revision of Canon Law," *RfR* 26:19-45 (January 1967). M. Basil Pennington. "The Integration of Monastic Law in the Revised Code," *Jur* 25:345-50 (July 1965).

2. Cf. CC 613, 614, 615, 620, and 684, §3.

3. C 17.

4. C 6, §2.

5. "Norms Concerning Association with the Confederation," (private) (undated) accompanying letter of Richard Yeo, "To All Benedictine Abbesses and Prioresses," dated June 1983.

6. E.g., C 684, §3.

7. Cf. C 622 (below).

8. Cf. "Cum admotae" (Sec. St., Rescript, November 6, 1964) *AAS* 59–374 (Faculties of Superiors General of Pontifical Clerical Religious Institutes and of Abbots President of Monastic Congregations, *CLD* 6:147).

9. C 622.

10. CC 1405, §3; 1427, §2; 1438, 3°.

11. Cf. C 6, §2.

12. C 27.

13. Cf. C 684, §3.

14. Cf. discussion in Introduction, since the Code does use the term "congregation" within this canon.

15. C 615.

16. William Skudlarek, ed., *The Continuing Quest for God. Monastic Spirituality in Tradition and Transition* (Collegeville: The Liturgical Press, 1982) 184.

17. E.g., CC 589, 594, 595, 625, 628, 637, 638, 686, 688, 691, 700.

18. Cf. C 684, §3.

19. The canon uses only the term "congregation." For further discussion on this topic, see the Introduction.

20. Cf. C 686 below.

21. C 576.

22. For a discussion of the denial of Benedictine women's monastic rights and tradition, see Joan Chittister, et al., *Climb Along the Cutting Edge, An Analysis of Change in Religious Life* (New York: Paulist Press, 1977) 23, 75-76, and William Skudlarek, *The Continuing Quest for God, Monastic Spirituality in Tradition and Transition* (Collegeville: The Liturgical Press, 1982) 183–86.

23. For examples see C 119 on quorum; C 127, §1 on majority vote requirement; CC 119, 164–79 on elections; CC 1271–1276 on alienation of property, especially since alienation now includes any transfer of property or act which lessens the rights on property, e.g., a lease.

24. In a few monastic congregations, the members take vows to the congregation rather than to an individual community, e.g., the Hungarian Congregation and the Sylvestrian Congregation.

25. *AAS* 62–548 (*CLD* 7: 536).

26. See Introduction.

27. See Introduction and C 622.

28. See Introduction.

29. C 17.

30. Cf. C 615.

31. The four minor orders were replaced by the institution of the two ministries reader and acolyte in a *motu proprio* by Pope Paul VI, dated August 15, 1972. An abbot retains the authority to confer these ministries on his monks.

Glossary

SHARON HOLLAND, I.H.M.

ABSENCE: the permission given to a religious by the major superior with consent of the council, to live apart from a house of the institute for an extended period of time for a just cause. An absence of more than one year can be granted in cases of sickness, the pursuit of studies, or the exercise of an apostolate in the name of the institute.

ADMINISTRATION (of goods): transactions involved in acquiring and managing temporal goods. Ordinary administration involves day to day operations which do not require special permission. Extraordinary administration involves transactions which are beyond those authorized by approved budgets and guidelines. Statutes of institutes must express limits and procedures for the authorization of extraordinary acts of administration.

ALIENATION (of property): the transfer of ownership of temporal goods to someone else. Property owned by public juridic persons in the Church is ecclesiastical property, and can be alienated only with the necessary authorization in order to protect the patrimony of the institute. The canons also require this authorization for any transaction which could endanger the patrimony of the juridic person.

APOSTOLIC SEE: a term, referring not only to the Sovereign Pontiff, but also to the Secretary of State, the Office for the Public Affairs of the Church, the Tribunals, Congregations, and other organs of the Roman Curia.

BONDS (sacred): the vows, promises, oaths, or consecrations by which members of institutes of consecrated life bind themselves to the observance of the evangelical counsels. Religious profession always implies public vows. Secular institutes may use a vow, oath, or consecration for assuming celibacy and vows or promises for obedience and poverty.

331

CESSION (of administration): a juridic act by which the administration of personal properties is turned over to another party who is willing to assume the obligation. This is effected through a document similar to the power of attorney. Religious must complete cession papers before first profession.

CHAPTER (general): the highest extraordinary authority in a religious institute. Except in very small institutes, this representative body is composed of ex officio and elected members; it functions collegially. It is charged with preserving the spiritual patrimony of the institute, renewing according to that patrimony, electing the highest superior, and dealing with the major affairs affecting all.

CLERICAL INSTITUTE: a religious or secular institute which by reason of the end intended by the founder or due to legitimate tradition is under the governance of clerics, assumes the exercise of Holy orders, and is recognized as such by Church authority.

CLOISTER: a restriction on entrance into or exit from a religious house. Minimal cloister reserves part of the house for the use of members; stricter observance is called for in monasteries ordered to the contemplative life. In monasteries of nuns which are totally ordered to the contemplative life, "papal" cloister is observed, more exactly regulating entrance into the monastery by outsiders or departure from the monastery by the nuns.

COMMON LIFE: the observance particular to religious life, by which all things are held in common, and members are dependent upon the institute for their material needs.

COMMUNITY LIFE: the term commonly used to refer to religious living together, and sharing a common life. It also may refer to the *vita fraterna* or communitarian spirit lived by secular institutes, or to the life in community shared by members of societies of apostolic life.

CONSECRATION (of life): the consecration to God by a "new and special title" effected through profession of the evangelical counsels of chastity, poverty, and obedience in religious or secular institutes. The rite of consecration in a life of virginity is received by the candidate through the blessing of the bishop.

CONSENT (of the council): a positive vote by a majority of the councilors required in certain cases for valid action by a superior. This consent is sometimes called a deliberative vote. In contrast, "hearing the council" requires that the councilors at least be consulted before action is taken.

CONSTITUTIONS: the primary book of proper law by which an institute of consecrated life is governed. It contains the expression of the institute's nature, end, and spirit, its way of formation, incorporation, living and governance. Constitutions are often supplemented by other collections called directories, statutes, or the like.

CONTEMPLATIVE LIFE: the life of institutes which have prayer as their primary focus and which are not engaged in external apostolates or are so engaged in a very limited way. Solitude, silence, prayer, and penance characterize this vocation and the Church recognizes it as having great apostolic fruitfulness.

COUNCIL: a body of advisors whose role is to assist those in governing offices. In cases designated in universal and proper law, their consent or counsel is necessary for the validity of acts.

COUNSELS: the evangelical counsels of chastity, poverty, and obedience based on the life and the teaching of Jesus. These express three dimensions of the one attitude of Christ's self-offering in the Paschal Mystery which those professing the counsels seek to enter more radically.

DEPARTURE: the definitive separation from an institute of consecrated life, formerly called secularization. An indult of departure *(indultum discedendi)* carries the dispensation from vows or other sacred bonds and the cessation of all rights and obligations flowing from incorporation.

DIOCESAN BISHOP: a bishop to whom the care of a diocese has been committed. If pastoral needs call for it, he may request one or more auxiliary bishops to assist him.

DIOCESAN INSTITUTE: a religious or secular institute erected by the diocesan bishop, with approval of the Holy See, and remaining under his special care. Where law calls for the intervention of ecclesiastical authority, it is usually the diocesan bishop who is competent for diocesan institutes.

DISMISSAL: a juridic procedure by which a member's incorporation in an institute of consecrated life is terminated on the initiative of the institute. This may be done only for the most grave causes, which are also external, imputable, and juridically proven. A decree of dismissal must be confirmed by competent ecclesiastical authority before it has effect.

DISPENSATION: a relaxation of the law, granted by competent ecclesiastical authority, e.g., as in the case of impediments which would invalidate entrance to the novitiate. Dispensation from vows follows from legitimately granted indults for departure from religious life or from decrees of dismissal.

ERECTION: the act by which an institute is officially established and recognized by competent ecclesiastical authority.

EXCLAUSTRATION: a temporary form of separation from a religious institute. The vows remain but the individual is exonerated from the obligations which cannot be observed in the new form of life; active and passive voice are lost.

EXEMPT INSTITUTE: an institute which has been removed, by the Sovereign Pontiff from the jurisdiction of the local Ordinary, and made subject to himself or some other authority. This is intended to serve the mission of the Church and the good of the institute.

HABIT: the traditional English rendering of the Latin *habitus* which is used in the canons on both the ecclesiastical garb of clerics and the clothing worn by religious as a sign of their consecration and a witness to poverty.

HERMIT (anchorite): a person who lives in greater seclusion from the world, in solitude, prayer, and penance, in praise of God, and for the salvation of others. The law recognizes this as a form of consecrated life when the evangelical counsels are publicly professed in the hands of the diocesan bishop and lived under his guidance.

IMPEDIMENTS: conditions which would invalidate, or make illicit, one's admission into an institute of consecrated life. These include such things as age, a marriage bond, or another sacred bond. Dispensation from the impediment must be sought before admission.

INCARDINATION: the affiliation of a cleric to his institute, or to a diocese for service in and support from, that institute or diocese. Religious clerics are incardinated in their institute; clerical members of secular institutes are usually incardinated in their diocese.

INCORPORATION: the act by which an individual becomes a member of an institute. This is effected through the profession of the evangelical counsels. Rights and obligations according to universal and proper law follow from incorporation.

LOCAL ORDINARY: a term which besides the Roman Pontiff, diocesan bishops, and those equivalent to them in law, also includes those enjoying ordinary, executive power, i.e., vicars general and episcopal vicars. The term "local Ordinary" does not include major superiors of pontifical clerical religious institutes and societies who are called ordinaries for their members.

MAJOR SUPERIORS: those who govern a whole institute, its provinces or equivalent parts, or who govern autonomous houses such as abbeys or priories, and their vicars. Abbot primates and superiors of monastic congregations are similar to major superiors but do not have all of the same powers.

NOVITIATE: the period of initial formation in religious institutes. The purpose of this time is to allow both the individual and the institute to more deeply examine the candidate's vocation to the institute, to allow an experience of the life of the institute and formation in its spirit and to evaluate the candidate's suitability. The comparable period of time in secular institutes is simply called "initial probation."

PATRIMONY (temporal): all of the goods in funds, properties, securities or any form, which belong to an institute. (Spiritual): the nature, end, spirit, and character of the institute according to the intent of the founder or foundress, and the institute's sound traditions.

PIOUS UNION: the traditional name for an association of the faithful destined to become a religious or secular institute. This is the first step toward approbation and is within the authority of the diocesan bishop.

PONTIFICAL INSTITUTE: an institute erected by the Apostolic See or approved by it through formal decree. Such institutes have usually been diocesan for some years previously. As pontifical, the institute is immediately and exclusively under the jurisdiction of the Apostolic See in matters of internal governance and discipline.

PROBATION: the time of formation and discernment prior to formal incorporation in an institute. Initial probation in religious institutes is called novitiate; in secular institutes, the term initial probation is used. The transfer process calls for a minimum of three years probation in the new institute.

PROFESSION: the formal act by which religious assume observance of the three evangelical counsels by public vows and are thus consecrated to God through the ministry of the Church and incorporated into the institute with the consequent rights and obligations.

PROMISES: a form of sacred bond, sometimes used by secular institutes, for assuming the counsels of poverty and obedience. Promises were allowed to religious on an experimental basis but are no longer provided for in the Code. Promises are addressed to the institute or moderators; a promise made to God is, by definition, a vow.

PROPER LAW: the law of an institute of consecrated life, including as a principle code, the fundamental law or constitutions, and other collections of statutes, norms, or procedures by which the institute is governed.

PROVINCE: the name given an immediate part of a religious institute, composed of several houses under the same superior and canonically erected by legitimate authority.

RELIGIOUS INSTITUTE: an institute of consecrated life in which members, according to proper law, pronounce public vows and lead a community life in common.

RENUNCIATION: a legal act by which a religious gives up personal ownership of monies or goods, in favor of the institute or some other person or group.

SCRIS: the Sacred Congregation for Religious and Secular Institutes, the organ of the Roman Curia dealing with institutes of consecrated life. The 1985 *Annuario Pontificio* has dropped the word "Sacred" from the titles of Roman Congregations, suggesting a new acronym, CRIS.

SECULAR INSTITUTE: an institute of consecrated life in which Christians living in the world, seek the perfection of charity, and work for the sanctification of the world, especially from within.

SECULARIZATION: the name previously used for definitive departure of a member from a religious institute.

SEPARATION: a general term for the various forms of temporarily or permanently being removed from the life of an institute. This may take the form of transfer, exclaustration (religious only), departure, or dismissal.

SOCIETIES OF APOSTOLIC LIFE: societies similar to institutes of consecrated life, whose members, without religious vows, pursue an apostolic end and lead a community life in common. According to their own mode, they seek the perfection of charity through observance of constitutions. In some societies, the evangelical counsels are assumed by a bond prescribed in the constitutions.

SUPPRESSION: a legal act by which the existence of a house, province, or institute is terminated as a juridic entity.

SUPREME MODERATOR: the major superior or moderator who has authority in the whole institute, its provinces, houses, and members according to proper law.

TRANSFER: the canonical process by which a perpetually professed or incorporated member of one institute changes his or her membership to another institute. After a period of probation a new profession is required, except between autonomous monasteries of the same institute, or federation or confederation.

VOW: a free and deliberate promise made to God. In institutes of consecrated life, the content of these vows is the evangelical counsels of chastity, poverty, and obedience, to be lived according to their constitutions. A vow is called public if received in the name of the Church by a legitimate superior; otherwise it is private.

Appendixes

Forms to Record or to Verify Canonical Acts

MARY DAVID OLHEISER, O.S.B.
DANIEL J. WARD, O.S.B.

Exclaustration

Release of Medical Information

Declaration Concerning Remuneration

Renunciation of Goods

Petition for and Approval of Transfer

Will of Testator

INTRODUCTION

A number of canons in the law for religious require forms to record or to verify canonical acts.

The forms illustrated here are models that can be adapted to the needs of religious institutes whether apostolic or monastic. The forms are selective, not taxative.

A religious institute should check with a civil lawyer for forms required by civil law. Such forms differ from state to state.

COMMENTARY

The two forms for authorization to erect a house of a religious institute illustrate the recording of the erection of an independent house by the competent authority of a congregation and the recording of the erection of a dependent priory by an autonomous monastery. The third form is included to illustrate the granting of rights and privileges of governance to a dependent monastic priory.

Agreement Between Diocesan Bishop and Major Superior

On this _____ day of _____in the

year _____, the _____

represented by _____

and the Diocese of _____ represented by

the Diocesan Bishop, _____ enter

into this agreement concerning the apostolic work of _____

_____

The specific terms of the agreement to be carried out is attached hereto.

This agreement was signed and declared by the above named Major Superior and Diocesan Bishop in the presence of each other on the day and year written above.

Signature of Major Superior _____

Signature of Diocesan Bishop_____

Cession of Administration of Personal Property

I, _____, who having made my

profession in the Congregation of _____,

on _____ hereby grant the power of attorney during my
(date)

lifetime in this Congregation of my personal property consisting of

Item	Amount
_____	$ _____
_____	$ _____
_____	$ _____
_____	$ _____
_____	$ _____

or any property subsequently acquired by me to be administered by

( ) the Congregation

　　　　or

( )_____ 　_____
　　　　　(name)　　　　　　　　　　　　(relationship)

_____
　　　　　　　　　　(address)

_____
　　　(city)　　　　　　　　(state)　　　(zip code)

The income derived therefrom shall be

( ) added to the principal

( ) given to the Congregation

( ) given to

_____ 　_____

_____

_____

Signature _____

Witnesses (1)_____

　　　　　(2)_____

Date _____

Petition for Indult of Departure
to Supreme Moderator

To: _____
(supreme moderator)

Congregation of _____

_____
(address)

I, _____ of the

_____ located at
(religious institute)

_____request
(address)

a dispensation from perpetual vows according to the provision of canon

law for the reason(s):

Signature _____
(petitioner)

Dated: _____

Place: _____

DEPARTURE
FORM II

Petition For Indult of Departure to His Holiness

Date _____

His Holiness
The Vatican
Vatican City

Most Holy Father:

I sincerely ask you to grant my petition to be dispensed as soon as

possible from the perpetual vows which I took as a member of the

Congregation of _____ of
(religious institute)

_____ on
(complete address)

_____.
(date)

The reason why I ask for this release from my vows is the fact that
I am not able to persevere in fulfilling them. The reasons why I am unable
to do so are:

(Here the petitioner should briefly but concretely detail the actual
reasons motivating the request. Indicate what means—spiritual,
psychological, or medical have been used in order to resolve existing
problems.)

I have consulted both with my immediate superior and my spiritual
director and they support my petition for dispensation.

With sentiments of reverence and devotion, I remain

Obediently yours in Christ,

_____
(religious name)

_____
(secular name)

DEPARTURE
FORM III

Curriculum Vitae of Petitioner

Curriculum vitae of _____
(petitioner)

Date and place of birth: _____

Date of first vows: _____

Date of final vows: _____

Apostolates: List all apostolates the petitioner has served in—giving place and date:

Apostolate	Place	Date

DEPARTURE
FORM IV

Letter of Approval to His Holiness by Supreme Moderator

Date _____

His Holiness
The Vatican
Vatican City

Most Holy Father:

I present for consideration the petition of_____

_____ for a dispensation

from perpetual vows professed on _____
(date of final vows)

in the _____ of
(religious institute)

_____ whose
(address)

motherhouse is in _____.

(Here are set forth the statements of the Supreme Moderator and that of his/her council.)

In view of the above statements I approve the request and recommend

that this petition for dispensation from perpetual vows be granted.

Asking your Holiness' blessing, I am

Most respectfully yours,

_____
(signature)

_____
(supreme moderator)

_____
(religious institute)

Acceptance of Indult of Departure and Waiver of All Claims

TO WHOM IT MAY CONCERN:

This is to certify that in view of my requesting a dispensation from

perpetual vows, and having received the dispensation from the Congre-

gation for Religious, Rome, Italy, Prot. No._____,

dated _____, releasing me from the membership

in the _____,

I hereby surrender and waive all claims I may in any way have had

against _____
                              (religious institute)
by virtue of my profession in it or my living as a member of this religious

congregation.

I acknowledge receipt of the following monies to assist with my

expenses:

Signature _____
                         (petitioner)
Dated: _____

Witnesses _____

_____

Dated: _____

DEPARTURE
FORM VI

Commission of Instruction for Dispensation from the Priesthood

I, _____, Superior General of the

Congregation _____,

hereby delegate _____ of the same

Congregation, _____

to conduct the process for Dispensation from Religious Vows and Priestly

Obligations in the above-named case.

_____
(superior general)

Congregation of _____

Dated: _____

Place: _____

DISMISSAL
FORM I

Declaration of Automatic Dismissal

TO: _____
              (name of religious)

AND ALL OTHERS CONCERNED:

_____, a professed member of
              (name of religious)

_____, has contracted marriage
              (name of institute)

contrary to his vows and thus has incurred the penalty of automatic

dismissal under C 694, §1, 2°.

The facts are as follows:

Wherefore, by virtue of canon law and the laws of the Congregation, I, the major superior, with the concurrence of my council, decree and declare that the above-named member of the Congregation is automatically dismissed from the Congregation. Vows, rights and obligations of the above-named member hereby cease (C 701), and the Congregation shall not be responsible in any manner for the above-named member nor for any of his or her obligations.

Given at _____

on _____   _____
                              (major religious superior)

                      _____
                              (secretary of the council)

DISMISSAL
FORM II

Statement of the Right of Defense

THE PETITION) MEMORANDUM
FOR DISMISSAL OF)
) STATEMENT OF THE RIGHT
)
_____) OF DEFENSE
)
)

_____

I, _____ of the _____
(religious institute)

of _____ declare that I have
(address)

had the opportunity to state my defense and that I have nothing further

to add in defense of myself to the Acts now presented to the Congrega-

tion for Religious and Secular Institutes in the Petition for Dismissal.

_____
(respondent)

Date: _____

Place: _____

_____
(advocate for the respondent)

NOTARY:_____

DISMISSAL
FORM III

First Canonical Warning

TO: _____
(name of religious)

In accordance with the provisions of canon law and the law of our Congregation, you are hereby given the first canonical warning required by C 697, 2° prior to being dismissed from our Congregation. Having heard the advice of my council, I now declare that you will be dismissed from our Congregation unless you

> [e.g., return to the Motherhouse within fifteen days from the issuance of this warning. You have been unlawfully absent from the Congregation for more than six months, and have refused previous requests and admonitions to return to community life.] (More details may be required.)

If you fail to comply within fifteen days of the issuance of this first canonical warning, you will be given a similar second warning. If you fail to comply with the second warning, I will proceed with the process of dismissal.

You have the right under law to self-defense, including canonical counsel, in this matter at all stages. You have the right to present your defense to me, in person or in writing, against this first canonical warning and proposed dismissal within fifteen days of issuance of this warning. You also have the right to communicate with and offer a defense directly to the Superior General in Rome.

Please be advised of the seriousness of this matter.

Given at_____

on _____   _____
(major religious superior)

DISPENSATION
FORM I

Petition for Dispensation from Temporary Vows

I, _____, a temporarily

professed member of the _____
(religious institute)

of _____ request an
(address)

indult to leave according to the provisions of canon law for the reason(s):

_____

_____

_____

_____

_____

_____

Signature _____
(petitioner)

Date_____

Place _____

DISPENSATION
FORM II

Dispensation from Temporary Vows

In accordance with the provisions of canon law, I, _____

_____, having obtained the consent of the
    (supreme moderator)

Council, grant an indult to leave to _____

_____ .
                (petitioner)

In accordance with the provisions of canon law the petitioner is

dispensed from vows and is free from all obligations arising through his or

her profession in the _____
                (religious institute)

Signed _____
           (supreme moderator)

_____
           (congregation)

Dated: _____

Place: _____

Accepted and signed by petitioner

_____

Dated: _____

Place: _____

ERECTION OF A HOUSE
FORM I

Authorization to Erect a House of a Religious Institute

The _____ of
(authorizing body)

_____   _____
(religious institute)   (address)

grants this charter in accord with the Constitutions of _____

_____ to and for the

_____ to be situated at
(new house)

_____ in the diocese of
(address)

_____.
(diocese)

The _____ authorized by the vote of
(name of new house)

the _____ on _____
(authorizing body)   (date)

is hereby founded with the approval of the Diocesan Bishop, _____

_____ of _____
(name)   (diocese)

on _____.
(date)

Signature _____
(for authorizing body)

_____
(title)

Signature _____
(for diocesan bishop)

_____
(title)

ERECTION OF A HOUSE
FORM II

Authorization to Erect a Dependent Priory of a Monastic Institute

The monastic chapter of _____
(monastery)

of _____ grants this charter of erection in
(address)

accord with the Constitution of _____
(federation)

to and for the _____ to be
(dependent house)

situated at _____ in the diocese of

_____.

The dependent priory authorized by vote of the monastic chapter on

_____ is hereby founded with the approval of the
(date)

Diocesan Bishop, _____ of

_____ on _____.
(diocese)   (date)

Signature _____
(for monastery)

_____
(title)

Signature _____
(diocesan bishop)

_____
(title)

ERECTION OF A HOUSE
FORM III

Governance of a Dependent Monastic Priory

_____ is hereby granted all the rights
      (dependent house)

and privileges and assumes the obligations of a dependent priory in

accord with the Constitution of the _____.
                                         (federation)

A. Motives for Founding the Dependent Priory.
(Motives for founding the dependent priory should be set forth
in this place.)

B. Purpose of the Dependent Priory.
The purpose of this priory is to establish monastic life according

to the _____ at
                      (Rule)

_____, _____
    (dependent priory)   (address)

C. The Works of the Dependent Priory.

_____ shall have as its works:
    (dependent priory)

(A listing of the works may be given here.)

D. Administration of Dependent Priory.
1. The Major Superior of the founding house is the major
superior of the dependent priory and has full jurisdictional
power over the dependent priory.
2. The superior of the dependent priory shall be elected by the
members of the dependent priory for _____ years, but
confirmed by the abbot/abbess of the founding house.
3. By virtue of appointment, the superior of the dependent
priory shall have all delegated authority necessary to serve

the priory, except: _____

_____.
(list any reservations of jurisdiction)

Given at _____

on _____.

_____
(abbot/abbess of founding house)

EXCLAUSTRATION
FORM I

Petition for Exclaustration

TO:_____
(supreme moderator)

Congregation of _____

_____

I, _____ a perpetually professed member

of the Congregation of _____

request an Indult of Exclaustration for a period of _____

_____ according to the provisions of canon law and of the

Constitutions of the Congregation _____

for the reason(s):

[e.g., to discern whether I wish to continue as a member of the Con-

gregation.]

Signature _____
(petitioner)

Dated _____

Place _____

EXCLAUSTRATION
FORM II

Indult of Exclaustration

Indult of Exclaustration for _____
                              Address:

In accordance with the Code of Canon Law and the request of the above-named religious, an indult of exclaustration is granted for a period of _____ year(s) from the date of acceptance of the Indult for the reason(s): _____

_____ (C 686, §1)
During the period of exclaustration, the religious is considered as dispensed from those obligations incompatible with his/her new condition of life except that the religious shall remain bound to celibacy and shall be subject to his/her major religious superior. The religious shall keep the major religious superior informed of his/her residence and telephone number. He/she may (not) wear the religious habit. The right to active and passive voice in the institute is suspended.

During the period of exclaustration, the religious shall be responsible for all his/her financial obligations and the religious institute shall not be responsible for any of his/her financial obligations whatsoever.

(C 639)

At the expiration of this indult, the religious shall be obligated to return to

_____, unless
further dispositions shall have been made.

Granted _____   _____
                                       (supreme moderator)

_____

on _____

Consent of the Council
given at _____   _____

(secretary of the council)

_____

on _____

I, the undersigned religious, hereby accept the Indult of Exclaustration
and its terms.

_____   _____
(date)   (religious)

Release of Medical Information

I, _____, do hereby

authorize any hospital or doctor, from whom I have received medical

services of attention, to release to _____

_____, any and all information from

records or personnel which may be in their possession. Such release of

medical information shall apply to all organizations and persons who

may have medical knowledge concerning my physical and mental health.

I further authorize such persons having knowledge about my case to

discuss all aspects of my physical and mental health with any represen-

tative of _____.

Dated this _____ day of _____, 19_____.

_____

Sworn and Subscribed
before me the

_____ day of _____, 19_____.

_____
(notary public)

Declaration Concerning Remuneration

I, _____ otherwise known in religion

as _____ of _____
                                        (religious institute)

_____ in the county of _____

and the state of _____.

IN CONSIDERATION of the law of the Roman Catholic Church concerning the remuneration of candidates, postulants, novices, and members of a religious community acknowledged by the Roman Catholic Church which law I fully know and deliberately acknowledge and to which I voluntarily and fully submit myself, and

FOR AND IN CONSIDERATION of the benefits accruing to me as candidate, postulant, novice, or member of the approved religious

community, incorporated as _____ existing
                                    (name of corporation)

under and by virtue of the laws of the state of _____.

DO SOLEMNLY STATE AND DECLARE, that I shall never claim or demand, directly or indirectly, any wages, compensation, remuneration, or reward, either in specie or by way of annuity or pension, for the time or for the services or work that I devote for or with

_____ during the time I may remain there or elsewhere in the name of or upon commission from

_____ .

IN WITNESS WHEREOF I have subscribed my name this

_____ day of _____

_____ .

Signature _____

Witnesses (1) _____

(2) _____

Renunciation of Goods

In consideration of the laws of the Roman Catholic Church concerning the renunciation of goods and the Constitution of the _____

_____ I, _____

renounce (all, part) of my goods amounting to $_____

and all goods which I may acquire in the future.

Signature _____

Witnesses (1) _____

(2) _____

I, _____, the major superior with

the consent of Council approve the request of _____

_____ to renounce (all, part) of his/her

goods amounting to $_____ and all goods which

he/she may acquire in the future.

Signature _____
(supreme moderator)

Signature _____
(secretary to council)

Date _____

Petition for and Approval of Transfer

To: Supreme Moderator
  (of petitioner's own institute)

and

To: Supreme Moderator
  (of institute to which petitioner requests to transfer)

I, _____, a perpetually
professed member of the _____
of _____
request permission to transfer from the said Congregation to the __
_____ of
_____ .

The transfer will be effective upon completion of the requirements of canon law and proper law.

My reasons for requesting a transfer are:

I understand that throughout the period during which the proposed transfer will be discerned I am subject to the Constitution of _____
_____ .

Signature of Petitioner _____

Dated _____

This request is approved and formalized as of the date below and by the signatures of the supreme moderators of the releasing and receiving religious institutes having the previous consent of their Councils.

Signature _____
      (supreme moderator of
        releasing institute)

Dated _____

Signature _____
      (supreme moderator of
        receiving institute)

Dated _____

Will of Testator

I, _____, also known as _____,

of _____, revoke any prior wills

and codicils, and make this my will.

ARTICLE ONE
PAYMENT OF EXPENSES AND TAXES

1. My personal representative shall pay from the residue of my estate the expenses of my last illness and funeral, valid debts including any taxes owed by me at my death, expenses of administering my estate, including non-probate assets, and any estate and other death taxes, except any generation-skipping transfer tax, which become due because of my death, including any interest and penalties. There shall be no apportionment of any such taxes, and I waive on behalf of my estate any right to recover any part of them from any person, including any recipient of property passing apart from this will.

ARTICLE TWO
SPECIFIC GIFTS

2. I give the following:

2.1 I give my tangible personal property as follows:
(Here list specific gifts)

2.2 I give all interest (real or personal) in real property as follows:
(Here list real property)

ARTICLE THREE
RESIDUE

3. I give the residue of my estate consisting of all property which I can dispose of by will and not effectively dispose of by the preceding articles of this will, except any property over which I may then have a testamentary power of appointment to

_____ .

ARTICLE FOUR
PERSONAL REPRESENTATIVE

4. I nominate the person holding the office of _____

_____, at the time of my death, as personal representative.

4.1 The Superior at the time of my death shall have the power to nominate any additional or successor personal representative.

4.2 No bond shall be required of any personal representative nominated by the Superior or me.

4.3 My personal representative, in addition to all other powers conferred upon him/her by law that are not inconsistent with those contained herein, shall have the power, exercisable without authorization of any court:

4.3.1 To sell at private or public sale, to retain, to lease, and to mortgage or pledge for the purpose of borrowing money, any or all of the real or personal property of my estate;

4.3.2 To make partial distributions from my estate from time to time and to distribute the residue of my estate in cash or in kind or partly in each, and for this purpose to determine the value of property distributed in kind.

4.3.3 To exercise or not exercise any selection or option granted my personal representative by the Internal Revenue Code or the tax statutes of any state, without making any adjustment to estate principal or income that may be affected by such exercise or non-exercise.

ARTICLE FIVE
GENERAL GOVERNING PROVISIONS

5. The following provisions shall apply to the interpretation of my will and the administration of my estate.

5.1 The rules of law and statutes of the State of _____, insofar as legally possible, except as altered by this will, shall govern in all respects the meaning and legal effect of this will and the administration of my estate. Except as I have otherwise provided, all references to applicable law and _____

_____ Statutes mean those in force and effect on the date of my death and shall include any amendments and successor provisions thereto.

5.3 Where appropriate, the feminine includes the masculine, the singular includes the plural, and vice versa.

5.4 I direct unsupervised administration of my estate and that my estate be administered in as informal a manner as my personal representative deems advisable and applicable law permits.

I have signed this will consisting of _____( ) pages, this

page included, on _____, 19_____.

_____
Testator

We certify that in our presence on the date appearing above in the State

of _____, _____ signed the foregoing instrument and acknowledged it to be her/his will, that at her/his request and in her/his presence and in the presence of each other, we have signed our names below as witnesses, and that we believe her/him to be of sound mind and memory.

_____ residing at _____

_____ residing at _____

Self-Proved Affidavit

THE STATE OF _____)

COUNTY OF _____)) ss.

We, _____ and _____
(testator)   (witnesses, respectively)

_____ whose names are signed to the

attached or foregoing instrument, consisting of _____ typewritten pages, being first duly sworn, do hereby declare to the undersigned authority that the Testator signed and executed the instrument as his/her last will and testament that he/she signed willingly, and that he/she executed it as his/her free and voluntary act for the purposes therein expressed; and that each of the witnesses, in the presence and hear of the Testator, signed the will as witnesses, and that to the best of their knowledge the Testator was at the time 18 or more years of age, of sound mind and under no constraint or undue influence.

_____
(testator)

_____
(witness)

_____
(witness)

Subscribed, sworn to and acknowledged before me by _____

_____, the Testator, and subscribed and sworn to

before me by _____ and _____

Witnesses, this _____ day of _____, 19_____.

_____
(notary public)

Canons That Refer to the Constitutions and Proper Law of Institutes of Consecrated Life and Societies of Apostolic Life

JORDAN HITE, T.O.R.

One of the principles used in preparing the 1983 Code of Canon Law for institutes of consecrated life and societies of apostolic life was that the common law should contain only the general principles leaving to the institute or society suitable freedom to apply the principles in accord with their own particular purpose and spirit. This was done to avoid a "leveling off" by the use of excessively specific norms in the common law while at the same time indicating in the common law the areas in which the institute or society should develop its own norms.

This resulted in a series of over one hundred canons that refer to the constitutions and proper law of institutes and societies. It is helpful to have a list of them so that constitutions and proper law can be prepared in accord with the canons. It should be noted that the matters covered in the canons do not exhaust the material for constitutions, since SCRIS may expect additional material. [1]

In regard to proper law, the intent of many of the canons is to alert the institute or society that if the matter is important or relevant it should be in the proper law. In fact, the majority of the references are relevant to most communities although some may not be an important concern for a particular institute or society. The canons referring to proper law do not state the level of proper law in which a particular item should appear: a directory (Book II), policies, procedures, etc. The book in which an item appears is a guide to the level of authority required to change it, thus, constitutions need the approval of SCRIS or the diocesan bishop (if a diocesan institute), a directory usually needs the approval of a chapter and policies and procedures the approval of the council. Whatever the term used for the proper law of an institute or society, the authority to change it should be a part of its law.

In addition, there are some canons or areas of life of an institute that invite the development of proper law even though not referred to specifically in the canons. Thus, although the list will be a guide to the canons it is not exhaustive in the sense that the life and needs of the institute will be the foundation for its proper law. The list is divided into sections, one containing the canons that use the term constitutions, the other using the term proper law. In some cases in which the use of the term proper law appears to include constitutions it is listed under constitutions. The following are paraphrases of the canons and the full text should be consulted for accuracy.

1. See *Report of the Council* of the "16," April 29, 1983 providing a similar list of canons referring to the constitutions and proper law. The list in the *Report* includes canons that do not have a reference to matter to be placed in the constitutions (CC 580, 585; 588, §3; 598, §2). It is noted at page 5 of the *Report* that SCRIS can ask that certain norms appear in the constitutions rather than in secondary codes. See also the list in Guttiérrez, A., "The New Code of Canon Law and the Internal Law of Institutes of Consecrated Life" *ConLife* 9 (1984) 81–97 at 90–95.

Canons Using the Term Constitutions or Referring to the Constitutions

Book II, Part III, Section I

Title I: Common Norms

1. C 573, §2 The faithful profess the evangelical counsels according to the *proper laws* of the institute.
2. C 578 The nature, spirit and character of the institute according to the founder, are to be ratified by the competent Church authority (describing the *constitutions*).
3. C 581 Dividing, erecting or forming parts is according to the *constitutions*.
4. C 587, §1 Besides the things stated in C 578 the *constitutions* contain norms regarding governance, discipline, incorporation and formation of members, and the object of sacred bonds.
5. C 587, §2 The *fundamental code (constitutions)* is approved by competent authority and can be changed only with its consent.
6. C 587, §3 Spiritual and juridical matters are to be suitably joined together in the *fundamental code (constitutions)*, but norms should not be multiplied.
7. C 595, §1 The bishop of the principal seat of a diocesan institute approves the *constitutions* and changes therein.
8. C 595, §2 The diocesan bishop can grant dispensation from the *constitutions* in certain cases.
9. C 596, §1 Superiors and chapters enjoy authority over members which is defined in the *constitutions*.
10. C 598, §1 The *constitutions* should define the manner of living the evangelical counsels.
11. C 601 Obedience obliges one to superiors who rule according to the particular *constitutions* (cf. poverty, C 600 where proper law is used).

Title II: Religious Institutes

Chapter I: Religious Houses: Their Erection and Suppression

12. C 609 Houses are erected by the competent authority according to the *constitutions*.
13. C 613, §1 Houses of regulars and monks are autonomous unless the *constitutions* state otherwise.

14. C 614   Monasteries of nuns attached to an institute of men main-
              tain their order of life and governance according to their
              constitutions.

15. C 615   The superior of an autonomous monastery enjoys true
              power as determined by the *constitutions*.

16. C 616, §1 A religious house can be suppressed by the supreme
              moderator in accord with the *constitutions* (after con-
              sultation with the bishop), but proper law provides for
              disposition of goods.

17. C 616, §3 Suppression of autonomous houses belongs to the general
              chapter unless the *constitutions* state otherwise.

18. C 616, §4 When an autonomous monastery of nuns is suppressed
              by the Holy See, the *constitutions* are to be followed
              regarding its goods.

Chapter II: Governance of Institutes

Article 1: Superiors and Councils

19. C 623   For the valid nomination of a major superior a suitable
              time after perpetual profession is required and this time
              is to be determined by the *constitutions*. (For other
              superiors by proper law).

20. C 624, §1 Superiors are to hold office for a certain period of time
              unless the *constitutions* state otherwise for the supreme
              moderator or a superior of an autonomous house.

21. C 625, §1 The supreme moderator of an institute is to be designated
              by canonical election according to the *constitutions*.

22. C 625, §3 Other superiors are to be constituted according to the
              constitutions.

23. C 627, §1 According to the norms of the *constitutions* superiors
              should have their own council.

Article 2: Chapters

24. C 631, §1 The general chapter has supreme authority according to
              the *constitutions*.

25. C 631, §2 The composition and power of a chapter should be de-
              fined in the *constitutions* (proper law should further
              define the order and procedures).

Article 3: Temporal Goods and Their Administration

26. C 634, §1 Unless the *constitutions* exclude or abridge the capacity,
              institutes and their parts which are juridic persons can
              acquire, alienate, etc. temporal goods.

Chapter III: Admission of Candidates and Training of Members

Article 2: Novitiate and the Training of Members

27. C 648, §2 The *constitutions* can establish periods of apostolic exercises to be done outside the novitiate community (beyond the twelve-(12) month novitiate).

*Chapter IV: The Obligations and Rights of Institutes
and Their Members*

28. C 662   The *constitutions* should express the way the institute follows Christ.

29. C 667, §3 Nuns who do not observe the cloister according to the norms given by the Apostolic See should observe cloister according to their *constitutions*.

30. C 668, §1 Cession of goods should be made before first profession unless the *constitutions* state otherwise.

31. C 670   An institute must furnish everything members need according to the *constitutions* to achieve the goal of their vocation.

Title III: Secular Institutes

32. C 712   *Constitutions* are to determine the sacred bonds by which the evangelical counsels are taken in the institute and define the obligations flowing from the bonds.

33. C 714   Members are to lead their life according to the norm of the *constitutions*.

34. C 717, §1 The *constitutions* prescribe the manner of governance, the time during which moderators hold office and the way in which they are chosen.

35. C 720   Admission for probation or to sacred bonds pertains to the major moderator and council according to the *constitutions*.

36. C 721, §2 The *constitutions* can establish other impediments to admission, even for validity.

37. C 722, §3 The manner and time of probation is to be defined in the *constitutions*, but no less than two (2) years.

38. C 723, §2 The first incorporation, no shorter than five (5) years, is to be temporary according to the norm of the *constitutions*.

39. C 723, §4 The effects of definitive or perpetual incorporation are to be in the *constitutions*.

40. C 724, §1 Formation after first sacred bonds is to be continued according to the *constitutions*.

41. C 725   Other Christian faithful can associate themselves to the institute by some bond determined in the *constitutions*.

42. C 727, §1   A perpetually incorporated member of a non-pontifical institute may seek an indult to leave from the diocesan bishop according to the *constitutions*.

43. C 729   The *constitutions* may determine additional causes of dismissal.

Section II: Societies of Apostolic Life

44. C 731, §1   Members live the life of the society through the observance of the *constitutions*.

45. C 731, §2   Members embrace the evangelical counsels by some bond defined in the *constitutions*.

46. C 734   Governance of the society is determined by the *constitutions*.

47. C 736, §1   Clerics are incardinated in a clerical society unless the *constitutions* state otherwise.

48. C 737   Obligations and rights of members are defined in the *constitutions*.

49. C 738, §1   Members are subject to the particular moderator according to the *constitutions* regarding internal life and discipline.

50. C 738, §3   Relations of a member incardinated in a diocese with his proper bishop are defined by the *constitutions* or particular agreements.

51. C 739   Members are bound by the *constitutions* and the common obligations of clerics unless something else is evident from the nature of the matter or its context.

52. C 741, §1   Societies are juridic persons as are their parts and houses unless the *constitutions* state otherwise.

53. C 742   The departure and dismissal of a member not definitively incorporated is governed by the *constitutions*.

54. C 743   An indult of departure can be obtained from the supreme moderator with the consent of the council unless reserved to the Holy See by the *constitutions*.

Canons Outside the Section on Institutes of Consecrated Life and Societies of Apostolic Life

55. C 832   Members of religious institutes need the permission of their major superior in accord with the norm of the *constitutions* to publish writings on questions of religion or morals.

56. C 833, 8° Superiors of clerical religious institutes and societies of apostolic life in accord with the norm of the *constitutions* are to make a profession of faith in accord with a formula approved by the Apostolic See.

57. C 968, §2 Superiors of a clerical religious institute or society of apostolic life of pontifical right who in accord with the norms of their *constitutions* possess executive power of governance enjoy the faculty to hear the confessions of their subjects and others staying in religious houses.

58. C 1019, §1 The major superior of a clerical religious institute or clerical society of apostolic life of pontifical right is competent to grant dismissorial letters for the diaconate or presbyterate for subjects who have become perpetually or definitively members of the institute or society in accord with their *constitutions*.

59. C 1174, §1 Members of institutes of consecrated life and societies of apostolic life are bound to perform the Liturgy of the Hours according to the norm of their *constitutions*.

Canons Using the Term Proper Law

Title I: Common Norms

1. C 597, §1 Any Catholic can be admitted to an institute in accord with universal and *proper law*.

2. C 598, §2 All members must live according to the *proper law*.

3. C 600 Poverty brings with it dependence in the use or limitation of goods according to *proper law*. (Obedience refers to the constitutions, C 601).

Title II: Religious Institutes

4. C 607, §2 Members pronounce public vows according to *proper law*.

Chapter I: Religious Houses and Their Erection and Suppression

5. C 616, §1 Suppression according to the canons. *Proper law* provides for disposition of goods.

Chapter II: Governance of Institutes

Article 1: Superiors and Councils

6. C 617 Superiors should exercise their power according to the norms of *proper law*.

7. C 622   The supreme moderator holds power over provinces, houses and members to be exercised according to *proper law*.

8. C 623   To be appointed or elected a non-major superior, a suitable time after perpetual profession is required, which is to be determined by *proper law*.

9. C 624, §2   *Proper law* should provide a time limit for a superior to hold office without an intermission in office.

10. C 624, §3   Superiors can be removed or transferred for reasons determined by *proper law*.

11. C 626   Superiors in the conferral of offices and members in elections should observe the norms of universal and *proper law*.

12. C 627, §2   *Proper law* should determine cases in which the superior should obtain the consent of the council (beyond those stated in universal law).

13. C 628, §1   *Proper law* should designate the visitator and the norms for visitation.

14. C 629   Superiors should reside in their own house. They may be absent according to the norms of *proper law*.

15. C 630, §2   According to the norms of *proper law*, superiors should be solicitous that confessors are available.

Article 2: Chapters

16. C 631, §2   *Proper law* determines order and procedures for elections and other matters in chapters.

17. C 631, §3   In accord with *proper law*, anyone can send suggestions to the general chapter.

18. C 632   *Proper law* should determine all which pertains to other chapters and gatherings.

19. C 633, §1   Organs of participation or consultation should carry out duties entrusted to them by *proper law*.

Article 3: Temporal Goods and Their Administration

20. C 636, §1   The finance officer is to be constituted according to *proper law*.

21. C 636, §2   The finance officer and others should render an account of their work to the competent superior in accord with *proper law*.

22. C 638, §1   *Proper law* should define acts which exceed ordinary administration and the procedure necessary to validly perform such an act.

23. C 638, §2 *Proper law* should designate those officials besides superiors who can perform juridic acts of ordinary administration.

Chapter III: Admission of Candidates and Training of Members

Article 1: Admission to the Novitiate

24. C 641   Major superiors may admit candidates to novitiate according to *proper law*.
25. C 643, §2 Impediments to admission can be established by *proper law* (even for validity).
26. C 645, §3 *Proper law* can require additional testimony about suitability and freedom from impediments.

Article 2: Novitiate and the Training of Members

27. C 650, 1   The program of training is to be according to *proper law*.
28. C 653, §2 Novitiate can be extended according to *proper law* but not more than six (6) months.

Article 3: Religious Profession

29. C 655   The length of time for temporary profession may be defined in *proper law*, but no less than three (3) nor more than six (6) years.
30. C 657, §2 The time of temporary profession can be extended in accord with *proper law*, but for not more than nine (9) years.
31. C 658   *Proper law* can require additional conditions for perpetual profession.

Article 4: The Formation of Religious

32. C 659, §2 The *proper law* should define the program of formation.

Chapter IV: Obligations and Rights of Institutes and Their Members

33. C 663, §3 The liturgy of the hours should be celebrated in accord with *proper law*.
34. C 667, §1 Cloister should be observed according to *proper law*.
35. C 668, §2 *Proper law* should designate the competent superior to give permission regarding a change in disposition of temporal goods.
36. C 668, §3 Unless otherwise stated in *proper law*, pensions, etc. are acquired for the institute.
37. C 668, §4 *Proper law* can provide norms for the renunciation of goods.

38. C 668, §5 After renunciation, goods accruing to a member belong to the institute according to *proper law*.

39. C 669, §1 Religious should wear the habit of the institute made according to *proper law*.

Chapter VI: Separation of Members from the Institute

Article 1: Transfer to Another Institute

40. C 648, §3 In transferring from one autonomous monastery to another of the same institute, it is sufficient to have the consent of the major superior of both monasteries and the chapter of the receiving monastery without prejudice to other requisites stated in *proper law*.

41. C 684, §4 *Proper law* should set the time and mode of probation for the professed member in a new institute.

42. C 685, §2 The transferring religious is obligated to obey the proper law of the new institute from the beginning of the probation period.

Article 3: Dismissal of Members

43. C 696, §1 Additional causes for dismissal can be stated in *proper law*.

44. C 696, §2 Lesser causes stated in *proper law* suffice for dismissal of a member in temporary vows.

Title III: Secular Institutes

45. C 716, §1 All members share actively in the life of the institute according to *proper law*.

46. C 718 The administration of goods is ruled by Book V and the *proper law*. *Proper law* is to define the financial obligations of the institute toward members who carry on work for it.

47. C 719, §1 Prayer, retreat and other spiritual exercises are to be carried out according to *proper law*.

Section II: Societies of Apostolic Life

48. C 735, §1 Admission, probation, incorporation and training are determined by *proper law*.

49. C 735, §3 *Proper law* must determine doctrinal, spiritual, and apostolic method of probation and training.

50. C 740 Members live in a house or community and observe common life according to *proper law* which also governs absences.

51. C 741, §1 A society and its parts which are juridic persons can acquire, possess, administer and alienate goods according to Book V, CC 636, 638, 639, and the norm of *proper law*.
52. C 741, §2 According to the norm of *proper law*, a member can acquire, possess, administer and dispose of goods.

Other Terminology Referring to Proper Law

1. C 587, §4 Other norms established by the competent authority are to be suitably collected in other codes
2. C 608 A religious community must live in a house constituted under the authority of the superior designated according to the *norm of law*.
3. C 635, §2 Each institute should state *appropriate norms* for the use and administration of goods.

APPENDIX 3

Authority in Institutes of Consecrated Life and Societies of Apostolic Life

Jordan Hite, T.O.R.

The lines of authority applying to institutes of consecrated life and societies of apostolic life can be divided into those outside the institute or society and those within the institute or society. Outside the institute or society authority is exercised by the Supreme Pontiff, the Apostolic See, and the diocesan bishop. Within the institute authority is exercised by the chapter, the supreme moderator, the major superior, and lower level superiors. Superiors may act alone or with the consent or consultation of a council.

In twenty-nine (29) cases the institute or society is to seek approval, consultation, or act in accord with the direction of the Supreme Pontiff or Apostolic See. In forty-five (45) cases the institute or society needs the approval of or is in some way subject to the diocesan bishop. In the seventeen (17) cases which require the approval of the bishop, twelve (12) apply to institutes of diocesan right or autonomous monasteries of C 615. In other cases the canons refer to the competent Church authority, which may mean either the Apostolic See or the diocesan bishop.

Within the institute or society there are only three (3) canons that refer directly to the authority of a chapter; however, since the grant of power is broad the small number of canons is not indicative of the authority of a chapter. Superiors acting alone or according to a norm of law to be established by the institute or society have authority in twenty-four (24) cases, while in seventeen (17) cases superiors need the consent of council or act with the council (the sole case of a superior acting collegially with the council is in issuing a decree of dismissal). In canons which specify action in accord with the norm of law, the proper law of the institute or society may require the consultation or consent of council before the superior acts. In nine (9) additional cases the superior is to seek the advice, opinion, or vote of the council. A few canons refer the matter to the competent authority of the institute or society, which means the proper law should designate the appropriate authority to fulfill the responsibility.

I. RELATIONSHIP TO AUTHORITY OUTSIDE THE INSTITUTE

Cases for the Approval of the Apostolic See or the Supreme Pontiff

Book II, Part III, Section I

Title I: Common Norms:

1. C 582   Mergers, unions, federations, and confederations are reserved to the Apostolic See.
2. C 583   Changes in institutes which affect matters approved by the Apostolic See cannot be made without permission of the Apostolic See.
3. C 584, §1 Suppression of an institute belongs to the Apostolic See (including disposition of goods).
4. C 589   An institute is of pontifical right when erected or approved by the Apostolic See.
5. C 590   The Supreme Pontiff can exempt institutes.
6. C 605   Approving new forms of consecrated life is reserved to the Apostolic See.

Title II: Religious Institutes

Chapter I: Religious Houses and Their Erection and Suppression

7. C 609, §2 The permission of the Apostolic See is necessary to erect a monastery of nuns.
8. C 616, §2 Suppression of the only house of an institute belongs to the Holy See including the disposition of goods.
9. C 616, §4 Suppression of an autonomous monastery of nuns belongs to the Apostolic See.

Chapter II: The Governance of Institutes

Article 3: Temporal Goods and Their Administration

10. C 638, §3 The permission of the Holy See is required for acts of alienation and transactions in which the patrimonial con-

dition is adversely affected if it goes beyond the amount allowed in the region, items given to the Church in virtue of a vow, or items of precious art or historical value.

Chapter VI: Separation of Members from the Institute

Article 1: Transfer to Another Institute

11. C 684, §5 The permission of the Holy See is required to transfer from a religious institute to a secular institute or society of apostolic life or from them to a religious institute.

Article 2: Departure from the Institute

12. C 686, §1 Extending an indult of exclaustration beyond three (3) years for an institute of pontifical right is reserved to the Holy See.
13. C 686, §2 The Apostolic See grants an indult of exclaustration to nuns.
14. C 686, §3 The Holy See can impose exclaustration for a member of an institute of pontifical right.
15. C 691, §2 An indult to depart for a perpetually professed member of an institute of pontifical right is reserved to the Apostolic See.

Article 3: Dismissal of Members

16. C 700 A decree of dismissal in an institute of pontifical right does not take effect unless confirmed by the Apostolic See.
17. C 703 The process of dismissal can be referred to the Apostolic See in cases of exterior scandal or grave imminent harm to the institute.

Chapter VIII: Conferences of Major Superiors

18. C 709 The Holy See erects conferences of major superiors and approves their statutes.

Title III: Secular Institutes

19. C 727 An indult to leave is obtained from the Apostolic See for a member of an institute of pontifical right.
20. C 730 Transfer to or from another institute of consecrated life requires the permission of the Apostolic See.

Section II: Societies of Apostolic Life

21. C 743 An indult of departure can be obtained from the supreme moderator with the consent of the council unless it is re-

served to the Holy See by the constitutions.

22. C 745   Transfer to or from an institute of consecrated life requires the permission of the Holy See.

Cases Calling for the Consultation of the Apostolic See

Title I: Common Norms

1. C 579   A diocesan bishop can erect an institute of consecrated life providing the Apostolic See has been consulted.

Title II: Religious Institutes

Chapter V: Apostolate of Religious

2. C 679   A bishop can prohibit a member of an institute from living in his diocese if the major superior has been advised and neglects to act. The matter should be referred to the Holy See.

Relationship of Institutes to Apostolic See

Title I: Common Norms

1. C 590, §1 Institutes are subject to the supreme authority of the Church in a special manner.
2. C 592, §1 The supreme moderator should send a report on the life of the institute to the Apostolic See.
3. C 593   Institutes of pontifical right are subject to the Apostolic See in internal governance and discipline, but with due regard for C 586.

Title II: Religious Institutes

Chapter IV: Obligations and Rights of Institutes and Their Members

4. C 667, §3 Monasteries of nuns totally ordered to the contemplative life must observe cloister according to the norms given by the Apostolic See.

Chapter VI: Separation of Members from the Institute

Article 3: Dismissal of Members

5. C 704   The report sent to the Apostolic See mentioned in C 592, §1 is to mention members separated from the institute in any way whatsoever.

Cases Calling for Approval of Bishop

Title I: Common Law

1. C 579   Diocesan bishops can erect institutes in their own territory (must consult Apostolic See).
2. C 589   An institute is of diocesan right when erected by a diocesan bishop.
3. C 595, §1   The bishop of the principal seat of the institute approves constitutions and confirms changes in them, handles business matters beyond the power of the internal authority of the institute (unless it belongs to the Apostolic See), and consults other bishops if the institute has spread to several dioceses.
4. C 603, §2   A hermit is under the direction of the diocesan bishop.
5. C 604, §1   Virgins are consecrated to God by the diocesan bishop.

Title II: Religious Institutes

Chapter I: Religious Houses and Their Erection and Suppression

6. C 609, §1   Houses of an institute are erected by an institute with previous written consent of the diocesan bishop.
7. C 612   The consent of the diocesan bishop is necessary if a house is established for apostolic works different from those for which it was constituted.

Chapter II: The Governance of Institutes

Article 3: Temporal Goods and Their Administration

8. C 638, §4   For the transactions covered by C 638 autonomous monasteries of C 615 and institutes of diocesan right must have the written permission of the local Ordinary.

Chapter VI: Separation of Members from the Institute

Article 2: Departure from the Institute

9. C 686, §1   Exclaustrated religious priests need the consent of the local Ordinary to remain in his territory. Extending the indult of exclaustration beyond three (3) years belongs to the diocesan bishop for institutes of diocesan right.
10. C 688, §2   In institutes of diocesan right and monasteries mentioned in C 615, departure during temporary vows can be granted by the supreme moderator with consent of coun-

cil, but validity depends on confirmation by the bishop of the house of assignment.

11. C 691, §2 A member of a diocesan institute in perpetual vows may depart by receiving an indult from the diocesan bishop of the house of assignment.

Article 3: Dismissal of Members

12. C 699, §2 For autonomous monasteries of C 615, the decision on dismissal pertains to the diocesan bishop.

13. C 700 A decree of dismissal takes effect for a member of an institute of diocesan right when confirmed by the bishop of the diòcese where the house to which the religious is assigned is situated.

14. C 701 A dismissed religious cleric cannot exercise sacred orders unless a bishop permits him to do so.

Section II: Societies of Apostolic Life

15. C 727, §1 A perpetually incorporated member who does not belong to an institute of pontifical right obtains an indult of departure from the diocesan bishop.

16. C 733, §1 A house is erected by the competent authority of the society with the prior written consent of the diocesan bishop who must be consulted for its suppression.

17. C 745 A clerical member of a society who receives an indult to live outside the society is to have the permission of the local Ordinary to reside in his territory.

Responsibilities and Powers of the Bishop

Title I: Common Norms

1. C 586, §2 Ordinaries are to safeguard autonomy of institutes.
2. C 594 An institute of diocesan right is under the special care of the diocesan bishop.
3. C 595, §2 A diocesan bishop can grant dispensation from the constitutions in particular cases.
4. C 605 Diocesan bishops should strive to discern new gifts of consecrated life and aid the promoters.

Title II: Religious Institutes

Chapter 1: Religious Houses and Their Erection and Suppression

5. C 615 An autonomous monastery with no major superior beyond its own moderator and not associated with any

other institute is committed to the special vigilance of the diocesan bishop.

Chapter II: The Governance of Institutes

Article 1: Superiors and Councils

6. C 625, §2 The bishop of the principal seat presides at the election of a superior of an autonomous monastery mentioned in C 615 and of the supreme moderator of an institute of diocesan right.

7. C 628, §2 The diocesan bishop is to visit even with respect to religious discipline autonomous monasteries mentioned in C 615 and houses of institutes of diocesan right in his territory.

8. C 630, §3 In monasteries of nuns, houses of formation, and numerous lay communities, there are to be ordinary confessors approved by the local Ordinary after consultation with the community.

Article 3: Temporal Goods and Their Administration

9. C 637 Autonomous monasteries (C 615) must render an annual account to the local Ordinary and the financial report of religious houses of diocesan right is to be made known to the local Ordinary.

Chapter III: Admission of Candidates and Formation of Members

Article 1: Admission to the Novitiate

10. C 644 The local Ordinary is to be consulted before a secular cleric is admitted to the novitiate.

11. C 645, §2 To admit a cleric to the novitiate the testimony of the local Ordinary is to be obtained.

Chapter IV: The Obligations and Rights of Institutes and Their Members

12. C 667, §4 The diocesan bishop for just cause can enter the cloister of nuns in his diocese and permit others to enter and nuns to leave for a necessary period of time.

Chapter V: The Apostolate of Religious

13. C 678, §1 Religious are subject to the authority of bishops in regard to care of souls, public exercise of divine worship, and other works of the apostolate.

14. C 678, §2 In exercising the external apostolate religious are under their own superiors. However, a bishop may enforce fidelity to the discipline of the institute if the case arises.

15. C 678, §3 Diocesan bishops and religious superiors should consult with each other regarding works of the apostolate.

16. C 679 A diocesan bishop for serious reason can prohibit a religious from living in his diocese.

17. C 680 The bishop should moderate cooperation between religious and diocesan clergy.

18. C 681, §1 Works entrusted to religious by a diocesan bishop are under the authority and direction of the same bishop.

19. C 681, §2 Written agreements are to be drawn up between the diocesan bishop and the competent superior for works entrusted to religious by the bishop.

20. C 682, §1 If an ecclesiastical office in the diocese is to be conferred on a religious, the religious is to be named by the bishop after presentation or with assent of the competent superior.

21. C 683, §1 The bishop during pastoral visitation can visit the works entrusted to religious for the faithful, etc., but not schools open only to students of the institute.

22. C 683, §2 The bishop can correct abuses if he has advised the religious superior who has failed to act.

Chapter VI: Separation of Members from the Institute

Article 2: Departure from the Institute

23. C 686, §3 For grave reasons a diocesan bishop can impose exclaustration on a member of an institute of diocesan right.

24. C 687 An exclaustrated religious remains under the care of superiors and, if a priest, also the local Ordinary.

25. C 691, §2 An indult of departure can be granted by the diocesan bishop of the house of assignment for a member of an institute of diocesan right.

26. C 693 For a religious cleric an indult of departure may not be granted before a bishop will incardinate him or receive him experimentally. Unless the bishop refuses a religious cleric received experimentally is incardinated by law after five (5) years.

Title III: Secular Institutes

27. C 715, §1 Clerical members incardinated in a diocese depend on the diocesan bishop.

28. C 715, §2 Clerical members incardinated in an institute depend on a bishop in a way comparable to religious.

Cases Committed to the Competent Church Authority

Title I: Common Law

1. C 573, §2 Those who profess the evangelical counsels in institutes of consecrated life canonically erected by competent Church authority are joined to the Church and its mystery in a special way.
2. C 576 It belongs to the competent authority of the Church to interpret the evangelical counsels, to regulate their practice by law, and to constitute stable forms of living by canonical approbation.
3. C 578 The intention of the founders about the nature, purpose, spirit, character, and traditions of the institute are to be ratified by the competent Church authority.
4. C 587, §2 The fundamental code or constitutions are to be approved by the competent Church authority.
5. C 588, §2 An institute is clerical for certain reasons and is recognized as such by Church authority.
6. C 588, §3 An institute is lay for certain reasons and is recognized as such by Church authority.

Title II: Religious Institutes

Chapter V: The Apostolate of Religious

7. C 682, §2 A religious can be removed from office by will of the authority who committed the job to him or her.

Chapter IV: Separation of Members from the Institute

Article 2: Departure from the Institute

8. C 691, §1 A petition to depart from an institute should be presented to the supreme moderator who should transmit it to the competent authority.

II. AUTHORITY IN THE INSTITUTE

The General Chapter

Title II: Religious Institutes

Chapter I: Religious Houses and Their Erection and Suppression

1. C 596, §1 Chapters enjoy that power over members defined in universal law and the constitutions.
2. C 616, §3 Suppression of an autonomous house (C 613) belongs to the general chapter unless the constitutions state otherwise.

Chapter II: The Governance of Institutes

Article 2: Chapters

3. C 631, §1 The general chapter has supreme authority in the institute in accord with the constitutions.

Superiors Acting Alone or According to the Constitutions or Proper Law

Title II: Religious Institutes

Chapter I: Religious Houses and their Erection and Suppression

1. C 596, §1 Superiors enjoy that power over members defined in the universal law and the constitutions.
2. C 596, §2 Superiors in clerical institutes of pontifical right possess ecclesiastical power of governance for both the external and internal forum.
3. C 601 In accord with the evangelical counsel of obedience, members are to obey superiors when they command according to the constitutions.
4. C 616 §1 A religious house can be suppressed by the supreme moderator according to the constitutions after consulting with the diocesan bishop.

Chapter II: The Governance of Institutes

Article 1: Superiors and Councils

5. C 617 Superiors are to exercise their duty according to the norm of universal and proper law.
6. C 622 The supreme moderator holds power over all provinces, houses, and members, exercised according to proper law. Other superiors have power within the limits of their office.
7. C 625, §3 Elected superiors need the confirmation of the competent major superior.

Chapter III: Admission of Candidates and Formation of Members

Article 1: Admission to Novitiate

8. C 641   Admitting candidates to novitiate pertains to major superiors according to the norms of proper law.

Article 2: The Novitiate and Formation of Novices

9. C 647, §3 A major superior can permit novices to live for a stated period of time in another house of the institute.
10. C 649, §2 The competent major superior can permit anticipation of first profession by up to fifteen (15) days.
11. C 653, §2 Novitiate can be extended by the major superior according to proper law but not more than six (6) months.
12. C 657, §2 The time of temporary profession can be extended by the competent superior according to proper law but not for more than nine (9) years.

Chapter IV: Obligations and Rights of Institutes and Their Members

13. C 665, §1 Religious may be absent from the house with the permission of the superior.
14. C 668, §2 To change a cession or a will, a member needs the permission of the competent superior in accord with proper law.
15. C 668, §4 A member may renounce goods with the permission of the supreme moderator in accord with proper law.
16. C 671   A religious should not accept duties and offices outside the institute without permission of the legitimate superior.

Chapter V: The Apostolate of Religious

17. C 678, §2 In exercising the external apostolate religicus are also subject to their own superiors (in addition to the bishop).
18. C 681, §2 For works entrusted to a religious institute by a diocesan bishop a written agreement is to be drawn up between the diocesan bishop and the competent superior.
19. C 682, §1 To accept a diocesan office the religious is to be presented or receive the assent of the competent superior.
20. C 682, §2 A religious can be removed from diocesan office by the will of the superior having notified the diocesan authority.

Chapter VI: Separation of Members from the Institute

Article 1: Transfer to Another Institute

21. C 684, §3 For a religious to transfer from one autonomous monastery to another, the consent of the major superior of both monasteries and the chapter of the receiving monastery is required.

Article 2: Departure from the Institute

22. C 690, §1 The supreme moderator can determine a suitable period of probation for temporary profession and in vows prior to perpetual profession in a case of readmission.

Article 3: Dismissal of Members

23. C 703 In the case of serious exterior scandal or grave imminent harm to the institute, a member can be expelled from the religious house by the major superior—or if danger of delay by the local superior with consent of council.

Section II: Societies of Apostolic Life

24. C 738, §1 All members are subject to their particular moderator according to the norm of the constitutions in matters which affect internal life and discipline.

Superiors Acting with the Consent of Council or Acting with the Council

Article 3: Temporal Goods and Their Admission

1. C 638, §3 For the validity of alienation etc. the written permission of the competent superior with the consent of council according to the norm of law is required.

Chapter III: Admission of Candidates and Formation of Members

Article 2: Novitiate and the Training of Members

2. C 647, §1 The erection, transfer, and suppression of a novitiate is by the written decree of the supreme moderator with the consent of council.

3. C 647, §2 By concession of the supreme moderator with the consent of council, novitiate can be made in another house of the institute.

Chapter IV: Obligation and Rights of Institutes and Their Members

4. C 665, §1 The major superior with the consent of council can permit a member to live outside the house but not for more

than one (1) year unless for illness, studies, or apostolic work.

Chapter V: The Apostolate of Religious

5. C 684, §1 A member in perpetual vows cannot transfer to another institute without the consent of the supreme moderator of each institute with the deliberative vote of their respective councils.

Article 2: Departure from the Institute

6. C 686, §1 A supreme moderator can grant an indult of exclaustration for up to three (3) years with the consent of council.
7. C 686, §3 If a supreme moderator with the consent of council petitions, exclaustration can be imposed for grave reasons by the Holy See for pontifical right institutes and the diocesan bishop for diocesan right institutes.
8. C 688, §2 During temporary profession, the supreme moderator with the consent of council can grant a member an indult to leave.
9. C 690, §1 One who has left legitimately after completing novitiate or making profession can be readmitted by the supreme moderator with the consent of council.
10. C 690, §2 Superior of an autonomous monastery has the facility of C 690, §1.

Article 3: Dismissal of Members

11. C 694, §1, §2 A major superior with the council can *ipso facto* dismiss a member after having collected proofs and made a declaration of fact to establish it juridically.
12. C 699, §1 With the council, which must have four (4) members for validity, the supreme moderator can issue a decree of dismissal.
13. C 703 In certain cases if there is danger in delay, the local superior with the consent of council can expel a member from a religious house.

Title III: Secular Institutes

14. C 726, §2 A temporarily incorporated member can obtain an indult to leave from the supreme moderator with the consent of the council.

Section II: Societies of Apostolic Life

15. C 743   A definitively incorporated member can obtain an indult of departure from the supreme moderator with the consent of the council, unless reserved to the Holy See by the constitutions.

16. C 744, §1   It is reserved to the supreme moderator with the consent of the council to grant permission to a definitively incorporated member to transfer to another society.

17. C 745   The supreme moderator with the consent of the council can grant a definitively incorporated member an indult to live outside the society for up to three (3) years.

Superiors Acting with the Advice, Opinion or Vote of Council or Others

Title II: Religious Institutes

Chapter II: The Governance of Institutes

Article 1: Superiors and Councils

1. C 625, §3 Suitable consultation is to precede appointment of a superior.

Chapter III: Admission of Candidates and Formation of Members

Article 3: Religious Profession

2. C 656, 3° Admission by the competent superior with the vote of council is required for temporary profession.

3. C 658   Admission by the competent superior with the vote of the council is required for perpetual profession.

Chapter VI: Separation of Members from the Institute

Article 2: Departure from the Institute

4. C 689, §1 When temporary profession has expired, if just cause is present, a member can be excluded from subsequent profession by the supreme moderator after listening to council.

5. C 691, §1 A petition for an indult to leave is to be presented to the supreme moderator, who is to transmit it to the competent authority with a personal opinion and that of the council.

6. C 694, §2 The major superior and council collect proofs and make a declaration of fact for automatic dismissal.

7. C 697, §1 The major superior after hearing the council and believing the process of dismissal should be started should collect the proofs, warn the member, and if the warnings are useless, transmit all the acts to the supreme moderator.

Title III: Secular Institutes

8. C 720 The right of admission or assumption of sacred bonds (temporary or perpetual) pertains to the major moderator with the council according to the norm of the constitutions.

9. C 726, §1 When the time of temporary incorporation has elapsed, a member can be excluded from renewing sacred bonds for a just cause by the major moderator after hearing the council.

Cases Committed to the Competent Authority of the Institute or Society

Title I: Common Norms

1. C 581 Dividing an institute into parts, erecting new ones, and joining or defining parts pertains to the competent authority of the institute in accord with the constitutions.

2. C 585 Suppressing parts of an institute pertains to the competent authority of the institute.

3. C 587, §4 The competent authority of the institute is to establish other norms (in addition to constitutions).

Title II: Religious Institutes

Chapter I: Religious Houses and Their Erection and Suppression

4. C 609, §1 Houses of an institute are erected by the competent authority according to the constitutions with the consent of the diocesan bishop.

Chapter III: Admission of Candidates and Formation of Members

Article 2: The Novitiate and Formation of Novices

5. C 653, §1 The competent authority of the institute can dismiss a novice.

Section II: Societies of Apostolic Life

6. C 733, §1 A house is erected by the competent authority of the society.

Appendix 4

Table of Canons